Current readings in

URBAN EDUCATION

College Readings Inc.
Post Office Box 2323
Arlington, Virginia 22202

Current readings in
URBAN EDUCATION

Library of Congress Catalog Card Number 74-159576

To Darlene

PREFACE

The preparation of today's students for urban teaching is an extremely difficult task because of the daily advances being made through experimentation and application. The newest textbooks published on this subject are not truly current because of the great period of time required by the author to assemble his thoughts into book form and then the extended time lag inherent in the publication of any regular text. Therefore, instructors are forced to scan countless magazines and journals in search of material pertinent to their subject and to correlate their findings effectively into teaching outlines. During this planning period, they must constantly be searching for material which is both current and relevant. This book has been especially designed to help the instructors meet these objectives.

To meet the need for current material, this book consists of articles drawn from 1969, 1970 and 1971. The absence of articles earlier than 1969 in no way infers that excellent articles were not being written then, but it is believed that the better ideas from that period were either expressed in later articles or are by now included in the newer texts. Also, for the sake of currentness, the book publication time for this text has been cut to less than four months.

To meet the need for relevancy, I have evaluated many hundreds of urban education articles from almost one hundred different publications from the years 1967 to 1971 and have selected those most pertinent and presented them in this book.

Another feature of this book is the presentation of many diverse viewpoints — innovative, conservative, reactionary, idealistic, realistic, controversial, conceptual, and many others as expressed by seventy-seven different authors in sixty-one articles from thirty-four publications.

URBAN EDUCATION, a current and relevant anthology, is subdivided into eight separate chapters dealing with compensatory education, curriculum, decentralization, disadvantaged children, black positions and viewpoints, ghetto, teachers and administration, and big city problems. Each article also includes thought-provoking and project-oriented questions. It, thus, constitutes an ideal textbook for graduate or undergraduate study.

I would like to express my appreciation to the authors of the selected articles for putting their ideas into print and to the publishers, institutions and organizations which granted me permission to reprint their material, and to my family and friends whose time and encouragement have greatly helped make this book a reality.

Richard R. Heidenreich
Racine, Wisconsin
April 16, 1971

TABLE OF CONTENTS

COMPENSATORY PROGRAMS
AND SPECIAL EDUCATION:
IS THERE A DIFFERENCE?

By JAMES L. OLSON
RICHARD G. LARSON

There is agreement among many special educators that a sizeable percentage of the urban retarded in schools are in fact not retarded, but are environmentally handicapped, or disadvantaged. Nonetheless, this concern has not materially affected placement procedures. School systems too often place disadvantaged students in special classrooms. In short, there are not more retarded among the poor; there are more poor among the retarded, simply because we have put them there. Thus, students consider themselves retarded because of our expectations.

During the last several years, compensatory programs for disadvantaged students have become common among urban school systems. Their existence is acknowledgment of the fact that large numbers of urban children have learning problems that need treatment in the regular classroom setting. This reality renders inconsistent the placement of large numbers of the poor into special classes for the mentally retarded.

We thus seem to be faced with the paradox of educating the urban poor in two conflicting ways. On the one hand, we provide compensatory programs; on the other, we accept standardized intelligence test results at face value, label poor children mentally retarded, and place them on waiting lists for special classes. Is the paradox real? What are the relationships between the two efforts?

The writers have gathered some information relevant to this question, and to related issues: Does one program affect the other? Do special educators play a role in compensatory programs? If so, what is the nature of that role? The purpose of this paper is to present and discuss our interpretations of this information.

PROCEDURE

Questionnaires were constructed to be sent to major American cities, including 105 with populations over 100,000 and the largest 175 cities with populations less than 100,000. One questionnaire was designed for directors of special education programs and another was prepared for curriculum directors. A table of random numbers was utilized to divide the group into "special education director" and "curriculum director" cities. Size of city was equated between the samples. The rationale for varying distribution was to ascertain the extent of agreement between the two offices involved in the study. An effort was made to maintain brevity for respondents. Final total returns were 83.6 per cent of the original sample of 280 cities.

Reprinted with permission from the *Journal of Negro Education* (Spring 1970).

RESULTS AND DISCUSSION

Major results are presented in table form.

The data in Table I show that most cities have both compensatory education programs and special education programs for educable mentally retarded. Data also show that both directors of special education and curriculum directors feel there should be a relationship between special education and compensatory programs.

The responses to question four, Table I, indicate that departments of special education assume administrative responsibility for programs for the disadvantaged in 50 per cent or less of the cities contacted. (Consultation, coordination and administration for remedial reading, Headstart, and teacher aides would seem to constitute the bulk of their responsibilities. Special educators perceived 20 per cent more responsibility for teaching than was perceived for them by curriculum directors. Conversely, a research function for special educators was perceived 19 per cent more often by curriculum directors.) While special education was thus involved in roughly one-half the cities contacted, responses to question five, Table I, indicate that 85 per cent of the school

TABLE I

THE PERCEIVED RELATIONSHIPS BETWEEN COMPENSATORY PROGRAMS AND DEPARTMENTS OF SPECIAL EDUCATION

Questions	Responses			
	Curriculum Directors		Special Education Directors	
	% Yes	% No	% Yes	% No
1. Is there a department of special education or similar administrative unit in the school system?	96.7	3.3	96.4	3.6
2. Is there a special program for educable mentally retarded children?	99.1	.9	99.1	.9
3. Are there compensatory programs for disadvantaged children within the school system?	97.4	.6	96.3	3.7
4. Does your department of special education have any responsibility for the operation of programs for the disadvantaged?	55.6	44.4	37.8	61.3
5. Do you think that city school systems should attempt to build a relationship between programs for the disadvantaged and the department of special education?	85.8	12.4	84.8	15.2
	(1.8% undecided)			

TABLE II

ESTIMATES OF ADMINISTRATIVE FUNCTIONS OF SPECIAL EDUCATION DEPARTMENTS IN COMPENSATORY PROGRAMS

Questions	Response Percentages	
	Curriculum Directors	Special Education Directors
1. Check the type of programs for disadvantaged children in operation in the school system.		
Headstart	81	76
Remedial Reading	93	84
Community Agents	32	35
Work-Study	59	52
Follow-Through	24	20
Teacher Aides	67	69
Other	38	32
2. Check the type of responsibilities for programs for the disadvantaged performed by the department of special education.		
Administration	53	58
Coordination	64	58
Teaching	38	58
Consultation	83	78
Research	47	28
3. Check the following statements which you think might result from a relationship between programs for the disadvantaged and the department of special education.		
A. An increase in the number of classes for the educable retarded	44	39
B. An increase in the number of special education personnel (excluding classroom teachers)	58	53
C. A reduction in the number of classes for the educable mentally retarded	20	17

systems felt that the departments of special education should relate to programs for the disadvantaged. The discrepancy between actual and desired relationships indicates a need for change.

Directors of special education and curriculum directors, however, do see a somewhat different allocation of responsibility for the operation of programs for the disadvantaged. Responses to question four, Table I, indicate that 55.6 per cent of curriculum directors perceive that departments of special education have responsibility in programs for the disadvantaged while only 38.7 per cent of the directors of special education perceive that they have some administrative responsibility. This discrepancy of perception may be attributed to: (1) the broader instructional responsibility of the curriculum director; (2) the special educator's need for greater involvement; and (3) the curriculum directors' assumption of involvement through intermediary offices, when in fact such involvement does not exist. Chance, of course, may be a factor.

The investigators feel the major finding was that a like percentage of curriculum directors and special education directors agreed on the anticipated results of a relationship between compensatory programs and special education. Only one respondent in five perceived that such a relationship would result in cutting the number of special classes for the educable retarded. Substantially greater percentages felt that more special classes would be needed. Therefore, the concept of special classes for children labeled "atypical" seems more pervasive and more firmly grounded than concerns about hidden human intelligence and the segregation of children on socio-economic grounds. Perceptions of those in authority seem to reflect either an acceptance of special class placement procedures as adequate, a pessimism about the possibilities for their change, a lack of awareness of the problems caused by placing disadvantaged children in special classes, or, most damning, a lack of desire to come to grips with critical social issues.

About half of both administrative groups felt that an increased relationship between special education and compensatory programs would result in an increased number of special education personnel. To the extent that these personnel were perceived as supplements to regular classroom programs, the above argument must be tempered. Conversely, if this is not the case and an acceptance of the current "drain pipe" philosophy does in fact exist, what are the chances for change? How can teachers in regular classrooms be convinced that their responsibilities extend beyond the average middle-class child, as they perceive him? Will existing placement procedures facilitate needed curriculum changes? Will we continue to label "mentally retarded" those children from disadvantaged backgrounds? The perceptions of those in authority continue to determine the answers.

Questions:

1. Why do you feel that large numbers of compensatory-type students are placed into mentally retarded classes?
2. In your opinion, what significance is there in having compensatory programs under the administrative responsibility of the special education director or the curriculum director?

WHO NEEDS IT?

COMPENSATORY EDUCATION

By JOSEPH T. DURHAM

In the 1960's American education became aware of the large number of children enrolled in our public schools who were being ill-served. Whether the children were at fault or whether the school system was to be blamed was not clear, but considerable discussion was directed at the question of the proper designation for these children in educational trouble. Reissman preferred the term "culturally deprived."[1] Others preferred "socially denied," "socially disadvantaged," and "educationally disadvantaged." Whatever terminology was used, it was clear that the children being considered were offspring of the poor, and were victims of all the corroding defects that the culture of poverty could produce.

It was further discovered that the "target population" was not homogeneous in racial composition. In the ranks of the disadvantaged were American Negroes concentrated in the urban ghettoes; American Indians shunted aside on depressed reservations; Appalachian whites in lonely enclaves of rural poverty; Mexican Americans in the Southwest; Puerto Ricans again in the big cities, and even children in the lumbering and fishing areas of Maine and New Hampshire. All of these children were deprived not of culture but of a genuine opportunity to succeed in our middle-class oriented schools.

With the realization that educational disadvantagement was a serious problem, numerous remedies were proposed. One of these remedies was the institution of compensatory education programs for disadvantaged children. The basic notion was that disadvantaged children had certain deficits that had to be overcome.

In the State of Illinois, compensatory education was defined in the School Code as follows:

Compensatory education program means a program of instruction and services, supplementary to the regular public school program, for educationally disadvantaged children including those enrolled in school, those who have dropped out of school before graduation, and those who have not yet entered first grade.[2]

Perhaps it will be instructive to take a brief historical look at the growth of the compensatory education idea. Beginning with the research findings of Martin Deutsch, Benjamin Bloom, Samuel Shepherd and others, educators decided to organize and initiate special programs to upgrade the education of disadvantaged children.

Reprinted with permission from *Clearing House* (September 1969).

One of the early compensatory programs was the Demonstration Guidance Program of New York City.[3] The program, known as Higher Horizons, attempted to identify junior high school students with limited cultural backgrounds. It provided a program of remediation and enrichment for them.

The efforts of the federal government and private foundations also stimulated the growth of compensatory education. Perhaps the most telling federal effort to date has been the Elementary and Secondary Education Act of 1965, signed into law by President Lyndon B. Johnson. Title I of this act specifically mentions educationally deprived children. In the private sector, the Great Cities Project under the aegis of the Ford Foundation was an outstanding example of compensatory programs.

With funds coming from both governmental and private sectors, programs of compensatory education have increased in number. These programs evince wide variations in size, scope, and quality. Though most of the existing compensatory programs claim that they are designed to achieve the twin goals of remediation and prevention, most of them have been longer on remediation than prevention. It may be that the heavy emphasis on the lacks, deficits, and weaknesses of disadvantaged children has led us into a *cul-de-sac* in our theory of how to best educate them.

In 1966 an exhaustive study of compensatory education programs was conducted by Edmund Gordon and Doxey Wilkerson.[4] Gordon and Wilkerson found that most compensatory programs embodied the following eight characteristics:

(1) Heavy emphasis on reading and language development.
(2) Different curricular approaches; team teaching, *e.g.*
(3) Extra-curricular innovations such as field trips.
(4) Parental involvement.
(5) Community involvement.
(6) Teacher recruitment and training.
(7) Emphasis on guidance.
(8) Use of specialized personnel such as social workers and psychiatrists.[5]

A cursory examination of this list reveals that the programs studied did not contain anything really "new" or innovative in education. Indeed, the characteristics mentioned should be a part of a good educational program for any child. It is precisely on this score that most compensatory education programs have failed or have ended in ambiguous results. Thus, compensatory education, which was once thought to be the answer to the problem of disadvantagement, is now under criticism. Why? Let us examine the evidence.

Martin Deutsch has stimulated much interest in the field of early childhood education, and pre-school compensatory programs of the Headstart variety have been numerous. Studies of pre-school compensatory programs have reported positive results, but the early gains seem to wash away when the youngsters enter kindergarten and first-grade classes.

In a study by Wolff and Stein, *Six Months Later,* children who have attended Headstart classes were compared with non-Headstart children in kindergarten six months later. They concluded that the Headstart children showed greater readiness, but no educational gains were apparent.[6] From a study conducted in Racine, Wisconsin, comes even stronger language concerning Headstart:

Potentially, the most useful conclusion which can be drawn . . . is that "one-shot" compensatory programs would seem to be a waste of time and money. The fact that differences between groups disappeared and that in several areas the rate of growth of both groups regressed during the first year supports this conclusion.[7]

Recently, the second annual evaluative report of Title I programs found that though disadvantaged children in Title I schools were making relative progress in reading, for example, yet 60 per cent of Title I youngsters in some districts were reading far below the level expected of them.[8]

These critical comments are typical of those being currently directed at the results of compensatory educational programs. Moreover, additional criticism of the idea of compensation is coming from another quarter.

Oddly enough, civil rights proponents have scored compensatory education programs. When they demanded the integration of school children they were most frequently offered improved segregated facilities with compensatory programs. If one were devious enough, he might suspect that some communities have settled for an educational *quid pro quo:* substitute compensatory education programs for persistent efforts to achieve integration, or at least racial balance.

Thus, when we examine the national picture, programs of compensatory education are being conducted almost exclusively in segregated schools, mainly in the ghetto. There is some evidence to suggest that neither compensatory education nor integration taken alone can be effective. Integration must, however, be an essential ingredient in any meaningful program of compensation.

So far, it has been stated that compensatory education has been criticized because (1) many programs have not achieved viable results; (2) many programs do not really contain anything that is new; (3) in some communities, educational compensation has been offered as a substitute for integration, thereby disenchanting the militants in civil rights and the black community in general.

This discussion now turns to a deeper level of critical comments about compensatory education, and that is an examination of the nature of the theory of compensatory education itself. Several philosophical considerations are raised in this section.

In educational theory, a basic postulate is that the characteristics of children must be taken into account in conceiving a program for them. The flood of literature on the disadvantaged contains a full listing of the characteristics of this population. This listing, however, is essentially negative, placing heavy emphasis on the weaknesses and deficits of disadvantaged children. It may be that the almost romantic emphasis placed on the deficits of these children has resulted in what Kenneth Clark has called "The Cult of Cultural Deprivation."[9] Suppose, says Clark, a child does not know one color from another, how long will it take him to learn the colors of the spectrum? Does this lack constitute a permanent barrier to learning?

It has been assumed that there is a cause and effect relationship between the negative environmental influences exerted on the disadvantaged and their deficient educational performance. The deficits are assumed to account for the high incidence of school failures. It is true that growing up in the atmosphere of modern urban poverty does not usually facilitate academic achievement, yet there seems to be no clear evidence that such upbringing makes educational development impossible. There are disadvantaged children who do succeed despite their growing up in the ghetto. It may be instructive to recall that The Honorable Carl B. Stokes, Mayor of Cleveland, was an ADC child. His brother, Louis, is a member of the Ohio delegation in the U.S. House of Representatives.[10]

Our doting on the negative characteristics of disadvantaged children may have resulted in educators taking a posture which is essentially defeatist; consequently, we do not expect them to learn. This posture is the inevitable result of our assumption that there is a high positive correlation between the characteristics of their environment and what we perceive as their educational inadequacies. Perhaps the burden of proof (from the standpoint of performances) should be removed from the shoulders of the students and placed on the school system. Is it the child who is deprived, or is it the school system which is disadvantaged?

This leads to another consideration. How much revision has our school system undergone as a result of compensatory education programs? Present thinking about compensatory education seems all too ready to accept the present school system as its proper setting. This is being done in spite of the evidence that a "third educational world"—the Jobs Corps and educational programs of the Armed Services—is successfully competing with the public school and is achieving with persons who were pushed out of public schools. The success of the "third educational world" is further highlighted when we recall that one of the most successful compensatory programs today is not being conducted in a public school but in a downtown department store. This is the "World of Inquiry" in Rochester, New York.

When we consider the successes of these two extra-school occurrences against the advocacy of Milton Friedman and Christopher Jencks that parents of disadvantaged children should be paid subsidies with which they can compete on the open market for the best available education for their children, whether it is provided by industry, by private schools, or by public schools, then perhaps the question of whether compensatory education should be contained in the public school should be re-examined. At best, we may be forced to make changes in the structure of public education itself.

The unexpressed purpose of most compensatory education programs seems to make disadvantaged children as much as possible like the kind of children with whom the school has been traditionally successful. It is not at all clear that this goal is appropriate for the disadvantaged. Do we need to make all products of the public schools middle-class creatures? If a person is happy as a member of a class other than the middle class, does he not have the right to "the pursuit of happiness" at that class level? What will be the effect of imposing contrary middle-class attitudes on a disadvantaged child if his environment (which might be facilitative for him) remains the same? Can a program of compensatory education even at its best be salutary without altering the disadvantaged environment which caused the disadvantaged child? Of course, the ultimate question is what right have we as educators to change his environment—all or in part?

Various models for compensatory education programs have been tried. The special education model has been popular. The essence of this model was to make an application of principles derived from work with brain injured and cerebral palsied children to the building of compensatory programs for the disadvantaged. However, Milton Schwebel contends in *Who Can Be Educated?* that we cannot yet cope with the learning problems of the tiny proportion of people who have brain and other neurological defects.[11] If this is true, perhaps special education is inadequate as a theoretical model for compensatory education.

Possibly, the behavioral sciences can be a better model. In structuring compensatory programs greater attention should be given to the effect of intra-group interaction on the learning, motivation, and accomplishments of students. There is strong evidence from the Coleman Report and from the report of the U.S. Commission on Civil Rights, *Racial Isolation in the Public Schools,* that racial and social class composition of student bodies has a powerful effect on the academic performance of children. Nevertheless, few, if any, programs of compensatory education take account of the factors of racial and/or social composition of students in the design and execution of programs of intervention.

If the student body is the immediate medium in which instruction and learning occur, its collective advantagement or disadvantagement can facilitate or impede intellectual growth. Hence group dynamics and the frontiers of the behavioral sciences might be revisited as sources of fruitful leads toward the building of a more adequate theory of compensatory education.[12]

The two landmark reports, *Equal Educational Opportunity* and *Racial Isolation in the Public Schools,* have escalated discussion of what constitutes equal educational opportunity. In the wake of the 1954 Supreme Court Decision, it was assumed by some that equal facilities—teachers, buildings, books, equipment, etc.—constituted equal educational opportunities. However, Dr. James S. Coleman documents the fact that these measurable facilities were not the most influential forces affecting a child's education.[13] There is a persistent attempt to equate equality of educational opportunity with the effectiveness of a school to overcome the differences in the starting points of children who come from differing social groups. A school which can perform this feat is thus conceived as providing equal educational opportunity.[14]

Compensatory education programs have not solved the problem of how best to educate the children of the poor. Yet the education of the disadvantaged is one of the major tasks before the schools today. It has been estimated that there are 30,400,000[15] children who need compensatory education, and the cost of implementing truly effective programs has been set in the staggering billions.

The ultimate challenge to American education is to eliminate the need for compensatory education *vis-a-vis* educational disadvantagement. The challenge is to relegate compensatory education to the museum of educational antiquities along with corporal punishment and the Lancastrian system. This is a task to which the whole society must be committed; it cannot be done by the school acting alone. What is needed is a massive reordering of social and political power so that education again becomes a national passion. But in addition, the American people must be willing to sanction this reordering and to strive assiduously for a truly "open" society in which all children will have equal access to quality education.

REFERENCES:

[1] Frank Reissman, *The Culturally Deprived Child* (New York: Harper and Brothers, 1962), p. 3.

[2] *The School Code of Illinois,* 1967. p. 159.

[3] Jacob Landers, *Higher Horizons: Progress Report* (New York: Board of Education of City of New York, 1963), *et passim.*

[4] Edmund W. Gordon and Doxey A. Wilkerson, *Compensatory Education for the Disadvantaged* (New York: College Entrance Examination Board, 1966), 299 pp.

[5] *Ibid,* pp. 31-53.

[6] Max Wolff and Annie Stein, *Six Months Later* (New York: Ferkouf Graduate School of Education, Yeshiva University, 1966), p. 83.

[7] *Consultants' Papers.* The White House Conference on Education, 1965, p. 111.

[8] *Title I/Year II.* The Second Annual Report of Title I of the Elementary and Secondary Education Act of 1965, School Year 1966-67 (Washington: Government Printing Office, 1968), p. 7.

[9] Harlem Youth Opportunities Unlimited, Inc. *Youth in the Ghetto* (New York: HARYOU, 1964), pp. 239-240.

[10] See Ebony Magazine, February, 1969, pp. 56-65.

[11] Milton Schwebel, *Who Can Be Educated?* (New York: Grove Press, 1968), pp. 204-205.

[12] Cf. Eli M. Bower and William G. Hollister, *Behavioral Science Frontiers in Education* (New York: John Wiley & Sons, Inc., 1967).

[13] James S. Coleman, *Equality of Educational Opportunity* (Washington: Government Printing Office, 1966), p. 22.

[14] David L. Kirp, "The Poor, the Schools, and Equal Protection," *Harvard Educational Review* (Fall, 1968), pp. 635-638.

[15] Adelaide Jablonsky, "Some Trends in Education for the Disadvantaged," *IRCD Bulletin* (March, 1968), p. 2.

Questions:

1. Describe the general provisions of Title I in the Elementary and Secondary Education Act of 1965.

2. What changes or additions to current compensatory programs would you make to overcome the "long-on-remediation" objection?

3. Discuss your interpretation of the following phrase: "A truly 'open' society in which all children will have equal access to quality education."

PERFORMANCE OF HEAD START AND NON-HEAD START PARTICIPANTS AT FIRST GRADE

By JOHN F. CAWLEY
WILL H. BURROW
HENRY A. GOODSTEIN

INTRODUCTION

Although comprehensive educational activity at the preschool level for disadvantaged children is a relatively recent innovation, there is little doubt that society has developed great expectations for this endeavor. The expectations of society appear to focus upon the notion that participation in Head Start will alleviate developmental deficiencies in disadvantaged children; and, that participants in Head Start will perform significantly higher than non-participants. While these are appropriate considerations, they are only moderately inclusive and subject to numerous limitations.

The most obvious limitation to the expectancies of society is the proposition that preschool education must alleviate the deficits in the developmental status of disadvantaged children. A more proper consideration is that Head Start should initiate a gradual intervention with the pattern of educational disability which so frequently accompanies economic and social impoverishment.

The existence of differences in developmental characteristics between children of divergent socioeconomic backgrounds as young as four years has been well documented.[1] Because the school is unable to overcome many of these environmentally determined handicaps, Deutsch [2] suggests that the child should be better prepared to meet the school's demands before he enters first grade, hence preschool. However, we have yet to determine the most effective elements of a successful preschool program.

In a comprehensive review of the literature relevant to initial reading instruction, Cawley and Goodstein[3] observed that it would be desirable to structure the learning situation ior the child in order to refine and direct the maturation of developmental characteristics. Accordingly, preschool and kindergarten education should consider a diagnostic-prescriptive learning orientation. This orientation has implications in terms of the capability of Head Start to alleviate deficiencies which hamper educational progress. To illustrate, Feldman and Deutsch[4] assessed the impact of auditory perceptual training on the reading abilities of third grade disadvantaged children. The effects of this training were minimal, and the suggestion was offered that training in the perceptual skills should precede reading training. Silvaroli and Wheelock[5] found that auditory discrimination abilities of disadvantaged kindergarten children could be signifi-

Reprinted with permission from the *Journal of Negro Education*, (Spring 1970).

cantly increased by training. Tachistoscopic training on the recognition of capital letters has been shown to be beneficial on visual discrimination tests with letters. [6]

Bereiter and Engelmann[7] note that preschool is an appropriate time to formalize the process of learning; and it is suggested that disadvantaged children with mental ages of four years and above can be successfully introduced to reading.

Previous research[8] has shown that the psycholinguistic characteristics and learning aptitudes of preschool children are significantly changed as a result of participation in Head Start. When the performance of children of different intellectual levels was contrasted, it was found that the effects of Head Start were varied. Brighter children tended to benefit more than children of lesser ability, although there was an overall population deficit in visual attention for objects, vocal encoding, motor encoding and auditory-vocal automatic abilities.

Curtis and Berzonsky[9] studied the academic, psycholinguistic and intellectual development of preschool experimental and control subjects. As measured by the Metropolitan Readiness Test, at the end of kindergarten, there was no firm pattern of significance favoring the experimental group. There was no pattern favoring experimental subjects at the conclusion of first grade, as measured by the Metropolitan Achievement Test. These samples experienced summer programs. Another sample participated in a year-long preschool program. In this phase of the study there were no differences between participants and non-participants in academic achievement at the end of first grade or at the end of second grade.

Similar patterns of results were observed by Larson and Olson[10] in a pilot study of the effects of an all-day kindergarten program for disadvantaged children. Experimental subjects scored significantly higher on seven of the nine subtests of the *Illinois Test of Psycholinguistic Abilities* (experimental edition), whereas the contrast group showed statistically significant gains on only two of the nine tests. The two groups were also assessed upon completion of first grade. Significant gains were attained on only one of the nine subtests by each sample and the experimental group actually lost ground on five of the subtests.

DiLorenzo and Salter[11] have studied the effects of preschool upon disadvantaged and non-disadvantaged children. They note that preschool programs do have an impact upon the disadvantaged. The pattern of the impact is somewhat different from one year to the next and for one method of assessment in contrast to another. To illustrate, Stanford-Binet differences between experimental and control groups for the 1965 sample occur as a result of a larger I.Q. drop by the control group than by the experimental group, (C = 90.75 to 88.20, E = 90.97 to 90.07); whereas, in the 1966 sample, E's rose from 92.66 to 96.71 while C's regressed slightly, 90.97 to 90.01. The pattern for the PPVT showed considerable gain for both groups. The differences resulting from preschool were maintained through kindergarten for the experimental groups, although there was no further differentiation.

Klaus and Gray[12] have studied the developmental status of experimental and control subjects in the Southeastern part of the country. One sample participated in three ten-week summer sessions and another had two ten-week summer sessions. A local and a distal control group were established. Specific to academic attainment as measured by the Metropolitan Readiness Test, the Gates

Reading Readiness Test and the Stanford Achievement Test, the effects of preschool education consistently favored the participants.

Weikart[13] reports on the intellectual and academic progress of children who were studied from preschool through the completion of second grade. With respect to intelligence, preschool participants demonstrated a change from a mean of 78.4 at the beginning of preschool to a mean of 91.1 at the conclusion of a one-year experience. Control subjects rose to 82.2 from an initial mean of 75.0. Experimental subjects showed a gradual decline over the next three years and at the completion of second grade the means were 85.5 and 83.9 for participants and non-participants. Differences between the two groups at the end of first and at the end of second grade, on measures of reading, arithmetic and language skills, were significant on five of six tests. However, the mean percentile rank of the participants decreased from 22 at the end of first grade to 18 at the conclusion of second grade; the control group decreased from a mean rank of 5 to a rank of 3 during the same period. In spite of the fact that participants and non-participants were significantly different on academic measures, it appears that both groups were considerably below expectancy.

Meyers[14] suggests that preschool kindergarten programs should be flexible and that they should contain experiences that will modify the degree of incapacity which is observed in learning and behavioral problems of children. Our own position is in concert with this. To be even more explicit, we propose that (1) Head Start should identify and intervene with incipient and demonstrable psychoeducational disabilities in preschool children; (2) the differential characteristics of preschool children should be identified, and they, in turn, should become the basis for program development; and (3) experimental programs of many types must be developed and assessed in order that they might ultimately be organized into comprehensive systems of successful education.

Simple exposure to preschool is an inadequate basis for the expectancies of society. Active participation in a system of successful education is a more fundamental consideration. Head Start is only one part of this system. The present project was undertaken for the purpose of comparing the developmental status of Head Start and non-Head Start subjects. This developmental comparison represents only one step in the total system.

PROCEDURE

In order to fulfill the purposes of the present study, three samples of first grade children were identified and located. The first sample, hereafter referred to as the Primary Head Start Sample (PHS), was composed of fifty-eight children who were among the participants in a previous research effort.[15] These subjects were located after a search of disadvantaged schools. In the major part of this study, the sample was reduced to fifty-four subjects because four were absent at various times during testing. We retained only those who received the entire first-grade battery, plus four who received the Stanford-Binet, L-M; the Illinois Test of Psycholinguistic Abilities; the motor speed and precision test and the visual attention for objects tests of the Detroit Tests of Learning Aptitude during the preschool year.

It was felt that there might be some effect as a result of the previous testing experience of the PHS. In order to compensate for this, a Secondary Head Start Sample (SHS) was identified. This sample consisted of seventy-seven subjects who had also attended a year-long preschool program during the same period as the PHS. They had not been previously subjected to the instrumentation utilized herein. These children were chosen by selecting the names of Head Start participants who alphabetically followed the PHS. In many instances, more subjects than necessary were selected in order to handle attrition. The result was that seventy-seven subjects received the entire battery.

The major contrast group consisted of seventy-eight non-Head Start subjects (NHS) who alphabetically followed the SHS on the school roster. These children were not exposed previously to the instrumentation used in this project. They were residents of the community during the period when others were enrolled in Head Start.

RESULTS AND DISCUSSION

Comparisons Between Head Start and Non-Head Start Children

Comparisons at Kindergarten: The initial comparisons among Head Start and non-Head Start subjects are based upon data obtained from the cumulative files of the cooperating school system. This particular system, because of its own interest in acquiring information relative to the children in it, administered a battery of tests around March of the kindergarten year. The data, which are contained in Table I, do not provide any indication of significant differences between children who experienced Head Start and children who did not.

The intelligence quotients and mental ages, as measured by the *Peabody Picture Vocabulary Test,* tend to be somewhat lower than that which is defined as average. Comparable data at the beginning of kindergarten, or at the conclusion of preschool, would establish a firmer basis for conclusions relative to the immediate impact of Head Start. As the data stand, midway through kindergarten, measures of selected developmental characteristics do not demonstrate significant differences.

Comparisons at First Grades: The more comprehensive comparisons among the three samples were conducted on a basis of assessments conducted at the beginning of first grade. There are no significant differences among the various comparisons. The mean I.Q.'s of the various samples are within the lower limits of the average range — 91.56 for the SHS, 93.77 for the NHS, and 94.02 for the PHS. Mental age is slightly lower than that which is to be expected when contrasted with chronological age — (Mental Age means are: 69.98, PHS; 69.44, NHS; 67.05, SHS; Chronological Age means are: 74.24, PHS; 74.53, NHS; 74.56, SHS).

At no time do the data for the *Developmental Test of Visual Perception* show any significant differences between the mean scores of the Head Start and Non-Head Start children. The data were transposed to Perceptual Age equivalents. The three samples show perceptual age equivalents which approximate their chronological age in the area of "Eye-Motor Coordination." The basic requirement for this task is the ability to draw straight, curved or angular lines between boundaries of various widths or from point to point without guided lines. Disadvantaged children in the present samples appear to manifest this ability quite adequately — (with mean scores of 11.68 for the PHS, 12.82 for the NHS, and 12.10 for the SHS).

TABLE I
COMPARISONS AMONG HEAD START AND NON-HEAD START CHILDREN IN KINDERGARTEN

	Primary Head Start (n=55)	"t"	Non-Head Start (N=73)	"t"	Secondary Head Start (N=63)
Draw-A-Man (MA)	M 72.45 SD 10.72	.55	M 71.38 SD 11.02	1.13	M 69.10 SD 12.05
Design Copying	M 64.15 SD 8.47	.24	M 63.78 SD 8.28	.94	M 62.20 SD 11.16
PPVT (MA)	M 60.13 SD 12.13	2.13	M 55.49 SD 12.28	.64	M 56.82 SD 11.38
PPVT (IQ)	M 88.33 SD 14.80	1.42	M 84.25 SD 16.97	.66	M 86.08 SD 14.36

The remaining four measures of visual perception are characterized by developmental inadequacies ranging from nine months to one year below chronological age. These discrepancies point up the fact that the lack of significant differences between samples cannot be interpreted as an indication that the developmental status of these children is free from deficit.

Comparisons on measures of learning aptitudes show that the PHS is significantly different from the NHS sample on motor speed (means of 33.06 and 24.65, respectively), auditory attention span for unrelated words (means of 34.81 and 32.99, respectively), visual attention for objects (means of 33.52 and 31.24, respectively), and auditory attention for related words (means of 39.89 and 33.15, respectively). At the same time, there are no differences, at the .01 level, between the SHS and the NHS. The Primary Head Start sample had been exposed to the tests of motor speed and visual attention span for objects at the beginning and at the end of the year in which they were enrolled in Head Start.

The mental age equivalents of the *Detroit Tests of Learning Aptitude* were graphed. The profiles are characterized by wide discrepancies in the developmental equivalents in each of the aptitudes which have been assessed. Memory-for-Designs is an area of comparatively adequate development, with two of the samples attaining levels equal to their chronological age; the third is only slightly below level. Attainment in motor speed extends downward from fifteen months to twenty-one months below expectancy. Performance also extends downward from fifteen months to thirty months in auditory attention for unrelated syllables. Auditory attention for related words appears to be another area of considerable deficit for all subjects.

Visual attention span for objects show the widest range of mental age equivalents among the areas measured. The peak of six years, nine months in the

PHS exceeds the level of attainment of the Secondary Head Start sample by twenty-one mental age months. The figure clearly indicates considerable variation in measured aptitudes in the areas assessed. Throughout the profile, the status of the Primary Head Start sample is developmentally superior to the other samples. There is, however, no basis for attributing these differences to participation in Head Start, inasmuch as the achievement of the Secondary Head Start sample failed to show a similar pattern.

Psycholinguistic development among disadvantaged children is an area of great concern. The *Illinois Test of Psycholinguistic Abilities* has been the workhorse of research workers in a substantial portion of the projects that have measured psycholinguistic development. Previous research[16] with the primary sample also utilized the ITPA as an evaluative instrument.

The data in the present study show that there are no significant differences between the Primary Head Start sample and the Non-Head Start sample; and, between the Secondary sample and the Non-Head Start sample. The total language scores for the three samples are approximately nine months below age expectancy.

Major deficiencies exist in auditory-vocal-automatic, (means of 7.83, PHS; 8.00, NHS; 8.77, SHS), motor encoding (means of 12.41, PHS; 11.73, NHS; 11.51, SHS), and auditory-vocal association (means of 22.48, PHS; 21.24, NHS; 21.48, SHS), whereas the strengths are exhibited in the visual-motor-association (means of 14.19, PHS; 14.58, NHS; 15.12, SHS), and auditory-vocal sequential abilities (means of 22.48, PHS; 21.24, NHS; 21.49, SHS). The latter ability has been shown to be an area of strength among disadvantaged children.

The *Metropolitan Readiness Test* was administered to each of the samples in this study in order to obtain some indication of academic preparedness. There was no evidence of significant differences between Head Start and Non-Head Start participants on any of the six subtests, or on the total score. The *Metropolitan Readiness Test* does not provide any firm basis for transforming the subtest scores into any form of age or grade equivalency. A rough comparison of the means of the three samples, with the quartile for each subtest, indicates that the subjects in the present project tend toward the first quartile (25th percentile). The percentile rank for Total Score for the PHS (mean, 38.82), NHS, (mean, 35.81), and SHS (mean, 33.12) groups are the 22nd percentile, the 17th percentile and the 14th percentile, respectively. Clearly, the indications are that the readiness skills possessed by these children are substantially inferior upon entrance to first grade.

The final basic comparison among the samples in the present study was conducted on a test of letter recognition. This was accomplished by typing the typewriter keyboard on five-by-seven inch cards. The cards were presented to the youngsters and they were requested to name as many letters as they could. Only upper case letters were used. The score was the number correct. The mean number correct for the Primary Head Start samples was 5.63 with a SD of 7.13; the Non-Head Start sample mean was 6.61, SD 7.32; and, the mean for the Secondary Head Start sample was 5.29, SD 7.66. There were no significant differences, at the .01 level.

A review of the data reported herein indicates that differences beween Head Start and Non-Head Start children are infrequent and the few that do occur are probably attributable to chance. The general curriculum approach to

Head Start, without planned follow-through, does not appear to yield significant developmental difference between participants and non-participants. The need for curriculum and methodological demonstration programs is apparent, particularly those that have a relationship with some form of follow-through.

Overall, there is no tendency toward significant differences between those who participated in Head Start and those who did not participate. The lack of differences was measured as early as March of the kindergarten year and a comprehensive assessment at first grade yielded a continuation of this pattern.

It is difficult to attribute the lack of differences to any particular factor or series of factors, inasmuch as experimental and control groups were not intact from the beginning of preschool. More extensive research with a paradigm that provided for control and experimental subjects would furnish the foundation for more adequate generalizations. It may prove valuable to conduct the assessments on experimental and control subjects at selected intervals during the year, rather than always at the beginning and the end.

The tragic aspect of these data are not the differences, or lack of differences, between participants and non-participants. The tragedy rests in the fact that the overall developmental pattern of these youngsters is so replete with deficits. It does not seem rational to expect Head Start to compensate for these. Rather, Head Start should be the beginning of a comprehensive system of education that will produce an individual that is adequately skilled for today's world. This suggests that the notion of a twelve-year system of education is irrational. Most Head Start programs deal with the disadvantaged child sometime after the fourth birthday. From the little that is known about early childhood development there can be no doubt that the learning habits of all children have been considerably developed by four years of age. This would suggest that planned intervention strategies might begin, not at age four or five, but as early as eighteen months. Although obvious research problems would exist when dealing with such a population there can be no denial that such research should be undertaken to determine the effects of very early planned intervention.

Society's present course of action is predicated upon the notion that Head Start will enable these youngsters to "catch up." If they don't, then failure in the traditional public school curriculum, often based upon chronological age expectancies for performance, seems obvious. A more logical approach suggests that the guidelines of our system of graded education need to be revamped.

REFERENCES:

[1]S. Stodolsky and G. Lesser, *Learning Patterns in the Disadvantaged* (Cambridge, Mass.: Harvard University Press, Reprint No. 6, 1967).

[2]M. Deutsch, "Facilitating Developing in the Preschool Child: Social and Psychological Perspectives," *The Merritt-Palmer Quarterly*, X (1967), 249-264.

[3]J. Cawley and H. A. Goodstein, "Initial Reading Instruction" (paper presented at the Workshop in Behavioral Modifications, Seattle, Washington, 1968).

[4]S. Feldman and C. Deutsch, *A Study of the Effectiveness of Training Retarded Readers in the Auditory Perceptual Skills Underlying Reading* (New York: New York Medical College, NDEA, Title VII Project, No. 1127, 1966).

[5]N. Silvaroli and W. Wheelock, "An Investigation of Auditory Discrimination Training in Beginning Readers," *Reading Teacher*, XX (1966), 247-251.

[6]W. Wheelock and N. Silvaroli, "Visual Discrimination Training for Beginning Readers," *Reading Teacher,* XXI (1967), 115-120.

[7]C. Bereiter and S. Engelmann, *Teaching Disadvantaged Children in the Preschool* (Englewood Cliffs, N.J.: Prentice-Hall, Inc., 1966.

[8]J. Cawley, "Psycholinguistic Characteristics of Pre-School Children," *The Training School Bulletin,* LXIV (1967), 95-101; and J. Cawley, "Learning Aptitudes Among Preschool Children of Different Intellectual Levels," *The Journal of Negro Education,* XXXVII (1968), 179-183.

[9]C. Curtis and M. Berzonsky, "Preschool and Primary Education Project, 1966-67," (Annual progress report to the Ford Foundation, Harrisburg, Pa., 1967).

[10]R. Larson and J. Olson, "Compensatory Education: How Much is Enough?" *The Journal of Negro Education,* XXXVII (1968), 164-167.

[11]L. DiLorenzo and K. Salter, "Second Year Report of an Evaluative Study of Pre-Kindergarten Programs for Educationally Disadvantaged Children" (paper presented at Educational Research Association, New York, 1967).

[12]R. Klaus, and S. Gray, "The Early Training Project for Disadvantaged Children: A Report After Five Years" (Nashville: George Peabody College for Teachers, 1968).

[13]D. Weikart, "Preliminary Results from a Longitudinal Study of Disadvantaged Children" (paper presented at the Annual Convention, Council for Exceptional Children, 1967).

[14]W. J. Meyers, "Quarterly Progress Report to the National Laboratory on Early Childhood Education," Syracuse University, 1968. (Mimeographed.)

[15]J. Cawley, *An Assessment of Intelligence, Psycholinguistic Abilities and Learning Aptitudes Among Preschool Children* (Storrs, Conn.: University of Connecticut, Office of Economic Opportunity, Project No. DED-1336, 1966), p. 64.

[16]*Ibid.*

Questions:

1. Give two examples to illustrate the following: "The differential characteristics of preschool children should be identified, and they, in turn, should become the basis for program development."

2. Reviewing some of the results of Head Start, one could view this program as unnecessary. What do you feel would be the reaction of your community to the elimination of Head Start?

3. Suggest several reasons why the status of the Primary Head Start sample is developmentally superior to other samples.

PROJECT ASPIRE:
HELP FOR HOPELESS KIDS

By DIANE DIVOKY

Forget about the usual education rhetoric for a minute. The awkward name: ASPIRE–*A Student-Planned Innovative Research Experiment.* The ESEA Title III forms that dissect the experience into *statistical data*–"a one-year self-contained program for 25 to 30 tenth-graders (some already 18 years old), staffed by two full-time teachers and supporting staff"; *project goals*–"to foster in the unmotivated, disenchanted student a more positive attitude toward himself and his education"; and *financial report*–"$31,000 a year in federal aid, $17,000 in nonfederal support." Or even the newspaper piece that proclaims that this is how to "salvage the dropouts."

Take a cue, instead, from the comment of the Vermont Department of Education team which evaluated the program: "Anyone proclaiming to do things for kids should watch the kids at ASPIRE."

The kids at ASPIRE are teenagers trying to grow up, or fit in, or just get through Burlington (Vt.) High School. But they are the kids you see in any high school in any town in this country—bored and vacant-faced in the back of a classroom, a little out of step in the halls, a little out of place wherever they go. They're the kids who never make it to the honor rolls, or the prestige activities, or any kind of achievement or distinction on their way through school. Teachers notice them most when they don't do homework, or their grades slip from low C's to D's, or they "goof off" in class, or ultimately slip away altogether from the school roster.

They can't be explained away with handy labels: they're not "disadvantaged minority group youngsters," "slow learners," "exceptional students," "hard-core delinquent problems," or even "the culturally deprived." What they do have in common is a strong conviction that school is a waste of time, a place where you learn to live with boredom and failure. Usually they remain in the shadows of the educational process, barely noticed in the rush to enrich the gifted and save the handicapped.

Burlington High School's big step forward three years ago was first to identify these students who were wasting away in its classrooms. Since then, the challenge has been to figure out what works for them. That job is still going on.

Eight-thirty a.m. Monday morning at Burlington High School—an attractive, modern school with a house plan, modular scheduling, and no bells. At the hub of the school, behind a door with psychedelic decorations, are two rooms and an office set aside for ASPIRE. Rock music is playing as a trio of

Reprinted by permission from *Scholastic Teacher*, (February 2, 1970), © 1970 by Scholastic Magazines, Inc.

sullen-looking girls drift into the complex and slump into seats. A boy comes crashing through the door.

"You got a problem?" a stout girl asks him.

"Yeah, you. You're always here," he comes back in defense.

In the small office, the atmosphere is brighter. A gum-cracking girl is pecking away at a typewriter, working on a report, she explains, which is part of a project she "contracted" to do under a new system which encourages independent work for credit among ASPIRE students.

"Evie, does this sound okay for an opening?" she asks a small-boned dark-haired woman. Evie is Mrs. Evelyn Carter, one of the ASPIRE teachers. She wears a peace medallion, wonders whether schools should exist, and has five children of her own.

As Evie makes suggestions about the report, another student—a sociable fellow—volunteers particulars about a contract he has just completed: He read an article on black models in *LIFE* magazine and did a little research on racial minorities in advertising. He likes being in ASPIRE, he says. "When I finished ninth grade last year, I wasn't really ready for high school. But the only reason I didn't learn last year was that the teacher just stood up there and—*blah, blah, blah.* That can be pretty sickening."

A few minutes later the lights go off in the big room as a dozen students examine the newly developed slides they took of the Vermont countryside. The pictures flash on the screen. Some are praised by the group; others "knocked." Photography is part of a communications media project that ASPIRE is using as its central learning theme this year; Nikkormat cameras and an array of other A-V equipment are at the students' disposal.

After the viewing session, a handful of students gather in a corner with John Williams, a young bearded free-lance photographer who conducts a photo seminar for class volunteers two days a week. One girl is hesitant about joining the group. Her own photographic efforts—displayed on the screen a few minutes before—had been failures. Her confidence is shattered. Evie notices her chagrin, urges her to join the group, then finally leads her by the hand to the session. The other students go off to their own activities—one to letter a sign, another to do a crossword puzzle (a project required of all ASPIRE students each week, decided by class consensus), and two girls simply to talk.

Other students straggle in. Evie talks to one late-arrival about his "wreck" project. He is going to rebuild a wrecked car he bought for one dollar. The photography students take off for the beach on Lake Champlain, a few hundred yards from the school, to shoot pictures. Evie and Chick Ash, the other teacher, circulate among the remaining students, talking to them. Chick, a good-natured burly man, is gentle and low-keyed with the boys who often gather around him. The program originally had its own guidance counselor, but the students began on their own to turn to the teachers for advice. Staff members now see themselves as teacher-counselors.

Visitors drift in—an ASPIRE alumnus now in eleventh grade, two senior activists who want to use ASPIRE's library on blacks and civil rights. At 11 a.m. Evie and Chick call the students together for a short session on "where we are." In spite of months of open, spontaneous discussion, the students are still a bit nervous and pained with the kind of honesty in a teacher who admits: "I have no idea if this will work" or "We don't know if we can help you." And they're still "psyching out" each other—and some of them remain uneasy with ASPIRE's lack of structure, with the feeling that none of this may be getting them anywhere, that mindless busywork and arbitrary grades would be safer than this freedom. "I think this class needs more direction," a boy suggests.

"What you're all saying is that this isn't learning as you're used to it," Chick responds to a complaining faction. "What changes would you like?"

As the class has grown into a closely knit group, crises and conflicts occasionally erupt. "Everybody in this class is still scared of each other," someone blurts out.

"It's been rough," another boy agrees. "But I think things are okay now. We're getting together slowly."

Getting together has been slow, often discouraging work. The teachers' weekly journal shows the ups and downs of the program:

Sept. 17: "This has been a week of difficult decisions, including decisions to rework our original plans, based on a couple of confrontations, painful and constructive, with the whole class. Evie and Chick found that each was holding back, waiting for the other to lead . . . we needed to find a better way to demonstrate our sense of direction, a direction we understood but were not making clear to the students. This day was an experience of honesty and purpose that we can hold together . . . . This week we continued our writing and science, ending with a film, *Glooscap Country,* taken in Nova Scotia. . . .We followed this with a short discussion and hike along the shoreline to gather materials for our terrarium. . . ."

Sept. 30: "We continued the science, writing, and camera work. Attendance picked up, we felt the group was getting together, interest growing in several directions. On Wednesday we went bowling, Thursday discussion and classes, Friday a short story, 'The Sea Devil,' and a film, *World Without Sun.* . . On Thursday we attacked the class head on about commitment: What are you doing here? What do we want the group to be? Out of this harangue and give-and-take, a couple of quiet people opened up afterward."

Oct. 3: "Monday everything seemed to fall apart again. . . . The discussion ranged over many topics, including parents, school, drugs, freedom, responsibility, using people, honesty—we wish we could reconstruct the discussion. The most interesting thing about it was that more and more kids dropped in until the room was packed with former ASPIRE students, friends of kids in the class, and a couple of teachers. Tim taped most of it. . . . Afterward he said he began to see what it was all about. . . . Monday night Evie took a group to see the ballet. Steve walked all the way in from Malletts Bay on a chilly night to see the ballet—seven miles. . . . The next day he was excited: 'You guys should've come. It was great!' "

The students have learned to be candid about their reactions to the program. After the first month, they too wrote comments: "ASPIRE means nothing to me because when we go to our 'group talks' only about one fourth or so take it really serious. The others just think of wisecracks to go along. . . and the whole room is nothing but a three-ring circus."

Another wrote: "I think ASPIRE is okay. The class is great. But I don't like the people in it, for the simple reason they don't like me. I'm sick of their foolish insults, their immature behavior."

And another: "ASPIRE is a good thing. You give the kids freedom and they may do things for you. It helps you learn things here and on trips and places."

At 12:30 the ASPIRE students begin to leave for the day, a few to an additional course they're taking within the school, some to jobs. The teachers begin assessing the day's dynamics and telephoning the day's numerous absentees. They talk about recruiting a candidate who has been recommended for the program, and about how to utilize a boy's keen involvement in archaeological diggings to bring him to the center of the group.

The staff explains that the style and structure of the program have varied during its three years. The first year the idea was complete freedom, and for the first month the teachers tried to convince the kids they were free to speak their mind and then let them holler about what a bad place school was. Then the group got down to planning its curriculum. As a result of student evaluation, more structure—and greater integration into the larger school program—was introduced last year, when students worked with programmed materials in math, English, and social studies. This year ASPIRE is looking for a balance between the two approaches.

In keeping with a philosophy of evaluation on the basis of "performance" rather than "time," ASPIRE students are graded with a bar graph indicating progress—not with traditional report cards. As experiments, students are sometimes asked to grade themselves or each other. Close contact is maintained with students' homes. Students and parents are interviewed together in their homes before they make a decision to enroll in ASPIRE. Parents, sometimes wary of the unconventional aspects of the program at first, usually welcome it when "good reports" from school replace the unpleasant contacts of former years.

The program sets aside other school requirements. Even regular physical education courses are replaced by informal group activities: skating, mountain-climbing, skiing, hiking.

ASPIRE teachers could simply boast of the best experiences of the three years: the student-planned social studies curriculum which resulted in class trips to EXPO, the Florida Everglades, the Boston Freedom Trail; the independent project on juvenile delinquency which culminated in interviews with the governor and other state officials; the full-scale model of the World War I biplane, the Sopwith Camel, now housed at a nearby hangar (the boys became so engrossed with its construction that they worked late into the night, and Northern Airways donated $500 in cowling).

If the goal of ASPIRE were simply to "save" students who are borderline dropouts—or reclaim those already out of school—the results are also impressive. A majority of the enrollees in the first two years have gone back into the school's regular program as eleventh-graders, much-strengthened in their confidence as well as in basic academic skills. For kids who have never before "made it" in the system, succeeding is often an exhilarating experience. One alumnus, a true believer, returns daily to the project to lecture current enrollees on the importance of working hard and getting the most out of ASPIRE—so they can succeed in school as he's doing.

But ASPIRE wants to produce more than individual success stories. It aims to be a catalyst for the entire educational community, to inspire innovation throughout the school, and "to bring about an awareness on the part of administrators and faculty that change in our educational institutions is not only necessary, but a definite good." ASPIRE's initial American Studies program is now a two-year unit in the general school curriculum. The school's "Our World Today" course—using team teaching and a humanistic approach—is also an offshoot of ASPIRE. The new receptivity to change brought about by ASPIRE has led to a completely nongraded, elective English curriculum this year, as well as teacher in-service programs focusing on educational change.

Burlington High School is learning from the project in other ways, such as the "talk-ins" sponsored by ASPIRE for the entire school community. A recent "talk-in" on education ran half a day, with students and teachers dropping in during free periods to confront the tough questions: "What is the responsibility of the public school?" "If you set up a class just the way you wanted it, what would it be like?" "Who should evaluate teachers?" "Does a grade help you learn?"

These are not academic questions for ASPIRE teachers, who continue to challenge established practice while taking on the job of serving the students everyone else has given up as hopeless. The program's staff members raise more questions than they answer, and refuse to believe that a student has been sufficiently aided if his reading ability improves but his problems at home—or with himself—are as overwhelming and perplexing as ever.

ASPIRE is more of an idea than a technique, its proponents explain, and the idea is that kids are never going to do what they might in school or out until they start feeling good about themselves and their world. Venturing into that world—which educators usually define as outside their realm—is a messy business. There are no lesson plans to deal with the backlog of failure and resentment, the fragility of hope, the complexities of human problems. Progress is tenuous and disappointments are frequent. The teachers—like their students— become human beings, vulnerable to each other and the kids, to their own limitations and successes. It's about time it's begun to happen!

———

Questions:

1. What do you feel is ASPIRE's greatest attraction to potential dropouts?
2. Evaluate the use of ASPIRE alumni to affect this program's students in terms of peer group influence.
3. Draw up a list of at least three innovations or deletions that you would make effective if you were in charge of Project ASPIRE.

LANGUAGE DEVELOPMENT AND
CULTURAL DISADVANTAGEMENT

By FREEMAN McCONNELL
KATHRYN B. HORTON
BERTHA R. SMITH

Abstract: In a 3 year study directed at the prevention of learning problems in school, the failure to achieve, and the subsequent school dropout, a daily program of language and sensory-perceptual instruction was provided to children enrolled in 2 community day care centers. The program was designed to counteract the inhibiting effects of cultural deprivation on language and perceptual learning during the important formative preschool years, and thus it placed emphasis on beginning education with the nursery age child. Preliminary results from the first 2 years demonstrated significant gains in intellectual, linguistic, and perceptual functioning in comparison to control groups which did not undergo the same instruction but which were receiving many elements of the traditional kindergarten type program.

A major focus in education today is upon the achievement levels of children from the large urban pockets of poverty ridden homes in cities throughout the nation. Through the use of speech and hearing personnel in programs such as Head Start, public school speech clinicians and other speech and language specialists have become involved in efforts to ameliorate some of the adverse effects of this environment. The scope of this social and educational problem is emphasized by Riessman (1962), who estimated that one-third of the children in the 14 largest cities of the United States are culturally deprived. He characterized cultural deprivation as "those aspects of middle-class culture—such as education, books, formal language—from which these groups have not benefitted."

It is widely recognized that these social class differences may be expected to inhibit or retard the mental development of the culturally deprived child (Bereiter & Engelmann, 1966; Bloom, Allison, & Hess, 1965; Deutsch, 1963; Jensen, 1966; McCandless, 1952). Jensen (1966) has estimated that 80 percent of the variability in measured intelligence is a result of genetic influence, while 20 percent may result from the environment. A major concomitant of this environmentally induced mental retardation appears to be retarded language development. The writings of a number of investigators (Luria, 1961; McCandless, 1964; Myklebust, 1960; Vygotsky, 1939; Whorf, 1956) have pointed to the theoretical position that high levels of cognitive ability, concept formation, problem solving ability, and intelligence as now measured are dependent upon high levels of linguistic ability. In fact, growth of intelligence appears to depend in large part upon the adequate development of language, and

---

Reprinted with permission from *Exceptional Children* (April 1969).

language depends upon the verbal climate in which the child lives as well as upon an intact sensory and neurological system.

Raph (1967) has suggested the role of the speech clinician may be changing as a result of the widespread interest in the culturally deprived child's failure to achieve in school, which appears to stem from a basic handicap in verbal skills. It was this facet of the problem which motivated personnel of the Bill Wilkerson Hearing and Speech Center to embark upon a planned program of sensory-perceptual and language training which would purportedly demonstrate that the use of methods and materials known to be effective with deaf and hard of hearing, cerebral palsied, and aphasoid children might well be applied to the child with an environmental rather than organic language disability. Thus in effect the project was viewed as a means to demonstrate further that speech pathologists, audiologists, and teachers of the deaf, by virtue of their preparation and long experience in disorders of communication, should be making major contributions to the overall planning in this area of socioeducational reform.

This article presents preliminary information gathered from the first 2 years of a research and demonstration project funded by the US Office of Education. The program described here reflected the philosophy that the disadvantaged child needs instruction early in life and of a type that differs from that of the traditional preschool. It attempted to counteract as much as possible the inhibiting effects of cultural deprivation on language learning during the important formative preschool years. The major premise was that the period in which normal language development occurs is crucial; thus, major emphasis was placed on instruction in the early preschool years, beginning with the 3 year old.

SUBJECTS

Five teacher clinicians provided daily instruction to 128 children (111 Negro and 17 Caucasian) ranging in age from 2 years 8 months to 5 years 11 months. These children, constituting the experimental population, were enrolled (1967-68) in two separate community day care centers located in the lowest socioeconomic areas of the city of Nashville, the urban population of which numbers close to a half million. The control group was comprised of 57 children enrolled in two separate but similar day care centers. For the first year (1965-66) the experimental population numbered 40 children, all from one day care center, and the control group numbered 18. In the second year (1966-67) the project was expanded to include two day care centers, which together provided an experimental population of 106 children, with 24 children in the control group.

HOME VISITS

The services of a caseworker were added in the third year, providing individual visits to the families of each child in the project. During the initial visit she not only assessed the family background and home environment but also instructed the parents specifically about the program, what the children were learning, and how it would help them to become better prepared to enter school. If the child was at home, he was encouraged to take part in the discussion of his activities. She endeavored to impress upon the parents how important it was for them to listen to their child and to let him know they were really interested in what he was learning.

The home visits were valuable both to the program and to the child and his family. In an age of numerous surveys, samplings, and studies, the family was assured that the child was not being used as a guinea pig but was really profiting by his experience. As a result, he received more encouragement at home and the staff members were provided with information which helped them to evaluate the children's progress both individually and as a group. The caseworker thus acted as a liaison between the project, the day care center families, and the community resources. Her services resulted in a variety of other activities, such as making the necessary arrangements for transportation for children who needed to be called back for testing, visiting other day care centers and instituting action for providing the program with control groups, keeping relations between the project staff and the day care center staff on a mutually satisfactory basis, obtaining many free materials for the teachers in the day care centers, and making arrangements for medical attention.

Through the home visitation program the families of 151 different children in the project were visited by the caseworker in the third year. Of this number 21 percent were living in federal housing projects, 20 percent in homes owned by the families, and 59 percent in nonfederal rental housing. Forty-one children, or 27 percent, were in homes sufficiently dilapidated to be classified as substandard housing. The average home contained 4 rooms and had 6 occupants. Since the number of magazines regularly subscribed for or purchased is one indication of the cultural enrichment present in a home, a survey of this factor was also made. One out of six homes had no magazines at all, and more than two-thirds of the homes had three or less.

The number of homes in which both parents were present was also determined. The parents of one-fourth of the children were separated, and one child in five was living with an unwed mother. The mean educational level expressed in highest grade completed was eleventh grade for both fathers and mothers. The mean age of the mothers was 30.8 years and that of the fathers was 35.1 years. Their mean occupational rating (Warner, Meeker, & Eells, 1960) was 6.0 for the mothers and 6.1 for the fathers; categories of occupation here were graded from 1 to 7 with 7 being the lowest rating.

EXPERIMENTAL CURRICULUM

The children receiving the training were divided by age into nursery and kindergarten groups, both of which were further subdivided into groups of six and seven each for the instructional program presented 5 days a week on a half day basis. The head teacher was a trained teacher of the deaf, three teachers were trained speech pathologists, and the fifth was a trained elementary teacher. Each of the teachers, except the latter, held the masters degree.

The four particular phases which constituted the daily curriculum were the opening exercises, the language program, the sensory-perceptual training program, and the music and story hour. The procedure used in opening exercises consisted of the flag salute, calendar work, and weather news. For the older children, increased emphasis was placed on the development of seasonal concepts during the opening period. Specially prepared teacher charts were used to develop these concepts.

The entire group participated in the opening exercises, while the language and sensory-perceptual training units were presented to the smaller subgroups previously mentioned. The types of units comprising the language series were presented in units such as The Child (Body Concept) and His Family, The Home, Clothing, Food, Toys, Science, Transportation, Farm Animals, Community Helpers, and Zoo Animals. These basic units were presented to all children, but with greater elaboration for the older children. Field trips and actual demonstrations of materials were used whenever possible. As part of the language instruction, an aid to grammar and syntax was presented by means of the Fitzgerald Key headings ("who," "what," "where," "how," "why," "what color," and "how many") which were borrowed from education of the deaf methodology. Printed forms are normally accompanied by pictorially presented concepts.

During the first year, emphasis was placed on the receptive aspects of language and on increasing listening skills and attention span. When at the end of the year it was found the children were still quite defective in expressive aspects of language as well, plans for the second year were modified to include increased emphasis on sentence structure, verb endings, and word forms. This emphasis was motivated by the present investigators' own test findings as well as those reported by other researchers, which revealed that grammar and syntactic functioning are one of the verbal areas of lowest performance in the disadvantaged child. Many of the procedures used in this aspect were delineated by Bereiter and Engelmann (1966) and by Frostig (1964). Additionally, the Peabody Language Development Kit, Preschool Level (Dunn, Horton, & Smith, 1968) was presented to all groups on a daily basis.

The sensory-perceptual training program emphasized development of the visual, auditory, and tactile senses. An innovation in the third year was the use of the Montessori materials to aid in developing size, form, number, and color concepts, although the extent to which the Montessori training was presented varied at the two day care centers. For the group which had more suitable physical facilities, the structured periods were supplemented by nonstructured periods devoted to the examination and use of the Montessori materials in which the individual child was particularly interested. For the kindergarten group, the Frostig Program for the Development of Visual Perception was used.

The music and story hour was a period in which a variety of activities were presented to sharpen visual and auditory skills. Of particular interest were the original stories using the P. Mooney theme developed initially at the Bill Wilkerson Center especially for use in this program and later incorporated into the Peabody Language Development Kit, Preschool Level (Dunn et al., 1968). P. Mooney is an imaginary character who solves life's everyday problems by dipping into the P. Mooney bag for solutions, which of course always work. When presented on attractively colored posters, P. Mooney and his friends seemed to appeal highly to the imagination and fantasy of the young children. Also, poems, finger plays, songs, and dramatizations constituted part of the instruction, as well as a eurhythmics program designed to increase body awareness and control and to correlate these functions with auditory experiences. The eurhythmic activities varied from the "let's pretend" type to complex dance patterns.

RESULTS

To evaluate the effects of the instruction program each child in both the experimental and the control group was tested at the beginning and at the end of the 9 month school year. This evaluation included a battery of tests adapted and designed for assessing overall language and learning capacity. Major areas assessed were language, intelligence, memory and attention, and visual-perceptual motor capacity.

Gains in intellectual functioning. Data support the contention that the program did significantly affect the children's intellectual functioning. The first year of instruction for three first year groups over a 2 year period resulted in highly significant increases. Table 1 presents the Stanford-Binet IQ data, for which the gain curves are illustrated in Figure 1. The gains of the experimental groups after one year of instruction were highly significant statistically at less than the 1 percent level. In Figure 1 it may be noted also that the 21 children who were in the program for 2 years (1965-67) maintained this gain through the second year of the program. In contrast, it may be seen that the control groups, although in a daily kindergarten-nursery program, achieved no change in intellectual functioning. In fact, for both the 18 in the first year and 24 in the second year, the mean IQ score was slightly less than that at the beginning of the experimental period, although the difference in both cases was not statistically significant.

When intelligence was measured by the Peabody Picture Vocabulary Test (PPVT), the gains were not so marked nor were the differences between the groups as great, as may be noted in Figure 2. Since this test is highly specific with respect to vocabulary, it would appear not to be as well suited for assessing the intellectual functioning of children from deprived environments. A total of 114 children with one year of instruction gained a mean of 15.9 IQ points, which was about equivalent to the gain on the Binet test, but despite this gain the children were still at a lower IQ level than they had achieved on the Binet test. The traditional day care program may have also exerted a favorable

TABLE 1

The Mean Stanford-Binet IQ Levels for Each of the Designated Populations Following First 9 Month Experimental Period

Group	N	Mean age	Mean pretraining IQ	Mean posttraining IQ	Mean gain
I. Experimental groups					
1965-66	35	4-1	90.5	107.0	16.5
1966-67	54	4-1	93.8	109.4	15.6
1966-67	17	3-6	88.0	112.8	24.8
Total first year	106	4-0	91.8	109.2	17.4
II. Control groups					
1965-66	18	4-1	98.4	98.2	−0.2
1966-67	24	5-3	93.0	91.0	−2.0
Total	42	4-9	95.3	94.1	−1.2

**FIG. 1.   Stanford-Binet IQ levels before and after language training program of
three experimental and two control populations.**

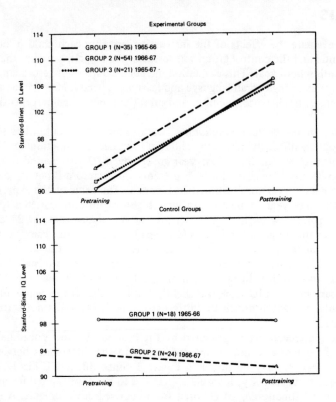

**FIG. 2.   Peabody Picture Vocabulary Test IQ levels before and after one year language
training program for experimental and control populations.**

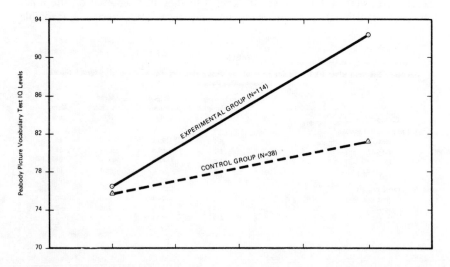

influence on PPVT level, since the control group did gain 6 points (from 75 to 81), although this amount was much less than that shown by the experimental group.

These results suggest, however, that retardation in language in these children in relation both to their chronological age and to their intelligence potential was present. Performance on the Binet comprehension items computed separately for all children in the first year of the study was superior to the PPVT by 9.4 mental age months, a rather significant difference for children at this age level.

Gains in sensory-perceptual and linguistic skills. Brooks (1968) studied the effects of the instruction program on visual perceptual ability, as determined by the Frostig Developmental Test of Visual Perception. Figure 3 illustrates the gains on each of the five subtests of the Frostig Test for the two groups during the first year experimental period. The group receiving instruction made statistically significant gains on four of the five subtests, while the control group gained significantly on only one, progressed minimally and not significantly on two, and regressed on the remaining two. The best indication of the significance

FIG. 3. Comparison of pre- and posttraining Frostig subtest mean scores for the experimental and control groups.

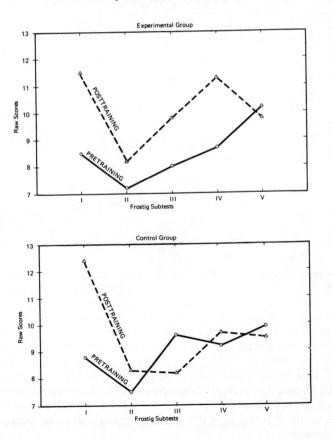

of the gains achieved by the experimental group can be seen in a comparison of
the Perceptual Quotient (PQ) scores for the two groups. The experimental
subjects gained 19.1 points in their pre- to posttraining PQ scores, while the
control group gained only 6.6 points, an amount one-third the gain evidenced by
the children undergoing specific sensory-perceptual training.

A more detailed study of language functioning was carried out by use of
the Illinois Test of Psycholinguistic Abilities. The ITPA results in Figure 4 were
obtained on 39 children in the first year of the study (Foote, 1966). The mean
Language Age of the group was 7 months below their mean Chronological Age,
with results on two-thirds of the ITPA subtests showing retardation of 8 months
or more. The poorest level of functioning was reached on the Auditory-Vocal
Automatic subtest, which assessed their use of correct grammar or syntax. This
finding no doubt reflected the meagerness and inarticulateness of their linguistic
environment.

**FIG. 4. Mean performance levels on Illinois Test of Psycholinguistic
Abilities for 39 culturally disadvantaged preschool children.**

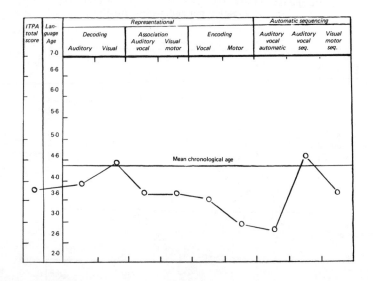

Another interesting finding from the ITPA was the superiority of visual
capacities over auditory capacities on the decoding subtests. In pursuit of this
trend, we further undertook an analysis of data from Binet tests and subtests
derived from the Nebraska Test of Learning Aptitude and the Gesell and Cattell
developmental schedules, which showed equivalent superiority of visual versus
auditory abilities. Specifically, each child in the first year of the study was
compared with reference to his performance on tasks of attention, discrimination, and memory for visual material as contrasted to his performance on the
same tasks for auditory material. When group differences were analyzed, a mean
developmental lag of 6 months in auditory functioning for the group appeared.
When one recalls that this lag was present in a group with a chronological age of

less than 4 years, its significance is heightened. The culturally disadvantaged children appeared not to be developing at equivalent rates with reference to all of their sensory capacities for learning. The significance of lags in auditory development is quite apparent when one considers the very important role that audition plays in school performance.

Pre- and postinstruction testing with the ITPA was not accomplished until the second year (1966-67). Data obtained from a group of 19 experimental subjects, compared with a group of 22 control subjects, demonstrated essentially the same pattern of linguistic functioning, with auditory-vocal automatic functioning (use of grammar) at the poorest level. After 9 months of instruction the experimental group gained in Language Age by 15 months, while during the same 9 month period the control group gained only 2 months, and were thus still further behind in Language Age compared to their Chronological Age than before the experimental period began. Such a finding would suggest that language, like intelligence, in the culturally disadvantaged may be characterized by the unfortunate feature of cumulative deficit unless appropriate steps of intervention are taken.

A major objective of the present study was to prevent the very common occurrence of school failure in the child from a culturally disadvantaged background. In essence, through a specific program of instruction planned to stimulate and enhance the development of linguistic skills, the child's functioning in a number of areas was positively affected. Not only had linguistic functioning improved, but also intellectual and visual-perceptual functioning showed significant gains. To determine the effects of the present instruction program on school readiness, the Metropolitan Readiness Test was used in the second year to assess all children in both the experimental and control groups who were preparing to enter the first grade in public schools the following September. This battery of tests purports to measure the extent to which school beginners have developed in the several skills and abilities that contribute to readiness for first grade instruction (Hildreth, Griffiths, & McGauvran, 1965). Although the population in this age group was small (16 experimental, 9 control subjects), the amounts by which the experimental subjects excelled the control subjects, on the average, is clearly evident from Figure 5.

The median total score for the control subjects was 13, which placed them in the lowest 7 percent of children entering first grade. According to the authors of the test, for children who score below 24 the chances of difficulty are high under ordinary instructional conditions; they postulated that further readiness work, assignment to slow sections, or individualized work is essential. The experimental group of 16 children achieved a mean total score of 44, which is almost at average range—it is the highest score in the Low Normal range. While these samples are small, the present authors believe the instruction program presented to the experimental subjects may have raised their readiness level by at least one score range.

DISCUSSION

Proponents of the traditional preschool philosophy contend that a program such as the one described in this article is too structured for the child of this age. As Bereiter and Engelmann (1966) have pointed out, however, what

FIG. 5. Comparative achievement of 5 to 6 year olds in experimental and control groups on subtests of Metropolitan (School) Readiness Tests after one year experimental period.

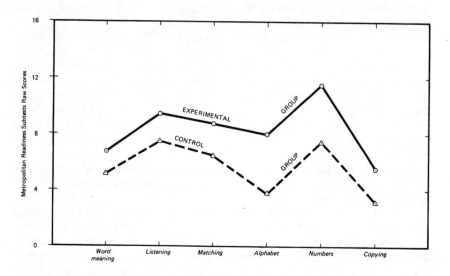

these proponents overlook is that the traditional nursery school is uniquely middle class and is designed to provide what middle class children need to round out their already rich diets of experience. Although the good nursery school may help the upper middle class child develop his intellectual abilities, he has the abilities before he enters, and he is not hampered intellectually if he does not attend nursery school. To the extent that environment has anything to do with the superior academic abilities of the child from such a background, the crucial factors, then, must lie in the complex of verbalism, parental stimulation, achievement motivation, and orientation toward the future, none of which characterize the deprived environment. For the disadvantaged child, a sharp departure from the traditional nursery school appears necessary if he is to compete successfully in society.

The authors have taken the position that it is indeed the language deficit which constitutes the greatest hazard to later school learning and subsequent life achievement. The lags produced in the early preschool years create, furthermore, what has been called a cumulative deficit which results in learning disabilities too marked to overcome in the ordinary school classroom. The effects produced are, therefore, often irreversible if not counteracted early. Thus, the authors believe it is necessary to concentrate efforts on the very young child in order to combat the lag in the crucial period of language development that should be occurring during the time from 2½ to 4½ years of age. Increasing chronological age simply adds to the pervasiveness of the problems, none of which are alleviated or reduced.

On the other hand, emphasis on language and sensory-perceptual training, if implemented in the critical preschool years, may be expected to combat in an effective way the sociologically induced mental retardation of such children.

Both the receptive and expressive aspects of their language functioning need to be stimulated, increased, and improved. When one considers that in the traditional nursery program a given child has very little opportunity for direct conversation with the teacher, one can appreciate the need for the small group interaction in which exchange of conversation and individual attention on structure and syntax of language are actually emphasized by direct teaching methods.

It was noted that auditory abilities were poorer than visual by several methods of assessment (McConnell & Horton, 1966). This difference, which has been found by other investigators, has interesting ramifications. One may indeed conjecture that language and vocabulary functioning will be reduced when auditory functioning is reduced, but, one might ask, what factors could be operating to produce such an auditory lag when hearing itself is normal? It is quite probable that most of these children come from homes in which the sound environment is extremely random and unstructured. For example, if a youngster has been living in a 4 room home in a family of seven or eight people, it is quite probable that the noise level in the home would be quite high and that there would be many extraneous sounds which the child would gradually learn to ignore. He thus might block out auditory patterns from the first days of life, as it were, because they are so profuse that he cannot handle them selectively at this stage in his auditory development. This blocking of auditory stimulation would thence directly affect the child's transmission of sensory stimuli by ear, which is the chief method by which the child learns language.

A problem which is yet unsolved is whether the basic auditory and perceptual skills learned by most children in the first years of life, if not learned because of the particular environmental milieu (as in cultural deprivation), would directly contribute to the child's lack of facility in language and subsequent poor educational achievement. Continued study of these and the many other different facets which combine to present the problem of sociologically induced mental retardation in our society is necessary if effective ways of remediation are to be found.

REFERENCES:

Bereiter, C., & Engelmann, S. *Teaching disadvantaged children in the preschool.* Englewood Cliffs, N.J.: Prentice-Hall, 1966.
Bloom, B., Allison, D., & Hess, R. *Compensatory education for cultural deprivation.* New York: Holt, Rinehart, & Winston, 1965.
Brooks, S. A study of visual perception in culturally disadvantaged children. Unpublished masters thesis, Vanderbilt University, 1968.
Deutsch, M. The disadvantaged child and the learning process. In A.H. Passow (Ed.), *Education in depressed areas.* New York: Teachers College Press, Columbia University, 1963. Pp. 163-180.
Dunn, L., Horton, K.B., & Smith, J. *The Peabody Language Development Kit-level P.* Circle Pines, Minn.: American Guidance, 1968.
Foote, E. An exploration of the language abilities of young, culturally deprived children using the Illinois Test of Psycholinguistic Abilities. Unpublished masters thesis, Vanderbilt University, 1966.
Frostig, M. *Frostig visual perception program.* Chicago: Follett, 1964.
Hildreth, G.H., Griffiths, N.L. & McGauvran, M.E. *Manual of directions, form A, Metropolitan Readiness Tests.* New York: Harcourt, Brace, & World, 1965.
Jensen, A. R. Social class and perceptual learning. *Mental Hygiene,* 1966, 50, 226-239.

Luria, A. R. *The role of speech in the regulation of normal and abnormal behavior.* New York: Pergamon, 1961.

McCandless, B. R. Environment and intelligence. *American Journal of Mental Deficiency,* 1952, 56, 674-691.

McCandless, B.R. *Children and adolescents.* (2nd ed.) New York: Holt, Rinehart, & Winston, 1964.

McConnell, F., & Horton, K. B. Language characteristics of the culturally deprived preschool child. In Foundation for the Help of the Deaf Child, *Proceedings of the First American Congress on Auditory Disorders and Language.* Buenos Aires, Argentina: The Foundation, 1966. Pp. 584-589.

Myklebust, H. R. *Psychology of deafness.* New York: Grune & Stratton, 1960.

Raph, J. B. Language and speech deficits in culturally disadvantaged children: Implications for the speech clinician. *Journal of Speech and Hearing Disorders,* 1967, 32, 203-214.

Riessman, F. *The culturally deprived child.* New York: Harper & Row, 1962.

Vygotsky, L. S. Thought and speech. *Psychiatry,* 1939, 2, 29-54.

Warner, W. L., Meeker, M. & Eells, K. *Social class in America.* New York: Harper & Row, 1960.

Whorf, B. J. *Language, thought, and reality.* New York: John Wiley & Sons, 1956.

Questions:

1. Describe the role in an elementary school of the speech clinician regarding the language development of the culturally disadvantaged.

2. List four or five factors that lead a number of experts to conclude that the traditional nursery school is uniquely middle-class.

3. Defend or reject the following statement: The home is the most important school that a child will ever have, and his mother his most important teacher.

EARLY SCHOOL ADMISSIONS

By ALICE CURRY HARDING

Five years ago, I visited Baltimore's Early School Admissions Project—a small-scale experimental prekindergarten program for four-year-olds living in the inner city. In the article I wrote about the program, I said:

"The story of the Early School Admissions Project is as exciting as a serialized mystery story. If only the conclusion can fulfill the hopes that the first installment raises, it will be a best seller."

Recently I paid a second visit to Early Admissions and found that it has indeed become a best seller. A project no longer, Early School Admissions is now a regular part of the Baltimore City school system. Educators and laymen alike regard it as a potent weapon in the war against poverty and ignorance.

At the time of my first visit, the Project was nearing the end of its second year. The children originally enrolled had gone on to kindergarten and a second group were nearing "graduation."

The indications seemed to be that the Project was achieving its goal—that it was giving a better chance for school success to children whose home conditions deprived them of many of the experiences that enrich other childhoods. The children who pioneered in the enrichment program had gained considerable understanding of concepts and had improved markedly in their ability to communicate and socialize. Their mental maturity test scores were higher than they had been when they entered the program. The youngsters who had already gone on to kindergarten had been kept together in special classes because kindergarten teachers considered them too advanced for work designed for children who had not had the Early Admissions experience.

Educators connected with the Project were understandably hopeful that the experiment would show the way to avoiding the school failures that so often lead to dropping out. They realized, however, that they had no conclusive proof of success:

"They're doing fine now," cautioned Baltimore's then assistant superintendent for elementary education, "but what will happen when they get to third grade? Will they taper off or fall behind? Will these children have an advantage that will persist through the grades? . . . We won't know for years."

In the five years between my visits, the superintendent's first question had been answered. The school records of children who took part in the program several years ago indicate that they have an advantage that persists at least through the third and fourth grades.

Reprinted with permission from *Today's Education* (November 1969).

Perhaps even more significant are the gains these youngsters have made in areas where progress can't be assessed by paper and pencil tests. Elementary teachers have found that Early Admissions children are better equipped to cope with schoolwork than children from their neighborhoods who have not had the experience. For example, a first grade teacher says, "You can begin earlier to do real work with them. They seem to be more mature and you can communicate with them on a higher level."

Typical comments by elementary principals are: "I would not want to be without the Early Admissions program," and, "Teachers say to me, 'I hate to think of the difficulties these children would have experienced if they hadn't had Early Admissions.' "

The school district has demonstrated its belief in the value of Early Admissions by allowing the program to expand. Early Admissions started in specially designed spaces—called Centers—in two elementary school buildings. Last year, 44 groups of preschoolers were enrolled in Centers housed in 22 elementary schools. More parents each year try to have their children enrolled in the program, and those parents whose children have participated are eager to have some of the special features of Early Admissions extended into kindergarten and the grades.

Early Admissions has been a stable program. Many of the elements outlined for the original program are little changed, and many of the professional staff members have been with the program since the beginning. Youngsters in the 1969 groups engage in the same kinds of tasks as did the children in 1963. They participate in similar horizon-expanding experiences—playing active games, pretending, taking trips, listening to stories and talking about them, making things, and wondering. The children receive a nourishing lunch every day and have the services of nurses, doctors, psychologists, nutritionists, and social workers.

Other aspects of the program have changed, however. Although Baltimore's early childhood educators have realized for several years that they have a good thing going, they have not been smugly satisfied with the program. While hundreds of Baltimore children have been learning at Early Admission Centers, the adults who work with them have been learning, too, and the program reflects what they have learned.

Originally, Early Admissions was somewhat isolated from the rest of the school system. Now that it is an integral part of the system, principals and teachers work closely with Early Admissions staffs and make every effort to carry Early Admissions-type experiences through kindergarten and the first three grades.

When Early Admissions was in the project stage, sessions lasted all day, and 35 children made up a class. The ratio of adults to children at a Center was about 1 to 9. Today, the proportion of adults is higher, because experience has shown that the more individualized attention a child receives and the more one-to-one encounters he has with interested adults, the more he benefits from the program. Class size has been cut in half by means of scheduling two half-day sessions at each Center; a Center staff now consists of two teachers and two aides, assisted by a fifth adult, the program assistant, who spends about a day a week at each of the four or five Centers she is assigned to.

The presence of so many adults in the Centers means that a grown-up is always on hand to admire a drawing, to help with a word that is hard to pronounce, or to comfort someone who has a bruised knee or hurt feelings. At lunchtime, an adult joins each group of four or five at its table.

The high ratio of adults to youngsters makes it possible to have many activities that would be impractical in a situation where only one or two adults were present. For example, on my last visit, the children at one Center were making fruit pies. With five adults present to supervise and suggest, the four-year-olds turned out real pies, ready for the oven. One doesn't need much imagination to picture what a bunch of four-year-olds might have done with piecrust mix and canned fruit if only one harassed teacher had been presiding over the operation.

Why make pies? For these children, the pie-making session provided a number of learning situations. First, the children scrubbed the tables, then their hands. Next they assembled the materials and equipment and did the necessary measuring. The adult and the children at each table worked together to make one pie. Each youngster had the chance to be in charge of one step in the process. Baking was to take place the next day and the children learned why the uncooked pies had to go into the refrigerator instead of being stored on a shelf.

Over the years, experience has dictated some changes in the makeup of the Center staffs. Program assistants and parent liaison workers—positions new since Project days—are now important in the staff structure.

Program assistants are highly experienced early childhood specialists who have been teachers in the Early Admissions program. A program assistant, who divides her time among four or five Centers, coordinates programs, helps teachers with planning or with particularly severe problems, and works with individual children. With program assistants serving as back-ups, teachers constantly have opportunities to improve the quality of the educational program.

The parent liaison workers are women who have served as aides in the program. Assigned to Centers in their home neighborhoods and familiar with the program, they spend enough time working with the children presently enrolled to know what is current in the classroom. Since parents look on the liaison worker as part of the neighborhood rather than part of the school, the worker can often get through to a parent whom a teacher cannot reach.

From the outset, Early Admissions has sought to reduce the home-school gap by involving parents, but many inner-city parents have such ingrained resentment or fear of school and everything pertaining to it that teachers are almost unable to communicate with them. Now, thanks in large part to the efforts of the liaison workers, parents have become increasingly involved in the program. For instance, parents are now eager participants in the Parent Advisory Committee. This group, composed of parent representatives from all the Centers, meets monthly to learn about and to make suggestions about the program. Members are no longer timid about telling what they (and the parents they represent) like and don't like about activities at the Centers.

A program assistant has this to say about how parents' reactions have changed. "When I was first teaching in the program, parents would accept everything I said—no questions asked. But now when I go back to a Center where I used to teach, it's no longer a case of 'The teacher said it, so it's right.' Now it's 'I want to know about . . . .' They raise more questions, even to the point of asking, 'Where is my child going, now that he's leaving Early Admissions? What is the kindergarten program going to be?' "

The original plan for Early Admissions called for measuring progress by comparing the school performance of children in the Early Admissions groups with that of control groups of children in the same neighborhoods who would have qualified for admission to the Project had numbers not been limited. Unfortunately, however, urban renewal and migration from project areas have resulted in such a population shift that this kind of group evaluation has been impossible.

The professionals who work in Early Admissions agree on the need for some means of evaluating individual performance in the program. They feel that as a child progresses from Early Admissions to kindergarten and beyond, the successive teachers need to know what he was like when he came to Early Admissions and how far he has advanced. One teacher illustrates the need to have such information available by citing the case of a little boy who did not speak when he came to Early Admissions and did not even know his own name. By the time he was in fourth grade, however, he was reading at second grade level. The teacher pointed out that this child had been highly successful in overcoming tremendous obstacles, yet someone who didn't know this story might regard him as a failure.

Some of the schools that house Centers are now trying to develop a means of keeping a four-or-five-year cumulative record for each child, so that as he advances from one grade to another, the teachers will have a picture of what he was when he started and of how he has progressed. Possibilities being explored range from a simple checklist to a maturity profile in which each year's record would be indicated in a different color.

The professional staff of Early Admissions has ample opportunity to work on such problems as evaluation. Every second Friday, while parent liaison workers fill in for Center teachers, program administrators, teachers, aides, and parent workers meet for in-service sessions that take the form of workshops, lectures, demonstrations, and discussion groups.

To this observer, the philosophy behind the in-service sessions deserves much of the credit for the success of the Early School Admissions program, although the carefully planned play/work experiences and the individualized attention certainly contribute, as does parental involvement. Other important elements are the well-prepared staff; the planned continuity with the regular school grades; and the medical, psychological, and other supplementary services. However, a certain spirit of purpose and optimism that seems to permeate the program may well be the factor most responsible for making Early Admissions a best seller in Baltimore. This spirit shows in what individual teachers say and in the tone of group discussions: "We've really got a good thing going. Let's make it better and better."

Questions:

1. What factors do you feel make Early Admissions a stable program?
2. List the possible advantages and disadvantages that you feel could result from the decision to cut the school day, as well as the class size, in half.

PERSPECTIVE ON THE JENSEN AFFAIR

By WILLIAM F. BRAZZIEL

In the Winter 1969 edition of **HARVARD EDUCATIONAL REVIEW,** *psychologist Arthur R. Jensen, of the University of California at Berkeley, wrote a lengthy article, "How Much Can We Boost IQ and Scholastic Achievement?" which has provoked unprecedented controversy.[1] As Jensen himself later described it, the article is "a comprehensive summary of my research and thinking on the subject of educationally relevant individual differences, ·vith reference especially to their genetic base." [2]*

Others have characterized his paper as an unfortunate revival of the nature-nurture argument, with disturbing claims about the heritability of intelligence, racial differences, and speculations about eugenic-"solutions" to learning problems of black children. Recently William F. Brazziel, professor of Higher Education of the University of Connecticut, presented a forthright summary of Jensen's major contentions and others' rebuttals in a presentation at a Head Start Regional Conference held in Washington, D. C. What follows is a shortened version of Dr. Brazziel's analysis.

Now that the dust has about settled on the Jensen controversy, it behooves us to search for the underlying causes of the conflagration, to try to repair the damage done to the children involved, and to determine that public Indian wrestling of this sort must never happen again.

The latter determination will be the hardest. Heredity-environment arguments seem to erupt every twelve or thirteen years. No one has a ready explanation of this phenomenon; I am tempted to blame it on the appearance of sunspots.

These observations do seem crystal clear:

1. The Jensen Affair resulted from the compounding of one or two basic and seemingly honest errors.

2. The controversy has been placed in proper perspective by statements from officials of the American Psychological Association, the American Genetics Association; by comment from Jensen's colleagues; and by comment from Jensen himself.

3. It is time to bring down the curtain on the argument and get back to making schools work for poor children.

The compounded errors were committed first by the editorial board of *Harvard Educational Review* in failing to call in outside help to edit thoroughly

Reprinted by permission of William F. Brazziel and the Association for Childhood Education International, 3615 Wisconsin Avenue, N. W., Washington, D. C. Copyright © 1970 by the Association. *Childhood Education* (April 1970).

the manuscript and then by Jensen's insistence on slanting the piece so severely as to insure its failure to pass the test of objectivity. Graduate students run *HER*—completely—and in this situation they were simply in over their heads.[3]

As a result, Jensen has had to shift his positions, constantly it seems, thereby creating utter confusion and disarray in all quarters. Statements of clarifications, reversals and retreats from his original positions have been recorded in the Summer 1969 issue of *HER*, in interviews for *Science News* (April 5, 1969, p. 326), in a summer issue of the *New York Times Magazine*,[4] and in a letter to a subsequent issue of the latter.

What then (hopefully for the last time) did Jensen say? When? Where?

In his original article in the Winter 1969 issue of *HER*, Professor Jensen began by accusing workers and supporters of compensatory education of attempting to violate all laws of individual differences and raise (or lower) all children to a median level of achievement and intelligence—a sort of homogenization process as it were. He then stated rather sternly that success in this effort was not possible due to the hereditary constraints involved and that he would prove this thesis in the next 122 pages of his article.

This argument is a straw man. Compensatory people are not ignoring individual differences in children. Nor are they engaged in a Great Test Race. They are trying to do what President Johnson charged them with in his statements in signing the various bills to run these programs: to make it so every child can get as much education as possible. The testing apparatus is only one of several means of trying to get feedback from the programs. It is not the most important means. Teacher judgments, grades, parent comment, school persistence and many other indices are used to good advantage in highly successful programs.

(When apprised of these facts by rebuttals of a team of psychologists and geneticists in the Spring issue of *HER*, Dr. Jensen retreated from his accusation by explaining to a *New York Times Magazine* interviewer that he made it to give emphasis and draw attention and interest to his article. He said his English teachers always urged him to begin his papers with a provocative statement.)

Dr. Jensen then proceeded in his original article to re-hash the old co-twin studies of the nature-nurture controversy. He selected three of these studies and computed a simple heritability index involving an analysis of variance. He then claimed to have proved environment accounted for no more than 20 percent of the development of the mature human's intelligence and that the other 80 percent was a product of heredity.

Jensen's colleagues immediately pointed out the errors, inadequacies and general cant in his claims. Martin Deutsch and a group of associates at the Institute for Developmental Studies at New York University identified seventeen statistical transpositions in Jensen's computations—all in favor of his heritability thesis. (See Fall 1969 issue of *HER*.) Others have noted that Jensen also failed to analyze thoroughly one of the three classic co-twin studies (Newman et al)[5] he used as the mainstay for his heritability index.

Ernest Hilgard and Richard Atkinson have analyzed the same study (in their *Introduction to Psychology,* New York: Harcourt Brace, 1967, p. 454) and shown that environmental deprivation is indeed a potent factor in IQ development and measurement. Hilgard and Atkinson observed that while most co-twin studies involve moving children into a similar environment, four of the nineteen pairs in the Newman study were placed in widely contrasting environments (like suddenly becoming poor, turning black and taking up residence in Sunflower County, Mississippi!). The resulting IQ scores were so different that, according to the authors, the entire correlation was dragged down significantly. Such a difference, if analyzed properly, would lower Jensen's heritability index considerably and shed light on the racial storm he managed to stir in still another set of comments. The rebuttal team also reminded Dr. Jensen that an IQ gene as such has never been identified and may not exist.

When apprised of these errors Jensen stated in the Summer 1969 issue of *HER* that he did not seek to be definitive and all-inclusive but that he was attempting to re-assert the importance of heredity in human development.[6] He stated that this concept had been pushed into the background by the environmentalists over the past decade or so and that he simply wanted teachers and others to consider heredity when confronted with individual differences in children.

In an astonishing statement for this day and time, Dr. Jensen then assured his headlines and controversy by toying with the hypothesis that black people thought differently from white people and by citing one or two studies showing gaps in black-white IQ scores. The analysis here was brief and far from objective. I looked in vain, for example, for treatment of the half dozen or so classical studies showing black-white comparability in IQ scores. In scholarly, objective articles on this subject, these *always* find a place. None did here—even in the bibliography.

Omitted were such classics as H. A. Tanser's work showing black-white IQ comparability in rural Kent County, Ontario;[7] Eli Ginsberg's *Negro Potential*,[8] showing black soldiers from some states scoring higher than white soldiers from some states in World War II testing; and the works of Otto Klineberg[9] and E. S. Lee,[10] which documented big jumps in the IQ of Negro children when taken north from southern farms and villages.

In answer to a written request I personally sent to Dr. Jensen for clarification of his real stand on race and IQ, I received a form-letter response. Jensen stated in this letter that his main interest was in ethnic learning styles. Further, Jensen complained to interviewers from *Science News* that he devoted less than 5 percent of his article to race but that 95 percent of the news coverage was on this subject. I will never understand, however, why he failed to include some of this material. We now find, for example, that the school with the highest IQ in the largest city in Jensen's own state is 90 percent black (see the January 1970 issue of *Phi Delta Kappan* for a report of Windsor Hill School in Los Angeles).[11]

Startled and confused at being denounced as a white supremacist by his colleagues and at being embraced as one by Klan-type groups, Jensen denied such labels in the Summer 1969 issue of *HER* (p. 480) and, to the consternation of some Birch-type groups, declared that Oriental people were superior in abstract intelligence. Jensen also softened his stand on black inferiority by attributing black-white IQ gaps to large black slum families and small black middle-class families. He emphasized his belief that there are no yellow, black or white IQ genes as such but only IQ genes.

Finally, and most cruelly, Jensen said that compensatory education had failed and that eugenics was the long-range and manual training the short-range answer to people mired in poverty.

When apprised of the fact that he had literally ignored thousands upon thousands of success stories, Dr. Jensen reversed his position and stated in a letter to a fall issue of the *New York Times Magazine* (November 16, 1969, p. 15) and in an interview with an editor of *U.S. News and World Report* (June 2, 1969, p. 54) that compensatory education had not failed, that it could help poor children learn better, and that it could raise test scores where people considered these as being very important in the educative process. He claimed that he meant to imply in his original article that compensatory education had been spread too far too fast and that model research and development should precede federal grants to operate the programs.

What to do? I suggest we write the whole thing off as one of those natural disasters that come along from time to time. And, at the risk of some unemployment in the measurement industry, I suggest that psychologists take the advice of the National Academy of Sciences;[12] i.e., suspend racial comparisons on tests until black, brown and red people match white people in jobs, income, housing, quality of education and, most important, in respect and in complete participation in the day-to-day affairs of the country. We should make the same suspension for any child who is growing up poor.

I suggest, also, that we heed the advice of concerned educators who urge us to eliminate IQ tests from the schools and that we follow the lead of those school systems who are building their testing programs around readiness, achievement and diagnostic testing.[13] The problems caused by IQ tests far outweigh any possible good they can ever do in the schools.

Some defense lawyers are using Jensen's original statements in desegregation cases. They should be disbarred for malpractice. Some administrators and government officials are slackening the pace and vigor in planning and executing programs of instruction for poor children. They should be fired. Teachers with poor children in their classrooms should re-dedicate themselves to helping these children get all the education they can. Incidents such as the Jensen Affair must not derail us in our drive to bring this about.

REFERENCES:

[1]Arthur R. Jensen, "How Much Can We Boost IQ and Scholastic Achievement?" *Harvard Educational Review* 39 (Winter 1969): 1-123.

[2] . "Reducing the Heredity-Environmental Uncertainty: A Reply," *HER* (Summer 1969): 449. See also a brief summary by Celia Stendler Lavatelli in the February 1970 issue of CHILDHOOD EDUCATION, pp. 240-41.

[3]As noted on the title page of each issue, *"The Harvard Educational Review* is a journal of opinion and research in the field of education. Articles are selected, edited, and published by an Editorial Board of fifteen graduate students in Harvard University, and the editorial policy does not reflect an official position of the Faculty of Education or any other Harvard faculty."

[4]See L. Edson, "Jensenism, *n.,* The Theory That IQ Is Largely Determined by Genes," *New York Times Magaine,* August 31, 1969.

[5]E. B. Newman, F. N. Freeman, and K. H. Halzinger, *Twins: A Study of Heredity and Environment* (Chicago: University of Chicago Press, 1937).

[6]*Harvard Educational Review* 39, 3 (Summer 1969): 449-83.

[7]H. A. Tanser, *The Settlement of Negroes in Kent County, Ontario* (Chatham, Ontario: Shephard Publishing Co., 1939).

[8]Eli Ginsberg, *Negro Potential* (New York: Columbia University Press, 1960).

[9]Otto Klineberg, *Negro Intelligence and Selective Migration* (New York: Columbia University Press, 1935).

[10]E. S. Lee, "Negro Intelligence and Selective Migration: A Philadelphia Test of the Klineberg Hypothesis," *American Sociological Review* 16 (1951): 227-33.

[11]"What Would Jensen Say?" From Newsfront Department of *Phi Delta Kappan* LI, 5 (January 1970): 292.

[12]See April 17, 1967, report of NAS Committee on Racial Testing. Committee issued statement in response to requests of William Shockley, Stanford physicist, for the NAS to sponsor racial studies in intelligence.

[13]See Elliott Carlson's analysis and report of deletion of IQ testing from New York, Philadelphia, St. Paul, Cleveland, Washington and Los Angeles schools because of test bias, *Wall Street Journal,* June 12, 1969, p. 1.

———

Questions:

1. What are the main objections to the theory that heredity is the main factor of intelligence?

2. Defend or reject the following statement: The problems caused by I.Q. tests far outweigh any possible good they can ever do in the schools.

3. List what you feel are the reasons why the heredity-environment controversy erupts every twelve or thirteen years.

KIBBUTZIM FOR THE DISADVANTAGED

By BEATRICE R. METALITZ

On every side, teachers are confronted with children who can't learn in our schools—especially those children who come from slum neighborhoods. Much of the money and effort poured into making changes in our educational methods has turned out so far to be too little, too late.

Even crash programs for the cradle crowd have proved largely ineffective, for the child learns first from his family, and his learning patterns are established in the home before he goes to kindergarten, Head Start class, or nursery school. In the case of the ghetto child, his parents are so caught up in the deprivations of poverty that they often cannot equip him with values conducive to learning in our schools.

Perhaps the time has come for us to try a dramatically different method with such children—communal child rearing. This method has been tried with considerable success in Israel in the collective societies called kibbutzim. When the kibbutz program was first started in the early 1900's, Israeli parents in the kibbutz had many problems that are similar to those of parents who live in our ghettos today. They are:

1. *Deficient housing.* The Israeli pioneers lived in flimsy tents under primitive conditions. Their children needed something better, substantial housing and sanitary living conditions. The parents couldn't afford this for themselves, but for their children, it was a must. (Slum dwellers in this country live in crowded, rat-infested ghettos. New public housing is scarce, and, for a variety of reasons, quickly becomes abused and deteriorates. Better housing should be provided for slum children immediately, even if it cannot be provided for their parents at the same time.)

2. *Inadequate diet.* The collective settlements were poor. Funds had to be used to buy equipment and machinery so the community could turn the barren land into productive farms. Adult rations were at a subsistence level, but the children had to have a nourishing diet for healthy growth. (Slum parents, too, are poor, but their children must not be permitted to suffer from malnutrition.)

3. *Women's economic role.* In every kibbutz, the labor of every member of the settlement was sorely needed to drain swamps, reclaim deserts, and make the land productive. While each mother could not spend her time caring for her children, their welfare was not sacrificed. (The slum mother, because her skills are sometimes more employable than her husband's, is also a working mother and she, too, must have assurances of adequate care for her children.)

Reprinted with permission from *Today's Education* (December 1969).

4. A change of values. This is perhaps the most important similarity. The kibbutz parents had themselves been children of the ghetto. Their values were fashioned in a minority environment. Hazardous situations forced them to become facile at accommodating themselves. In Israel, these newcomers wanted to break with the past. They wanted to develop a confident self-assured generation for the new homeland. (The slum parent is faced with the same need to develop a generation that can escape the debilitation that results from a ghetto environment.)

Recently, I visited four Israeli kibbutzim—one in the hills of Galilee in the north, one near the Mediterranean shore, another near a large city, and a fourth in the desert in the south. They differed in their childrearing methods as vastly as they differed in geography. However, I found some characteristics generally true in each of these kibbutzim.

Children are raised communally with their peer group. Babies live in the nursery from the time their mothers return with them from the hospital. Then, they progress to the toddler's house and from there to other houses appropriate to their age—always moving with their peer group.

The kibbutz provides facilities and personnel for the children's changing needs as they develop into adulthood. Settlement members who have been specially selected and trained for their role in the childcare process staff the children's houses: Teachers; nurses; nutritionists; and metaplot (usually women, 21 to 35, who provide care, socialization, and education) make up teams that are immediately responsible for the children's daily welfare. But in reality the children are the responsibility of the whole community. The parents, as members of the kibbutz, help set the goals for child rearing.

Parents work all day at their jobs in the settlement. The work may be in the fields, in the communal kitchen, or in the communal laundry. Since parents' cottages require only minimal housekeeping care, and since such things as meals, laundry, and mending are provided on a communal basis, mothers and fathers are free after work to visit with the children and to pursue recreational and hobby projects with them until the evening meal is served in the communal dining room. (Adults eat their meals together, and children eat with their peer group.) In many kibbutzim, children sleep at home.

Children visit their parents' cottages too. During my trip, I was impressed to find that teen-agers voluntarily come to socialize with their parents each day. I saw parents and children working on a tile mosaic for the social hall, constructing play equipment, and even building a harpsichord.

The children are the pride of the whole kibbutz, and all adults serve in an avuncular role. Community devotion to the needs of the children is limitless. In one kibbutz in the Negev desert, I was surprised to see a four-year-old girl spraying precious water into a sandbox. In that parched areas of Israel, it seemed tantamount to a criminal offense. When I commented on it, a kibbutz adult assured me that the kibbutz allotted some of the rationed water for this purpose.

In the kibbutz, there is no demarcation between education and living. The school is the community and the community is the school. Everything the child learns, the community needs to have him learn. Little tots know that their work is needed and useful. For example, the products of the children's farm are marketed right along with the rest of the harvest.

Socially each child is secure in his relations to his peer group. He has no fear of loneliness. There's no need for competitiveness or possessiveness about people or things. All property is collectively owned. Each child knows his role and is eager to do his best for his kibbutz and his country.

Of kibbutz-reared children, about 85 percent elect to apply for kibbutz membership after their army service. They either return to their settlement or join with their peers in forming new kibbutzim. Membership is always voluntary. Any adult is free to leave at any time, but very few do so because they believe that the kibbutz way is the best way to live. While only 4 percent of the Israeli population lives in collectives, the kibbutz supplies more than its proportional share of national leaders.

Now it must be asked, why not try communal child rearing for ghetto children in the United States? To many, advocating separation of mother and child is shocking. Foremost among the horrified will probably be the middle-class working wives who have entrusted the upbringing of their own children to the tender ministrations of untrained, although devoted, cleaning women—perhaps the very domestics who are the mothers of those children that cause so many educational problems. At the other end, I anticipate, will be outraged militants of various minority groups. For those of us who are in between, let us see how this communal child rearing might be approached.

It doesn't require the wisdom of Solomon to know that the real mother, if she has a choice, wants the best food, housing, medical care, education, and social environment for her child. The ghetto mother can't provide them on her own, but she can join with others in providing a good, total environment for her child. One building and a small, qualified, round-the-clock staff would be the basic requirement.

Since the ghetto parent has many of the same economic, cultural, and psychological handicaps to overcome as did the founding kibbutz members, ghetto leaders may very well come to see collective child rearing as a solution to the myriad problems that plague their society.

In case the zeal and purpose that fired the pioneers in Israel may be missing from our slum people, substitute inducements can be found. Parents might be willing to enroll their children in residential schools if they were given the incentives of financial allotments and transportation for daily visits with their children.

Eventually, minimal housekeeping units could be built near the children's house. Communal dining and recreational facilities for the parents could also be provided. And, most important, small industries could be developed so that parents could earn their livelihood in the collective.

Instead of disrupting the family organization, voluntary, communal child rearing can strengthen the family sociologically as well as economically. Cultural and psychological confidence can develop in such a community-oriented educational system. And I would hope that, as in Israel, communities of varied cultural backgrounds could be integrated into a unified nation with high educational goals and achievements.

The Israeli kibbutz found a solution and influenced basic value changes in just one generation. Scholars and researchers indicate that the changes are generally good.

Here in the United States, we must believe that the vicious cycle of poverty can be broken. Perhaps we can effect a change in less than a generation. The time has come to try, and we must begin at the beginning—at birth.

———————

Questions:

1.   What are some of the positive things that exist today in our urban society that would tend to make kibbutzim a reality?

2.   What are some of the negative things that exist today in our urban society that would tend to make kibbutzim unrealistic?

3.   Discuss the one factor regarding life in kibbutzim that you feel most benefits a child's educational life.

CURRICULUM FOR THE DISADVANTAGED

By ROBERT J. HAVIGHURST

In writing usefully about school programs which will be valid for the coming decade in the education of the economically disadvantaged, it is important to look ahead at the shape of things to come, and to avoid being turned to stone by the backward look at the ways of the past.

What is the probable social setting in the 1970's for children of the poorest 20 percent of the American population? With considerable assurance we can predict the following:

1. Increased real income and greater stability of that income. Some reform of the welfare system is sure to come very soon to provide a basic family allowance for every poor family. It will operate to keep fathers and mothers together with their children.

2. Higher educational level of low-income parents. The increase in grade-level attainment since the war is reflected in the young adults whose children are now beginning to enter school. Lower-income parents will be better able to appreciate the school experience of their children, to read to them, etc.

3. Pre-school education for at least one year before the age of five. An improved and amplified Head Start program is now ready for widespread use, and teachers trained in one of several programs proven successful will be available in increasing numbers. These successful programs are raising the I.Q. level of disadvantaged children by an average of 10 to 15 points and keeping this gain for three years, at least. In another year or two, we will know whether these children retain their improved learning ability up to the third- or fourth-grade level. If they do, we will be able to employ a curriculum for the intermediate grades which is based on the assumption of very little reading retardation of children in inner-city schools.

4. Improved methods of working in primary grades with disadvantaged children. This is part of the situation we have just described. Once a child from a disadvantaged family has been aided substantially by a pre-school program, he will continue to be aided by primary school teaching that gears in with his Head Start experience.

5. Slowly decreasing racial and economic segregation in the schools. The pattern of residential segregation by race and income which was set in the 1950's and supported by public housing practices will only slowly be overcome by the forces now at work to produce integration in the central city and the suburbs. While we may expect substantial change in the direction of integration, it will

Reprinted with permission from *Phi Delta Kappan* (March 1970).

not affect large proportions of disadvantaged children during the decade immediately ahead.

6. A gradually decreasing gap in material style of life and in social attitudes and values between the middle class and the disadvantaged lower-class group. Though the gap will continue throughout the decade, it will become less noticeable. The "subculture of poverty" which dominates the life style of many poor families today will lose much of its grasp.

To some readers this may appear to be an overoptimistic view of the immediate future, but it seems essentially realistic to me. It is far better for the schools to "tune up" to the future than to prepare for a disappearing past.

The goal of education for all children, rich or poor, from literate or illiterate families, is the same if it is expressed in general terms. This is to help the child become a competent and happy person, now and in the future, in a democratic, productive, and increasingly urban society. There is no distinction here between social classes. It does not make sense in this society to talk about "turning a lower-class child into a middle-class child" as though this were a good or a bad thing to do. There are common goals of competence and happiness in a productive and socially integrated society. Children will differ individually, because of social group differences, in their progress toward these goals. The school's mission is to help all children move toward these common goals.

There are two important questions to be answered with respect to the curriculum for economically disadvantaged children. One has to do with *methods* of teaching, the other with *content* of the curriculum.

METHODS FOR THE DISADVANTAGED

There is a growing body of data on the relation of reward to learning among children which supports the following propositions.*

1. There are differences among socioeconomic groups and ethnic sub-cultures in the reward systems they teach and use with their children. External rewards (material, or intangible—such as praise) and punishments are to be contrasted with internal (superego and ego) rewards and punishments.

2. In general, external rewards (material or intangible) have greater positive value for disadvantaged or failing children.

3. Appropriate teaching methods can help a child evolve from the external to the internal reward system.

Thus a system of deliberate external rewards (material things like toys, gold stars, edibles) and praise should be employed with disadvantaged pupils.

A CHILD-ORIGINATED CURRICULUM?

When children do not learn well in school, we naturally ask ourselves whether there is something wrong with the curriculum or the way it is presented to the pupil. There are two contrasting answers to this question. One is that we adults are imposing a limited, rigid curriculum on children and putting their

---

* These propositions are developed more fully in my article on "Minority Sub-cultures and the Law of Effect," *American Psychologist,* 1970 (in press).

minds in a strait-jacket. The other is that we do not present the curriculum in such a way that the child can understand what he is doing and where he is going.

The first view has had considerable play during the last few years, in a revival of the child-centered curriculum movement which was popular in the 1920's and 1930's. Among its persuasive presenters are John Holt and George Dennison, authors of books recently published. Holt, in his book, *How Children Learn,*[1] says, "Only a few children in school ever become good at learning in the way we try to make them learn. Most of them get humiliated, frightened, and discouraged. They use their minds, not to learn, but to get out of doing the things we tell them to do—to make them learn. In the short run, these strategies seem to work. They make it possible for many children to get through their schooling even though they learn very little. But in the long run these strategies are self-limiting and self-defeating, and destroy both character and intelligence. The children who use such strategies are prevented by them from growing into more than limited versions of the human beings they might have become. This is the real failure that takes place in school; hardly any children escape. . . . What is essential is to realize that children learn independently, not in bunches; that they learn out of interest and curiosity, not to please or appease the adults in power; and that they ought to be in control of their own learning, deciding for themselves what they want to learn and how they want to learn it."

As expounded by Holt, this proposition seems to apply more to middle-class children than to the economically disadvantaged group. However, Herbert Kohl's *36 Children*[2] appears to present much the same kind of case, based on experience in a Harlem ghetto school.

Kohl describes how he worked for a year with a class of 36 Negro slum children who were below average in academic skills. He did get results. There is no reason to doubt this. His method of encouraging them to write about their fears, their hates, and their likes, about the bad and good things they experienced in their homes and streets, loosened their pens and their tongues, added to their vocabulary, and got them interested in school.

What Kohl appears to have done was to attach school learning to the impulses of the children. By helping them to talk and write about the things that were most impelling in their daily lives, he made school relevant to them. To put this into psychodynamic terms, Kohl was marshaling the forces of the id on behalf of learning, just as Holt proposes to do. But Holt talks in "safe" middle-class terms about children's curiosity and interests, while Kohl faces the slum realities of children's fears and hates.

But how far can a system based on children's felt needs go? How far can a slum child (or a middle-class child) go toward mastery of arithmetic, of English sentence style, of knowledge of science and history, if he is motivated only by his drive to express his feelings or to satisfy his curiosity, or possibly also by his desire to please his friendly and permissive teacher?

We do not know how far this kind of reward will carry a child's learning. We might guess that it would carry children up to about the seventh-grade level. Therefore, we should ask Kohl and others of this school of thought to prove that their methods will carry children to the eighth-grade level. No such claims appear to have been substantiated, except in the case of socially advantaged children, such as those attending A.S. Neill's school at Summerhill, England. And some observers of this school argue that it can only work with children who have a strong British middle-class superego, and can profit from teaming their somewhat starved id with the superego in the pursuit of learning.

The contrasting view of curriculum calls for more rather than less adult-created structure than the pupil generally gets today, but a structure which is carefully fitted to the student's present knowledge and to his motives. It aims to achieve "a real dialectic of authority and empathy in the classroom," which Donald Barr, headmaster of the Dalton School, called for in his criticism of Holt's position.[3]

The essential element is the pupil's perception of the connection between what he does in the classroom or in his school work and a result which he wants. When this condition is met, the pupil's ego can come into action to guide his effort and reward his success.

Programmed learning is an example, where it is used skillfully. The pupil accepts an assignment to learn a particular lesson or set of facts, and he is informed immediately of every successful step he takes toward this goal.

According to this view, the pupil must accept the notion that he has hard work to do which will require effort on his part in order to achieve the goal that he sees clearly.

Another example is the Mastery Program which Benjamin Bloom has helped to work out in schools in Puerto Rico, a program now ready for general use. The work assignments are divided into relatively small units with frequent tests for mastery. The pupil works for the mastery of his assignment and keeps on working until he has demonstrated mastery. No matter how slow he is, compared with the rest of his class, he achieves mastery before going on to the next assignment. Bloom has found that the slow pupils move along much more rapidly than he had expected. Not only do pupils learn more effectively, they also come to enjoy learning. Bloom says,[4] "The clearest evidence of affective outcomes is the reported interest the student develops for the subject he has mastered. He begins to 'like' the subject and to desire more of it. To do well in a subject opens up further avenues for exploration of the subject. Conversely, to do poorly in a subject closes an area for further study. The student desires some control over his environment, and mastery of a subject gives him some feeling of control over a part of his environment. Interest in a subject is both a result of mastery of the subject [and] a cause of mastery."

The successful innovative programs for high-school-age students also contain this element of motivation toward a clearly understood goal. For example, the storefront academies that give high school dropouts a chance to prepare for the G.E.D. test and high school diploma equivalency probably are successful because they work with young people who have become convinced that they need more education; they see clearly the connection between their study in the storefront academy and the achievement of this goal.

The Upward Bound and High Potential programs for disadvantaged high school and college youth, where they are successful, seem to combine the element of motivation to succeed with a clearly outlined program of study for a summer or a semester. Such programs can be seen as a long step forward by the student.

EMPHASES FOR THE DISADVANTAGED

The argument to this point has been as follows: Economically disadvantaged children have difficulty in the school system for two reasons:

1. Their family environment limits their perceptual, conceptual, and linguistic experience in their early years, thus preparing them poorly for school. But this family factor is improving, due to the reduction of poverty and the increasing level of education among low-income parents.

2. Teaching methods in the schools have not been well-adapted to the learning styles of economically disadvantaged children. But recent research has shown the way to improved methods of teaching these children.

This line of reasoning suggests that there is no special need for a special curriculum for the disadvantaged child.

Still, there are certain topics and subject areas that might well be given special stress in a school that serves diadvantaged children and youth. These have one or the other of two kinds of value:

1. *To meet specific deficiencies in the life of the child.*—For example, it is well established that the diet of children in poor families is very likely to be inadequate, partly because the family lacks money to pay for essential foods and partly because the child and his family lack knowledge about nutrition. Therefore it would seem wise to put special emphasis on the study of nutrition at two levels of the school—the third- or fourth-grade level, with simple and clear rules about diet, and the ninth- or tenth-grade level, with science-based information about nutrition.

2. *To meet self-image needs in the child and adolescent.*—Several disadvantaged minority groups have been given shabby treatment in American history and literature, which gets into the school curriculum and tends to undermine the self-esteem of children of these groups when they meet this material in front of their classmates. Three groups have suffered the most from this kind of experience — Negroes, American Indians, and Mexican-Americans.

For the sake of all American youth, the study of these minority groups should be more accurate, truth-based, and positive.

For the sake of minority group members whose forefathers are presented as inferior, cruel, savage, or servile, and who are themselves subject to discrimination in contemporary society, there may be some value in special readings and projects which give them a more positive picture of the past and present status of their own ethnic group.

CONCLUSION

Thus my conclusions concerning the education of the economically disadvantaged are:

1. We need a pre-school program of at least one year's duration aimed at improving the cognitive and language development of disadvantaged children.

2. Elementary school teachers need to learn more effective methods of rewarding disadvantaged children for effort and achievement in school.

3. Elementary school teachers need to create and maintain an orderly classroom regime in which pupils are convinced that they will be rewarded in the future for consistent effort today.

4. A relatively small adaptation of the ordinary school curriculum should be made to fit specific knowledge deficiencies and self-image needs of disadvantaged children and youth.

REFERENCES:

[1]John Holt, *How Children Learn.* New York: Pitman Publishing Company, 1967.

[2]Herbert Kohl, *36 Children.* New York: New America Library, 1967.

[3]Donald Barr, "The Works of John Holt," *The New York Times Book Review, Special Education Book Supplement,* September 14, 1969.

[4]Benjamin S. Bloom, "Learning for Mastery," *Administrator's Notebook,* April, 1968 (Midwest Administration Center, University of Chicago). See also B. S. Bloom, J. T. Hastings, and G. Madaus, *Formative and Summative Evaluation of Student Learning.* New York: McGraw-Hill, 1970.

Questions:

1. Describe four or five main ingredients of a pre-school program which would improve the cognitive and language development of disadvantaged children.

2. Explain the main parts of a program that you would institute to reward disadvantaged children for effort and achievement in school.

3. List three or four improved methods of teaching economically disadvantaged children.

METHODS, MATERIALS, AND THE CULTURALLY DISADVANTAGED

By EDWARD F. DeROCHE

Stripped of all its glamor and jargon, education is concerned with three basic elements: the student, the teacher, and the environment beyond the school.[1] Many of the problems encountered in classes are a result of student values nurtured by their social environment. The usual approach to teaching the culturally deprived has been, in general, similar to methods of teaching all youth. We herd them into schools, separate them into classes, label them according to their abilities, teach them by the same old group methods that we were taught by, and then wonder why things are not going well. One out of four drop out, others "hang around" and cause problems, and some try to make the best of it.

Teaching the culturally disadvantaged is not easy. But neither is being poor. Our task is to explore some ideas about teaching methods and materials in a hope that they will contribute to helping youngsters become both more effective and more efficient learners.

THE STUDENT AND HIS ENVIRONMENT

A culturally disadvantaged youngster has many obstacles to overcome the minute he sets foot inside a school. Problem one, he speaks a different language. He knows English, but it's different than that spoken in the school. His communicative skills are limited. He relies a great deal on nonverbal language, but the school's entire structure flourishes around verbal communication.

Problem two, he has limited experiences in what the teacher is saying or doing. Thus, he is always trying to catch up to basic learnings the teacher has taken for granted. And yet, because there is too much going on around him, too many other things competing for his attention, he almost never succeeds. So, early in his educational life, he experiences frustration.

Problem three, he generally has a low self-concept and much of what he experiences in school reinforces his feelings of inadequacy. He has things to contribute in class but can't, because the opportunity to do so seldom comes his way. He finds little motivation to learn, to do school work. The teacher talks about books, stories, values, and attitudes to which he cannot identify. "This is unreal," he says to himself. "The real world is out there." "Out there" is where he finds opportunities to be motivated and to learn.

Problem four, he has values but they usually conflict with those of the school. He values honesty, responsibility, and loyalty—but only when his family

---

Reprinted with permission from *The Clearing House* (March 1970).

or friends are involved. In terms of others, well, "It's a rough world, Mac, so I have to get mine while I can." This doesn't mean that his values are poor ones. It only means that they are different. These differences can be useful to the school. As James Olsen says, "It seems much more reasonable to reduce the social distance between the school and its students by finding out what the content of the lower class culture is and then modifying or changing some of what we teach and how we teach it."[2]

THE TEACHER'S TECHNIQUES

Any teacher who works with culturally deprived youngsters will tell you that typical teaching methods are not realistic or usable. There needs to be a different approach in teaching methods and realistic instructional materials must be used. In actual teaching, methods cannot be divorced from instructional material. But for our purposes, the two will be discussed separately.

Open-system. The first technique for teaching the culturally deprived is the "open-system" technique. The teacher should examine what these youngsters can contribute to the school, and for the time being, stop worrying about what the school can give to them. This means that their values and attitudes are allowed to operate freely and openly in the classroom. There will be controls, however. Discipline will be appreciated as something necessary and worthwhile, both to the individual and to the group.

We have to overcome the guilt feeling that if we spend time being concerned about their values, attitudes, or social skills, we are not teaching anything. As Bettelheim said about teachers of the culturally deprived, "One recurrent problem was the teachers' anxiety that if they were to take time away from the teaching of the subject matter of the three R's, they would be falling down on their job."[3]

Discussion techniques. As our first technique implies, we have to make greater use of discussion techniques. The classroom should be arranged to provide communication between teacher and student. The typical rows of desks facing in one direction does not contribute to this objective. There should be ample opportunity for group discussion—in their language. The important element in discussion techniques, however, is the fact that it can represent what we mean by democracy. Through these techniques, youngsters can experience democracy in action.

When a teacher has properly planned for effective discussion, the culturally deprived youngster learns to appreciate group work, develop skills in group interaction, improves his social attitudes, and enhances his thinking abilities. It is all the more meaningful if viewed as a means of improving one's self-concept. As Snyder says, "The individual's behavior is largely determined by his self-concept, which emerges from the social situations in which the individual participates. . . . By modifying the situation the individual's self-concept can be modified."[4]

Emphasize the Present. Teachers of the culturally deprived should emphasize the present, rather than the past or future. Youngsters from the low social class see little value in education for the future. They want to see immediate results. Remote goals must give way to immediate goals. Goals that are attainable. Goals that are meaningful. The teacher has to incorporate this "emphasis on the present" into his teaching repertoire.

Problems for discussion must be meaningful to the student. "Problems of Tenement Living" have to replace "The Role of the U.S. in Southeast Asia." Panel discussions about slum landlords may, for the present, replace discussions on the democratic way of life. Vocational skills should be emphasized because youngsters see immediate benefits in such skills. How to buy clothes, food, and a car may be more meaningful than how to construct a parallelogram or how to write a complex sentence.

Activity. Techniques that employ more doing and less saying should be employed. Although this may seem to contradict the use of discussion techniques, it does not. In teaching academic skills, teachers must prepare activities that cause the student to *do* something. Where instruction in higher social classes rely on verbalization, the low social class youngster needs activity. Verbalization is his handicap. They like to be "where the action is." And the action is in doing the thing he is learning; role playing, acting it out.

The teacher reduces the verbalization in teaching a concept and provides more activity. For example, the student learns to divide by actively engaging in a problem involving division that is meaningful to him. And only after he has various experiences with the active process of dividing things does the teacher rely on verbalization.

Transfer of training. Teachers must consistently help these youngsters relate the skills and concepts they are learning in school to the environment outside of school. Transfer of skills and concepts is not automatic, it must be taught. Only when it is taught will youngsters appreciate school and find meaning in the things they learn there.

In summary, we have by no means exhausted the number of useful techniques for teaching the culturally deprived. We suggested, however, that the classroom become an arena for their ideas; that discussion and activity become the vehicle for these ideas; that the present be emphasized and vocational skills developed. Finally, we indicated the value of assisting youngsters in developing meaningful relationships between what they learn in school and what they do outside the school.

INSTRUCTIONAL MATERIALS

The materials used in teaching the culturally deprived should reflect teaching technique and the "real" world. Thus, several suggestions may prove valuable.

Replacing the textbook. We have to explore the possibilities of replacing the "sacred" textbook, at least for a while, with more meaningful media. The daily newspaper is probably the best of several types of printed media. Magazines, comic books, travel flyers, and trade books are very meaningful to culturally deprived youngsters. These can be used to teach most subjects. As Dale says, "Books can tell us what happened in the past. Newspapers usually give us the thin slice of the present and are now moving to a more interpretative approach. But magazines can provide a link between the useable past and the up-to-date present."[5] We should examine the possibilities of having youngsters write their own textbooks, particularly for use in the language arts.

8mm film. We have to explore and examine the usefulness of 8mm films in the classroom; not only commercially prepared films, but films made by the youngsters and teachers of their own experiences. These should make excellent instructional material.

Commercial television. We should examine the contributions commercial television can make to the improvement of reading, writing, spelling, and listening skills. Most youngsters watch television anyway, so teachers should suggest programs to watch, provide learning activities based on these programs, help students differentiate between propaganda and truth, fact and fiction, and the like.

Skill material. The introduction of "skill material" into the curriculum for the culturally deprived may prove beneficial. How-to-do-it books and magazines are very useful. For example, filling out tax forms can be an activity that helps all youngsters. After they know how to complete an income tax form, "tax-history," the how, why, when, and what of taxes can be examined. Drivers' manuals and tests can be very meaningful. Automobile licenses, hunting and fishing licenses can be discussed in detail. Culturally deprived youngsters should be taught how to fill out applications; mock interviews should be demonstrated; job opportunities examined.

When buying a car many skills are necessary, as any purchaser knows. Youngsters are most interested in owning cars and once teachers have captured their interest, instruction can be similar to the following: the history teacher uses the automobile as a focal point to trace the economic and social changes in the United States; the English teacher uses automobile advertisements and brochures to teach the skills and concepts of his subject; the mathematics teacher uses the problem of car-buying to teach skills in decimals, percentages, interests, and the like. A team approach is essential and beneficial to students and teachers.

Toys and games. Very little has been done to explore the use of toys and games as instructional aids. They may serve as excellent motivational devices. Many games can be used to increase vocabulary, to improve reading skills, and the like. Think of the instructional uses that could be made of the game of Monopoly alone.

Tape recorders. Extensive use of the tape recorder should help youngsters improve communicative skills. It is also a useful tool for helping youngsters examine their attitudes and values, their ideas and prejudices.

Community resources. Community resources should be used to their fullest advantage. Concerts, movies, plays, sporting events are but a few activities that should supplement the formal teaching-learning process of the classroom.

Success stories. Stories of "those who made it" must take precedent over the usual middle-class stories. The emphasis here is not only on those who are the leaders, but also on the plumber, the service station manager, the chef who, because of their skills, are capable of earning a decent living.

SUMMARY

Obviously, this article does not touch upon all the teaching methods and materials useful for helping culturally deprived youngsters learn effectively and efficiently. Its major purpose was to initiate ideas about this most important problem. We are not going to solve the problem of teaching the culturally deprived youngster by placing the most experienced teachers in these schools, or by developing a system of rotation, or by providing teachers in these schools with more money. We will provide tentative solutions by allowing teachers the experience of exploring various methods and materials and thus attempting to substantially change the attitudes of hopelessness that sometimes permeate schools serving the deprived.

Thus, the methods and materials used for teaching the culturally deprived should not reflect the attitude that school is a place where one passes or fails. The entire school atmosphere should indicate that it is the *best* place to learn about things, where one is taught to think, to develop useful skills, to have a chance to contribute and progress according to one's abilities. As teachers, our influence on the culturally deprived is only limited by our imagination.

FOOTNOTES:

[1] Austin, Ernest H. Jr., "Cultural Deprivation—A Few Questions," *Phi Delta Kappan,* 47:69, October, 1965.
[2] Olsen, James, "Challenge of the Poor to the Schools," *Phi Delta Kappan,* 47:82, October, 1965.
[3] Bettleheim, Bruno, "Teaching the Disadvantaged," *National Education Association Journal,* 54:8, September, 1965.
[4] Snyder, Eldon E., "Self-Concept Theory," *The Clearing House.* 40:243, December, 1965.
[5] Dale, Edgar, "The Reading of Magazines," *The News Letter,* 31:1, November, 1965.

Questions:

1. What obstacles must a culturally disadvantaged youngster overcome when he enters school?

2. Describe the three techniques which you feel are most effective in teaching the culturally deprived.

3. What suggestions for innovative uses of instructional materials for the disadvantaged are made by Professor DeRoche?

PROBLEMS IN TEACHING SCIENCE
TO THE URBAN CHILD

By JOSEPH C. PAIGE

Approach, methodology, and content in science have always been problems to those of us concerned with quality education. Somehow, we have not been able to reach agreement on what to teach or how to teach science at any level. These problems take on additional dimensions and complexities in a dialogue pertaining to what to teach and how to teach the urban child. There are many reasons for this. The rhetoric is generally directed toward minority groups and toward blacks in particular. In my judgment, this is not unreasonable. With respect to quality education, the urban child, particularly the urban black, has been victimized by fraudulent if not criminal instruction practices at almost all instructional levels. Those of us in science education have done little, if anything, to change the situation. We talk a lot; we make broad generalizations; and we become quite academic in our discussions. We do little more than provide lip service to the notion of improving the quality of science education to children in the urban school.

I am convinced that most science educators, regardless of their levels of professionalism, status, competency, or degree of liberalism have been so systematically programed over the years that even with all of their good intentions, they are incapable of understanding the practical dynamics of dealing with children of urban minorities. Yet, sadly, these well-meaning, misguided educators—the sophisticated elite in science education—are the ones who write the textbooks, who supervise curriculum development for the big cities, who make judgments on content and methodology. They are the ones delegated by the major federal and state agencies, the foundations, and industry to make the final decisions with respect to the establishment of priorities and the subsequent allocation of resources for support of special science programs for the so-called culturally disadvantaged. They decide on both the nature and types of programs to be supported and, in many cases, have veto power with respect to staff selection.

Our problems in the teaching of science to the urban child lie first in the fact that the decision hierarchy is dominated by a misguided, misinformed, educationally egotistical elite, otherwise meaning well, but lacking in even the most elementary understanding of the population we wish to reach. They lack both knowledge and appreciation of the life styles and basic chemistry of some of the youthful, soulful inhabitants of our big cities.

Reprinted with permission from *The Science Teacher* (October 1969).

Teacher education colleges and departments of education are also problem sources. They show little evidence of having learned anything about urban problems over the past century. The science educators in these colleges or departments of education, while concerned and dedicated, seem to be ill equipped to do meaningful, creative things with this population. They seem, for the most part, to be always in search of sophisticated methodology and of highly theoretical practicums and experiences. At least to me, they seem to reject that which is simple, relevant, or meaningful. They seem to prefer the difficult, confusing, and irrelevant.

With respect to overall influence, it is my sincere view that textbook publishers, because of their profit orientation and their often conservative reading of the public pulse, contribute greatly to our current problems. In their search for the mighty dollar, they have found it convenient, as a general practice, to sacrifice principle for expediency. In all too many cases, they know what is best, but they are generally only too willing to sacrifice a quality effort for a mighty "buck."

My experience has been that teachers tend to teach what publishers print. Likewise, students tend to believe what the books say. And in general practice, both teachers and students are programed by the process which characterizes the book or teacher's guide, almost without exception, exactly as stated in the text or guide.

I believe that these are our major problems. I believe that they are much more severe than is the cultural deprivation of the urban child or his readiness level in specific subject areas as indicated by tests or other criteria.

While my experiences in dealing with science educators on problems related to the urban child have been disappointing, they have provided helpful and up-to-date insights into the basic nature, problems, interests, aspirations, and needs of the economically poor, both young and old, irrespective of ethnic origin. These experiences have helped us identify for this population some of the major issues and problems relating to (1) life styles, (2) socialization needs, (3) coping skills needed for successful interaction on the job, at home, and in the neighborhood, and (4) learning patterns.

The involvement also helped facilitate the clarification of what appear to be reasonable goals and priorities in the design of instructional strategies for teaching urban children and their parents. We believe that we are in a position now to assist in the design of more relevant preservice and inservice programs for teachers and administrators, including curriculum development and materials for children.

The urban child is very much a part of the social revolution. His frustrations, joys, and basic energies seem to be related to that which is current. The notion of relevancy to him, whether in science or social studies, math or language, has meaning only in terms related to the "now" aspects of his life experiences. In this context, teaching science to the urban child takes on new dimensions, touching on such areas as race, sex, crime, religion, and war. It is concerned with drugs and narcotics, cigarettes, alcohol, space, electronics, and all of the current socioeconomic issues that make the news today. To the urban child, science must be a living thing with live, swinging, soulful people.

I consider a large amount of the current social confusion a reflection of failure of science educators. I consider the violence, the unprecedented increase in crime by youth and adults, the growing polarization between the races, as reflective of something sad and sinfully unAmerican, requiring the best of your talents and mine. Hence, to do "our thing" in science education we must address ourselves to the health ethic, the legal ethic, the political ethic, and the social ethic. All of these ethics or concerns are intimately related to an umbrella socioeconomic "thing," which at the moment emerges, for blacks, in the rhetoric of various interpretations of black power. Science, more than any other area, ought to be able to help point the way to involve young people with these ethics.

Never before in the history of our country has the United States been this close to catastrophic confrontation of the races. Never in this century has our country been so close to such critical crossroads. Never before have we been so close to bloody social rebellions. And the irony of the situation is that these conditions exist in our America, even though our nation has had the fortunate opportunity of having a more comprehensive view of the ideas, beliefs, perceptions, and frustrations of its citizens than has any other nation of the world. As a nation, we seem not to learn, even though we say we care. The view of the revolutionists is that we really don't care, that all is a farce, and that we will continue with our lip service. Science ought to be able to help change this view.

An effective, relevant science education program, including meaningful community involvement, combined with school and home mechanisms and integrated with other major content and enrichment areas, provides, as I see it, our only real hope for salvaging an otherwise lost society. I see the problem as being neither black nor white, but rather a human one.

As I talk with groups around the country, I often think that perhaps the medium of humor might be one of the most precise kinds of social criticism available at this time. I am reminded of a story I heard some time ago about an aging, tired black man in Detroit who was praying, and at the end of his prayer, he said: "Lord, may I ask you a few questions?"

And the Lord said, "Yes, my son, go ahead."

He said, "Lord, why did you make me black and all of the people in charge around me white?"

The Lord said, "Well, my son, I made you that way because you were running through the jungles and swamps of Africa, and it was hot, and if you hadn't had that protective coloration you would have burnt up."

He said, "Well, Lord, why did you make my hair short and kinky and, again, make all of the people in charge around me with long flowing silky hair?"

And the Lord said, "Again, it was for your own protection: Your running through those wildernesses—through the forests—if you would have had long flowing hair, your hair might have caught on a low limb and you might have strangled and killed yourself."

He said, "Lord, why did you make my feet so big?"

The Lord said, "Well, my son, it is for the same protective reason. You were running up those hills and through the swamps, and you needed big feet in order for you to have a solid foundation on earth."

Whereupon, the old black man said, "Well, Lord, with all of this special equipment, what am I doing in Detroit?"

I have talked to so many children of the urban poor and their parents and listened to their problems and frustrations—the repeated incidents of discrimination because of race or color, age or sex, and the lack of relevancy in practically all of the activities imposed upon them by a previously insensitive white society. Many of them ask in sincerity, "If this society ain't for me, then what am I doing here?" Actually, the entire social revolution, is a reflection of the "What am I doing here?" thing. And science ought to provide some answers.

Somehow, those of us who are responsible must help to recapture the spirit of America for all Americans. Somehow, we must combine the teaching of science with that of history, sociology, and philosophy. Somehow, in science, we must accommodate and provide explanations for the notions of black power, white power, and brown power under a single American umbrella, all sharing in the production and use of "green" power, or any other positive critical power. If we cannot do this, we must give up.

It has always been my feeling that if a science education program is to have any real meaning or personal relevance to the youngsters we teach, it must, in its broadest dimension, be community or neighborhood oriented, tailor-made to fit the individual needs of each participant, at least initially. Likewise, it appears to me that the science program of any school should make maximum use of public and neighborhood facilities. For example, science programs ought to be designed to encourage maximum family and community participation. They should have a special relevance to the school neighborhood, its assets and liabilities, its needs and problems, and most especially, the aspirations of the neighborhood residents. In other words, science programs for urban children ought to provide well-rounded experiences for their parents as well. How can we begin to organize such programs? From my own experience I would like to suggest that a systems approach offers the best framework.

For the past two years, I was the director of the Urban Adult Education Institute in Detroit. The Institute has developed and tested a variety of approaches to teaching and working with the extreme "hard core" of the disadvantaged, following the guidelines of the educational sciences. The experimental design of our unique approach to the development and refinement of instructional methodology is the brainchild of Joseph Hill, president of Oakland Community College, Bloomfield Hills, Michigan. I am convinced that this approach is worthy of consideration in the development of instructional strategies for the teaching of science. It has a workable pattern of organization and allows for the flexibility and innovations so important for adapting a program to the needs of special groups.[1]

I believe that with respect to instructional strategies, the major problems relate to process. Our results from the application of the educational sciences suggest the following as a process.

The "educational sciences," at present, are composed of seven strata: (1) the symbol and its meaning; (2) "cultural determinants" of the meaning of symbols; (3) modalities of inference; (4) the memory function (recognition, retention, recall, and association) expressed in terms of neurological, electrochemical, and biochemical aspects of the nervous system; (5) cognitive styles of individuals—sets of Cartesian product combinations of elements included in strata (1) through (3); (6) teaching, administrative, and counseling styles (defined in the context of the "sciences"); and (7) systemic analysis and decision-making in educational administration and management.

STRATUM I: SYMBOL AND MEANING

The *theoretical symbol* (T) can be defined as that symbol which presents to the "awareness" (the consciousness) of the individual something different than that which it (the symbol) itself is. There are two main types of theoretical symbols: the auditory and the visual.

Auditory theoretical symbol. The sound of the word "cat" is the auditory symbol. It brings to the awareness an imagery different from the sound itself.

Visual theoretical symbol. The written or printed word. For example, the printed word "cat" brings to the awareness an image different from that printed arrangement of letters. When an individual sees the word "cat," he may associate an image with that word, but the image is different from the written word.

The *qualitative symbol* (Q) is that symbol which presents and represents to the "awareness" of the individual that which it (the symbol) itself is to him. To exemplify, the shade of red of a particular object presents to the awareness of the individual, and henceforth represents itself to the awareness system of the

The Educational Sciences

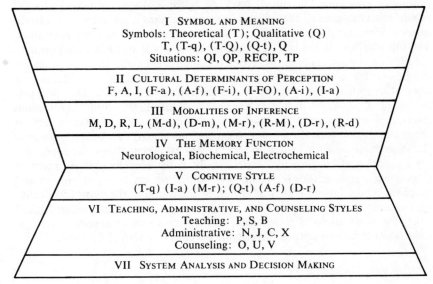

I SYMBOL AND MEANING
Symbols: Theoretical (T); Qualitative (Q)
T, (T-q), (T-Q), (Q-t), Q
Situations: QI, QP, RECIP, TP

II CULTURAL DETERMINANTS OF PERCEPTION
F, A, I, (F-a), (A-f), (F-i), (I-FO), (A-i), (I-a)

III MODALITIES OF INFERENCE
M, D, R, L, (M-d), (D-m), (M-r), (R-M), (D-r), (R-d)

IV THE MEMORY FUNCTION
Neurological, Biochemical, Electrochemical

V COGNITIVE STYLE
(T-q) (I-a) (M-r); (Q-t) (A-f) (D-r)

VI TEACHING, ADMINISTRATIVE, AND COUNSELING STYLES
Teaching: P, S, B
Administrative: N, J, C, X
Counseling: O, U, V

VII SYSTEM ANALYSIS AND DECISION MAKING

Capital letters indicate dominant and small letters indicate subordinate values of the same characteristic.

Symbols:	T — theoretical Q — qualitative	Teaching Style:	P — predominant S — switcher B — flexible
Situations:	QI — qualitative independence QP — qualitative predominance RECIP — reciprocity TP — theoretical predominance	Administrative Style:	N — dominant J — adjusting C — cooperative X — passive
Perception:	F — family A — associates I — individual	Counseling Style:	O — nondirective U — situational V — highly directive
Inference:	M — magnitude D — difference R — relationship L — appraisal or evaluation		

individual, that which was perceived by the individual. In order for two or more persons to share knowledge of the particular shade of red exhibited by that particular object at the time it was originally observed, it would be necessary for the two persons to observe the object at the same point of time. The residue of the stimuli resulting from the observation of the color of the object is, in essence, that which is referred to as the qualitative symbol.

Champlin and Villemain have interpreted an "educational" situation in terms of the two types of symbols and have classified four different kinds of "situations": (1) qualitative independence (QI); (2) qualitative predominance (QP); (3) reciprocity (RECIP); and (4) theoretical predominance (TP). Let us illustrate a possible application of the theory: If an educator is attempting to motivate students to listen to a particular type of music, he might merely play three different recordings of scores that exemplify the qualities of the music in question. This approach would provide a situation of "qualitative independence" for the listener—a type of situation frequently advocated by music lovers as the best for developing an appreciation for music. If the educator is attempting to teach students how to appreciate the type of music involved beyond that of the previously undefined "listening" level, he might make a few remarks to the group concerning, say, the unique rhythm patterns that prevail at certain intervals throughout each of the recorded scores, and then play the recordings. The introduction of the brief explanation (theoretical symbolization) prior to the playing of the records for the group (qualitative symbolization), provides the conditions for a "qualitative predominance" situation. If the educator is attempting to teach technical aspects of the type of music, as well as the appreciation of it, he might decide to play each of the three records, but at given intervals of time interrupt the musical presentation to explain certain aspects of the music. If the intervals devoted to explanatory remarks are of approximately the same duration as those devoted to the musical presentations, the conditions for a situation of "reciprocity" exist. Finally, if the educator delivers a lecture (theoretical symbolization) on the type of music under consideration and supplements the lecture with a modicum of the sound of the music (qualitative symbolization), the conditions for a situation of "theoretical predominance" exist. The implications of these examples for the instruction of music should be self-evident in various settings throughout the educational establishment.

STRATUM II: PERCEPTION

Both types of symbol, the theoretical and qualitative, can be perceived in a different fashion by different individuals. The general culture of the individual sets certain limits on his patterns of perception. Further structuring of meaning is effected by the individual's family background, occupation, economic class, sex role, and other related social factors. There are various theories of perception both in social-psychological terms and in more universal terms. The purpose of this statum of the educational sciences is the application of the pertinent aspects of these theories to educational problems. Three essential "effects" are employed in this stratum: family (F), associates (A), and individuality (I).

STRATUM III: MODALITIES OF INFERENCE

The human being can draw both deductive *conclusions* and inductive *inferences* (probability conclusions). Inductive modes of inference (*inferences* can be either inductive or deductive) are of maximum value for the educational sciences as they apply to the process of education. In the employment of the inductive process, man can only advance three hypotheses and can draw only four inferences. The three hypotheses are classified as (1) magnitude (M), (2) difference (D), and (3) relationship (R). The four inferences are: (1) magnitude (M), (2) difference (D), (3) relationship (R), and (4) appraisal or evaluation (L).

The implications of Stratum III are similar to those of Stratum I (Symbol and Meaning) in that once an individual student's characteristic mode of inference is identified, then any teaching of that individual should take into account this characteristic mode of inference. This statement should not be interpreted to mean that the teaching of an individual should only be limited to those areas that reinforce the strongest aspects of the student's mode of inference. The appropriate task of the educator might well be that of identifying the weakest aspects of the student's "mode" and then working with educational approaches that tend to correct these deficiencies. Diagnosis of the individual educational needs in terms of the previously delineated strata may be the most important function of the educational sciences in their beginnings.

STRATUM IV: MEMORY

There are certain aspects of the basic theories of the neurological structures and the electrochemical and biochemical processes of the brain that have bearing on human memory and thought. These aspects have not been as fully developed as they need to be to form a proper stratum of the educational sciences. However, they hold much promise for the future.

At present, modifications of the hypotheses of Holger Hydn (neurologist, Göteborg University, Sweden) are serving as points of departure for studying possible neurological, biochemical, and electrochemical aspects of memory and learning. One of the present hypotheses is that memory is effected by certain configurations of protein substance stored in neuroglial cells that envelop the synapses of neural pathways. These configurations are the memories of the stimuli that generated them. The configurations of the protein substance are formed in the neuroglial cells called ("glial cells") as the result of electro-chemical stimuli (nerve stimuli) distributed throughout a given neural pathway. The protein substance is composed of three basic acids, the structures of which are capable of forming an infinite number of permutations that yield configurations that (it is hypothesized) are unique to their associated sets of stimuli.

Biochemists now are probing methods of encouraging and inhibiting the "flow" of protein in neuroglial cells. If the above hypothesis is valid, the memory function of the brain can be improved by controlling the "flow" of protein. Thus, the possibility of using memory pills for certain types of educational tasks might become a reality in the relatively near future.

STRATUM V: COGNITIVE STYLE

At present, the cognitive style of a student can be defined in terms of the first three strata of the sciences: (1) symbolic orientation, (2) perception, and (3) modality of inference. The fourth stratum, neurological, biochemical, and electrochemical aspects of the brain, although important to the definition of cognitive style, is not sufficiently developed to include at this time.

The first three strata of the educational sciences offer a means of analyzing, interpreting, and evaluating educational activities in a manner different from those employed today. For example, suppose a student is confronted with an educational task (an algebra lesson, for example) calling for a predominantly theoretical (TP) symbolic approach, and suppose his cognitive style is (Q-t), (A-f),(D-r). This characterization of the student indicates that his capabilities for being able to solve problems are most easily used by him if the problem or phenomenon is cast in the qualitative symbolic, in a context in which his associates have opinions about the solutions being sought, or to a lesser extent, his family has or has had experience in "solving." Suppose, further, that providing the "setting" of the problem includes "contrasts" or "analogies" through which solutions to the problems might be derived. Given these circumstances, the educational scientist would know that the study of the algebra lesson would tend to be very difficult for the student. If the student *must* study mathematics—and although it is contrary to what advocates of modern mathematics wish to educate the student in terms of—the point of departure and the bulk of his instruction, whenever and wherever possible, should be carried out in terms of the qualitative symbol (e.g., pictures, graphs, objects). On the other hand, if the student: is mainly *theoretical* in *symbolic orientation* (T-q), has *perceptions* (I-a) that are mainly affected by his individuality (I) and to a lesser extent by his associates (a), and is mainly *appraisal inferential* (L), then his being educated in modern mathematics (as it is taught today) would present no problem. Computers are now being employed to match the cognitive styles of students with programed instruction materials on the basis of the cognitive style of the "programer." For example, if the student's "style" is (T-q), (I-a), (M-r), and he is going to use programed instruction materials on a modern math unit, the computer would seek from the store of those appropriate units that had been programed the one which was programed by an individual with a cognitive style that was somewhat similar to the student's, e.g., (T-q), (A-I), (L). This approach has been termed: "Computer Assisted Management of Learning" (CAMOL).

STRATUM VI: TEACHING, ADMINISTRATIVE, AND COUNSELING STYLES

Teaching style. From the information provided by certain doctoral studies and certain field-testing results, it became clear that analysis and predictions in the student-teacher relationship could not be totally explained in terms of the cognitive styles of the respective individuals involved. For example, an excellent teacher might be called upon to prepare programed instruction materials in a subject matter unit in which the teacher had previously had great instructional success. But students who had cognitive styles that were significantly different from that of the teacher had considerable difficulty in attempting to pass the proficiency examination associated with these materials. It should be noted that the frames included in the programed instruction materials had highly satisfactory reliability and validity indices as did the proficiency test attached to the respective units. When the teacher was allowed to teach the same students in a face-to-face relationship, they were able to handle not only these units but others at a level of greater difficulty with comparative ease. The factor at work actually was a tight-loop feedback circuitry between the students and the teacher in the teaching situation. It was through this feedback circuitry that the teacher was able to adjust her approaches in order to accommodate the cognitive styles of the students, which were significantly different from the teacher's.

It should be noted that all teachers are not able to adjust their cognitive styles in the fashion noted here. Many teach in a rather set pattern. These types of teachers have been classified as those who possess a predominant (P) teaching style. The teacher who is able to teach a student "where she finds him," so to speak, in terms that are amenable to his cognitive style is said to have a teaching style that is flexible (B). Finally, the teacher who uses the student's cognitive style as a point of departure for instruction and moves him in the direction of his being able to accommodate her cognitive style is said to be an adjusting— "switcher"–type (S).

Teaching style is a necessary aspect of the educational sciences. It is used to analyze and predict occurrences associated with face-to-face teaching situations of various types and those involving programed instruction approaches.

Administrative style. Although the cognitive style of the administrator is an aspect of his approach to administration, it is not a sufficient element to explain his total administrative behavior. Employing a systemic analytical approach, it has been discovered by persons working in the field of educational sciences that it is helpful to be able to classify the administrative style of persons holding administrative positions. There are four classifications of administrative style: dominant (N); adjusting (J); cooperative (C); and passive-custodial (X).

In certain field tests, administrators with highly similar cognitive styles have chosen decidedly different administrative behaviors while performing the same administrative tasks. The systemic approach which was used to analyze these behaviors noted whether the administrator was "persons" oriented, "processes" oriented, or "properties" oriented in his administrative decision-making approach. This fact, coupled with the administrator's attitude toward who should set the goals (the group or himself) and whose approach to the task should be employed (his or the group's), provides the essential elements for determining the administrative style of an individual.

Counseling style. The cognitive styles of the individuals involved were, as in the case of teaching style and administrative style, found to be a necessary but not sufficient entity for explaining and predicting behaviors manifested by the student and the counselor in various types of counseling situations. In those cases where the counselor was highly directive, regardless of the situation involved, his counseling style was classified as (V). In those cases where the counselor was directive in some instances and nondirective in others, depending upon the situation, his counseling style was classified as situational (U). Those counselors who demonstrated to a high degree nondirective activity, regardless of the counseling situation, were classified as nondirective (O).

STRATUM VII: SYSTEMS ANALYSIS AND DECISION MAKING

Using the approach that all the activities occurring under the rubric of education could be classified either as microcosmic systems and/or macrocosmic systems, in which decision making coupled with tight-loop feedback circuitry results in the desirable feature of self-adjustment, a selected set of systems models has been field tested in pilot study demonstrations in the areas of analysis, evaluation, and simulation. Further work is being carried out in this stratum in large-scale projects involving various types of educational decisions, concerning personnel, facilities, and equipment.

FOOTNOTE:

[1] Most of the material on the educational sciences is extracted from Urban Adult Education Institute Technical Memo No. 8, May 10, 1968, based on a position paper prepared by Joseph E. Hill.

———————————

Questions:

1. What course of action would you follow to effectively bring about a change in the science program taught to culturally deprived urban children?

2. Defend or criticize the use of a basic text book in a sixth grade urban school science class for culturally deprived children.

3. Select a particular grade level and then list three or four items in the science curriculum that you feel are irrelevant. Then mention the changes you would make to bring about relevancy in these items.

AFFECTIVE ASPECTS
OF BLACK LITERATURE

By BARBARA DODDS STANFORD

"Volcanoes of creative energy" is how my college methods teacher described high school students, and this image burns the pit of my stomach as I watch my leaden-eyed students shuffle listlessly into the room and stare blankly into space waiting for their buttons to be pushed. I am pained to see them so unhappy and bored, but I can get no more excited than they about reading *Silas Marner* or discussing elliptical clauses, parts of the prescribed curriculum. The dryness and irrelevance of school irritates me further, because I know that most of my students have real problems in communication: they continually complain that they cannot talk to their parents; they sit nervously, afraid to speak to any of their classmates except their own small circle of friends; and most of them are completely unnerved when confronted with a member of another race. These are the communication problems the English class must deal with, not the intricacies of the theory of tragedy or nominal clauses.

Black literature is a godsend to the teacher who wants his class to deal with genuine communication problems in the classroom. Writers like James Baldwin, William Melvin Kelley, Richard Wright, and Gwendolyn Brooks confront deeply, honestly, and humanly the issues that our students fearfully struggle with alone in their inner worlds. What a relief it is to recognize our own struggle to find ourselves in Baldwin's *Notes of a Native Son,* for Baldwin's frank discussion reassures us that this is a normal human question and aids us in our own quest. Robert Teague's *Letters to a Black Boy* gives parental advice to a black child, but it also gives the white reader honest reactions which will help him communicate with the blacks around him who may not be as open. Claude Brown's *Manchild in the Promised Land* shows the devastating toll of human life and happiness that the city slum takes, and students who are worried about their own friends and family—or even themselves—can gain some courage and insight from Brown's escape. Lorraine Hansberry's *A Raisin in the Sun,* James Baldwin's *Go Tell It on the Mountain,* and Paule Marshall's *Brown Girl, Brownstones* portray young people struggling to assert their own independence and identity against their parents. Most black writers deal with sex openly and without embarrassment as in William Melvin Kelley's short story "Connie," which tells of a pregnant girl who must decide what to do with her baby.

But even if we rush to our classes with exciting samples of black literature, we may still face the blank, turned-off faces of our students. Instead of vibrant communication about real issues, we may find actual resistance to discussion. What can the problem be? Obviously their silence and apparent lack of interest is not irrelevance of material as it was with *Silas Marner,* for they read eagerly and comment on how much they like the books. But during discussion they are silent and look the other way.

I began to understand my students' silence and apparent apathy better when I myself was a participant in a discussion group. In this group I found that though I had plenty to say, I was very reluctant to talk, even when the silences became uncomfortable. I hid within myself weighing each comment carefully, wondering how the rest of the group would react to my revelation. Would they dislike me or make fun of me or refuse to associate with me if I said what I was thinking about? And in this particular group I was with people I probably would not see again. How much more frightening it must be for students to reveal their feelings to classmates whom they see daily and who control their social success or failure.

Their fears are well-founded. Several weeks ago two girls from an all-white school were explaining why they did not want a certain boy to go on a trip with them. Their main objection to him was that he was prejudiced, and they based their judgment on an incident several years earlier when they had heard him call a Negro by a derogatory name. Of course, in another social group, a student could be ostracized for being too friendly to Negroes. Naturally, students are reluctant to participate in serious discussions when the social consequences can be so disastrous. Not only can a person be penalized for the wrong response by ostracism for years in the future, but he often does not even know what response his fellow classmates want.

If dealing with relevant material is so dangerous, then maybe we had better put Baldwin back on the shelf and resurrect "Idylls of the King." And that is the "cop-out" many of us use. But there are two answers to any problem in teaching: One is to give up; the other is to accept the challenge and develop new techniques and ideas to solve the problem. It may be that in the long run the greatest contribution of black literature to the English class will be that it will force us to find ways to deal with and use strong feelings in the classroom.

One of the first skills I found that I had to develop to teach black literature effectively was simply to listen. While watching my apprentice teacher imitate me, I realized that in presenting my well-developed lesson plan explaining a literary work, I was so concerned about getting my own ideas across that I could not give any of my attention to the ideas my students were generating. As an experiment, I tried going into the class every day without any preparation other than reading the assignment. I would ask a very general question such as "What do you want to talk about from yesterday's chapter?" and would wait for the students to present their own ideas. Although there were several periods of silence, the discussions were much more effective than usual, and I gained much insight into my students, and myself. Since then I have found it very effective to begin discussions of black literature or other controversial materials with such open-ended questions. With slower students, the question may need to be more focused, and the students may require some direction to be able to express their ideas. For example, after reading aloud "The Debut" by Kristin Hunter, a story which shows how a social climbing girl learns about her power over men from watching a girl from the streets handle a group of boys, I asked the students to make their minds blank and then to think about the story and to tell me which scene came to their minds.

"The girl's mother."

"What did you notice about the girl's mother?"

"The way she was trying to make the girl be something that she wasn't."

"How did you feel about the mother?"

"I didn't like her."

Another student added, "Yeah, she thinks she is better than anybody else," and the students continued in an effective discussion of social climbing. As the discussion began to die down, I told them that I was surprised by the statement that the mother interested them the most, for I had noticed that they all seemed to be much more attentive during the scene where Lucy Mae was talking to the boys. "Who did you like most, Judy or Lucy Mae?"

By now they were ready to quit intellectualizing about social climbers and to express their feelings about the two girls, particularly their hostility toward Judy, who thought she was better than Lucy Mae, with whom they identified. With little direction, they heatedly discussed their resentment of people who think they are better than anybody else because of money or color, and they criticized the story because from their view of the world the story was unrealistic. In their world a girl like Judy would end up tragically. They discussed the story with depth and explored on their own most of the significant themes as well as applying sophisticated critical skills.

This technique also works well with books which students may have strong reactions to. The question "What makes you angry about this book?" revealed that my students felt that the author of *To Kill a Mockingbird* was very prejudiced, and they did not understand that the comments of characters like Mrs. Dubose did not necessarily express the author's opinion. This discussion led naturally to the concept of point of view.

But an effective class that can deal with black literature needs more than a teacher who can listen. It also needs students who can listen, who can tolerate differences of opinion, and who can trust each other not to hold differences of opinion against them. The biggest aid in helping students talk to each other is letting them see that they have many ideas and problems in common.

The "Secret Sharing Game" is a very effective way of showing students how many problems they share with their classmates. For this activity, students are given identical sheets of paper and instructed to write about a personal problem. Then the papers are exchanged and the person who receives the paper must read it as if it were his problem. Usually students will see that most people have basically the same problems. I particularly like to use this exercise while reading a play like *A Raisin in the Sun* and have students extend the exercise by presenting Beneatha's, Walter's, Ruth's, Mama's, and the white visitor's problems in the same way.

Variations of role-playing activities can also help to build trust within a group as well as helping students empathize with the characters in a book. Students could be assigned to the roles of the father, mother, son, brother, and aunt in *Go Tell It on the Mountain* and asked to respond to such open-ended statements as "I am most afraid of . . .," "I would like to . . .," "I hate . . . ," and "I don't understand. . . ." Students then could continue by filling in the blanks as they apply to their own feelings. A discussion of this type might give students enough confidence to talk about the touchy subjects of religion and illegitimacy that the books raises.

Besides the ability to listen and a spirit of trust within the class, effective teaching of black literature requires honesty and a willingness to face painful self-revelation. We all like to think of ourselves as good, kind people; black literature forces us to recognize the murky prejudices, hatreds, and fears that lurk in our subconscious. A white girl who thinks of herself as tolerant may be horrified upon reading *Julie's Heritage* to realize that she has done the same things that wounded Julie. This revelation may be so painful that she cannot face it herself, and certainly she will not want to talk about it to her classmates. At times like this, silence may be the best sign of success.

Last year the black revolution hit our school, and I was aware of the identity crises my students faced as they both flirted with and tried to avoid militant groups. Ellison's *Invisible Man* seemed the ideal book to help them understand the conflicts within them, but the questions the novel raised were too personal and confusing for effective class discussion. This time a partial answer was dividing the class into small groups where students could explore their ideas with less threat because the group was smaller. But even here, discussions could not reach the depth of the struggle the more perceptive students were engaged in. Two of the students attempted to create order out of their chaos by their own literary efforts—one with a nightmarish short story, obviously imitating the style of *Invisible Man* but dealing with the students' own problem, and the other with a very creative poem.

And isn't that what literature is all about? Isn't good literature an attempt to create meaning out of the chaos of our lives? Isn't literature a way of not only releasing our feelings, but of using them to create beauty and understanding? If we allow our students to listen to honest writers struggling to deal with this very frightening world, perhaps they will not only experience the comfort of knowing that others have faced these same problems and the insight of seeing different perspectives on the problems, but perhaps they will also see that literature can be, for them, too, a way of dealing with the world, a way of handling and using their feelings, a choice of weapons.

―――――――――

Questions:

1. List the advantages of this type of literature in class discussion groups.

2. What things must a teacher be aware of in order to carry on an effective class discussion of the type described?

3. Name the difficulties that you can see confronting a teacher trying to get at the real issues through the use of black literature.

ESTABLISHING A SCIENCE CURRICULUM
FOR AGGRESSIVE CHILDREN

By BOAZ COHEN
HOWARD L. JONES

Children with aggressive and/or inappropriate behavior in our public schools continue to be a major concern of parents, teachers, and administrators. Children exhibiting these behaviors have been labeled as "emotionally disturbed," "socially maladjusted," "problem children," or just "bad."

Special facilities, ranging from special classes or schools to after-school recreation and study centers, have been established in an attempt to deal with, and hopefully alleviate, such aggressive student behaviors. But the hard truth of the matter is that the public school teacher is the person responsible for intervening in school crises involving aggressive children. Another harsh reality is the fact that no matter how many times a child can be "referred" out of a classroom—a procedure which requires close examination in terms of the child's being repeatedly rejected or thwarted—the teacher must still contend with the presentation of the "normal" curriculum programs as they are found in the vast majority of public schools.

Implementing appropriate science curriculum materials into classrooms which include aggressive children is no mean feat. This fact is echoed by the unfortunate response of many teachers: "Science, how can I teach science? These kids can't even read, write, behave, etc." (The reader should add his own appropriate verb.)

Two most perplexing questions, then, are what methods should we use to teach (not just manage) the aggressive child and what, in terms of science content and skills, should we teach him? To answer these questions, we must ask ourselves how we can best bring about a reduction of maladaptive behaviors and an improvement of the child's positive life adaptation while mastering some part of science.

There are two particular reactions to the process of schooling which most aggressive children exhibit. One reaction is anxiety. The imposing structure of the school as an institution delegated to caring for the child for almost half of his waking hours often contributes to an increase in the child's anxiety level. Another reaction is brought about by the imposition of standard middle-class values in the structuring of many of our classrooms. Teacher-expected and teacher- or principal-enforced "middle-class" behaviors frequently contribute to increased problems of impulse control on the part of the aggressive child.

In planning a science curriculum for aggressive children one must consider these factors of anxiety and impulse control. For example, science instruction

Reprinted with permission from *The Science Teacher* (November 1969).

that is purely a group text-reading exercise calls for library-quietness on the part of students. Such an imposition of standards often raises the anxiety levels of aggressive (and other) children. Any means of "blowing off steam" for these children may just be the start of a cycle of anxiety, problem behavior, punishment, etc.

The use of manipulative materials in science instruction is one way to decrease the amount of "science-reader" use. Certainly the exemplary materials developed and greatly emphasized by the AAAS, COPES, ESS, Minnemast, and SCIS elementary science programs have brought about the increased usage of manipulative materials in the teaching of science.

Attempts have also been made to develop curriculum materials specifically for the aggressive child. The Board of Education of the City of New York has prepared a basic curriculum in all subject areas for socially maladjusted and/or emotionally disturbed children, and particularly for the aggressive child in special schools. Topics for this science curriculum were selected in terms of the degree to which they supposedly are related to the immediate needs of the aggressive child and to the realistic aspects of the child's daily environment. The proposed science curriculum consists of three basic units: (1) transportation, (2) communication, and (3) machines.

Note, however, that in each of the national curriculum projects and in the New York materials, the teacher or the text is called upon to be the mediator in imparting knowledge and skills to students. With the exception of some ESS units and some other selected "advanced" materials of the other curriculum projects, the child normally gets little chance to select for study that which is of interest to him. The structure of what, when, and how to do or learn something is still imposed upon the child from outside.

Another difficulty for aggressive children with most existing science texts and materials is the lack of appropriate success measures. Most curriculum designs have evaluative materials to measure the child's reaching specified or unspecified objectives. But the aggressive child needs more than a number score on an examination to demonstrate his success or lack of success. This child, probably more than any other, needs a feeling of competence. Successful remedial reading teachers report that their big problem in helping poor or non-readers to learn to read, or to read more proficiently, is building a confidence in them that *they can read*. There is little doubt that when a child finds that he can do something in a consistently efficient and successful manner, he will be highly motivated to repeat that activity, or a similar one. This is especially true for children who have experienced earlier failures. To the authors, helping aggressive children see that they can learn science is the most important outcome of the science curriculum.[1] Success measures, then, for aggressive children should be specified by the individual child and his teacher to answer the question: "Does the child feel that he has learned to do something that he wanted to learn to do?"

The present authors would also like to suggest that *there is a need for modifying present programs and curriculum content* to make additional tools for channeling aggressive impulses into positive learning experiences. There might be special therapeutic objectives of science education for the aggressive child. Many aggressive children have a distinct deficit in their senses of order and routine, responsibility and planning. Thus, in the selection of science concepts, principles and skills which stress order and balance in the universe would have particular therapeutic value. These principles might include the following: night follows day, the sun rises and sets, the reestablishment of order follows the destruction and chaos of storms, earthquakes, and tornadoes.

In addition, perhaps an emphasis on man's capacity to use his knowledge and learning to control physical and natural forces has an important implication for aggressive children, many of whom feel victimized by vague forces in life over which they have no control. For these reasons, knowledge and skills in the physical and life sciences can serve to improve the child's self-concept through increased mastery and control over his own destiny. The order, balance, and system underlying all science can serve as a model for the possibilities of establishing order in the child's own life.

Along this line, Cohen [1], in an evaluation and critique of the New York City curriculum, suggested a closer look at the curriculum's themes in terms of their emotional meaningfulness to aggressive children. She suggested the inclusion of more human themes which stress the science of man and the world of living plants and animals as a source of nurture and as a tool for the survival of man.

What the present authors are proposing is that the foundation of science education for aggressive children be teacher-pupil-initiated, pupil-performed, and pupil-actualized success-producing tasks that enhance the child's self-concept and promote his ego growth.

To meet these ends demands that science curriculum materials be considered from a different point of view from that used to describe the "normal" science curriculum. Often school systems adopt *in toto* texts or curriculum materials for system-wide classroom use. However, since teacher-pupil-initiated activities are to be included in the curriculum for aggressive children, no one set of texts or other materials will suffice. Materials must be *adapted* for individual classes, and more specifically, for individual students.

Teacher-adapted instructional materials might well include present program or text materials, but they must include planning and selection on the part of both students and teachers. The UNIPAC concept described by Kapfer and Swenson [3] might be a possible solution here. Kapfer and Swenson describe methods for the development of short lessons, with one or two objectives, designed to be used by individual students who want to learn a concept, principle, skill, or just more about something they find interesting. Two main features of the UNIPAC idea that make it a viable tool for use with aggressive children are the shortness of the lessons and the necessary self-selection procedure by which the child selects what he wants to learn. Certain UNIPACS (or parts of some) could be developed by the teacher to emphasize the child's control over his life, perhaps using as content vehicles such things as order in the universe and the balance of nature. These topics may have the needed therapeutic value described earlier.

Certainly the role of the teacher must be considered if he is to meet the individual differences of students in classrooms where there are some, one, or all aggressive children. Goodlad [2], in discussing prepackaged curriculum projects, has noted that "the well-designed package, like love, is not enough." The authors of this article feel that the well-designed package for aggressive children must be developed or, at least, adapted by the teacher for his students.

In adapting appropriate materials the teacher must be willing to accept the fact that there are probably more important things in the aggressive child's world than the science concepts that, as a teacher, he would like the child to have. Rubin [4] describes primary skills as those skills that are necessary for the individual's physical and emotional well-being. These skills are the ones that the teacher of aggressive children must keep in mind at all times. The secondary skills or knowledge, which may be the laws of motion, probability, or cell division, might be important but must be relegated to vehicles by which the child gains in ego development and competence.

If the science curriculum suggested by the authors is implemented, finding enough time for the individual teacher to develop, adapt, and/or prescribe the components of a "well-designed package" will be of paramount importance. Certainly, teachers are presently adapting curriculum materials to their own methods, materials, and content backgrounds. The plan suggested here, however, calls for the "adaption" of curriculum materials to the individual needs of children as well. This would more than double the present science curriculum planning and implementation time needed. We feel that the time spent is well worth it to the school, and, more importantly, the students.

FOOTNOTE:

[1] In the same vein as White's suggestion of competence as being an intrinsic psychological motivating force. [5]

REFERENCES:

[1] Cohen, Rosalyn S. *Redevelopment of a Curriculum for Socially Maladjusted and Emotionally Disturbed Children with a Corollary of Teacher Training.* Center for Urban Education, New York. 1966.

[2] Goodlad, J. "Directions of Curriculum Change." *NEA Journal* 55: 33-37; December 1966.

[3] Kapfer, P. G., and Swenson, G. "Individualizing Instruction for Self-Paced Learning." *Clearing House* 42: 405-410; March 1968.

[4] Rubin, L. S. "The Object of Schooling: An Evolutionary View." In Rubin, L. S. (Ed.) Life Skills in School and Society. *Association for Supervision and Curriculum Development,* Washington, D.C. 1969.

[5] White, R. W. "Motivation Reconsidered: The Concept of Competence." *Psychological Review* 66: 297-333; 1959.

Questions:

1. List some of the reasons why aggressive children exhibit anxiety toward schooling.

2. Describe how you would increase the aggressive child's feeling of competence in a science program.

3. Do you see science programs being adapted by teachers to fit their students as a weakness or a strength? Explain.

BLACK STUDIES IN THE
ELEMENTARY SCHOOLS

By WILLIAM E. ADAMS

Learning is a continuum which has its beginning at birth. We must draw from this statement one major fact, the greatest number of black children have been conditioned to failure. Due to years of civil and human injustices, black parents do not experience various social and economic opportunities that provide educational or intellectual stimulation.

Once the child is taken from his mother at birth, then the multiplicity of learning experiences begins. Many of these experiences are not good. Each new pattern introduced to him has some impact on the formation and molding of his personality. At this very early age the child becomes an individual, although dependent, with a profusion of needs, but an individual, no less, with the power to sense his new surroundings. From a hard slap on the rear, to the nursery where he may or may not receive the fullest attention; to home where he must make the greatest adjustment. The home is very often cold, dark and extremely rejecting. To begin life under conditions that do not foster intellectual growth, the child must adopt certain patterns that contribute to his survival only.

In the struggle for survival the young child must eat what it is given. Although malnutrition is not hereditary, the mother of the black child is in many cases malnourished because of her own way of life. This is passed on during stages of pregnancy and still further during post natal care.

There is growing evidence that nutrition may affect intellectual, behavioral, as well as physical growth. Mental retardation can be the result of a lack of protein during stages of prenatal development. Continued use of the wrong diet after the child is born further retards mental growth. Families that live in deprived areas use foods which are very high in starches and low in protein. The results of a survey show that multiple deficiences of specific nutrients occur in varying degrees, but in higher than expected proportions in black areas. Misinformed mothers whose knowledge of diets, food substitutes, and sanitary conditions — coupled with inadequate prenatal care — are the major factors contributing to malnutrition.[1]

The brain may be damaged during the period when growth is supposedly fastest. This occurs during the first 10 months after birth. At the end of the first year, the brain has reached approximately 70 per cent of its adult weight. At the end of the second year the brain has practically completed growth. Therefore, it goes without saying that the lack of sufficient protein of expectant mothers affects brain development of the unborn child. Severe malnutrition 6 to 10

Reprinted with permission from *Journal of Negro Education* (Summer 1970).

months after birth impedes further development of brain tissues. Intellectual impairment is associated with severe malnutrition. This does not mean that mental retardation *will* occur from lack of protein or diet deficiency. However, more than likely, severe malnutrition affects the rate of learning among the poor and the indigent, into which category most Black Americans fall.

The child in order to be a "normal" learner must benefit from adequate prenatal care so as to assure proper brain development. The most critical time for brain development is in the 33 months following conception.

THE PARENT OF THE BLACK CHILD IN OPPRESSED AREAS

At a very young age the black child is burdened with a profusion of problems which co-exist with deprivation. He has no one to work with him in doing the things that he finds interesting. As a matter of fact, those things that are of interest are often discouraged. Quite often the child's ideas are suppressed by his parent, who may be totally unaware that she is impeding his creativity. This frequently kills the child's initiative.

Parents rarely engage in activities with their children. As a consequence the children engage in their own activities, which often are not constructive. Those activities termed as not constructive cause not only social rejection, but social and emotional immaturity.

No one is available to listen to the concerns of small children who give freely of their thoughts; and frequently give clues to their feelings. The aches and pains of youngsters are often shrugged off by the parent. Thus, they have to live within themselves. Many parents are out working, or they are too busy "doing their own thing" to be conversant with their children. Many black parents do not encourage or reward their children when they show some achievement. These parents have been deprived of an adequate educational opportunity. This in conjunction with poverty and social deprivation leaves them frustrated and of little help to their children.

Many black children live in broken homes and are, therefore, limited to either a maternal or paternal identity, which tends to create a personality deficiency. Many children do not meet adult male relationship until they reach the upper elementary or the junior high school level. Here again there is lessening of social growth.

In homes that are broken, grandma, who may be tired of raising children, very often takes the reins. As the home goes, so goes the child. If the home is "empty" then the child's life style is meaningless. Children need attention and affection. Love of children should be included in conception. Some parents think they have fulfilled their obligation to humanity when they give birth to a child. They fail to realize the high commitment that goes with child growth and development. Tenderness has a very definite place in rearing children.

Many black parents are insecure about raising children. Psychologically they run from their responsibilities because they are lacking in the fundamental knowledge of child care. Very often they are too young and too immature to take on the tremendous burden of being a parent.

When the young black child comes to school, he is, for the most part, undernourished, lacking in love, lacking in care and understanding; lacking in educational, intellectual and social experiences; lacking in the ability to make decisions; and lacking in the ability to be conversant about his problems or concerns.

To "throw" something as complex as black studies on the young troubled mind of a 5-year-old, would serve only as a further obstruction to what he as a young learner really needs. The young black learner must be awakened to a new life style. He must be awakened to a different form of living, a discovery of events that lead him to identifying himself as a personality; free to create, to think, to converse, to relate to others, to take something home to share with his parents or whoever is there. His early formal education must provide all of the things he missed in his pre-school years, including *love* and *nutrition.* Both the nourishment of values and the nourishment from vitamins are necessary because the mind and body need stimulation toward the *wholesome* aspects of modern living.

Educating the young black child must be firmly based on truth, virtue, and social judgments, rather than hypocrisy and emotion.

THE SCHOOL

Educating all children by one standard seems to be the rule in this country rather than the reality. Tests, for example, are based on middle-class white standards. Books are written seemingly to serve the needs of white middle-class children. It appears as if education today, throughout our country, is divided; those to be educated as first class citizens and those to be educated as second class citizens. Those who do not meet the specifications established by old testing standards are dropped out along the way. Much of today's curriculum is still geared to antiquated forms of testing.

Black children entering school for the first time may meet one of four kinds of teachers: (1) the white teacher whose set pattern of life dictates white middle-class standards, thus dooming the unsuspecting child to failure in his first formal educational experience; (However, this concept does not wholly apply to white teachers.) (2) the black teachers who feel that "they're got it made", have no real concern for a child who appears to have "nothing going for him;" (3) the teacher who has an oversized class and who overlooks the child who needs all the help and attention he can get; (4) the teacher who loves all children and cares about their needs.

A child has the right to attend school, the right to an education, and the right to success. When the school and its teachers are committed to quality education for *all* who enter, then, and only then, will educational experiences prove to be a series of happy, successful events.

Children come to school alone. It is only through the spirit of communication that teachers reach out to the loneliness of the child and help him. The child's play time is much occupied with activities that duplicate, as lifelike as he can, the attitudes, gestures, tones, speech and other incidents of adult behavior that has impressed him.

The teacher may not like the child that is standing before her, but must see beyond the dirt, the language spoken in communicating, and the behavior exhibited. The young child is doing all that he knows how to do.

Once the teacher overcomes this invisible barrier that is between her standards and the child's inner-self, a base for learning new things can be established.

I have purposely not referred to black studies in the elementary school. I feel the real job of the elementary school, especially the lower elementary, is one primarily of building wholesome attitudes, principles of love, dignity of self, pride, the evolution of constructive thought patterns; developing truths in conviction, and creating different styles based on human values.

I believe the burdening of past events, the inhuman treatment of blacks in the annals of time should not be pursued at such a formative age. Such corrosive influence is not psychologically sound.

To begin implanting ideas in young minds which are already depressed, would tend to cause them to view life as being unrewarding. Children see others happy (especially on T. V.) and desire to put themselves in the same place. The molding of good moral character, the ability to form hypotheses and the ability to exercise good judgment should precede Black Studies.

> Jesus loves the
> little children
> All the children
> of the world
> Red or Yellow
> Black or White
> All are precious
> in His sight
> Jesus loves the
> little children
> of the world
> ("Jesus Loves the Little Children")

Some may disagree with my reference to the deity. However, this simple verse is strong in human understanding that all children are loved. Therefore, they should love each other as they are loved.

Children must be taught by one who is compassionate and understanding, be he black or white.

The elementary school is subdivided into two main categories. One is considered early elementary the other is later elementary.

Black children should establish, as soon as possible, codes of acceptable social behavior. This means, among many things, developing a genuine capacity for friendship, and a discipline for helping each other. Teachers must help young children develop a philosophy of life that fosters the golden rule so as to make peace and brotherhood a reality. Young children can adopt this philosophy easier once their reasoning powers are developed.

Incorporated in their learning of the brotherhood of man, interpretation of books and stories about contemporary blacks should be used to assist in stimulating a progressive spirit and, also, a feeling that the world has a place for them. When young black children bring to school a deep feeling of depression or rejection, the teacher can, through books, stories, T.V. programs and play acting, reshape or reform their aggressive temperament, to one which often accompanies a zest for living.

As educators, our responsibility is to help individuals to know themselves and their own power. Black children must learn the importance of their role. They should learn that they cannot become effective or productive without a set of operational skills, the primary skills of *reading* and *thinking*. The first three grades of school *must provide* the young black child with these two main skills if he is to look at reality and fit constructively within the social order.

Reading and thinking are the response mechanisms the young learner must use in the rebuttal of problems that are concurrent with daily living. All stops must be pulled out to make black children avid readers before grade four. Too many teachers are caught up in the racial "hang up," which is imparted to the child either by reference, by innuendo, by emotion or by lecture. If a child can read, and think, he will not so easily be influenced, but rather be able to draw his own conclusions; based on his own reasoning.

In the upper elementary school a curriculum that will include black studies should be geared toward a developmental process that will help the child achieve social and economic objectives.

Black Studies in the upper elementary should be a blend of skills learned in lower grades, (which are prerequisites) interrelated with social objectives. The children should be able to call upon their curriculum to serve as a kind of self teacher. With further extension of skills, they will be able to use their abilities to recognize their needs or problems, state them in rational terms, and reach desired competency in performing tasks to meet their objectives. This approach further allows for flexibility in choosing areas of black studies to pursue. Under such conditions, enthusiasm will be high, motivation and interest up, and the performance level almost superior. A greater understanding of subject matter and feedback will take place among individuals and groups of individuals.

Black children *can* manipulate at an upper elementary level within a structured or unstructured curriculum if they are relatively free of restrictive measures for advancing ideas. It is imperative that black children become equipped with skills for future performance. Competency in basics must evolve in the elementary grades.

Secondary education sets a high priority on acquired skills and abilities, as it should. Independent competencies bear greatly upon achievement in secondary school. The gap between abilities to comprehend and required performance rapidly widens as the child progresses through the secondary grades if he lacks skills, especially in reading. At some point in time, those who can not cope with curriculum demands will subsequently drift away from formal education and drop by the wayside.

Unfortunately most of the children who drop out of school have been, through no fault of their own, conditioned to failure. Their intellectual development has not been adequate from birth. When the basic skills of reading and thinking are forfeited in the elementary school the child cannot keep pace.

By a concerted effort of the teacher, the child and the parent, countless thousands of black children will be spared intellectual retrenchment. They must be lead to study all major disciplines including social sciences and the humanities. This can be done with an emphasis on contributions of contemporary black Americans.

Black children must come to believe in man and that *they are a part* of mankind. Thus, young black children can work within the systems developed by man, and sense changes that need to take place. Once the need becomes significant, then the idea is conveyed in order to properly effect the change. Young blacks must be taught that they can creatively improve the system in which they are to interact.

GUIDELINES FOR BLACK STUDIES IN THE ELEMENTARY SCHOOLS

I would like to conclude by offering a few basic guidelines that should precede an effective program for Black Studies in the elementary school:

(1)   The school where young black children begin their formal education should have certified teachers in grades K-3. No provisional or probationary teachers should be placed in those grades. The major emphasis *must* be on reading — thinking skills.

(2)   The teacher of black children must have the temperament to work with black children. They must be sensitive to the needs rather than condemn the children they're teaching because of their apparent shortcomings.

(3)   The teacher's attitude must be flexible enough to instill in all children a worth of being, to develop within them a sense of obligation to oneself, and to his fellow peers. This *includes moral, ethical,* and *aesthetic aspects* of life. A sense of appreciation is mandatory at an early age.

(4)   The teacher must not permit young black children to begin thinking that this country is not theirs. *It is,* black children are, *in fact,* born free. The Constitution of the United States gives to all born under it this privilege. As Americans they are free to move about as they wish. They are free to train and pursue the avocation of their choice. There are *no* man made barriers that are insurmountable.

In addition, young black children should not be made to believe that they will have to exist as a separate ethnic group. Although they may belong to a subculture of America, *they are* born Americans and their heritage is American.

(5)   The ghetto elementary school should have more adult males as administrators. The present elementary schools are dominated by females. A strong "father image" is needed, one which doesn't necessarily "spare the rod."

(6)   The school must promote the use of standard English. "Ghettoese" may be spoken in informal gatherings. However, the business world is not written in colloquialisms. Therefore, black children must learn to properly use the language of the society in which they must interact.

(7)   Instructional materials used in primary grades must furnish multi-ethnic illustrations in order to provide identity for the young learners.

(8)   The young expectant mother should be apprised of proper diets, to ensure proper brain development.

(9)   Black parents should reward and encourage their children when they (the children) show some achievement.

(10)   Black children should not be burdened with adult problems of family living.

(11)   Black parents should listen to their children and encourage conversation.

(12) Children have many interests, some more specific than others. Black parents must work with the things in which their children show an interest.

(13) Black parents who don't have a formal education should make every effort to get a formal education. This new self-improvement and confidence will be transmitted to their children who will learn faster because of the elimination of a psychological barrier. Parents will then be more conversant with their children, because they will share common problems.

(14) Teachers must understand how black children participate in class discussions. "They must not be closed out when their responses differ from the expectations of the teacher. If the children are turned off, they will soon learn to expect this and many will refuse to volunteer remarks."

FOOTNOTES:

[1]Merriel S. Read, "Malnutrition and Learning," *American Education,* V (December 1969), 11-14.

[2]"The Chalkboard," *Middle Grade Activities,* (Scott Foresman & Co., Spring Issue, 1970).

———————————

Questions:

1. Explain the various factors that retard brain development and thus lead to decreased academic performance.

2. Many experts agree that 75% of a child's attitudes and values are formed by age 5. Describe how this article suggests that the poor performance of Negroes is due in a large extent to environment.

3. Develop guidelines for primary teachers to follow to counteract the detrimental effects of ghetto life.

INTEGRATING AMERICAN HISTORY

By N. FRANKLIN HURT

Showing the Negro in his true role in American history is perhaps the most complex, important, and difficult as well as the most necessary task that a high school history staff will undertake in this generation. Pressures for the needed innovation have come from at least four quarters: the Civil Rights movement of the last dozen years, the new light shed on the role and treatment of the American Negro by recent studies, the realization that racial stereotyping is divisive and inimical to the development of an intelligent and constructive way of life in a pluralistic society, and the increasing demands on the public schools to assume responsibility to help society with its most pressing problems.

In 1963, the staff of the History Department at Thornton Township High School in Harvey, Illinois, began the task of "integrating" the history curriculum used in the integrated (two-thirds white, one-third Negro), comprehensive high school. The goal of the revised curriculum was to break down the racial stereotypes that existed in the minds of some of Thornton's students.

As a beginning, the staff developed a new course of study designed to help teachers show how Negroes have participated in our history. Department members revamped standard chronological units (the Age of the Federalists, 1789-1800; the Jeffersonian Period, 1801-1808; and so on, up to the present) so that each would include germane facts of Negro history for that period. A bibliography and a listing of audiovisual materials for each chronological unit provided teachers with significant source material classified for fast, average, and slow-ability groups.

The new course of study seeks to keep the Negro in focus as a constant and natural participant in U.S. history. Heretofore, only a fragmented or blurred conception of the Negro's role in our nation's past has emerged because he has tended to appear only infrequently and spasmodically in the history books.

As revised, the course of study brings to light the contributions of the American Negro in the context of each historical period and the handicaps placed upon him in each. In addition, it helps students question common assumptions or misconceptions. A common misconception, for example, is that prior to the Civil War, the Negro's sole contribution to the nation was picking cotton. This notion ignores the work of such an outstanding Negro as Benjamin Banneker—mathematician, astronomer, editor, and surveyor—who served on the commission that drew up the plans for Washington, D.C. It also overlooks Phyllis

---

Reprinted with permission from *Today's Education* (January 1969).

Wheatley, the eighteenth century Negro poet, and the powerful abolitionist leader, Frederick Douglass.

Students of the new course of study find that, contrary to prevalent assumptions, Negroes have distinguished themselves since the Civil War, not only as athletes and entertainers, but also as scientists and artists. The new look at history examines both the achievements of the American Negro and the obstacles that have been placed in his way.

To the revised course of study, the Thornton history staff added something new—a unit centered on the condition of the Negro from Reconstruction to 1900, the period in which racial segregation was legally sanctioned by a series of Supreme Court decisions.

In this unit, the student sees the casting of the mold that has systematically excluded Negroes from political participation, economic progress, and social acceptance. He learns how, in the Civil Rights Cases of 1883, the U.S. Supreme Court struck down the Civil Rights Act of 1875 and removed the public-accommodations provision covering hotels, theaters, and places of public amusement. He notes that the Court crippled the Fourteenth and Fifteenth Amendments and declared that interference with Negro voting rights by such private groups as the Ku Klux Klan was a matter beyond its purview. He hears how the Plessy *v.* Ferguson decision of 1896 legalized racial segregation in public facilities, including schools, and how the Supreme Court rationalized this under the "separate but equal" concept for almost six decades.

This specialized unit involves examination of other restrictions applied to the Negro during the last quarter of the nineteenth century. It also highlights discriminatory practices that have retarded economic development. For example, the student finds that by 1900 over 50 percent of the Negroes in the South were still engaged in agriculture and that until World War I most of the Negro population remained in the South because Northern industrialists preferred immigrant labor.

In short, the student learns that by the turn of the century restrictions on Negro housing and social conduct had reached national proportions and the foundations had been laid for a continued high rate of Negro illiteracy, public dependency, and crime.

When the student has completed this intensive unit, he is in a better position to examine thoughts he may harbor about the "inherent inferiority" of the Negro. As a result, he may better come to grips with immediate issues like school integration, open occupancy, the biased attitudes of his friends and neighbors, and simple slogan solutions.

Although standard U.S. history texts are improving, they continue to depict slavery as an abstract political issue with both favorable and unfavorable aspects. Too frequently, they play down moral issues while leaving slavery essentially untouched or sugarcoated as a human condition. Most texts fail to report the achievements by and for the Negro during the Reconstruction period and largely ignore the post-Reconstruction story of how the Negro was systematically and legally stripped of his newly gained rights.

To compensate for the inadequacy of the texts, Thornton uses supplementary material organized into classroom sets. Such works as *Black Cargoes: A History of the Atlantic Slave Trade* by Daniel Mannix and Malcolm Cowley (Viking, 1962) and *From Slavery to Freedom: A History of American Negroes* by John Hope Franklin (Knopf, revised edition 1956) depict the truly harsh nature of the slave trade and plantation system. Works like *The Era of Reconstruction: 1865-1877* by Kenneth Stampp (Knopf, 1965) and *The Strange Career of Jim Crow* by C. Vann Woodward (Oxford, revised edition 1966) may be used to dispel many of the common myths and misunderstandings about the nature of Reconstruction and the condition of the Negro between 1865 and 1900.

Two studies that deal very perceptively with the problem of Negro self-image and cultural identification are: *Negro Self-Concept: Implications for School and Citizenship* by William C. Kvaraceus et al. (McGraw-Hill, 1965); and *Crisis in Black and White* by Charles E. Silberman (Vintage Books, 1965).

Other supplementary sources useful in showing the Negro in his proper perspective in American history are: *The Negro in the Making of America* by Benjamin Quarles (MacMillan, 1965); a syllabus entitled *The Negro in American History* prepared by the Department of History of the Public Schools of the District of Columbia (1964); and a collection of documents, *The Negro in American Life,* edited by Richard C. Wade (Houghton Mifflin, 1965). Teachers find the Quarles book suitable for the fast and average students because of concepts and vocabulary, and the Washington, D.C., syllabus especially useful for the slow learner because of its very precise organization and terse narrative. Richard Wade's collection of documents can be used with all groups. Funds for these books can be obtained under Title II of the Elementary and Secondary Education Act.

Books are not the only helpful sources. Some of the audiovisual materials dealing with Negro history are remarkably well done, adaptable, and reasonable in cost. For example, a three reel, 16mm film series entitled "History of the Negro in America" (McGraw-Hill) covers the entire span of American history. The first reel begins with the fifteenth century slave trade and traces slavery up to 1860; the second reel focuses upon the Negro during the Civil War and Reconstruction; the third traces his plight from the 1870's through the Civil Rights movement of the 1960's. Each reel is 20 minutes long, costs $125, and can be used in a variety of ways, at various points, and for many purposes.

Filmstrips and records also prove to be excellent material. For example, an eight-part filmstrip series presents "History of the American Negro" (McGraw-Hill). Each picture frame is accompanied by a meaningful paragraph-long caption, and the result is something more than a string of celluloid clichés. This series costs $60. Other very good aids are phonograph records, such as "The Negro People in America" and "Songs of American Negro Slaves." These materials also can be purchased with Title II funds.

Many other excellent supplementary sources are available. For instance, *The Journal of Negro History* and the *Negro History Bulletin* carry articles that are scholarly and readily adaptable to classroom use. Both periodicals are published by the Association for the Study of Negro Life and History, which also publishes books dealing with Negro history. The Center for Human Relations of the NEA has contributed significant materials including *The Negro American in Paperback,* an annotated list of paperback books for secondary school students; "The Negro in American History," a filmstrip; and *An Index to Multi-Ethnic Teaching Materials and Teacher Resources.*

These are just a few of many very fine supplementary sources. Others are identified in useful bibliographies that have appeared recently, such as *Teachers' Guide to American Negro History* by William Loren Katz (Quadrangle Books, 1968), which lists pertinent audiovisual materials as well as books and periodicals; *The Negro in America: A Bibliography* edited by Elizabeth W. Miller (Harvard, 1966); and "The History of Negro History," an excellent bibliographic essay by Ernest Kaiser *(Negro Digest,* Vol. XVII, No. 4, February, 1968).

After developing the new course of study and acquiring supplementary materials, the staff made decisions concerning the actual classroom presentations of the new program, the strengthening of faculty preparation, and follow-up programs.

Guided by the following general conclusions, each Thornton history teacher works out his own method of presenting the new material:

1. The project would be doomed to failure if the new material were presented with sermons or if one day of the week were set aside perfunctorily or rigidly as "Negro History Day." The former approach would guarantee an indifferent response, and the latter would run the risk of ridicule. The successful program must help the students to "look at the record," a reasonably complete one, and come to their own conclusions.

2. The Negro must be included as a regular and functional participant in American history. Consistent and generally undramatic references to the Negro, whether his role is great or small in various units of study keeps him in proper focus as a constant factor in American history.

3. Students will recognize new content as a standard part of the course only if it is a standard part of the testing program. Desired outcomes must be planned and results must be tested. A revised testing program provides for evaluation of the new materials.

The history staff at Thornton recognizes that the additions to the curriculum bring with them the necessity for additional study. Teachers need in-service work in order to become familiar with the revised views of such topics as African civilization, slavery and the plantation system, Reconstruction, and contributions of the American Negro. They also need to develop a variety of approaches, as well as sensitivity and skill in presentation and in discussion management.

A monthly in-service seminar supplements individual study at Thornton. These meetings occur after regular school hours and require considerable outside research and preparation on the part of the teachers. In pursuing topical inquiries, the participants either concentrate on Negro history exclusively, or deal with major themes in U.S. history (such as growth of industry and labor) with considerable emphasis on the role of the Negro. From such systematic inquiry, the staff hopes to develop a coherent concept of the Negro's part in America's past and present that will contribute to informed and consistent instruction.

Other departments at Thornton have cooperated to provide valuable reinforcement and enrichment of the revised history curriculum. The English, Art, and Music Departments have introduced additional material by and about Negroes. For example, the Speech Department follows a rational and aesthetically acceptable policy of biracial casting for plays. It has also successfully presented the prizewinning Negro drama, *A Raisin in the Sun*. Similarly, in science class, students examine biological and anthropological aspects of race. Such interdisciplinary links seek to strengthen and deepen the student's knowledge and understanding, as a prelude to attitude change.

Arriving at this fairly comprehensive approach to putting the Negro into U.S. history has taken five years of planning, conferring, and experimenting. Responses of the students have ranged all the way from ill-concealed rejection to genuine interest and reappraisal of stock notions.

The next step is to evaluate systematically the results of the program. This year the staff has introduced an evaluative system to analyze the effectiveness of the curriculum revision with the primary objective of determining if, how, and to what extent an integrated American history course affects the racial attitudes of students.

The components of this procedure are: (a) administering a questionnaire about racial attitudes to U.S. history students at the beginning of the school year, (b) teaching one group of students a straight, integrated American history course without any particular attempt to deal with racial attitudes when discussing the Negro, (c) teaching another group an integrated American history course with special emphasis on racial attitudes, and (d) administering the questionnaire on racial attitudes again at the end of the school year. This follow-up procedure should contribute valuable data about the basic hypothesis that including Negro history in the regular U.S. history course will substantially improve racial attitudes.

The staff regards this U.S. history curriculum revision as a modest but significant initial step towards altering misconceptions about the Negro—a means of helping youth break through debilitating blocks to an intelligent and constructive life in our pluralistic society.

Questions:

1. Discuss your feelings as to how successful you think the Thornton Plan was in breaking down the racial stereotypes that existed in the minds of some of Thornton's students.

2. How important is it for a Negro to study Negro history in high school? Explain.

3. Explain your viewpoints regarding what type of teacher will be the most successful in teaching Negro history.

FURTHER CONSIDERATIONS IN THE
EDUCATION OF THE DISADVANTAGED

By VIRGIL A. CLIFT

The public schools in America are in serious trouble. In school districts across the nation hardly anyone wastes time quibbling over whether or not the public schools are really as bad as the critics say they are. Schools enrolling large numbers of poor or black people are deteriorating; they grow from bad to worse.

Children who enter school at the bottom of the socio-economic scale or who belong to one of the minorities—Negro, Puerto Rican, American Indian, Mexican American, etc.—generally achieve far below national norms. The longer they remain in school, the farther below grade level they fall; until finally they drop out, become delinquent, and join the increasing mass of unemployed youth.

We have reached the stage where the most compelling problem confronting American education is how to provide adequately for the disadvantaged. Seemingly it has become impossible to teach the disadvantaged. This is a strange and peculiar development for a nation where the public school has been the dominant institution in the control and socialization of youth. Until recently, it has been the major force in determining status transitions of youth; it helped people move up the socio-economic ladder from poverty to success with the result that today we have the largest middle class of any nation on earth. Because of what the public school did for the masses of poor, deprived people, Horace Mann referred to it as "man's greatest invention—the balance wheel of the social machinery."

But today the inability of the public school to serve black people and other poor people is beginning to have some serious and disturbing effects upon the broader society. The following comparisons are illustrations:

Nonwhite infant mortality in 1940 was 70 percent higher than the white rate. In 1960 it was 90 percent higher.

Maternal mortality among nonwhite mothers in 1940 was 2.4 times the white rate. In 1960 it was 3.8 times higher than the white rate.

A Negro boy born in 1962 had as much chance of surviving to 20 as a white boy had of reaching 37. A Negro girl could look forward to reaching 20 as confidently as a white girl to reaching 42.

In employment, the best years for Negroes only come up to the recession levels for whites. In 1964, a prosperous year, when white unemployment dropped to less than 3.5 percent, the Negro rate was still almost 10 percent.

Reprinted from *Educational Forum* (January 1970) by permission of Kappa Delta Pi, An Honor Society in Education, owners of the copyright.

That was half again as high as the worst white rate since the depression. These figures are for adults 20 and older. For 16- and 17-year-old Negroes, unemployment has not dropped below 20 percent in 10 years.[1]

President Kennedy stated the situation thus:

The Negro baby born in America today, regardless of the section or state in which he is born, has about one-half as much chance of completing high school as a white baby born in the same place on the same day; one-third as much chance of completing college; one-third as much chance of becoming a professional man; twice as much chance of becoming unemployed; about one-seventh as much chance of earning $10,000 per year; a life expectancy which is 7 years less; and the prospects of earning only half as much.[2]

The Selective Service Mental Test also provides a basis for some interesting comparisons. For the country as a whole, the failure rate is about 25 percent. Between June 1964 and December 1965, the rate of failure for the white applicants was 19 percent, for the Negroes 67 percent. On the other hand, Negroes in the State of Washington with 25 percent failure rate were close to the white national average and did better than white applicants in eight other states. Negroes in Rhode Island surpassed the whites in six other states. These data and others that could be cited seem to indicate that the poor showing of schools is not caused simply by an influx of Negro children. Rather, the schools are not meeting the needs of the children who are the victims of deprivation, neglect, and prejudice.

What can be done about it? The first task is that of helping teachers, administrators, and the general public to understand the social, psychological, economic, political, and cultural factors which account for deprivation. Much of the useless rhetoric on the education of the disadvantaged reveals that the educators who are writing on this subject do not understand the factors that account for it. The result is that we deal with symptoms rather than with root causes for the pathology itself. For example, what does it do to the individual child when he comes from a group that has been relegated to inferior status? To reply that he develops a negative self image and a deeply ingrained feeling of inferiority is a woefully inadequate answer. This does not establish a direct relationship between the events and forces in the life of the individual and the development of his ego and personality structure.

Many forces at work in American society exert a negative influence on minority children. We have considerable information on the effects of discrimination, segregation, poverty, and other forces. The struggle of the minority to improve its condition is not without its concomitant undesirable and negative influence on children. For example, we need to know how the Negro revolt and the civil rights movement are influencing our young people. It is already quite evident that many young people feel they are the scum of the earth. Others, when given an opportunity, fail to discharge responsibilities up to the level of their abilities. They use race, poverty, or discrimination as an excuse.

Another way of elaborating upon this idea is to take a look at what has happened to the Negro personality and to his institutions as a result of a long struggle in the courts to achieve school integration. For more than three decades, in court after court, including the U. S. Supreme Court, the Negro has been highly successful in proving to himself, the courts, and the entire society that the

Negro school is inferior and can never be equal. No one has really tried to measure the influence of this on the Negro school. During a part of this period there were some good Negro schools that were improving. This past decade, however, has seen a marked deterioration in hundreds of schools that at one time were of high quality. Seemingly the constant emphasis on the inferior quality of the Negro school has had a negative influence on a large number of such schools that had been doing well. The prevailing attitude seems to be that the school is inferior anyway, so why bother at all. In passing, the question should be asked of those who are now advocating a return to all-black schools: When the total society, including the Negro, has accepted the view that the all-Negro is inferior, is it really possible to make it superior? In sum, the point of this discussion is to emphasize that we need to understand the direct influence of events on certain institutions and on the personalities of individuals and groups. Until we do, we cannot deal very effectively with the problems of the disadvantaged.

Segregation and discrimination in the past have led to an intolerable existence for the minorities. Efforts to eliminate inequality have in themselves had serious negative influences upon the minority. This points up in a minor way how complex this problem is.

We have just begun to gain insights into the kinds and nature of language difficulties of the deprived child. Most teachers do not recognize that disadvantaged children use English in ways which differ from standard English in both syntax and grammatical structure.[3]

There is at present a great lack of analytical and remedial scholarship related to the language disabilities of the disadvantaged. But any attempt to identify the types and nature of the child's disabilities in language must be based upon research dealing with his unique and particular language deficiencies. Consequently, as things now stand, the teacher does not understand the child's language system, and the child does not understand the language system of the teacher. For example, the child says, "My mother, she be working," or "My mother, she working." In the first instance the child means that his mother has been working in the past, and she is still working. By the expression "My mother, she working" the child means that his mother is presently working. Another interesting observation on these two expressions has to do with the use of pronouns. The writer recently pointed out to a high school student that he was using an excessive number of pronouns. After having thought about it, the youngster came back the next day with the retort: "In the Bible it says, 'Thy rod and Thy staff, they comfort me.' I haven't heard middle-class people complaining about the number of pronouns in that sentence." With rare exception, the teacher treats the disadvantaged child as if he is speaking English in a careless manner rather than recognizing that the child's grammar—his whole verb structure—is different from standard English.

In trying to improve the child's speech the school treats the child as if he had a pathology similar to a cleft palate. Common sense dictates that these children should not receive the same type of speech therapy as that provided for children with organic difficulties. In schools, however, we continue to be concerned with pronunciation, vocabulary and slang because, as pointed out earlier, research has been inadequate; analytical scholarship has been shoddy.

The development of language and communication skills should be given high priority not only because it is essential to high level academic work, but because it relates to social acceptance or rejection. Nonstandard and socially unacceptable English may be the basis for discrimination in the school. It has a direct bearing on employment and success even in the service occupations.

Ways must be discovered for helping disadvantaged youth to deal with difficult trying situations. The inhospitable environment in which these youths live has caused the development of submerged, warped, and distorted personalities. This causes the child to be unable to cope with the normal flow of events and he may withdraw completely or "act out" in defiant and delinquent behavior.

Much has been written to establish the notion that the values of the disadvantaged are entirely different from those of the middle-class. This writer holds that there is a considerable amount of confusion on this point. Much of the behavior that is being attributed to lower social-class values should more accurately be attributed to mental health problems. Apathy, low levels of aspiration and motivation, resentment and hostility toward teachers and authority figures, and deep-seated anxiety are wide-spread among the disadvantaged, but not because their values differ from those of the middle class. Rather, children exhibit these personality traits because they have absorbed some of the mental and emotional problems which are commonly found in their families and peer groups.

Ways must be found to help children feel that they are respected, that they can be successful, and that what they do counts and is important. This is consistent with one of the most important findings in the Coleman study.[4] He found that students with a sense of control over their own destinies do better in school than those who are convinced that what they to will have little effect upon their ultimate opportunities.

The school has done very little to help the disadvantaged to become aware of the opportunities open to them if they become efficient students. All too frequently neither the parents nor teachers are aware of the many new opportunities. They do not know of the many sources of scholarship aid available to the disadvantaged. The fact that these young people see no relationship between the day-to-day activities of the school and the opportunities open to them in the future is the fault of our teachers.

The school's day-to-day activities must be organized to improve initiative and responsibility, high frustration tolerance, impulse control, orderliness, hard work (with satisfactory rewards), and deferred gratification to undergo educational and vocational preparation. There are broad categories of handicaps that are easily identified which make it impossible for the child to function in school up to an acceptable level. Unless the teacher is able to ameliorate these problems, teaching does not produce desired results.

Some changes will have to be made in the administration, organization, and operation of the schools if we are to educate the disadvantaged. Much of our difficulty stems from the fact that school board members, superintendents, and principals are not really committed to providing equality of opportunity for all people. In some instances, those in leadership roles are prejudiced; in other cases, they are uninformed and do not know what to do; still others are apathetic and hope that the problem will go away.

All too frequently, those responsible for policy and the administration of schools act as if they were convinced that the disadvantaged either cannot learn or that they should not be given an opportunity to learn. Far too many decisions are political rather than educational. Decisions are not being made because they are educationally sound or because they are consistent with sound principles for a democratic society. Rather, they are political in that they reflect what some pressure group wants.

In education, to provide equal treatment for unequals produces neither equality nor justice. The schools must reduce the inequity caused by the fact that a child may have been born of a certain socio-economic, racial, or ethnic background by providing an equitable foundation of mental skills and knowledge. This cannot be done by making the curriculum accommodate low motivation and low interests in academic work, both of which result from deprivation and exclusion. Rather, the school must help the student to overcome educational deficiencies and disabilities and then move him quickly into the main educational stream where he can gain skills and knowledge needed in the highly technical work of tomorrow. There can be no compromise on trying to raise achievement levels dramatically.

On the evidence available, it must be concluded that the major reason why an increasing number of Negro students fall below their grade level in performance is that *substandard performance is expected of them.* The majority are in programs of curricula where standards have been lowered "to meet their ability" or "to take into account their cultural differences." Less is expected of such pupils, they are rewarded for poorer performances, and the result is a steadily increasing gap between what they accomplish and what pupils of their grade level should accomplish.

Children enter school with individual differences in experience, skills, and attitudes which stem from differences in cultural or economic background. It has never been demonstrated that these differences constitute a permanent barrier to learning. The school needs to compensate for cultural deficiencies by concentrating on skills needed to do work on grade level. It needs to impose the same standards of performance that are expected elsewhere.

The American public school has demonstrated for more than 300 years that poor people, black people, and other kinds of disadvantaged people can learn and become productive contributing members of society. The tendency to lump all children of a racial ghetto under one heading of "culturally disadvantaged," and to label them as being therefore limitedly educable leads to the development and implementation of educational procedures which stunt the ability of the child to learn and results in the self-fulfilling prophecy that they cannot learn. If it is assumed that a child cannot learn, he will not learn.

The schools, probably unavoidably, are contaminated by the moral sickness of racism which afflicts the larger society. Yet all American children must be educated under conditions which will provide them with knowledge, skills, poise, goals, perspective, and other psychological equipment needed to deal constructively with other human beings who differ in race, customs, and culture. The present generation of children have only one life within which they can prepare for this and to take their places in American society. Our communities must stop evading and avoiding this problem and help the schools to achieve their purposes for all children. If they do not, a social and political catastrophe is inevitable.

REFERENCES:

[1] "Schools for An Open Society," *Integrated Education,* Vol. II, 2:11-12 (March-April, 1968).

[2] President John F. Kennedy, "Special Message to the Nation on Civil Rights," Feb. 28, 1963 (Reprinted in *The Keystone in the Arch, Compilation of Major Remarks on the Subject of Education by the Late John Fitzgerald Kennedy, President of the U.S.;* Committee on Education and Labor, House of Representatives, Eighty-eighth Congress, 2nd Session, April 1964, p. 64.

[3] Probably the most helpful and insightful work in this area is being carried on by William A. Stewart, Director of the Center for Applied Linguistics, Washington, D.C. The Urban Language Study is a pilot program of the Center and accepts the view that a Negro language exists.

[4] James S. Coleman, *et al., Equality of Educational Opportunity* (Washington: U.S. Government Printing Office, 1966), p. 21.

Questions:

1. Discuss the often-stated supposition that the Negro has the same chance for academic success as a white man, only the Negro is too lazy.

2. To what extent should a teacher accept the so-called "disadvantaged language"?

3. How does the attitude of "High Expectations" on the part of the teacher affect the academic achievement of disadvantaged children?

THE NEW URBAN STUDIES-
A WORD OF CAUTION

By ANDREW M. GREELEY

Undergraduate education is busy discovering the city. As the nation's urban crisis becomes so painfully obvious it can no longer be ignored by any responsible citizen, educators are trying to fashion an appropriate response to the challenges of the city. New courses in urban studies are being added to the curriculum, majors in urban studies are appearing all over the landscape, and eager undergraduates are going to the ghetto either on a day-by-day basis or to spend a semester or even a full year attempting to discover "how it is."

One can hear some cynics remarking, "This is where I came in!" It seems like we have witnessed this before. The last fashionable curricular "innovation" was nonwestern studies, complete with new courses, new majors, and "fun-filled" visits to nonwestern cultures. The cynics wonder what the next fad will be after urban studies have gone the way of previous fashions.

In this case, however, it may well be that the republic cannot afford to let concern over urban problems turn into an educational fad. Therefore, it seems appropriate to be specific about the goals against which urban studies programs should be evaluated. The goals must be *educational*. It is most unlikely that undergraduate colleges or undergraduate students can make a direct contribution to the solution of urban problems. The effect of the college would, at best, be indirect through the education of young people whose attitudes and skills would lead to ultimate solutions to urban problems. The cry that we must "do something about the city," heard on the undergraduate campus, is nothing but meaningless posturing unless the college faces the harsh reality that the only thing it can possibly "do" about the city is to educate people who will "do" something about it.

GOALS OF URBAN STUDIES

The critical question, then, is what kind of young people does the republic need in the 1970s if it is to cope with the problems of the city? The characteristics of these young people are the goals of urban studies programs.

1. The nation needs young people who are capable of understanding the problems and their complexity and who do not respond to complex issues with simplistic slogans. It therefore follows that the college graduate must be familiar with the tools and methods of research by which man comes to grips with

---

complex issues. He must also practice the intellectual humility needed to realize that there are many questions for which he does not yet know the answers and, indeed, for which no one may yet know the answers.

2. The young American of the 1970s must be more than intellectually competent; he must be open and sensitive to his own emotions and to those of others. The affective and emotive dimensions of his personality are required both to understand the problems in their emotional context and to obtain solutions responsive to the emotive dimensions of other people's personalities. But if the young person understands the importance of the nonrational dimensions of his personality, he does not confuse the nonrational with the irrational. He understands, rather, that just as intellect should not be permitted to destroy emotions, so emotions cannot be permitted to overthrow intellect; he can turn on without tuning out.

3. The graduate of the 1970s must have compassion for other human beings, whoever and whatever they may be. Hence, he has little need to find scapegoats; just as he has no need to blame urban problems on black people, so he similarly does not think "white ethnic racists" is one word, as the southern bigot of past generations considered "damn Yankee." (As one whose occasional writings on ethnology have made him something of an "expert" in a day when social and governmental elites are beginning to rediscover ethnic groups, I am out of patience with people who ask what should be done about or for white ethnic racists. First of all, they should not be called white ethnic racists. Some of this group are racists, but most are not. Many have very real problems in the urban environment which have nothing to do, except indirectly, with racism. Second, the thing that can be done "about" or "for" this group is to abandon the illusion that anything can be done about or for them. There was a time when white ethnic groups were poor immigrants who had to accept the ministrations of settlement-house do-gooders, whether they liked it or not, and they usually didn't. At this point, however, they are no longer immigrants, and they have sufficient wealth and power that nobody is going to do anything for or about them, but only "with" them.)

4. The student who has completed an urban studies program, one would hope, would be capable of realistic responses to human problems instead of the romantic perfectionism that demands—unnegotiably, of course—that society reform itself completely on the morrow. When society does not do this, the uneducated person then stalks away in disgust. The educated person, on the other hand, realizes that he stands on the shoulders of those who preceded him. He has inherited from the past the very principles by which he criticizes the present social situation.

NECESSITY FOR PROFICIENCY

5. The future college graduate should be convinced of the need for competency in solving problems and coping with social issues. Understanding the need to know what one is talking about, he should be able to come to grips with the various dimensions of problems. He would not be eager to replace competency with self-righteous moralizing or meddling missionary activities. He would not, for example, engage in the folly of some Chicago radical students

who attempted to alienate Polish workers from the Cook County Democratic organization without ever trying to understand the appeal of that organization or the reasons for the vast support it enjoys.

6. The graduates of this decade must be capable of long-range commitment to the solution of social problems. They must not be so alienated from their background that they are forced to seek personal validity by identifying with someone else, for if it is personal validity they are seeking in their social commitment, that commitment is to their own weakness and not to the world to be changed. The young person who is trying to find himself by identifying with someone else is unlikely to have the persistence, conviction, and strength of character required for long commitments. It is hoped that the graduate of urban studies would not be ashamed of being middle class, much less find it necessary to expiate guilt over his middle-class status.

(I am reminded of a meeting in which sociologists and social activists were discussing a book on anti-Semitism purporting to show that the most religious people were the most likely to be anti-Semitic. The sociologists were quite properly casting doubt on the methodology of the research, but a number of the social activists—particularly, if the truth be told in this ecumenical age, the Protestant social activists—began to argue that the methodology was irrelevant, that we were all guilty of anti-Semitism, and that we should begin to expiate that guilt. I turned to an Episcopal bishop next to me and said, "Bishop, why all this emphasis on expiating guilt?" The bishop drew himself up to his majestic height and said, "Young man, it is perfectly clear you don't know what it means to be a Protestant." An unfortunate contribution of the Vatican Council is that guilt expiation is becoming increasingly popular among Catholics, too. That is the last thing we need in the city.)

COMPREHENSIVE VIEW

7. The graduate of the 1970s must be able to see the big picture instead of focusing on one segment, much less glorying in the narrowness of his focus. He must be metropolitan in his viewpoint; he must understand that action in the city is everywhere, not just in the ghetto. The metropolis is a functional unit; the problems of the people in one segment are but the reverse of those in another. As Kenneth Keniston said, "You have to go up to Scarsdale to know how bad things really are." Suburban college students must realize that the city and its problems begin the minute they walk out their door. The romantic view that the problems are only in one section of the city and that the suffering is limited to one social class or ethnic group is destined to be disastrous.

8. The graduate of urban studies should be able to organize resources and articulate arguments to develop a climate for public consensus for the solution of urban problems. While he should not be afraid of occasional protests, he should understand that dramatic and ineffectual exhibitionism usually inhibits rather than facilitates consensus. He should realize that Saul Alinsky is always right when he says to radical reformers: "You need allies." He should know that to change the city the ethnic neighborhoods in the suburban communities as well as in the inner city must be involved in some eventual overarching political consensus.

9. The young person coping with the challenges of the city should be sensitive to suffering, wherever it is, even next door. He should not fixate on one crusade to provide a magic solution to all human problems, as well as a magic validity for his own troubled ego. He should have a sense of the tragic which would prepare him to understand that some of his best efforts to alleviate suffering would be doomed to failure, but he should also have enough hope to realize that there is much that man can overcome.

POSITIVE PLURALISTIC MODEL

10. The graduate of the 1970s should rejoice in diversity, rather than be threatened by it. He should not want everyone to have the very real virtues he sees in the black people, and he should not deny that there are distinct virtues in white people—middle-class, working-class, upper-class, Irish, Polish, Italian, German, even WASP. He should not romanticize one group or treat other groups as scapegoats. He should be well aware of the weaknesses of the different components in American society (if, for instance, he is Irish, he should not blind himself to the high rate of alcoholism among the Irish), but he should also be aware of the positive contributions these groups have made and will continue to make. He should know that the melting-pot model of American society is false and accept the pluralistic model, not as a necessary evil, but as a positive good.

11. He should be capable of learning from the wisdom and experience of the past, rather than narcissistically believing it necessary to start with a clean slate. He should not need to repeat the mistakes of the past so they will be his mistakes. While he surely should not be imprisoned by the rhetoric, constraints, and values of the past, neither should he be so in love with the virtues of his own generation as to be unaware that it, too, has faults.

12. Finally, he should seek clinical, objective, and pragmatic solutions without the need to project his conflict with his parents into fantasies of collective guilt. He should not need to create a mythological Establishment or System with which to wage war and on which to blame all problems. He should understand that there are both bad men and bad institutions in society, but that most problems are more likely to come from ignorance, confusion, fear, and distrust than from malice. Thus, he will be far more interested in building something new than in destroying something old. He should never knowingly maneuver his opponents into a corner where they must either surrender completely or fight to the death.

There is nothing especially new about these goals for programs in urban studies. For the most part, they are the traditional goals of liberal education, although they are not stated as eloquently as they have been by others, such as John Henry Newman. If they still need to be stated, it is because the goals of liberal education have been poorly achieved and frequently ignored.

EVALUATIVE CRITERION

Most of these goals are operationally measurable. The criterion for evaluating programs is the extent of their contribution to the development of

the graduate just described. Only the most naive would think that higher education can produce the complete urban man in only four years, but it is legitimate
to require that at least some progress in the indicated directions take place
during the college years, and it is certainly legitimate to ask that new, elaborate,
and expensive innovations in the higher educational enterprise be evaluated in
terms of their contributions to such development. (The old technologies must be
so evaluated, also.)

If we are unwilling to evaluate our fancy curricular innovations, our
exciting ghetto programs, and our intense efforts to do good among the poor
and the oppressed in terms of their educational accomplishment, then it does
not take a prophet to predict that in a few years urban studies will go the way of
nonwestern studies. They will become part of the curriculum with about as
much life and vitality as formal logic.

To a considerable extent, these goals go against the spirit of the time. A
young person who understands complexity and feels compassion for both white
and black, who is realistic in his evaluations, competent in his criticisms, capable
of long-range commitment and of seeing the big picture, skilled in organizing
resources and articulating ideas, sensitive to suffering wherever it may be,
capable of rejoicing in diversity and learning from the past, and devoted to
pragmatic solutions rather than unconditional surrender would find himself
somewhat in a minority among current reformers. I suspect he would also be in a
minority among junior faculty.

On the other hand, those who are the exact opposite—who must have
simple solutions, engage in romantic perfectionism, and find scapegoats; who are
alienated from their background and ashamed of being middle class; who see all
virtue and goodness in the black poor; who would much rather engage in
dramatic exhibitionism than obtain competency; who would reject the possibility of the past yielding any wisdom; who need to expiate personal guilt; and
who demand collective expiation from others—are most likely to want to go
slumming in the slums. God protect us from them all, and, particularly, God
protect the black poor from their ministrations.

COMPREHENSIVE EDUCATION

Programs in urban studies provide a remarkable educational challenge, for
they offer to the imaginative and creative teacher the opportunity for countless
links between classroom and life, not only in the humanities and social sciences,
but also in other disciplines. How can one study economics in the present world,
for example, and not see the relationship between tax structures and urban
problems? How can one study the chemical and biological sciences without
learning about pollution cycles? The urban dimension of the traditional
disciplines is apparent—at least to those capable of seeing beyond the classroom,
beyond the narrow careerism of professional academic guilds. Disciplines like
engineering and accounting must have urban dimensions that should not be
difficult to find.

Major in urban studies, new courses in urban studies, and programs in the
inner city are all well and good if they are part of a program that attempts to
integrate the development of the total personality, cognitive and noncognitive,

in one comprehensive educational experience. If they are merely a response to guilt feelings, merely an attempt by the college to "do something" about the inner city, however, they are probably doomed before they start.

I would not engage in that racism which sees the goals of education aimed at whites only; surely black people also have the right to pursue such goals. Ethnic studies programs can develop the characteristics previously described as well as, and perhaps somewhat better than, many other disciplines. The important consideration is not what is taught in the classroom, but the way it is taught. The pertinent issue is whether the teacher has the ability to link academic instruction with the world off campus and with the personality needs of the student. Because it is difficult for a teacher to ignore these personality needs and the social implications of urban studies, urban studies themselves contribute to linkage. But teachers have ignored linkage before. Only the imprudent would bet they will not do it again.

Questions:

1. List the characteristics of the "ideal" youth who will be able to make a direct contribution to the solution of urban problems.

2. Which one of the twelve characteristics listed would you consider to be of greatest value? Explain.

3. Evaluate the idea of a "comprehensive education" in terms of cost and community acceptance.

SHOULD GHETTOESE BE ACCEPTED?

By WILLIAM RASPBERRY

"By the time I get there, he will have gone."

"Time I git dere, he be done gone."

You and I were taught to recognize the first example as good English and the second as bad. According to a growing number of linguists, we were taught wrong.

The two sentences, these linguists tell us, don't represent proper and improper usage; they represent two distinct languages, equally consistent and, in that they communicate meaning, equally valid.

The first is standard American English; the second, the nonstandard English of the black slums. These linguists, who include some of the leading lights at Washington's Center for Applied Linguistics, are attempting to build on the validity of the second as a means of teaching the first.

English teachers don't find it necessary to make a Spanish-speaking child feel that his native language is bad in order to get him to learn English. But when confronting children who speak the native tongue of the black slums, too many of them do precisely that. One unfortunate result, the linguists tell us, is that slum children become ashamed of ·their language and, therefore, ashamed of themselves.

The child who points to the rose on his teacher's desk and says, "Dere go a flyvuh," will too frequently be told flatly that a rose is a *flower* and that it isn't going anywhere.

Such instruction is more likely to confuse than help. The child knows very well that his meaning would be unmistakable at home; his mother might have put it just the same way. Furthermore, if his efforts at free expression are criticized too often, he may simply shut up and say nothing at all.

And so the teacher dubs him "nonverbal," a typical label for the ghetto child.

Nonverbal, hell! Follow him out the schoolhouse door and listen while his playmate tries to get a word in edgewise.

The teacher has made a classical error. He has tried to teach his pupil a new language by condemning the pupil's old one. And the result is that the child shrinks from the teacher, making it very difficult if not impossible for him to teach the pupil anything at all.

Wouldn't it be better, the linguists ask, to accept the validity of the child's native language if that facilitates teaching him a new one?

Reprinted with permission from *Today's Education* (April 1970).

The answer would be obvious if the child's native tongue were French or Spanish. The difference is that French and Spanish are respected languages *and they don't sound like standard English.* Thus, *voici* and *voilà* aren't wrong; they simply aren't English. Their exact equivalent in ghettoese, "here go" and "dere go" are just close enough to standard English that teachers are tempted to brand them as bad standard English rather than good nonstandard.

Nonstandard English, or ghettoese, it must be admitted, is a lot easier to recognize than to describe. (Try describing *standard* English!)

The linguists emphasize two things about ghettoese: First, it is the language spoken almost universally among low-income black Americans (and understood by almost all black Americans) and second, it is consistent in syntax.

Ghettoese is not slang: The latter is little more than a one-for-one substitution of nonstandard words for standard ones. Nor is it simply mispronunciation of standard English words.

"Sue is a boss chick" is slang. Boss is a synonym for "fine" and chick for "girl." But the sentence isn't ghettoese, although something very like it might be heard among ghetto residents.

On the other hand, the statement, "Dat Sue sho a boss chick," is ghettoese—but not solely because of the mispronunciation of "that" and "sure," for "Sue a boss chick" is also ghettoese, although each word may be given the standard pronunciation. It is ghettoese because of the missing "is," a feature common to ghetto speech patterns.

The linguists make another point: Ghettoese is not necessarily less *precise* than standard English. In some instances, it may be more precise than the standard.

Ask a slum child why his father missed last night's meeting, and the answer might be, "He sick." Ask him why his father misses so many meetings, and he might answer, "He be sick." The first describes a temporary illness; the second, a chronic or recurring one. No such distinction exists in standard English. The answer to both questions in standard English would be, "He is sick."

This example seems to be a favorite among the linguists who want standard English taught as a foreign language, which had led me on occasion to refer to them as the he-be-sick school.

This designation suggests, unfairly, that the linguists who have been addressing themselves to the language problems of slum children are of a single mind. Not so. There is something less than unanimity among them even on the notion of teaching standard English as a foreign language.

For some, it is a direct analogy to the teaching of English to a Spanish-speaking child. For others, it means using some of the techniques that are used in the teaching of foreign languages.

It is pointed out, for instance, that one reason middle-class children learn to read more easily than slum children is that the former have to make but a single translation: from print to sound. A slum child, on the other hand, has to make a second translation: from the standard English to his native nonstandard, just as a French-speaking youngster would have to make the additional translation to his native French.

The argument loses a little in light of the fact that translation increasingly is thought of as a rather poor way of teaching foreign languages. Total immersion is the current trend. If you want to learn Russian in a hurry, you might find yourself in a classroom where only Russian is spoken. No tedious translations. You learn to speak Russian because you have to speak Russian to get along in the class.

The method has a lot to recommend it. After all, isn't that how you learned English?

If the total immersion system is an effective way of teaching foreign languages and if our linguist friends want to teach English as a foreign language, then why not total immersion in standard English?

As a matter of fact, that is what almost always happens. Good teachers don't spend their time reminding their pupils that the "flyvuh" isn't going anywhere. They are careful to say, "Here is a flower." They believe that if they say something in standard English distinctly enough and often enough the child will learn to say it that way, too.

That is a very great deal different from translating from nonstandard into standard, which some of the linguists seem to be suggesting.

At least one of them, William A. Stewart, explicitly makes that suggestion. He tells of the time a young "problem reader" from the inner city happened across his ghettoese translation of *The Night Before Christmas:*

It's the night before Christmas, and here in our house
It ain't nothing moving, not even no mouse.
There go we-all stockings, hanging high up off the floor,
So Santa Claus can full them up, if he walk in through our door.

Says Stewart: "Lenora was one of the 'problem readers' of the public schools; she read school texts haltingly, with many mistakes and with little ability to grasp the meaning of what she read. Yet, when she began to read the nonstandard version of the poem, her voice was steady, her word reading [was] accurate, and her sentence intonation was natural. . . .

"This unexpected success in reading so surprised Lenora that she began to discuss the experience with her little brother. They decided that there was something different about the text, but were unable to tell exactly what it was.

"To compare, I then had Lenora read the standard English version of the poem. . . . When she did, all the 'problem reader' behavior returned."

Stewart's point goes far beyond pronunciation; its essence is grammar. His translation closely approximated the grammar of Lenora's native ghettoese, leaving her to make the single print-to-sound translation. Clement Moore's original required her to make the second standard-to-nonstandard translation and, thus, exposed her as being a problem reader.

It is for this reason that some linguists have proposed that early reading material for inner-city children be written in the slum dialect. They point to experiments, notably in Sweden, which indicate that children who are introduced to reading through their own nonstandard dialects and then are switched to standard surpass those who use standard materials from the beginning.

If this is so, they suggest, then we should be able to improve drastically the reading abilities of young slum dwellers simply by first teaching them to read in their native tongue.

The theory makes a good deal of sense, but it may be asking too much to expect the average classroom to implement it effectively. The more likely result is either to hopelessly confuse such children or to reinforce their nonstandard speech patterns.

But more is involved here than the teaching of reading. Involved, too, is the assessment of a child's intelligence, an assessment often based on his language proficiency in standard English.

Joan C. Baratz of the Education Study Center makes that point in the September 1969 issue of *Child Development:*

"If the criterion for language development is the use of a well-ordered systematic code," she says, "then the continued use of measures of language development that have standard English as the criterion of a developed form will only continue to produce the results that the Negro, lower-class child is delayed in language development because he has not acquired the rules that the middle-class child has been able to acquire. . . ."

What that means, I think, is that there are two distinct questions to be asked: To what degree has this child developed language skills? To what degree has this child developed facility *in standard English?*

Most of our written tests pretend to ask the first question, when in fact they ask the second. The answer to the first question is obviously a more valid measure of intelligence. But that is not the end of it.

What you, I, and the linguists want is to have slum children learn the language that will help them get along in the American society. That means standard English.

It may be academically interesting to be aware that, from a purely linguistic point of view, nonstandard is just as valid as standard. Interesting, but not particularly useful.

If employers, personnel officers, and the others whom we find it useful to impress with our intelligence were fluent in nonstandard English and understood its validity and if books and newspapers were written in nonstandard, then it would be unnecessary to teach standard. (But in that case, nonstandard would, by definition, be standard!)

The reason we want slum children to learn standard is that nonstandard is a good deal less negotiable—just as trading stamps are less negotiable than cash.

But that doesn't mean that trading stamps are *bad.* It is here that the linguists make the heart of their case. The way we speak is such an integral part of who we are that to deprecate our speech is to deprecate us.

What the linguists want to do is to give slum children facility with standard English without forcing them to forget their native nonstandard—to give them cash without confiscating their trading stamps. The nonstandard, lest we forget, may be *the* negotiable language back home in the slum neighborhood or within the family, or on the playground. After all, you can't pay cash for that lamp at the redemption center.

What we are talking about, then, is the desirability of making slum children bilingual, just as most educated blacks are bilingual. (Forget the black teacher, recently escaped from the slums, who pretends she doesn't understand when Johnny says, "I'mo take me a brick an' bus' you upsi' yo' head." Her kind, happily, is disappearing.) Giving slum children this kind of bilinguality has far less to do with understanding the inner workings of ghettoese than with being sensitive to the inner workings of people.

No teacher expects a pupil to learn arithmetic if he calls him a dunderhead every time the child delivers himself of a wrong answer. Nor should the teacher expect him to learn standard English (or anything else, for that matter) if, by his attitude, he conveys "you are a dunderhead" every time the child opens his mouth. (This, however, is simply psychology, not linguistics.)

In that light, linguists who emphasize the beauties of ghettoese may be showing their contempt for teachers. Their implication is that teachers are too stupid to distinguish between form and substance, that if a child says something really clever—but in ghettoese—the teacher will hear nothing but the ghettoese.

If that is the case, if substantial numbers of teachers believe nonstandard equals stupid, then forget linguistics. Forget everything, for any teacher so insensitive that he will shame a child into silence every time he opens his mouth is beyond the help even of the Center for Applied Linguistics.

Questions:

1. Develop a simple plan for a teacher to follow so that children will not be ashamed of their Ghettoese.

2. To what extent do you feel that the same translation for a Ghettoese statement exists in the majority of our slums? Explain.

3. Early reading material for inner-city children should be written in the slum dialect. Defend or attack this statement, and explain your position.

PACESETTING PLAYGROUNDS:
CITY SCHOOLS GRAB THE LEAD

By MARILYN H. CUTLER

Unless you live near one, you probably haven't curbstoned an inner city school recently. A refresher: more than likely it was built about 1910, give or take 15 years. It has a patina, all right, if you like soot-stained walls and narrow, tread-worn stairways and cramped classrooms.

Directly north or east or south or west of it lies a dirty, barren, mean looking, fenced-in yard. Can you picture your child playing in that horrid spot? Playing there because it's the only place around the neighborhood where he can let off some steam in a peaceable way? Probably not — not if you have your say. And it is a fair assumption that you have just that. Thousands of parents possess sensitivities similar to yours. But so what? They are poor. Their kids aren't going to discover the crazy delight of dangling upside down on a gym set, looking at a green turfy, sweet-earth smelling world.

Although they do not experience the semi-sylvan playground pleasures that their once or twice-removed suburban cousins unconsciously enjoy, some inner city children are whooping it up these days in areas that feed the spirit, vitality and fantasy of early, middle and late childhood. They are youngsters who probably live near to and attend PS 166 in New York City and Buchanan elementary in Washington, D.C. Their playgrounds, winners of important awards in the school and landscape architecture fields, possess a relevancy to the urban scene that reaches not only the children but their families as well. These playgrounds, without doubt, signify ingenious approaches to regenerating dilapidated school grounds.

A public school, Buchanan represents a private venture as far as its playground is concerned. Situated on a one and a quarter acre site, the play plaza, as it is called, was underwritten by the Vincent Astor Foundation at an approximate cost of $400,000 (that includes everything in the plaza — from original sculptures to adult recreation areas). Similarly, the playground at PS 166, measuring a minuscule 100 feet by 175 feet, represents a $195,000 gift to the public from the same Astor Foundation.

Board members facing comparable playground problems should not be disheartened because there's little hope for support from foundations or private enterprise or because there's precious little money in the budget to revive aesthetically starved school yards. Buchanan and 166 are described and pictured here to offer playground possibilities, not all of which need or indeed should be copied in a slavish way. The intention is to help you generate an idea or two.

Reprinted, with permission, from *The American School Board Journal,* August 1970. Copyright 1970, the National School Boards Association. All rights reserved.

114

Urban Education

PS 166 is the engaging brainchild of M. Paul Friedberg, landscape architect who heads a Manhattan firm bearing his name and who is a one-time resident of the neighborhood served by 166, located at West 89th Street, between Columbus and Amsterdam. His effort thus far won Friedberg a 1970 citation for special projects in the design exhibit at the American Association of School Administrators, as well as an honor award from his own professional fraternity, the American Society of Landscape Architects.

One of the things that is so compelling about 166 is that it does a whale of a job of fascinating children on a postage-stamp slice of land. Most of the action involves youngsters ranging in age from about 5 to 12. Geodesic domes and arches and sand pits? They are there. But so are fanciful little thickets of wood blocks that you can climb in and around on; spring pads that gently bounce back in trampoline fashion when kids jump on them; big concrete cubes, hollow and open on two sides – perfect places to climb on, sit in or play peek-a-boo around.

It isn't only clever shapes and sturdy metal forms that make 166 interesting and fun for everyone in the neighborhood. Friedberg designed an amphitheater for the east side of the playground. It serves as a giant spray pool during hot summer days. Water jets recessed under steps spray out into the open arena. A big chalkboard, 6 feet by about 16 feet, offers a focal point where youngsters draw scenes and such to add atmosphere to their skits in the theater. The wall that buffers the theater from the remaining play area was designed in a playful, sculptural manner. Directly behind the board and buffer wall is a large granite block mound (looks a little like the bottom half of an Egyptian pyramid) that houses comfort stations and spray unit for the amphitheater. Illustrating how Friedberg integrated economy and, as it turned out, ingeniousness into his design, the mound serves as an area for slides and other play forms on its outside surface.

With Central Park only a couple of blocks away, it made sense to limit 166 to the preadolescent set. Older youngsters in the neighborhood can find ample play areas that appeal more to them in the big park. At one end of 166, play space is designed with two age groups in mind: preschool and slightly older youngsters usually use an area that contains equipment scaled down to their size; another area is bigger – in proportion to the youngsters. All of 166 is depressed three feet from street level to give it additional privacy, although it is clearly related to the environs through its design that connects the playground with a small adjacent area called a street sitting plaza. Here, parents and neighbors sit and keep and eye on children at play without actually entering the grounds. The plaza also doubles as a convenient waiting area for parents to meet children after school.

Buchanan, located at the corner of 13th and E streets in Washington's black southeast section, represents a collaboration between two Manhattan designers, one of whom is landscape architect Friedberg, the other is architect Simon Breines of Pomerance & Breines. Approximately twice the size of its New York relative, the playground contains many imaginative play forms developed by Friedberg for 166, plus a few different ones such as a giant spider web where children climb around on cables, become tangled up, and generally have a great time with little danger of getting hurt. Buchanan differs from 166 in another fairly significant way, because the amphitheater doubles as a basketball court where older children usually choose to play.

Nobody feels locked out at Buchanan. The playground merges with the public sidewalk to produce a feeling of oneness that has been received enthusiastically in the southeast section where countless scenes of anguished violence erupted following the assassination of Martin Luther King in 1968. Bordering the play areas on one street side is a series of small pavilions that house a snack bar, comfort station and administration office. A tree-canopied sitting plaza gives adults a place to relax while they watch youngsters play. Focal points in this area are two original sculptures by William Tarr. Statues they are not; columns, richly embossed with numbers and graphics and you-name-it shapes, are what they are. One is sort of squat, the other tall, and both are for climbing on or hanging from.

Attesting to Buchanan's design excellence are two notable awards: a 1970 citation from AASA's special exhibit section and an honor award from ASLA.

Questions:

1. What makes the playground at PS 166 so noteworthy?

2. Describe the improvements you would make to PS 166 to make it fit your concept of an ideal urban playground.

3. Compare the Buchanan playground with PS 166.

GET RID OF GYMNASIUMS IN BIG CITY HIGH SCHOOLS

By EUGENE EZERSKY
P. RICHARD THEIBERT

"Locking in" of pupils and curriculums into gymnasium boxes, despite their newness or aesthetic external appearance, perpetuates an archaic system which has proven to be ineffective in educating today's youth. What was perfect for teaching Swedish gymnastics or Turnverein drills or mass calisthenics is completely unsuited for teaching tennis, golf, softball, bowling, ice skating, sailing, and practically all other activities of today's physical education, or more important, what today's youth will be doing tomorrow. Practically every other discipline of education has recognized the need to change its facilities to keep abreast of changing curriculum needs and to modernize in keeping with the swift movement of American life and the revolutionary educational advances in progress. Language laboratories, carpeted classrooms, multipurpose rooms, closed circuit TV, and many other individualized approaches to learning which were once considered innovative are now commonplace.

In physical education, however, we still build the same space accommodating basketball courts and spectator seating, even though curriculum demands point strongly to the need to consider 100% of the pupils and the community, not merely the small percentage of pupils who now accrue most of the benefits.

We would propose an entirely new approach to physical education for large cities, an approach which is economically sound, sociologically imperative, and educationally effective.

The major considerations in espousing this new approach would include –

1. The high density population of the large cities which usually results in large schools and crowded classes.

2. The demonstrated lack of quality and quantity in instruction in lifetime sports in the large cities.

3. The high cost of building and of land acquisition in the large cities.

4. The need to actually participate in a sport in order to develop skills, enjoyment, and positive attitudes toward the sport. (Fragmented, mimetic instruction is deadly in sport skill instruction. If the "gestalt" was ever essential in any area of education, it is in learning to play.)

5. The recognition of the value of success in mastering sports skills (People will participate in games in which they have a reasonable degree of competency. It is desirable for a youngster to learn to play one or two of the

Reprinted with permission from *Journal of Health Physical Education Recreation* (April 1970).

lifetime sports with a degree of competency rather than be exposed to a host of activities in which he has no success.)

6. The beneficial results of the pupil-coach relationship. (This has particular implications for the disadvantaged ghetto youngster where a father image is so frequently lacking.)

7. The desirability and necessity of multi-use recreational facilities for school and community.

Our frame of reference here will be New York City, for it is with these schools that the authors have had experience and because New York City certainly reflects the sociological and educational problems of the big city.

As now constituted, the high schools house approximately 4,000 students each. Most schools are on an overlapping session, running from approximately 8:00 A.M. until 5:00 P.M. Students are involved in revolving door education, and they begin and finish their schoolday at several different times. The interscholastic program, of necessity, is adversely affected because the gym facilities are used for regular physical education classes. Because of split programming and overlapping sessions, freshmen and sophomores usually cannot participate in the after school program because they are in scheduled classes until five o'clock. The pupils are scheduled for four or five periods of physical education per week — periods usually of 45 minutes duration. Dressing time and other organizational necessities actually cut the instructional time to approximately 25 minutes. These classes generally contain about 150 pupils, although in many cases the class load is in excess of 200. Assuming the best of indoor facilities and the best of dedicated teachers, it is virtually impossible to teach many of our physical education activities effectively. Can you really teach tennis, football, baseball, golf, archery, or bowling to such large numbers in the traditional gymnasium set-up? Yes, you can walk through stroking, or footwork, or mimetically practice parts of the skill, *but you don't play the game and you can't grasp the exhiliration that comes with the mastering of a skill and the successful conclusion to a team game or an individual triumph.*

Let's look at another dollar problem in the big city. When pupils are scheduled for six academic periods plus a period of physical education they must have a lunch period in addition. The lunch rooms in New York City high schools are tremendous "catch basins" for as many as 1,500 pupils at a time. They catch the overflow of the overcrowded schools where there are no more classrooms or teaching facilities to accommodate them. They frequently are the focal point of student disorder since the elements of crowds, movable furniture, food service, difficulty in supervision, and youthful exuberance all contribute to noise and unpleasantness. The space allotted to large lunchrooms coupled with the tremendous costs of food equipment and personnel makes this a very expensive facility, second only to the cost of physical education facilities in the overall school construction budget. The proposal here will shorten the school day by two periods so that the need to supply school lunches to such large numbers is eliminated. It will permit these large schools to operate as two separate schools, with either five or six periods per session, with no overlapping and no overcrowding. There will be no need to crowd 4,000 pupils into a building at one time. One of the most immediate responses to student disorders in New York City is to attempt to operate on this basis. A school with 2,000 pupils in it at one time is better from every educational viewpoint than one with 4,000 pupils at a time. The concept is that simple.

If physical education can be improved and successfully scheduled away from the school, as we propose, the gymnasium and lunchroom space is no longer necessary. It is then conceivable to think in terms of saving nearly $3½ million in school construction costs per school. This money would then be used to build outstanding facilities for the school and the community.

The average New York City high school of 400,000 square feet now costs approximately $14 million to build. At least 15% of this space is used for physical education, and more for service areas, storage, locker rooms, etc. Conservative estimates on the part of school planners are that approximately 25% of the cost of a high school is appropriated for physical education. On this basis, $3.5 million of each $14 million goes for this purpose. Add to this the cost for elaborate lunchroom space, and it becomes apparent that these two facilities constitute a large portion of the school construction costs. A small lunch facility to service those who must eat in school could replace almost $3½ million worth of present construction.

Now let's look momentarily at an accepted (and successful) method of sports instruction, particularly the system used in our better preparatory schools. Those of us in public education cast envious eyes on˙the prep schools approach to sports, and with good reason. All boys participate, in different sports, on different competitive levels, and with a teacher who assumes the "coaching" relationship. They can participate on the lowest skill level or at the highest level of interscholastic sport. They choose two or three or more sports per year and spend concentrated time learning the skills of the sport.

One of the most frustrating experiences for New York City physical educators is to see literally thousands and thousands of high school students with inherent good athletic ability who never get a chance to improve or to participate on any formal level because they are lost in the mass of the gym class. On the other hand, prep school youngsters with considerably less native ability develop into good or even outstanding varsity players because they have been trained under a system which encourages participation and provides for learning a sport in its totality. The pupil is in close contact with his teacher, who establishes an optimum learning situation.

Traditionalists will argue that the prep schools have smaller classes and good facilities. This is true, but what is significant is that prep schools don't necessarily have good gymnasiums. In many cases, it is quite the opposite. What they do have, however, is good facilities for sports — tennis courts, fields, swimming pools, skating rinks, and usable space. What they do have also is a curriculum to which boys are drawn, because they can select their area of participation based upon interest and need. They are not lumped into one pot and sprinkled freely with many unrelated skills. Their physical education is not interjected into the middle of an academic schedule. It is after school, or before school, or in the evening, and it usually doesn't take place in the gymnasium. It occurs, sport by sport, at various facilities, near and around and even distant from the schoolhouse.

This pattern is possible and practical for our large city schools and can be designed to benefit the whole city. Rather than build these gymnasium complexes in the schools, where we are once again tied to the traditional approaches to physical education, *build specialized sports facilities* in several locations amid the city schools.

The whole country travels to school by bus. Why can't we transport city pupils to their physical education facility? The distances will be relatively short.

Specifics will better describe the plan. Suppose a new high school is constructed in Manhattan with its ensuing problems of space and cost. By eliminating the gymnasium complex, the academic facilities can have more space and be improved upon, with extra funds being utilized to engineer the structure so that the roof space may become a playground. The budgetary allotment for physical education has still not been touched. In less commercial areas and on less expensive land a magnificent tennis facility can be constructed. It could provide for many more courts than could possibly have been built in the school, as well as facilities for all the racquet sports. This would be a year round facility, not closed down for five months in the middle of the school year as most outdoor facilities are now. Pupils who now choose tennis are assigned directly to the courts and report there. The juniors and seniors go after school from 1:00 P.M. on, and the freshmen and sophomores, who go to school during the afternoon, report to their sports center before reporting to school.

Similarly, bowling facilities can be constructed at another low cost site, while sophisticated golf instructional facilities can be built elsewhere. Synthetic turfs and modern technology makes it possible to build year round baseball, soccer, and football facilities, in tiers, for reasonably low cost. When one eliminates the spectator aspect of stadium construction, costs are significantly reduced. According to this plan, five or six different sports activities, appealing to all pupils, can be running simultaneously at five or six different sites for all of the schools.

The site possibilities are numerous, even in the overcrowded cities—by seeking air rights atop garages, over railroad tracks, over piers and highways, under municipal building complexes, and, of course, in vacant lots and areas unsuited for housing or other commercial uses. Under the supervision of the Board of Education, with the cooperation of the Parks and Recreation Departments, vacant areas can be effective educational areas and add an aesthetic, eye appealing building where one might not otherwise exist. The playing surfaces may well be placed in the air.

The extras are numerous. These facilities can be used by many large high schools. The construction funds thus freed for several schools can provide the city with much needed recreational facilities. These combination teaching and recreational sites can be used evenings, weekends, and summers on a fee basis, with all of the funding considerations thus implied. Most important, however, they will be used by school pupils to *effectively learn to play the game,* not merely to try to digest a series of rote, unrelated, unsatisfying skills.

The concomitant benefits of sport—socialization, cooperation, fitness, and vigor—will be additional end products of playing the game. The phrase "playing the game" is not used in the rhetorical sense here, but rather to describe a condition which most city high school children do not now experience. Under this proposed decentralized prep school approach, boys and girls can choose their sports and be involved in playing the game on their own skill level. Varsity aspirants report to one teacher and beginners play in another group, with the broad spectrum of children falling in between, on an intramural, class, or junior varsity level. Their successes are exciting on any level. The form teams of the prep schools, the fraternity and dormitory leagues of the colleges, the class competition of the service academies, and the weight classified college leagues are all based upon this principle and have all proven to be very successful. These groups attract participants, and this is what we're after. It is an approach which has never been tried in large city schools, where only varsity players have heretofore benefited from real competition and tasted the fruits of enjoyable play.

Where large adjacent fields exist, such as in the suburban sections of the city, the problem is not as acute. However, where weather is a factor, and outdoor facilities are unusable during the winter, it is a problem certainly worthy of serious consideration.

What of the role of the teacher? At first reading, physical educators may call "foul." The fears of being phased out or of downgrading the subject are entirely unfounded. On closer analysis, this plan is one which provides for the full utilization of the skills of the physical educator. It restores him to a professional level. He is no longer a "numbers man" whose concern is primarily with discipline and movement and organization of large class groups. He no longer has hundreds of *bored pupils* packed into a gym box. Rather, he now can teach on the "coaching level," with fewer pupils, with measurably better and more satisfying results. His particular skills can be exploited and appreciated. He can specialize in ways hitherto undreamed of in city schools. In truth, this plan may prove to be the salvation of the profession in the cities, because, continuing the present trend, physical educators can be phased out by stern disciplinarians, by paraprofessionals who provide locker room security, and by a few teachers who have mastered the techniques of herding large groups of pupils through forty minute periods of inconsequential activity and undefined purpose.

Finally, what will our money buy for us in terms of these specialized facilities in New York City? Since building costs are determined by a long list of variables, an approximation will have to suffice. These figures, developed by Richard Dempsey of the New York architectural firm of La Pierre, Litchfield and Weidner, serve to suggest some possibilities.

1. An aquatics center of 225,000 square feet, containing a diving pool, a community recreation and competition pool, a junior training pool, an instructional core for high school age pupils, as well as lockers, classrooms, office and storage space, would cost approximately $5½ million.

2. A basketball center, with 18 practice courts and 2 competition areas with spectator accommodations, utilizing 275,000 square feet, would cost approximately $7½ million.

3. A racquet center, for tennis, handball, and squash, of 90,000 square feet, would cost approximately $2½ million.

4. An individual sports and gymnastics center of 120,000 square feet would cost $3½ million.

5. An ice center, for exhibitions, hockey, instruction, and free skating, would cost approximately $3 million.

On the face of it, an expenditure of close to $20 million seems rather steep. Actually, however, it is less money than would be required to build inferior facilities in seven high schools. These facilities would provide outstanding areas for seven or eight or more central city schools, as well as providing equally outstanding facilities for community residents.

It is conceivable that these facilities would serve half the high school student population of the borough of Manhattan. Moreover, they will enable city youths to receive a high caliber program of physical education. Is the cost too high? We think not. We think it might well be one of the cheapest investments in quality education ever undertaken for urban children—a cheap investment yielding very high dividends.

———————

Questions:

1.   Is physical education a program to develop the skills and abilities necessary for physical fitness or a program to teach contemporary athletic activities? Explain your position.

2.   What financial arrangements do you envision for the payment of these facilities? Consider local, state and federal governments as well as the school board and private investors.

3.   List and expand on two or three of the weaknesses that you detect in this proposed plan.

URBAN SCHOOL
DECENTRALIZATION

By DR. RICHARD L. FEATHERSTONE
DR. FREDERICK W. HILL

The large "urban" school system is so complex, and is such an inherent part of the political, social, and economic life of the entire urban community, state and nation, that it is highly unlikely that it can continue to be functional if fragmented into multiple autonomous districts. Instead, a new structural design is required to bring into balance the best qualities of both centralization and decentralization to help effect a functional urban organization dedicated to public education and other social purposes.

The design must also reflect the political, social and economic pressures that constantly bear on the educational organization. Some pressures tend to influence a centralized design, others demand a decentralized plan. The pressures that seem to require centralization relate to sources of revenues for education, the creeping legalism of court actions which require uniform programs, the growth of technological aids, the need for educational programs to meet citywide social goals, and the power of teachers' organizations which have gained strength through unification.

At the same time, the citizen demanding a greater voice in the education of his children or in the control of local community action programs has become a powerful social force that demands a form of decentralization. The need of all human beings for "uniqueness" as an individual rebels against the vastness of the urban social organism and each wants to break it down to "controllable size."

Fortunately these pressures can be acknowledged and a balanced design developed. A balanced plan is possible because the functions that should be centralized tend to be of a service or supportive nature.

By contrast, those functions that should be decentralized are generally educational in nature and relate to curriculum development and instructional activities. These functions include textbook selection, program articulation, etc.

Thus, the position that a balanced organizational structure can be composed of both centralized and decentralized functions is based on the premises that:

a. There are management and educational functions found in both centralization concepts and in decentralization concepts that are excellent, adjustable, and should be retained.

b. Certain management and educational support functions should be centralized, and are most effective when so centralized.

c. Certain educational and management functions should be decentralized, and are most effective when so decentralized.

Reprinted with permission from *American School and University* (September 1969).

d. These respective functions can be identified, and an organization can be designed to accommodate both centralized and decentralized operations. Further, it may be accepted that regional, social, and cultural pressures affect the design of the balanced organization and will provide for some degree of individuality from city to city or between districts within a city.

These premises are important in the construction of a balanced control plan.

MODEL #3 – A BALANCED CONTROL PATTERN

In order to present a model of an organizational plan that has a degree of balance, certain beliefs should be stated:

a. Central control boards are necessary and will continue to hold a major role in education. However, their responsibility and authority will be redefined, and certain of their functions may be distributed or decentralized.

b. In urban areas, there will be an educational manager for the total school enterprise. He will be responsible to and work with a central board of control and will manage the educational enterprise at the system level.

c. Technology will provide opportunities for the continual assessment of the educational health of the system.

d. Authority will be assigned at some specific level in the school system so that responsibility for the effectuation of democratic principles relating to human rights or legal interpretations of these rights may be identified.

e. Authority and responsibility for some aspects of the control of education; the administration of learning units, and development of educational objectives must be located at the local level.

Model #3 is based on the premises and beliefs presented. The components of the model, the control of education within the balanced structure, and the administration of education are expressed as follows:

The System (Central District). The system is all the components of education and service located in, or existing to serve, the legal entity known as the school district. The system may be a city district, a metropolitan area district, a county or state district, or a federal district.

Educational Service Regions (Local Community District). The educational service region is a *component* of the educational system. The composition of the region is flexible and may vary in the number of school buildings, types and levels of schools served or services provided, according to the immediate and predicted needs of the district. Educational service regions are created to reflect democratic social policy. If it is necessary to combine the personal services and physical facilities of more than one region to serve a changing neighborhood, the fusion can be made. If it is necessary to divide a region in order to provide more intensive services by an educational leader or specialists, the division can be made.

The Learning Unit (Educational Facility). The learning unit is a component of the region. It may be a high school, junior high school, elementary school, middle school, grade unit, continuing education class, or other yet-to-be-named educational experience or process (e.g. educational TV piped to homes, dial-a-drill math instruction, etc.) where teaching and learning are the major objectives.

The learning unit is not limited to size, geographical location, age of learner, or educational discipline. Instead, its major characteristic is that it will serve as an educational and social experience for all learners related to it.

Central Lay Board of Control (System). The central board of control will be responsible for and have authority to provide the logistic support, such as computer technology, financing, professional and student personnel records, etc., that is necessary to maintain the educational services required. The board shall review and recommend functions relating to the educational policy but will have authority and responsibility, including veto power, only over educational policy that has a direct relationship to the effectuation of social policy (e.g. implementation of democratic principles relating to human rights). Such a central lay board could be composed of representation (at least one member) from each educational service region to be selected by the regional board, with the educational manager in ex officio role.

Regional Lay Board of Control. The regional (local) board of control will be responsible for and have authority to decide educational policy at the local level. In addition the board wil be responsible for the review of the educational objectives and management procedures that implement central democratic policies. Again, in its most representative form, such a regional or local board could be composed of representation, or at least one member from each learning unit (with one professional educator) to be selected by election procedure.

Learning Unit Representation. Each learning unit will have representation on the regional board of control. The representatives will have voice and decision making power as a member of the regional board.

Central (System) Administration and Middle Management. The central administration functions are to provide service to the regions and to manage the educational enterprises by coordinating services. The system is headed by the chief educational manager. The central administration has three centers as major support and planning offices, each responsible for business planning, social planning, and educational planning.

Regional Administration. The regional administration is responsible and has authority for the educational program of the educational service region. It is headed by the regional educational executive who is responsible for all administrative functions relating to curriculum, student and professional personnel (exclusive of record storage, etc.) and budget preparation and defense.

Learning Unit Administration. The learning unit (any combination of teacher-student where learning is the prime objective) is headed by a unit educational leader who is an administrative specialist. He is responsible for the development of educational objectives and the evaluation of the effectiveness of his learning unit to attain the objectives. He has a prime responsibility to make his school relevant to the needs of its community.

The Education Leader and the Teacher. The educational leader and the teacher are responsible for the evolution of the educational objectives. These objectives should reflect broad educational policies established by the regional representative board and/or legally constituted authority. Whenver possible, and to the maximum feasible extent, however, the evolution of educational objectives should be the right and responsibility of the educational leader and teachers working in the local learning unit. The entire organization must have service to the learning unit area as its primary focus.

DECENTRALIZATION A SOLUTION?

Legislators, civic officials, school board members, community action groups, teachers' organizations, and educational administrators have praised or condemned decentralization as a solution to reorganizing urban school systems. All agree that reorganization of the nation's large urban school districts is a necessity, but there seems to be little agreement as to how to reorganize.

Decentralization seems to be the selected solution but intense battles are and will be waged over which functions are to be delegated to local representatives and which are to remain centralized. Decentralization has elicited controversy on the part of every power group in American education seeking control through the persuasion of social issues.

Individuals expecting the process of decentralization to solve questions relating to segregation and the control of education endow the decentralization process with a social purpose it cannot accomplish. Decentralization is a reordering of certain elements of the existing structure, and there is little likelihood that such a reordering of an existing structure will bring about major ideological changes in a society. In fact, there may be weakness in any plan that uses the structure of an organization as the catalyst to bring about ideological changes. Preferably, the structure should be designed to serve an ideology whatever it may be.

OTHER WAYS TO RESTRUCTURE EDUCATION

If not decentralization, is there any other way in which to restructure the organizational control pattern of a school district so that it better serves a democratic society? What values will provide the basis for a new structure? Should the structure reflect ideology by being a model for society?

If restructuring of the organizations serving urban school systems is necessary, it must first be recognized by the legislators, educational administrators, and relevant power groups that reconstruction cannot come from chaos. Group goals cannot be accomplished without order. *Order is the major element in power, and power can and is represented through organization.*

The legislative body is the body politic with power in any state to develop enforceable laws based on appropriate human values. The legislature, in its modification of educational law, must reexamine: (1) The legal power and authority of the legislature as delegated to the school boards and administrators of the state: (2) the teacher and other employee organizations as power groups: (3) student power groups: (4) community power groups.

SERVING A DEMOCRATIC SOCIETY

The structure for the new organization must serve the ideology. In our case, the structure must serve the furtherance of a democratic society. Thus, the restructuring of educational control must be derived from the values inherent in the Constitution of the United States and the Bill of Rights. The new structure cannot be built upon autocratic design within the framework of a democracy. The restructured control system must be designed to allow all participants to behave effectively in a democratic manner.

Thus, the behavior of the participants on a democratic basis within a structure that is designed to serve democracy should provide a democratic model of administration and participation for the society.

The authors believe that our present educational model is a centralized, authoritarian model existing in a verbalized democratic framework. The main ideological elements are therefore basically incompatible. Thus, we start our restructuring by stating our belief that the authoritarian model is passe.

Why is it passe? Is it possible that during the infancy of our nation, when the knowledge level of most people was at a relatively low plateau, the authoritarian procedure (benevolent authority) was necessary? Have we in education reached the stage where we have educated people so well with regard to their human rights that, for most of them, we no longer need the authoritarian control system? If individuals understand their rights in a democracy, have we in education also helped them understand their authority and responsibility?

Are we at the stage in our democracy where individuals demanding their human rights can be trusted to accept accountability for their actions? May they not be given the freedom to decide, to make mistakes, and to improve future actions as a result? If so, how can one apply these beliefs to a new structure?

An urban school system is made up of a fantastic range of levels of knowledge and sophistication on the part of parents, children, and educators. How does one restructure a system that must meet diverse problems and utilize such diverse resources? How can one design a structure that recognizes the need for centralization of service and at the same time provides voice to the citizen? How can one design a structure that serves democracy instead of becoming so intrigued with the structure that ideology is lost?

GUIDELINES FOR THE NEW STRUCTURE

The authors believe that the guidelines for the new structure must come from the following beliefs:

a. The value used to construct the new framework must be derived from the Constitution and Bill of Rights as interpreted by the courts of a legal system of the United States.

b. Authority, responsibility and accountability for each of the relevant power groups in the educational arena must be developed, tested, and implemented. (Power groups include legislature, school boards, administrators, teachers' groups, community groups and student groups.)

c. Change is constant. Therefore, a system of reevaluating control patterns is necessary and procedures for shifting control in an orderly fashion must be developed, tested, and implemented.

d. Clear, concise, linkage between the parent, child, and teacher, and the school unit and school system must be evolved.

e. Clear, concise linkage between the boards, administrators, and teachers must be evolved.

f. A balance of power (authority, responsibility and accountability) on the part of all relevant groups must be defined.

g. Priority must be given to ideological values and democratic goal setting procedures, and the structure of the control pattern must be the servant of the people (society).

h. Uniformity in terms of numbers of children per teacher, teachers per principal, etc., has little or no relationship to quality or need. Therefore new ways to measure educational need and to allocate resources in relationship to need must be developed.

THE NEW STRUCTURE — A BEGINNING

In a very real sense, all education is "decentralized." It involves a learner and a teacher and is at its best when there is a positive interaction between teacher and learner. Further factors which may provide support, motivation, and expectation level come from the parent and the society which the parent represents. All other elements of the educational system should exist to support the teacher-learner interaction.

Each individual in the educational arena has human rights. Each also exercises authority, has responsibilities and may be held accountable. The first step in the design of the new structure is to define the authority, responsibility and accountability of the individuals who are directly involved in the teaching-learning task. In a sense they need to develop an educational contract that provides the appropriate clauses explaining the rights and responsibilities of each.

The model suggested herein, does not provide a "perfect answer" to the trauma and travail which any large urban center may and will experience as it reaches out for new administrative patterns to operate its schools.

No one can yet imagine the ultimate form which "education" must take in the 21st Century, or beyond. At some point, however, the end product must be a unique human being, possessed of human aspirations and goals, and motivated by all the cultural heritages which one generation of individuals may transmit to another. Perhaps "schools" as we know them, may no longer exist.

Certainly, however, society will be best served, and so will mankind, when we have given maximum opportunity for development of the intrinsic worthiness of each individual human being. A decision to decentralize the centralized authority of the present urban school system may be a significant first step down that long, long road.

Question:

1. Evaluate A Balanced Control Pattern—in terms of community acceptance.

DECENTRALIZATION:
PROBLEMS AND PROSPECTS

By ALLAN C. ORNSTEIN

Writers in any field, especially in education, are susceptible of regurgitating and accepting "fashionable" ideas. Witness the addictic tendency of educators to elaborate on and call for decentralization. During the last two school years (1967-68, 1968-69), perhaps the two most respected and influential educational journals, the *Record* and *Harvard Educational Review,* had not one article against decentralization and community control, but more than ten in favor. Certainly decentralization can be beneficial, but there is an appeal with it for "confrontation politics," especially as the trend merges with black power, as illustrated by the recent and tragic events of Ocean-Hill Brownsville and subsequent teacher-community-student disruptions throughout the New York City schools.

Briefly, fears of a possible loss in security, either through harassment or preferential hiring and promotion of black personnel or violation of "due process," cemented an unusual alliance between teachers and supervisors during the 1968 New York City Teachers' Strike. Having gone into education for security, among other reasons—some of them noble, too—thousands of teachers and supervisors in New York City and other cities, now are forced to recognize that non-whites would rather have members of their own ethnic group teach and supervise their children, even if these personnel lack proper credentials.

The current decentralization plan enacted in Albany on April 20, 1969, which splinters the New York City schools into as many as thirty local districts and permits those districts whose students are scoring below the reading norm to have their local boards hire and promote personnel, should only be viewed as a temporary truce in a series of confrontations which may plaque the New York City schools. It is doubtful whether the people will ever be "fooled" into believing that educators can run the schools. A new genre of extremists and self-styled, grass-roots improvement organizations—black and white, Panther and Birch in nature—will probably enter the arena of educational policy-making. Nepotism, politics, corruption, and local "wisdom" will probably flourish, while teachers may be intimidated and local boards coerced by a minority, as in most rural and suburban areas today.

Keeping in mind that educational controversies often commence in New York City because of its size and pluralistic quality, and often spread to other cities, educators should take heed to the past events that have crippled and polarized this exhausted school and pervasively ill city, and learn some lessons

Reprinted with permission from *The Negro Educational Review,* January 1970.

from what happened and hopefully avoid educational war in their school systems and cities. Indeed, related efforts concerning decentralization and/or teacher-community-student disruptions are already fermenting in numerous urban school systems across the country: Boston, Camden, Chicago, Cleveland, Detroit, Philadelphia, Syracuse, Washington, D. C., and elsewhere.

Decentralization and black power must be understood in light of past and present social conditions. Many black people in our northern ghettoes have repudiated the idea of integration as a farce, a "honkie hoax," just another myth of white supremacy. It must also be understood that integration was not abandoned by black parents, but by almost all urban school systems which consistently failed to deliver on their promises to integrate the schools. The twin concepts of decentralization and black power are a reaction to this inaction. Both concepts are a response to the failure of the urban schools to educate black children, and a means for equal access of black parents to the process of making decisions essential to the education of their children. Thus, it is now demanded that black children be educated in black schools with black teachers and administrators. Indeed, white teachers can only intellectualize, never fully understand or know what it is like to be black in this society. A few pictures of black heroes, even of militants, or a curriculum on black history will soon no longer suffice according to the black community, for their children will still be taught by many white teachers whose bigotry will affect their ego-development.

Black teachers welcome school decentralization and local control; they envision these concepts as an opportunity to bolster black power, as well as their green power through administrative promotion which they generally have been denied. To be sure, it is legally and morally justified for black-controlled school boards to hire or promote qualified principals or superintendents on the basis that the individual is black.

Our laws have permitted other groups a degree of separatism, permitting them to establish their own schools in order to maintain their customs, identity, and religious beliefs. The white "liberals," whatever that term connotes to the reader, who belong to the N.A.A.C.P. and move to suburbia are often seeking "better" schools for their children. In effect, they establish their own school systems, and tend to favor individuals of their own ethnic group in their employment and reward practices. True, a policy that permits white or black people to control their own schools will probably accent racism, but since whites refuse to listen to blacks and share power unless messages contain a threat of violence, and since whites are condoning and perpetuating segregation through "neighborhood schools," then blacks ought to control their own schools.

For most whites, local control of the schools by the black community is construed as a black victory and white defeat. Much of the present demand for local control must be viewed in context with the present unrest in the ghettoes which is partially due to frustration arising from the fact that blacks have not been permitted to shake loose the albatross of dependency which has historically hung around their necks. The urban school systems are viewed as part of the white power structure, and the white power structure has often been viewed by blacks as the enemy. Now the pendulum is beginning to swing the other way; blacks are beginning to get their way too. But whites cannot accept the feeling of being outnumbered or out-voted by blacks. The exodus of whites from the inner cities and their bewildering statements such as "They want everything their way," "What do they expect from us?", "Will they ever be satisfied?", illustrate the whites' discomfort and their desire to maintain the luxury of supremacy.

While some blacks consider the ultimate reforms will justify the immediate trauma, others recognize they are trapped by their own rhetoric, and that each successful demand breeds more demands which eventually may foster white extremism—in quest and in defense of law and order—as a virtue. Although collective force is instrumental now in accomplishing black objectives, it also invites massive counter force. Even among "liberals" and among those whites who advocate decentralization and community control in print or in speeches, this author senses an underlying uneasiness, a sense of doubt, alarm, fear, even racism at certain times, in conversation with such "good" people. Behind closed doors and among friends, people who often profess to be the friends of the black community renege on their "principles," and blacks surely realize this and do not trust good intentioned whites.

In a pluralistic society—though the myth of the melting pot no longer exists—no group, including the majority, should have total control. Unquestionably local residents should influence the schools enough to shape policy, but not enough to terrorize teachers and force policy makers to surrender their logic in face of fear—rather than being able to peacefully change by means of sound, tested ideas of educational reform. Peace by capitulation to the forces of unreason only breeds more unreasonable demands. We fail to recognize that both groups may be weighted by a sense of guilt—blacks for being told they are "marginal" directed, and whites for being told they are racist—and therefore, they may be bowing to the jarring forces of storm, stress, and senselessness. We fail to recognize that more grievances are easy to create—and escalate into demands, threats, and coercion—especially in the throes of "confrontation politics." There is no guarantee that what happened in the New York City schools in the 1968-69 school year will not happen again there or in other cities.

How could educators allow the situation to deteriorate and then act so clumsily? Because they were never allowed to act any other way. The "wisdom" of their policies have rarely been seriously questioned. While professors have lived in "ivory towers," detached from the schools and professing their "common wisdom," school administrators have been perpetuating the status quo, reluctant to innovate and deluding themselves into thinking all was quiet and content because there were no overt signs of dissent.

It is time to realize that it is no longer possible for one group to tell another group what is best for it. This means that white educators cannot tell the black community what is best for the black community; likewise, the black community should not expect to tell white teachers and administrators what is professionally best for them. While legality and "due process" are essential, many blacks regard present political and educational systems as antithetical to their values and nonrepresentative of their objectives. What decision-makers say is important, but it is important that the local community also believe in these decisions. Urban school-administrators can no longer expect to tell teachers about viable policies that exclude the teachers' voice and vote. Similarly, school administrators and teachers can no longer expect parents, even secondary students now, to accept grandiose ideas that exclude their opinions. Whereas teachers can coerce and disrupt the school system by striking, parent or student groups will often resort to more extreme measures. Teachers, parents and/or students are reacting to their powerlessness and opting for power. However, the latter two groups often resort to substantial force and are less willing to compromise, because they start with less power and are more alienated. If, as it is often claimed, power breeds corruption, then powerlessness may breed alienation, conflict, and violence.

No single group should try to make policy without listening to and including the other groups in decision-making. Satisfying one group often antagonizes another group, which diminishes reality and fosters the myth of power. It should be evident that all groups want to participate in decisions that affect their lives, and when excluded from this opportunity, the powerless or antagonized group will confront the system and this will lead to the further polarization of the various groups.

One cannot underestimate the potential good of decentralization. Who knows what will happen to our ghetto schools? In that hopeless situation, perhaps, there is some hope. To sustain it, however, we cannot encourage those who want to merely subvert the school system or polarize the vested groups, nor can we retreat to some "ivory tower" and wait for a call that may never come or wait until racial discord and fear disrupt pell mell. The old cliche is still good: time is running out. Educators who attempt to maintain the status quo are unwittingly inviting disaster by default. Educators must be sensitive to the changing patterns of society; and those who seek improvement, including school administrators, teachers, and community groups must be willing to share power. The opinions of professional educators should be combined with the wishes of the people. Indeed, the merging critics of the teachers and school systems are uneasy allies, and it will be no easy task to keep them together, focused on the common concern which we tend to forget, of educating all youth, and especially poor youth.

REFERENCES:

1. Glazer, Nathan, "The Negro's Stake in America's Future," *New York Time Magazine,* September 22, 1969, pp. 30-31, ff.

2. Hamilton, Charles V., "Race and Education: A Search for Legitimacy," *Harvard Educational Review,* Fall 1968, pp. 669-684.

3. Levine, Daniel U., "The Need for Activist Role Among Teachers in Big City School Districts," *Journal of Secondary Education,* March 1969, pp. 122-128.

4. Ornstein, Allan C., "Anxieties and Discontents Which Mitigate Against Ghetto School Teachers," *Journal of Secondary Education,* October 1968, pp. 243-254.

5.   , "In Defense of Slum-School Teachers," *Record,* May 1968, pp. 758-766.

6.   , "Theory Practices for Teaching Disadvantaged Youth," *Journal of Negro Education,* Winter 1969, pp. 82-85.

7. Sizer, Theodore R., "The Case for Free Market," *Saturday Review,* January 11, 1969, pp. 34-36, ff.

Questions:

1. For what reasons would you favor decentralization in the large urban centers?
2. Evaluate decentralization as a concept in terms of black power.
3. As an administrator, what would you do to include all of the other concerned groups in policy-making in terms of decision-making?

DECENTRALIZATION:
DIALECTIC AND DILEMMA

By SEYMOUR W. ITZKOFF

Decentralization is a new term in education, perhaps the most important idea in a long while to suggest a *modus operandi* for finding a path through the current educational wilderness. In New York City, the Bundy report suggested that the school system be broken up into between 30 and 60 semi-autonomous districts having control over at least their curricular destinies. New York State now has a decentralization law. In the various poverty programs of the Office of Economic Opportunity, local responsibility and participation are seen as essential prerequisites to effective implementation. We hear less and less of the empire building represented by the "multi-versity" and more of the necessary intimacy provided by the self-contained residential college. Even among the leaders of the civil rights movement, equality and freedom are no longer thought of as synonymous with integration but rather with autonomy and community pride.

The call for decentralization has come in spite of great counter pressures from several sources. One derives from the new corporate giants who see education as a lucrative market for their varied electronic gear and other curricular products. Their intent is to absorb this national undertaking into the industrial fraternity of General Motors, International Business Machines, and American Telephone and Telegraph. The other pressure is the product of the bureaucratic hallucinations epitomized by the recent Chicago plan. This latter plan would integrate the children of that city by funneling as many as possible into several vast educational parks (*i.e.*, prisons). If decentralism can stave off such Orwellian seductions of these eager system builders it ought to be welcomed enthusiastically.

THE DIALECTIC: CENTRALISM AND PLURALISM

One wonders if the situation in the past few years has so radically altered as to be responsible for this turnabout in public opinion. I would suggest that rather than the situation changing, the climate of opinion has changed, so that what formerly was interpreted as a social and moral imperative (for educational progress) has through the catalytic agency of several crucial student and parent revolts been completely reevaluated. Shifts such as these may be seen as products of a dialectic between the unique and the universal that is inherent in human

Reprinted from *Educational Forum* (November 1969) by permission of Kappa Delta Pi, An Honor Society in Education, owners of the copyright.

thought and reflected in social action.₁ This dialectic periodically affects our attitudes towards the content and structure of education. Today we see these educational shifts manifested in the demands for local control, neutralization of large bureaucracies, in the call for "black power," indeed in the call for all minorities or communities to control their own educational destinies.

Public education in the United States under the persistent goad of égalitarian and assimilationist ideals was conceived, from the mid-nineteenth century on, as a designer of a national culture. In addition and perhaps more importantly, as we approached our own time, it began to fulfill an obligation induced by the state to feed the burgeoning industrial society with managers and technicans, workers and consumers. For this purpose, both form and content in education were stereotyped to the point that "Look, Sally, look," and its varying analogues stamped their indelible message upon the curricular tradition of the American school. Where these natural stereotyping processes in education have not succeeded completely, the federal government has now begun to eliminate any slack.

The achievement of great material advances, partially the fruit of our traditional educational patterns, made it easier for man to satisfy his basic physical requirements, potentially eliminating want. In addition, the growth of technology released vast human energies for creative yet tangible encounters with the physical environment. The social and ideological byproduct of the union of mathematical science with technology has been to reshape the cultural patterns of our world, create new classes, new political and economic entities, and in general give the words "growth" and "progress" not only an exhilarating significance, but a tangible meaning.

The social and educational patterns of the last century have gained acceptance because they have reflected the same basic persuasiveness as has science. The acceptance of science is due not necessarily to the material and social good, but rather to the fact that the scientific attitude constitutes a natural quality of human thought and action. Its success stems from the satisfaction of deep psychological and intellectual attitudes in man. It has contributed to progress, but not to permanent, unilinear, or objective progress. Science, technology, and economics have led to the exploration of merely one element of the social dialectic. We have utilized one intellectual model derived from physics and biology and have applied it to the changing face of society and education.

We have long believed that physics, especially in its Newtonian envisionment, described the ultimate nature of the real. As one interpreter recently put it, the progress of physics placed man on the advancing "edge of objectivity."² The thrust of the logic of scientific theory is towards a universal encompassing individual and concrete particulars. The scientific enterprise has never been satisfied unless it could translate and comprehend things and events *sub species aeterni.* The more successful the scientific theory the more convincingly it could claim to include increasingly larger congeries of things in terms of "for all time and in all places."

The theory of biological adaptation has had an analogical and persuasive effect on our perception of experience. It has given additional credence to the view that the purpose of man's tenure upon this earth in terms of his bio-social nature is fulfilled through brute physical survival. The economic achievements of man are viewed as *prima facie* evidence that the good of man is attained through the support of institutions which promote technical, scientific, and material growth. To the extent that political and social decision making has tacitly reinforced these assumptions and expectations, popular assent has been gained for a variety of educational programs whose intrinsic good might otherwise have been questioned. (Examples are large school districts, state-wide examinations, vocationalism in public schools, etc.) Our world has thus been remade by us and for us into what Jacques Ellul has called *The Technological Society*.[3] It is a world-wide society, and each year it becomes increasingly uniform in social structure and inner content.

But in education this seems to be changing. The aims of centralism are being questioned, especially in our metropolitan areas, where the full impact of our mass society can be felt. Here local control, social responsibility, and personal relevance have become the great educational issues. The educational situation is not that much worse than it was ten years ago, but our attitudes have changed radically. There now exists a real if inchoate awareness that our traditional social patterns and purposes have created a quality of life that is wanting. Decentralization in education is but one attempt to regain the social control to transform the pervasive atmosphere of educational failure into one of achievement. The hope is that in gaining a measure of autonomy, citizens will, in addition, be able to explore diverse patterns and emphasize values which might constitute new potentials within our culture.

Decentralization will inevitably act to restore that which has gradually been eviscerated in American life over the last half century — the unique. Our deprivation of the unique has not been conscious. Rather, it has been one product of an erosion of the institutional support necessary for "identity" and "community." As Robert Nisbet has demonstrated, since the seventeenth century the intellectual support for the institutions within which traditional allegiances were made meaningful—guild, church, clan, or community, and ethnic identity—has been subject to successive attacks by the increasingly powerful national state.[4] The incapacity of these traditional institutions to survive their intellectual debilitation and to adapt themselves to a world of scientific technology only enlarged the ideational vacuum within which the national state could assert its authority.

Centralism has made traditional communities irrelevant; it has transformed Karl Mannheim's elite, his *freischwebende Intelligentsia* (socially unattached intellectuals), into a universal condition of mankind.[5] The resulting fragmentation of interpersonal communication has destroyed the familiar nuances that lie at the basis of ritual, language, personal relatedness, even esthetic communication, except on the most superficial level. We have not planned this. We have assumed that these intuitive qualities of experience, so close to our own personal beings, would always occur naturally. But in fact they can only prosper when communities and institutions allow them the possibility of real social envisagement.

These non-discursive elements can be recognized in the poetic or colloquial dialects a community creates and molds; in the art forms that express the deepest perceptual meanings shared spontaneously by creator and communicant; in the religious identities which unite men not merely because of shared ritual or theistic beliefs but also because of their mutual historic allegiances; in man's sudden realization of the need to shape his mysterious and inexplicable humanness in terms of the sanctions and limitations that he chooses to give social behavior—what we call morals. These are all values which a community school would ordinarily incorporate into its basic curriculum.

Freud considered these factors as essential to clear consciousness of an inner identity, that which helps man to assimilate the various imponderable and insoluble circumstances of human existence. But it is more than therapeutic, for the non-discursive symbolic elements of thought also provide the foundation for creative enterprise. As Freud further hypothesized, it is in this, the secret familiarity of identical psychological construction, that the roots of reason and individuation are to be located. In this model for education within the community we have a vision of selfhood that can maintain the integrity of the individual. It is an enterprise that is integral, that can be secure from the artifice and sterility of a qualitatively undifferentiated mechanical form of life.[6]

There exist then two basic and seemingly antithetical trends in the structure of symbolic thought. One, the discursive or scientific, is directed outward towards a material world within which man creates always larger, unifying patterns of thought and behavior. The other, the non-discursive, more intangible and esthetic, needs the intimate dimension of human communication to flourish.[7]

Educators have always given outward approval to the values that are products of community life—the artistic and humanistic dimension of the curriculum, the concern for morality, idealism, and commitment, the achievement of individual creativity and the importance of a responding audience. They have hoped that these values would persist. Yet they have acquiesced to social forces that have strengthened the allegiance of education to the federal government, to transnational corporate and professional organizations.

As we have chosen a society where value is measured in quantitative terms, in material production and consumption, purely external human relations have preempted power at the expense of interpersonal commitments, the ideal of community, and cultural diversity. As a consequence, we have created a shallow, meritocratic educational ideal. It is no wonder that today we are experiencing a national moral reevaluation. To a significant extent this state of affairs has been produced by our reification of values—which are only partially reflective of a humane society—into a permanent and objective good.

OUR CONTEMPORARY DILEMMA

This contemporary state of affairs constitutes the basic impetus for the decentralization movement in education and the crux of our educational problem. Our current acceptance of the centralist ideals has made our educational institutions ever more uniform and meritocratic in purpose. They have become a model, as Edgar Friedenberg has noted, of the trap that is society.[8] As controls over the schools have become increasingly rigidified by government, the teachers have defended their own interests by forming themselves into large organizations—the NEA and the AFT. Today it makes little difference which one chooses; they both mirror in their orientation the power structure of those they oppose.

But the clientele of education, the ultimate judges of the legitimacy of the institution, have not been seduced. The brightest, most morally sensitive college youth today rail poignantly against the status quo. Our disenfranchised Negro young resort either to violence or to the empty slogans of "black power." The violence and anarchy reflect a need to express in some manner their vague feelings of disenchantment with the implicit assumptions of our way of life.

To protest against the illegitimacy and futility of their violent actions is not enough. We must become sensitive to the fact that their disorder and disaffection are evidence of a deeply rooted *malaise.* Behind the discontent of the varying groups lies the reality of a desire for a society which can use their superabundant energies for growth, change, and enrichment. Perhaps the only way to achieve this is to realize first that existing institutions and social patterns have exhausted their symbolic possibilities; the apogee of technological centralism may indeed have been reached.

Will decentralization alone act to rejuvenate, to infuse into our society those possibilities which are increasingly unavailable to the young? If we do allow a measure of choice and structural control to the local community we have to ask eventually: after decentralization, what?[9] What will happen to our society if the local community begins to make educational decisions which challenge the substantive value system of the administrative or teaching bureaucracies? Irving Kristol identifies these bureaucracies as the means by which numerous Negroes have made their way into the middle class and that with the closing off of these traditional educational and social avenues, we may once more see a ghetto-like segregation, albeit voluntary, of white and black.

We could likewise ask how we could be assured that our children would receive the kind of education in one of these community schools that would be useful in the wider educational context of college and graduate school and thence in any one of the important occupational adjuncts of our "organized system."

These concerns still reflect the fixed sense of possibilities that characterizes so much of our official thinking. They assume that human equality can only be achieved in one particular social setting, that, for example, a Negro middle class with substantive economic and cultural advantages can be propagated solely through the aegis of the bureaucratic establishments. The price of Negro equality certainly should not be the continued maintenance of the educational and political status quo of New York or Chicago.

The issue of educational incommensurability from district to district, given neighborhood control of the schools, is likewise a spurious one. If equal national economic support were given to education in every district, it is difficult to believe that parents would prevent their children from receiving the kind of education they need to compete in the technological, intellectual, and economic market place. Here we must all be products of a twentieth century education. Also, we ought not assume that our colleges and graduate schools will remain forever insulated from the current trend towards reform. We ought not predicate conservatism in the lower schools on the expectations of conservatism in higher education.

Finally, we must hypothesize that an education that is uniform in structure and content for all men, that does not reflect the intimate communitarian and cultural valences of human existence, will ultimately be considered no education at all. Such a "common schooling" might be likened to requiring the Japanese, Italians, Russians, and English to give up the particular values which constitute their national character in order to participate in our modern scientific world.

Decentralization in education will certainly not lead to such sharp distinctions. The movement is merely reflective of the desire of individuals who come together through free choice to make educational decisions for their children, to explore the possibilities inherent in which Sir David Eccles has described as "the secret garden of the curriculum." In so doing the partisans of local control serve not only the interests of the nation, in its most generic and universal sense, but the interests of the community—and our democracy—in its most intimate and pluralistic sense.

Decentralization as a social option is not without its dangers. It could become an instrument of fragmentation and divisiveness. But it does indicate to us the necessity for replacing many of the secure symbols, institutions, and power complexes of our society and venturing down a new and largely unpredictable path. In time, no doubt, we will learn to accept these new social and educational orthodoxies, predictably at the very moment when we will need to shift again towards more universal patterns. Hopefully we will have attained the requisite philosophical perspicacity and moral sensitivity to know when to begin the inevitable return.

BIBLIOGRAPHY:

[1]J. A. Talmon, *The Unique and the Universal* (London: Secker & Warburg, 1965).
[2]Charles Coulston Gillispie, *The Edge of Objectivity* (Princeton, N.J.: Princeton University Press, 1960).
[3]Trans. John Wilkinson (New York: Knopf, 1964).
[4]Robert Nisbet, *Community and Power* (New York: Oxford Press, 1962).
[5]Karl Mannheim, *Ideology and Utopia* (New York: Harcourt & Brace, n.d.).
[6]Erik H. Erikson, *Childhood and Society* (Middlesex, England: Penguin Books, 1965), pp. 269-276.
[7]See Ernst Cassirer, *The Philosophy of Symbolic Forms,* 3 Vols., trans. by Ralph Mannheim (New Haven, Conn.: Yale University Press, 1953-1957; originally published 1923-1929); Susanne K. Langer, Philosophy in a New Key, 3rd Ed. (Cambridge, Mass.: Harvard University Press, 1957).
[8]Edgar Z. Friedenberg, *Coming of Age in America* (New York: Random House, 1965).
[9]Irving Kristol, "Decentralization for What?" *The Public Interest* (Spring, 1968).

Questions:

1. How can a decentralized school system better effect the equalization of educational opportunities?

2. List the dangers that you feel will result from decentralization.

3. What do you feel would be some of the educational advantages that could be gained through decentralization?

THE OCEAN HILL-
BROWNSVILLE EXPERIMENT

By MARIO FANTINI
MARILYN GITTELL

The Ocean Hill-Brownsville school district in New York City resembles the elephant in the Indian folktale. It reflects different qualities according to who is viewing it, when, and the angle of vision. Standards of measurement for success or failure are becoming subjective because of the political struggle enveloping the district. Probably a majority of the education people judge the district strictly in terms of its obedience to existing educational standards and procedures. Any attempt to move away from these commonly accepted practices, they feel, constitutes cause to label the experiment a failure. Some, for example, think that the only thing being tested is the concept of parent participation, and that all else should remain static. How, then, do you test even that single variable?

In fact, the general reluctance to accept the experimental status of the demonstration district probably was a major factor in the conflicts which developed. Experimentation was interpreted by the district as a means of evolving changes in roles, particularly in the role of the community but also in the role of the various professionals. Deviations from established procedures were viewed by the participants in the experiment as a source of new ideas and an opportunity for self-renewal of the subsystem. Those in the larger system increasingly tended to look upon experimentation and change taking place in the subsystem as a challenge to established interests, traditions, and procedures and regularly sought to undermine such efforts.

For those committed to reform of the educational system, the creation of the demonstration districts is analogous to heart transplant surgery. Through the experimental district they saw an opportunity for developing an important revitalizing option to the conventional system. Rejection of the new subsystem (as in the case of heart transplant) was to be anticipated but hopefully avoided.

The Ocean Hill-Brownsville district is an educational and a political experiment. The two goals are in many respects inseparable. Any evaluation must take into account the underlying assumption in the creation of the district: that community involvement in the development of educational policy is not only a politically worthwhile goal but will produce a new effectiveness in educational achievement. This is not to suggest that community control offers a panacea for ghetto education. Rather, the experiment is predicated on the need to compensate for the political and educational failure of the highly centralized structure of the city school system, its lack of innovative educational policy, its inability to respond to local community needs, and its general policy of non-

Reprinted with permission from *Phi Delta Kappan* (April 1969).

involvement of parents and community in the decision-making process. Evaluation of the experiment then must relate to each of these goals and the underlying thesis—that new governance patterns in urban schools at the local level is directly related to educational policy and to school improvement.

The full implications of the Ocean Hill-Brownsville experiment cannot be appreciated out of context. The district was created in the summer of 1967 after a full winter of crisis negotiation related to the Intermediate School 201 controversy in East Harlem. The Board of Education was desperately seeking an answer to demands for increased community participation in school affairs. Ghetto parents were demanding responses to their questions regarding the continued failure of the present system to educate their children. What emerged was clear: Desegregation and compensatory education were not working and new options in educational reform were necessary. Direct community participation was to be the essential ingredient—not a startling conclusion for a political system which espoused that doctrine as primary to its heritage. This implied that participation was essential to learning and growth of children in the schools and to adults in the community. Under such a system the major socializing agents would work together to reform urban schools. Diversity of interests and views would produce a more viable school system more appropriate to the needs of a changing society.

Ocean Hill-Brownsville has been functioning since the election of its governing board in August, 1967. Some have challenged the election itself as an indication of nonparticipation. Actually, the election was one of the first fulfillments of the goal of community involvement. Without the registration lists of eligible voters (which were denied to the planning group by the Board of Education), the group canvassed the area and produced a larger turnout of voters than one gets in any local election in the district. Between 25 and 30 percent of those eligible voted. It is said that in a recent local election for assemblyman only 400 voters took part, whereas over 1,000 parents voted in the school board election.

One of the first acts of the local board was the selection of its unit administrator, Rhody A. McCoy. Both Mr. McCoy's credentials and his previous professional experience are impressive. His sensitivity to the concerns and aspirations of the community has become readily apparent through the public media. A series of staff appointments and the selection of eight new principals moved the district closer to the goal of subsystem experimentation. These appointments, while challenged for allegedly violating established personnel practices, warrant considered judgment in relation to the goals of the experiment. The diversity, competence, sensibility, and style of these professionals has added much to the educational policy of the district. For example, the appointment of the first Chinese and Puerto Rican principals in the city (if not the country) should not be underestimated. Luis Fuentes was the source of major educational innovation—including the much-heralded bilingual program. His recruitment of a Spanish-speaking staff and his rapport with parents and community have been of considerable importance to the district. David Lee, on the other hand—an iconoclast by nature—has attracted many of the Peace Corps, VISTA type teachers to his school.

On balance, the appointments in the Ocean Hill-Brownsville district are characterized by their diversity. For example, the unit probably now possesses the most varied teaching staff in the city. Over 70 percent is white and 50 percent is Jewish. There are more law students, graduate degree people, and liberal arts majors in the district than one is likely to find in most school systems.

Ocean Hill has a waiting list of candidates seeking employment. This is in sharp contrast with the personnel record prior to the establishment of the district.

For anyone who has visited schools, the contrast in Ocean Hill-Brownsville will be immediate. There is a sensitivity and enthusiasm in the teaching staff which has been sensed by most of the 3,000 visitors, including numerous reporters. Again, this experimentation with new sources of teacher recruitment might suggest expansion. For example, why not offer the possibility of two to three years of ghetto teaching to male students in lieu of military service?

By any standard, it is too early to measure educational outputs in the district. Nevertheless, there are some inputs worthy of mention, if only because they suggest the receptivity of the local board to new ideas and the strong desire to produce educational success. Project Read, for example, has been adopted by the district and is being implemented with the cooperation of the Behavioral Research Laboratory at Stanford. This individualized programmed learning project is viewed as a first step to providing a base of accomplishment for students in the district. The program was planned and developed by the teaching and administrative staff and involved a series of conferences with parents to orient them to procedures and objectives. Beyond the usual excitement that accompanies such innovations, there is the attitude of accomplishment already evident among students and staff. There is at the same time an acceptance by the staff that this is only a very small first step, and plans must be made for further development.

In the bilingual program experimentation is the by-word. The director of the program insists on the trial nature of current practices and the need to learn from experience. Regular conferences with parents serve to inform the staff of problems which have developed and to inject other judgments of workable procedures. The staff meets regularly to evaluate their progress. Cooperative teaching and joined classes are common and the use of paraprofessionals is quite extensive and imaginative. There is continuous attention to the need to train paraprofessionals to fill useful roles in the schools. In each new program consideration is given to an imaginative community and paraprofessional input.

The district is developing an Afro- and Latin-American curriculum center which is planning to emphasize the Afro-American experience in the regular curriculum. It also sees its role as providing training and background for staff and community. Materials will be available for other schools and school districts. Keith Baird is in charge of the program. Prior to his assignment to the district he served as director of a city-wide program in this area for the Board of Education. Montessori and Bereiter early childhood methods are being tested in different schools and an ungraded school was initiated in February, 1969.

There are other educational plans, on and off the drawing boards; these indicate continued movement in the direction of educational advancement. Perhaps more sophisticated observers will consider many of these projects the ordinary stock of current innovations. It should be remembered, however, that the initial mood in the district is probably to seek stability and to develop a foundation from which to build. It should be remembered that the subunit has inherited a negative learning situation. Thus the starting point is not zero but minus. A rather concentrated assessment effort is being conducted. Part of the test of the district's viability will be the ability to move beyond these first steps. Also, it should be remembered that even these changes are difficult to come by in the larger system. What is most significant is the atmosphere and attitudes discernible among staff and parents—the great confidence they share in the ability to move ahead and educate children.

Regarding the political aspects of the experiment, the goal of increased participation should be viewed as at least twofold: first, the degree to which various community leaders have been engaged in the policy process; second, by a more standard form of measurement, the degree to which the larger community has been participating. With respect to the former, certainly the elected local board has been directly involved in the development of school policy. They meet several times weekly and participate in the selection of all personnel for the district.

The local board itself is quite protective of its powers and has been constantly concerned with the need to be consulted in all matters. In fact, it might be said that one of the problems that should be worked out as experience increases is the proper use of professional talents and advice and a viable relationship between staff and community. It should be appreciated, however, that at least in the initial phases of increased local control there is a great desire by the board to hold its newly acquired powers tight to the vest. The training of professionals ill suits them to these new roles and workable relationships have to be developed over a long period of time.

The backgrounds of board members are worthy of mention from the political viewpoint. The Ocean Hill-Brownsville board largely includes parents of school children in the district. They are grass-roots people highly representative of the larger community. This is quite unlike the general character of school boards throughout the country. Their sophistication about local problems comes from their immediate personal experience; their contact with the community is direct.

Although there has not been a planned and organized effort to involve the larger community through a structured arrangement, there is an informal communication network to other community groups and schools. As reported in *The New York Times,* when a crisis develops they are able to turn out large groups of people. Public meetings in the district have attracted upwards of 600 people, almost unheard of in the past. Obviously, the current crisis situation has solidified the community behind the governing board, even though there may be differences in points of view and even disagreements on the board itself. Questioning of principals and staff indicates that parents in the community are becoming increasingly involved in school matters. Attendance at meetings in the schools has increased considerably. Parent willingness to come and complain or inquire about programs and teachers is also increasing. To some observers this may not appear to be a sound basis for judging participation, but it is a first important step for ghetto parents who have been generally reluctant to approach school officials.

The increased use of paraprofessionals in more functional roles in the schools also indicates a serious movement to greater participation and more meaningful involvement. A special community training program administered by the governing board calls upon young adults in the community to work with dropouts and truants and bring them back to the schools. Some groups have referred to their youth as "militants" who have access to the schools, ignoring the purpose they serve and also the governing board's desire to make them an integral part of the experiment, which gives them a stake in the community. A similar youth undertaking is being conducted by the New York Urban League with its street academies program.

Some of the less tangible results of the last year and a half in Ocean Hill are more significant to the future of the community and to public education in general.

For example, reports of governing board meetings and parent discussions indicate the great emphasis on quality education. A strong desire to bring educational standards to new heights pervades the district. The myth of black parent apathy has been almost completely destroyed. Not only have the parents proven themselves to be vitally concerned with education, but their standards for quality are quite high. They are obviously not satisfied with run-of-the-mill programs. They are generating new energy necessary for real reform.

The local governing board and staff have become an important community symbol. They represent in large measure a form of local government that is accessible. They are an indigenous government to which community people bring a wide range of problems.

The nature of the Brownsville community is such that the school experiment has thrown "middle- and lower-class" blacks together, forcing them to interrelate and work together for the mutual interest of the entire community. Although there are conflicts, they must be resolved in the context of community needs. Local political leaders are held accountable for their actions because public consciousness has been aroused.

It would be foolish to suggest that the evidence on Ocean Hill-Brownsville is conclusive. There have been developmental problems. The task of attempting to reverse the spiral of decline in urban schools is fraught with awesome problems. This experiment has made an extremely important beginning. It has been of benefit to other cities. And there is no turning back from the experiment. That is perhaps the largest measure of its success. Its preservation during the recent strike in the face of city-wide school closings indicates the recognition in some quarters of its significance. Brownsville has become an important symbol of an alternative to urban school reform; as such, it has become a rallying point for middle- and lower-class blacks. In ghetto areas throughout the country community people have identified their own struggle with that of Ocean Hill-Brownsville; we can anticipate movements in other areas which will emulate it. There are also rather good educational reasons for not turning back. The signs of progress, limited though they be, offer proof of a larger potential for growth and development. The acknowledged failure of the city school system has created a constituency for reform and institutional change. And self-determination is integral to the philosophy of this constituency. This is not to suggest that those with interests in the standard educational process will not continue to oppose and constrain any movement in this direction, but rather that change in this direction appears inevitable. There will be continued efforts to restrain the Ocean Hill-Brownsville district, to limit its power and restrict innovation. The district will in turn strain for expansion of responsibilities needed to continue its search for quality education.

Developmental friction between the central and local board will probably continue even if guidelines are defined more carefully. With the passage of time, however, the governing board should develop increased political sophistication and skill to bargain effectively for a significant share in policy decisions. Saliency of the controversy surrounding development of the subdistrict has undoubtedly aroused expanded community interest and we can anticipate demands for broader participation. New elections should activate new groups to compete for positions on the board. We hope that community and staff involvement will become more structured on the individual school and district level and provide appropriate channels for such activity. The expansion of programs for para-professionals should also contribute to an expansion of community participation.

Whereas politics predominated in the first year of the district's life, there should be greater emphasis on educational policy in the immediate future. There will be external as well as internal pressure to achieve standard quantitative academic results, particularly as measured in reading test scores. Gradual movement to more experimentation with individualized learning and "affectively" oriented curricula may have to await the establishment of a more basic foundation. There may be some internal conflicts among staff, parents, and the local board on definitions of sound educational policy. Many of the imaginative young people attracted to the district will be inclined to unstructured learning experiences, while parents may want discipline and structure. The development of a dialogue between these groups should be most constructive to final policy determination. There are already signs of movement to outside professionals as a source of alternative educational methods and models, and this should also be expanded. Such programs as the school without walls (i.e., the community as classroom), teacher strength training, and cross-age student instruction are already under discussion. Other changes are likely to emerge shortly, among them the notion of matching teacher styles to particular sets of educational objectives and to the style of learning.

Greater interaction among parents, community, and professionals in the development of educational policy should produce some interesting insights for evaluation of the participatory system. Of special importance will be the response of the local board and the community to their own professional staff. Will they be able to adjust their rejection of the role of professionals to their new circumstances? Conversely, will the professionals be able to cast aside their traditional dispositions and work cooperatively with the board and local groups? Only the process of growth over the next several years should suggest some of the answers.

The Ocean Hill district has become a training ground for community school personnel. The advantages of the young and vigorous teaching staff also present problems which must be met. In-service training and extensive recruitment procedures will have to be developed over the next two years. Ocean Hill is developing a new system which in turn is an important clinic for professional training. At present we have few options to the standard system for training. These needs can produce some exciting new programs in these areas, certainly involving new cooperative and flexible arrangements with colleges and universities.

All of the above suggests that there is a difficult period ahead for Ocean Hill-Brownsville as it moves towards institutionalization of the gains already made and those which will be made in the near future. There is a certain excitement about beginning any project. Some of this excitement dissipates as you get down to the more difficult tasks of maintenance. Hopefully, the district will be able to carry forth its elan to the next phase of its development.

We would not, however, want to be accused of false optimism. There exists a very real drive to abolish Ocean Hill-Brownsville. If this should happen, we should anticipate strong reactions, for the district has become a visible spiritual symbol. Positions on both sides would be hardened and ghetto leaders and community people will be even more impressed with the impossibility of achieving change within the present structure. Solutions and strategies will become more radical and confrontations will increase. In the end, however, our guess is that there will be many more Ocean Hill-Brownsvilles to take its place.

Questions:

1. What are some of the more important results of increased community participation in education?

2. List the advantages you can see for the hiring of non-white principals to serve minority group schools.

3. Why has the apathy of the black parents decreased in the Ocean Hill-Brownsville School District?

DECENTRALIZATION:
ISSUES AND COMMENTS

By DELBERT K. CLEAR

One of the most recent forces currently shaping public education is the demand for changing the large educational bureaucracies of urban school systems in order to relieve the impersonal, sometimes irrational attributes that have come to characterize them.[1] Although "decentralization" is the word that is used most frequently to describe the process through which the large organizations are to be made more responsive to individuals, all users of the word do not have the same things in mind.

A district that is heavily oriented to central office decision-making, for instance, could decentralize by increasing the decision making authority of local school principals and teaching staffs. It could also decentralize by providing local schools' constituents, both parent and student, a greater voice in the operation of their schools. Decentralization following the former path would result in diffusion of decision-making within the existing system. Following the latter course would result in bringing additional groups into the organizational decision-making structures.

Both of these arrangements are familiar to educators. Systems in which the principals and teachers have considerable authority are not uncommon, and constituent control of education is not revolutionary in American public education. It is one of its basic tenets.

THE FAILURE OF CENTRALIZATION

But large urban school systems typically have been so centralized that neither diffuse decision-making nor constituent control has occurred. Elected or appointed boards only vaguely represent the various sub-communities encompassed by urban systems. Size, alone, results in tremendous gaps growing between constituent desires and the capacity of representatives to reflect them. Organizational functionaries aggravate the situation when they lose sight of their status as public employees with a responsibility to serve not the systems' self-perpetuating processes but the organizations' clients.

Such lack of direct influence on schools does not often become an explosive issue so long as the schools generally reflect the values and expectations of constituents. But the evidence that abounds today in urban school systems indicates that some of the schools in the nation's cities do not,

---

Reprinted with permission from *The Clearing House* (January 1970).

generally, reflect the values and expectations of their constituents. Urban areas are made up of many sub-communities, some of which have or are in the process of developing distinct identities based on their unique ethnic, social, and cultural characteristics, and the practice of imposing standardized curricula throughout large systems has not been conducive to local diversity, and has, in many cases, resulted in educational offerings with which students and parents are unable to identify.[2]

Further, it seems apparent that the centralized systems have not been able to deliver a satisfactory educational product in many areas. In recent months, the increasing demand for decentralization has been led by constituents of local schools who are dissatisfied with the education their children are receiving, and there is no denying the stark fact that the systems have no defense against the charge that they have failed to educate many children beyond minimum levels of communication, computational, and social skills.[3] Thus, urban school officials must realize that demands for decentralization have been generated by the failure of current structures to meet the expectations of the people they have ostensibly been created to serve.

Consequently, it would be a serious mistake for the administration of a large, urban district to respond to community pressure for decentralization by merely shifting decision-making responsibility within the existing organization, such as giving building principals broader powers or giving teachers a larger voice in educational policy. When local urban communities request decentralization they have in mind increasing the amount of influence that flows directly out of immediate constituents into the day-to-day operation of their local schools.

Decentralization in this context means participation of local interest groups in policy determination and operational decision-making at the individual school level. Since there are few precedents for subdividing large bureaucratic systems in response to such demands, systems embarking on programs of decentralization need to consider the implications of the actions they contemplate.

THE PROBLEMS OF SUBDISTRICTING

The basic problem in such subdivision concerns defining the decision-making areas which are going to be delegated to local units for control, which are going to be retained by the central organization for overall control, and which are not going to be controlled by either, but will be covered by someone else, e.g., teachers' organizations, or student organizations. Lack of clear understanding both within and among these elements of school systems about their respective areas of jurisdiction can lead to sharp, sometimes acrimonious conflict. Major disruptions can occur if the bases for solving jurisdictional disputes are not clearly agreed upon prior to decentralization attempts. Consequently, discussions and negotiations preceding decentralization should include careful attention to establishing avenues of influence and defining areas of decision-making authority.

If it is assumed that any subdistricting plan will be a response to an actual or projected demand for increased local control over education, it becomes absolutely necessary for the macro-organization to survey carefully the expectations that the local community has for decentralization. Such surveys must be carefully designed and conducted so that the actual expectations, both of the community in general and of various sub-groups within it can be identified.

The characteristics of the local communities involved will determine the nature of the effort necessary at this step. If they are politically cohesive and have established local leadership and channels of communication, the task will be greatly simplified. If they lack cohesion and are represented by competing interest groups and individuals, it will be very difficult to identify community expectations in any manageable way. They will be so fragmented that programs to meet even a portion of them will be difficult.

MEETING COMMUNITY EXPECTATIONS

Whatever action is taken in surveying and assessing community desires and establishing mechanisms of action, care must be taken to avoid suggesting that all the expectations a community generates can be met. It will be impossible to please everybody, especially in fragmented communities where broad community feeling may be absent. State regulations and laws may place limits on what can be done, particularly in personnel, curriculum and certification. The traditions of the existing systems will not be easily broken.

Nevertheless, care must be taken to insure that some expectations will be met. The establishment must commit itself to finding areas where local communities can have influence. It must be imaginative in helping local communities to become involved in decision-making. It must not play an obstructionist role and serve mainly to discourage local communities from becoming active in the operation of their schools.

The educational experts in the existing systems must be particularly careful not to indiscriminately impose their judgments about educational policies on communities. All judgments are hypotheses, and, as such, are candidates for refinement through the development and testing of rival hypotheses. A local community needs to have just as much right to operate on its judgments as the experts in the systems have traditionally had to operate on theirs.

Both need, however, to recognize the mutual interest they have in providing children and young people with maximum educational opportunities. Resources must not be wastefully expended in arguments or competition over whose judgments are the most true. They must be expended in finding out how to provide the community's children with the best possible education.

DEVELOPING COMMUNITY COHESION

Although some organization and community cohesion will have to be present in a community before any decisions about meeting requests for control over schools can be made, it would be a mistake to be unduly restrictive on this point. Political sophistication can hardly be expected to develop without political experience, but if established organizations are overly cautious in delegating responsibility and acceding to requests for influence in decision-making, then political experience never can occur. There will be mistakes, to be certain, but experienced organizational functionaries must grant a wide toleration for error at the early stages. This is not a particularly revolutionary notion, for mistakes have never been exclusively the domain of the inexperienced—the experts make them too.

Further, it can be shown that cohesion is not necessarily a prerequisite to effective community action. The problem at hand, indeed, can generate cohesion where it seems to be absent. Both in New York City and in Washington, D.C., where community control of schools is being placed into effect, the communities involved developed cohesion and political sophistication very rapidly once they were given real responsibility for decision-making in the schools.[4]

It is the judgment of the participants and many observers of these projects that the potential for community cohesion exists virtually everywhere in our society. It only needs to be given opportunity to develop within a framework that is committed to the long-run wisdom of the democratic process and the capacity of people to learn from experience. Again, this is not revolutionary. Learning through participation is a tradition in American political history.

ESTABLISHING DOMAINS OF "SOVEREIGNTY"

Although pressure for decentralization and local control may come largely from sources outside of the existing school organization, as such, the capacity to make smooth changes toward decentralization is mostly within the power of the established system. A local community, for instance, might define successful decentralization to be local citizens contributing in a real and direct manner to what occurs in local classrooms. It might propose that local constituents have a voice in the selection and retention of local administrators and teachers or in the selection and use of instructional materials. It might expect to be able to control the expenditure of local budget allocations.

In most urban systems the power to make such decisions is currently held by organizational functionaries, frequently at the central office level. Hence, it is well within their power to provide for smooth transition from centralized decision-making to decentralization and local control. If they willingly grant restructuring of decision-making processes to meet the community requests, things can go well. If they resist, power struggles may ensue.

It is imperative, therefore, that the macro-organization and its sub-elements (e.g. the administrators', the teachers', or other employees' groups) be willing to relinquish decision-making power to the local communities. There can be no place for obstructionism based on the contention that a suggestion is impossible because it never has been done, or would be difficult, or would be complex, or might not work.

The organization must not restrict itself to conventional patterns of community influence—P.T.A.'s, advisory groups, etc.—it must be creative in providing for community participation in educational decision-making. Such devices as home visitations, student-parent surveys, student-parent classes, community organization, and parent-teacher conferences may have potential for obtaining constituent inputs, and the establishment of local school boards or councils with clear domains of "sovereignty" might be a good way to provide for community influence on the character of local schools.

There must be commitment that the range of possible practices is nearly infinite and no alternative to current procedures should be discarded until it has been well examined, including trial attempts, if necessary, and found wanting. And it must be assumed that constituents, though they may not be professionally trained educators, can be made part of this evaluation process.

This is occurring in Washington, D.C., where the system committed itself to the idea of decentralization by extending rather broad decision-making powers to the constituents of local school buildings. Thus, the system *helps* local citizens develop areas of authority. To date, it has been making a relatively smooth transition from centralized decision-making to local control.[5]

THE RELUCTANCE TO RELINQUISH AUTHORITY

Regardless of pressures, commitments, and even such experience as exists, however, realignment of decision-making authority within school systems will not come easily. Various sub-groups within them can be expected to give up or share decision-making domains reluctantly, especially where a tradition exists of one group or individual holding sole responsibility.

For example, school boards and administrators have not easily accepted the idea of sharing decision-making with teachers through negotiations. It has taken the force of state legislation, in most cases, to bring it into being.[6] There will likely be even more reluctance to sharing responsibility with local parent groups, for such groups would seem to be, at least initially, outside of the organization, as such.

This is in contrast to negotiations, which shifts responsibility *within* the organization, with the control potential of the organizational sanctioning structure (both positive and negative) remaining in effect. Such sanctions would be of little or no consequence to a community group, which would operate with some degree of sovereignty and, as such, be in a position to *control,* not be controlled by, the organizational functions it relates to. This potential, which is reminiscent of the community schools of days past, will cause organizational incumbents to be apprehensive.

Duly elected or appointed *central boards of education* will want to be certain that their own demise is not implied by any decentralization plans presented to them. But since local groups will want a degree of policy-making power for *their* schools, some changes in the central board's prerogatives seems to be necessary. If the board reacts to this with fearful protection of its responsibilities, little can come of decentralization, short of an open power struggle. But if the central board views the situation as an opportunity to move toward a division of responsibility, with provision made for both centralized and local level decision-making domains, the basis for accommodation is present.

Established boards must not view decentralization as a weakening process. It must view it as an opportunity to provide for decision-making at its most appropriate level. It might be useful for school boards to think of decentralization as giving them an opportunity to specialize to some extent, thus being able to develop real expertise in a limited sphere. Taxation, for instance, would be a natural central function. Negotiating master personnel policies might be another, as would be the establishment of specialized educational services.

Policy-making that might be allowed to vary according to specific community desire would include local work conditions, local curricular offerings, planning for local facilities and budget expenditures, all within the broad parameters of district and state legal frameworks.

Administrators, at all levels, will likely resist giving up decision-making authority. Part of their motivation will be a genuine, though not necessarily valid concern that the students will not receive a good education if policy decisions are taken out of the hands of professionalized educators. But part of their motivation will be opposition, in principle, to further weakening of their positions because most, if not all, of the so-called gains of teachers over the past decade have been won at the expense of administrators. They are not likely to accept easily even *further* erosion of their decision-making powers without some clear idea as to what the final role of the public school administrator is to be.

Systems going into decentralization should therefore define as carefully as possible what the administrator in the new system will be and do. Authority that will remain his should be clearly described. Areas he will share will need clear shaping, and areas where he will no longer have authority will need to be defined and accepted. This will be a monumental task because there is some suggestion that the new role of the school administrator will be substantially different than current ones.

Teachers, too, can be expected to be apprehensive about decentralization to the extent that it connotes their relinquishing decision-making authority or classroom sovereignty. They will be particularly reluctant to give up or share authority that they have recently gained through negotiations, especially if the victory was won only after protracted intra-organizational struggle. To give up or share any of such authority would seem to be backward or weakening moves.

Further, the professionalization of teaching will lead to resistance to relinquish decision-making. A basic tenet of the professional is that his field is specialized to such an extent that only those with long training and socialization are competent to make decisions in it. Consequently, any community desire to make curricular or instructional decisions will be resisted by the teachers.

Changes that threaten welfare and working conditions that teachers are accustomed to, will be even more sensitive, perhaps. These will be especially critical in systems where complex procedures and provisions are written into contracts and agreements, whether union or non-union negotiated. In such districts, it will likely be necessary to begin thinking in terms of master and sub-contracts. The former might cover general conditions, such as salaries, district tenure, etc., while the latter might cover such things as length of work day, alignment of duties and responsibilities, building tenure, etc.

STUDENT PARTICIPATION IN DECISION-MAKING

The student boycotts that occurred in some Chicago secondary schools during the Fall of 1968, the frequent student unrest in many colleges and universities, and the appearance of so-called underground newspapers in many secondary schools around the nation are evidence that students, too, are becoming interested in participating in the decisions that influence their lives. This will present even greater problems than increasing local community control.

Student groups, at least on the secondary level, may ask for decision-making authority in areas where the *community* wants it retained, either by school officials, or by the community—in any event, by *adults.* Even if school people decide to extend more responsibility to students, the communities may resist. Thus the schools may find that certain decisions aren't theirs to make. The result will be that the school people may find themselves in the middle of the students' struggle to win further emancipation from parental and adult control.

All representatives of adult society are likely to find this struggle a difficult one to evaluate. Granting real authority and responsibility to students is quite foreign to the traditions of American education. It goes against the value structures within which public schools are erected. Students, according to the traditional model, should be compliant recipients of the cultural wisdom handed down by adults.

Such programs as student government, student activities, and advisory committees are supposed to provide them training for the magic moment when they become full-fledged participating members of our decision-making processes. At the same time, the programs are supposed to provide an outlet for the students' fledgling yearnings to participate in the democratic processes. Unfortunately, provisions for adult veto tends to make a sham out of such programs. Or even worse, student recommendations are ignored, giving the impression that the process, not the substance, of participation is valuable.

At any rate, students are rarely allowed enough freedom to make errors of judgment (as defined by adults). But such protection may not be wise, in the long run, for it is doubtful if the responsibilities of decision-making can be learned without making a few mistakes and profiting from them. Whatever direction student participation takes, it seems evident that here, just as in community control, facsimilies of decision-making will not be sufficient. Some agreement must be made between the parents, the schools, and the students concerning acceptable and meaningful areas of student decision-making.

RESISTANCE BASED ON FEAR

Secretaries, custodians, and other service and maintenance personnel may be affected by giving local communities greater voice in school affairs. Although there appears to be less potential for conflict of interest between local decision-making and those intra-organizational groups than with the professional staff, the possibility must not be overlooked. Unions, in particular, will be very interested in any changes in decision-making that may result in their having to negotiate *separately* with each local unit. As with teachers' organizations, the master contract-subcontract approach may offer the best potential for a workable combination of centralized and local negotiating.

Individual occupants of positions throughout the existing systems will also resist changes in reassignment of responsibility for decision-making. Such resistance may be solely a manifestation of blind opposition to change, and will be difficult to deal with, since it may be based on various kinds of fear.

Fear may arise from threats to individuals' self-concept that changes in patterns of responsibility are perceived to imply. This will be particularly true where responsibility for certain decisions is taken from an organizational incumbent and placed somewhere else—either within the organization or without. Such a move implies that the existing decision-maker is inadequate, which is a direct threat to his status and self-concept. This could be softened by careful redefinition of old positions where possible to allow for increased effectiveness in a more circumscribed scope. Of course, if the position or task-area is being eliminated entirely and its responsibility transferred elsewhere, no amount of redefinition will alter the condition that retraining or reassignment will be necessary if the individual wishes to remain within the organization.

Resistance to realignment of responsibility may also be based on economic fear. If current functionaries are given smaller decision-making domains, justification for current levels of economic rewards is jeopardized. Individual incumbents, therefore, can be expected to resist any changes which take authority away from them. Indeed, when the pressure from outside begins to build, they will fight for their organizational lives, because transfer of responsibility to extra-organizational sources leaves them with nothing to do. The only solution to the obstruction that economic fear creates seems to be some assurance that all changes will be accompanied by humanitarian concern for the welfare of affected people.

Fear that is neither status nor economically based also arises, and is very difficult to deal with. Incumbents who have a sense of mission about their positions frequently develop assumptions that they, or at least their positions, are virtually indispensable to the education of the children of the district.

Consequently, when changes in the authority and responsibility structures are proposed, some persons can generate genuine apprehension over the organization's continued capacity to accomplish its goals. Arguments to the contrary encounter stubborn opposition, inasmuch as acceptance of shared or fragmented decision-making would connote willful acceptance of second-rate education for the children. This type of fear is reflected in the often-heard remark of school principals that "someone has to be responsible for seeing that the students in this school receive a good education."

SUMMARY AND CONCLUSION

Insofar as possible, the intra-organizational conflicts over decision-making domains should be settled prior to the time the community groups enter discussions. It would present a sorry picture, indeed, for local schools' constituents to be caught up in the system's internal power struggles. Real care, however, must be taken to insure that the intra-organizational discussions are predicated on the notion that as much decision-making authority as possible should be potentially available to constituents. The temptation to present the newcomers with an authority structure already divided up such that only innocuous realms of decision-making remain for them, must be resisted.

When urban school systems encounter requests from community groups for increased local decision-making, they must take the above variables into account. The existing power structures must not be threatened into inaction by the apparent inexperience of constituents in educational decision-making. The organization must commit itself to the long-run efficacy of the democratic process and operate from a base of liberal optimism about the capacity of people to learn from experience. Discussions about the division of decision-making authority will have to include the representatives of the administration, the teachers, the service personnel, and the students, as well as the community-interest groups.

These discussions will be complex. Changes will not come easily. But they must come. There will be mistakes, to be sure, but the established power structures must grant a rather wide toleration for error at the early stages. Learning from mistakes is a well-practiced tradition in American political history.

But the local communities must realize that power is not license. They must realize that heavy responsibility goes with making decisions; gaining credit, good or bad, is the legitimate by-product of making decisions. There will be no scapegoats to blame if their decisions do not provide the results they seek.

FOOTNOTES:

[1] A revealing report on the largest of the urban educational bureaucracies was provided by David Rogers, *110 Livingston Street: Politics and Bureaucracy in the New York Public Schools,* (New York: Random House, 1968). Numerous other books and monographs attest to the problems that plague large, urban systems. See, for instance, Aaron V. Cicourel and John I. Kitsuse, *The Educational Decision-Makers,* (New York: Bobbs-Merrill, 1963); Marilyn Gittell, *Educating an Urban Population* (Beverly Hills: Sage Publications, 1967) and William R. Odell and Associates, *Educational Survey Report for the Philadelphia Board of Public Education,* (Philadelphia: Board of Public Education, 1965). A review of recent critical accounts of urban systems was provided by Harold W. Sobel, "The New Wave of Educational Literature," Phi Delta Kappan, October 1968.

[2] Miriam L. Goldberg, "Factors Affecting Educational Attainment in Depressed Urban Areas," in A. Harry Passow, ed., *Education in Depressed Areas,* (New York: Teachers College, 1963) pp. 68-69; Clement E. Vontress, "Our Demoralizing Slum Schools," in August Kerber and Barbara Bommarito, eds., *The Schools and the Urban Crisis,* (New York: Holt, Rinehart and Winston, 1965) pp. 57-66.

[3] James B. Conant, *Slums and Suburbs* (New York: McGraw-Hill, 1961); Robert J. Havighurst, *The Public Schools of Chicago: A Survey Report,* (Chicago: Board of Education, 1964). Frederick Shaw, "Educating Culturally Deprived Youth in Urban Centers," in August Kerber and Barbara Bommarito, eds., *The Schools and the Urban Crisis,* (New York: Holt, Rinehart, and Winston, 1965) pp. 67-73; Charles E. Silberman, *Crisis in Black and White,* (New York: Vintage, 1964).

[4] This impression was developed by the author as he talked with participants in the New York City and Washington, D.C. decentralization projects. This development was said to have been particularly visible in the I.S. 201 area of the New York City system when the controversy over the placement of a new junior high school generated wide community cohesion for its control.

[5] This impression was developed by the author as he talked with participants in the District's Morgan-Hill School decentralization project. Support for this is found in various correspondence of the D.C. School Superintendent, Board of Education, and other district officials, May to December, 1968.

[6] Myron Liberman and Michael H. Moskow, *Collective Negotiations for Teachers: An Approach to School Administration,* (Chicago: Rand McNally, 1966) pp. 47-54; E. Wright Bakke, "Teachers, School Boards, and Employment Relationships," *The Quarterly,* Vol. 19, No. 4, June 1968. p. 3.

Questions:

1. Centralization has been described as a barrier to a good education. List three weaknesses of centralization which adversely affect education.

2. State your position regarding decentralization for the purpose of increasing local control over education.

3. Do the problems that you foresee resulting from decentralization affect education in a positive or negative manner? Explain.

MALNUTRITION AND LEARNING

By MERRILL S. READ

Increasing knowledge of the effects of malnutrition, combined with the social consciousness of the 1960's, has turned national attention to the nutritional status of Americans. Growing evidence that nutrition may affect intellectual and behavioral as well as physical growth has stimulated efforts to determine the extent of malnutrition in the United States and to assess its long-term impact.

Experts disagree about the extent of malnutrition in America partly because of a confusion of terms. Malnutrition is not synonymous with hunger but, of course, may result from long periods of insufficient food. Hunger can be easily and immediately relieved with food; malnutrition requires prolonged rehabilitation and may leave lasting effects.

Here malnutrition is defined as a state in which an individual lacks one or more nutrients to the extent that specific symptoms and conditions appear (such as anemia, goiter, rickets, or vitamin deficiencies) or retardation in physical development occurs. Severe malnutrition refers to two types of diseases resulting from prolonged protein and/or calorie insufficiency in early childhood: Marasmus results from severe restriction of food intake—particularly of calories—from birth or shortly after and is manifest in wasting of the tissues and severe growth retardation. Kwashiorkor, a result of inadequate protein intake, occurs most often when the child changes from breast or bottle milk to foods high in starch but low in protein. It produces extreme stunting of growth, water retention, skin sores, and discoloration of the hair to red or blond. Both diseases cause death if untreated.

Malnutrition is most often associated with poverty. Yet, determining its effects on a given individual is extremely difficult since many other factors influence human growth and behavioral development, including an individual's innate potential, his health status, the conditions in which he lives, and his relationships with his family and the rest of society.

The National Nutrition Survey, begun in 1968 and being carried out by the Department of Health, Education, and Welfare, is the first comprehensive effort to assess the nutritional status of the U.S. population. Preliminary results have been reported on the study of 12,000 people of all ages, randomly selected in poverty pockets in two States and several smaller areas; ultimately the sample will include pockets in 10 or more States. Because of the poverty orientation of

Reprinted with permission from *American Education* (December 1969), by permission of Department of Health, Education and Welfare, Washington, D. C. 20202.

these studies, the majority of people examined were Negroes, although other ethnic groups were included.

The survey found an unexpectedly high prevalence of symptoms associated with malnutrition. Four to five percent of the people examined exhibited symptoms sometimes associated with severe malnutrition, although very few cases of marasmus or kwashiorkor were found. One-third of the children under six years old and 15 percent of the total sample population were found to have low blood hemoglobin levels diagnosed as anemia or iron deficiency.

About 17 percent — nearly 2,000 of those examined—showed abnormally low protein levels in their blood. Vitamin D, necessary for the absorption of calcium and the normal development of bones, was found to be lower than normal in the blood of 58 children under six years of age, and 18 cases of rickets were diagnosed. Deficiencies in vitamins A and C and in iodine were also found in a significant number of persons examined.

Other surveys carried out in the United States generally confirm the existence among the poor of the nutritional problems found in the National Survey. One study compared 558 preschool children from several economic levels in 20 counties in Mississippi. The 210 children from poor families were found to eat fewer calories and to take in significantly less protein, calcium, and vitamin C than the other groups; they also were considerably smaller and lighter physically.

Surveys have shown that the average North American Indian family of five persons, living on a reservation, attempts to survive on an annual income below $2,000. A study of 195 Apache children between one and six years old disclosed that one-third of them had anemia and deficiencies in vitamins A and C. Virtually all 165 children examined in one clinic had dental disease; half the cases were described as severe. In another group of 126 families, marked growth retardation was seen in children through age five years. Cases of severe malnutrition in children have also been found on Navajo reservations in the Southwest.

The results of these surveys are preliminary and in many cases cannot be directly compared. However, in the absence of complete national statistics, these studies suggest that multiple deficiencies of specific nutrients occur in varying degrees and in higher-than-expected proportions among poor people. A major factor contributing to the poor nourishment of infants is the decline of breast feeding, combined with inadequate information about food substitutes and poor sanitary conditions in the use of alternate foods.

The consequences of malnutrition depend on the time in the life of the individual when nutritional deficits occur, as well as on their severity and duration. The brain may be damaged by various influences during the period of fastest growth, which in human beings occurs from about five months before to about 10 months after birth. At the end of the first year the brain has achieved approximately 70 percent of its adult weight, and by the end of the second year, it has practically completed its growth

The brain grows both by increase in the number of cells and by increase in the size of each cell. Experiments with rats, made by Myron Winick of the Cornell University Medical College in New York, show that severe malnutrition during the period of cell division permanently reduces the total number of cells despite subsequent nutritional rehabilitation. Severe food restriction later during

MALNUTRITION AND LEARNING

By MERRILL S. READ

Increasing knowledge of the effects of malnutrition, combined with the social consciousness of the 1960's, has turned national attention to the nutritional status of Americans. Growing evidence that nutrition may affect intellectual and behavioral as well as physical growth has stimulated efforts to determine the extent of malnutrition in the United States and to assess its long-term impact.

Experts disagree about the extent of malnutrition in America partly because of a confusion of terms. Malnutrition is not synonymous with hunger but, of course, may result from long periods of insufficient food. Hunger can be easily and immediately relieved with food; malnutrition requires prolonged rehabilitation and may leave lasting effects.

Here malnutrition is defined as a state in which an individual lacks one or more nutrients to the extent that specific symptoms and conditions appear (such as anemia, goiter, rickets, or vitamin deficiencies) or retardation in physical development occurs. Severe malnutrition refers to two types of diseases resulting from prolonged protein and/or calorie insufficiency in early childhood: Marasmus results from severe restriction of food intake—particularly of calories—from birth or shortly after and is manifest in wasting of the tissues and severe growth retardation. Kwashiorkor, a result of inadequate protein intake, occurs most often when the child changes from breast or bottle milk to foods high in starch but low in protein. It produces extreme stunting of growth, water retention, skin sores, and discoloration of the hair to red or blond. Both diseases cause death if untreated.

Malnutrition is most often associated with poverty. Yet, determining its effects on a given individual is extremely difficult since many other factors influence human growth and behavioral development, including an individual's innate potential, his health status, the conditions in which he lives, and his relationships with his family and the rest of society.

The National Nutrition Survey, begun in 1968 and being carried out by the Department of Health, Education, and Welfare, is the first comprehensive effort to assess the nutritional status of the U.S. population. Preliminary results have been reported on the study of 12,000 people of all ages, randomly selected in poverty pockets in two States and several smaller areas; ultimately the sample will include pockets in 10 or more States. Because of the poverty orientation of

Reprinted with permission from *American Education* (December 1969), by permission of Department of Health, Education and Welfare, Washington, D. C. 20202.

child's fear of the new hospital environment also may inhibit his response to learning opportunities. Pertinent recent studies have shown that social isolation may reduce the size and number of cells in rat brain much the same as malnutrition.

The evidence strongly supports the conclusion that early severe malnutrition is associated with intellectual impairment. However, carefully planned studies are needed to determine whether any effects are due solely to malnutrition or to the unique constellation of environmental factors surrounding the malnourished hospitalized child who has most often been the subject for these studies.

Another major question concerns the effects of mild to moderate malnutrition on intellectual growth. These levels of undernutrition do not necessarily imperil survival, and hospitalization is not normally required, but they may cause growth retardation. Here there are few studies upon which to base a judgment, but the effects, if any, would certainly be expected to be less than for protein-calorie malnutrition. Furthermore, the interplay between social, medical, genetic, and nutritional variables might be expected to play a more prominent role.

In an eight-year study of Mexican children, investigators found that intellectual performance at the time of entry into school appeared to be related to the child's history of malnutrition. After the children spent four to five years in school, however, this relationship disappeared, and differences in performance appeared to be related more closely to socioeconomic conditions and regularity of school attendance.

Hence, iron deficiency anemia is the most frequently observed nutritional problem among infants, preschool, and young children. Its effects upon learning and behavior have not been systematically investigated. One study of 28 children under the age of three who were admitted to an American hospital with iron deficiency has been reported. The subjects were matched with a group not having anemia. A year after discharge from the hospital, the children who had had anemia were found to have more illnesses, more feeding difficulties, and more behavioral problems than those in the other group. The investigators attributed the behavioral deficits to parental failure and family disintegration rather than to nutritional insufficiency.

A key problem in determining whether malnutrition, disease, or the social environmental factors of poverty have the greatest effect on mental development hinges on the timing of the testing. Intellectual and behavioral measurements are best made in middle childhood, whereas the nutritional insult, if it has an effect, probably occurs in infancy. Long term studies monitoring nutritional intake and behavior development are essential.

A study that may provide some answers is now being done in Guatemala where many people still live in small, isolated villages, subsist on an inadequate diet, and till the overworked fields of their ancestors. Without adequate medical care many babies die before their first birthday, and those who survive are short and underdeveloped. In the villages under study, all participants receive heretofore unavailable medical care with special attention given to pregnant women, infants, and young children. The villages are studied in pairs so that they are as much alike as possible on socioeconomic, public health, cultural, and other bases. Each village in a pair receives added stimulation through a carefully planned visitation and examination program. One village in each pair also receives a specially designed nutritional supplement. Thus the investigators hope to define the effects of better nutrition as they follow the growth and development of the children over the first seven years of life.

Up to now it has been generally assumed that intellectual deficits would be proportional to the degree of malnutrition imposed. On the other hand, it is also possible that there may be a level of malnutrition in infancy below which neurological structures are so altered that retarded intellectual development is irreversible. Above this threshold, however, under-nutrition would have no serious consequences for neurological development itself. Genetic endowment and sociological factors surrounding malnutrition would then be expected to exert increasingly significant effects on intellectual ability.

Those who have worked with undernourished or hungry children know that they exhibit behavioral alterations. These include apathy, lethargy, inability to pay attention, and perhaps, overconcern about food to such a degree that responses to classroom stimuli do not occur. A child in such condition no longer meets the expectations of his family or teachers. He begins to live in a world of his own and may seek recognition or gain attention by ways that disrupt learning experiences.

Learning is increasingly recognized as progressing in stages, each stage becoming a foundation for the next. By not responding to early stimulation, the child gradually becomes unable to benefit from "normal" experiences at a later period. He fails to learn, not because the genetic potential or neurological structures are absent, but because he lacks the experiential foundation. Improved nutrition alone will not correct this deficit. Neither will improved educational opportunities by themselves. Both must be provided in a coordinated program to develop the child's potential.

Foremost among the problems requiring resolution is the development of a battery of tests that can measure the behavioral and social variables involved and that are applicable to varied social groups. These tests need to be addressed to the changes that we now suspect are related to malnutrition. It is hoped that they will detect those low levels of change that might be expected under less severe nutritional conditions.

Before firm conclusions can be drawn that malnutrition per se is the cause of mental subnormality, carefully designed studies will be required to clarify the role of parents and of the social and environmental factors that accompany malnutrition. Because research cannot at this time give an unequivocal or complete answer to the question of what effect malnutrition has on intellectual development is no reason to delay programs for improving the nutritional status and eating practices of mothers and infants. Information demonstrating the benefits of good nutrition in improved health and physical growth already justify such efforts.

Question:

1. Prepare a brief description of a compensatory program you would design to limit or eliminate the brain damage which occurs from five months before to ten months after birth.

AGGRESSION IN THE CLASSROOM

By FRITZ REDL

● There's plenty of minor aggression in the classroom that nobody objects to. The real problem is the aggression that prevents good teaching and good classroom life. This aggression comes primarily from three areas.

First, it is an input from the home or from the community. A teen-ager gets hopping mad at his old man, but he doesn't dare let off steam until he gets to school. Now, the teacher didn't produce the aggression, but it's there and he's got to handle it.

Second, is the discharge from within. Some youngster sits there daydreaming, and all of a sudden during a wild fantasy, he thinks of something that upsets him and he conks his neighbor on the head. None of them has done anything to him, and the teacher hasn't either. Something just burst out from within. (If youngsters are seriously disturbed, most of the aggression comes from way within, and neither they nor anyone else knows why.)

Third, the aggression is engendered right there in the classroom. It may be triggered either by what the teacher does that's right but that doesn't happen to fit the kid, or by God knows what—the kid's reaction to the group or to other kids, or to something that maybe the teacher wouldn't have done if he had stopped to think. But anyway, it's reactive to something in the environment at the moment.

Now, if I were a classroom teacher, I would like to know how much of which of those three packages is exploding before me, because it makes a difference in terms of long-range planning. It also makes some difference in terms of what to do at the moment. Most of the time we are not sure, but different sources of aggression smell different when we are confronted with them. Experienced teachers develop an uncanny skill at sensing "This is something the kid brought with him. I've got to help him recover from it before he acts it out." The outsider, though, wouldn't know.

Some aggression does not affect us directly because certain youngsters may be model pupils in the classroom, but then after school they may go out and rape or murder someone. So a youngster may be full of sick aggression without being a classroom problem.

On the other hand, there may be a great kid sitting over there who's bored stiff. He likes you a lot, but he gets mad at the fact that you bore him stiff. Finally, he's just had it, and he runs out and slams the door. A normal youngster like that whose aggression is classroom-produced is our problem. Too often, an

---

Reprinted with permission from *Today's Education* (September 1969).

article on aggression in the classroom concentrates on a few examples of youngsters who should have been in a mental hospital for the last 10 years anyway and ignores all the other kids who bother us.

The term *aggression* is so overused now, you've got to watch out for it. Don't ever let anybody trap you into discussing aggression without first asking him: "Listen, brother, which aggression are you talking about? What actually happened?" Because aggression has a wide range—all the way from reacting to boredom to wrestling at the wrong time in the wrong place with another pupil.

Discharge of surplus energy or of displaced needs from the home or neighborhood; loss of control in the face of seductive equipment like a slingshot or a knife or whatnot; personal battles with adults, other kids, the group, or the teacher—all these fall under the heading of aggression.

The way Joe or Jane expresses aggression, while not the end of what we're looking for, certainly should be the starting point. Unless you know what lies behind their behavior, you will have trouble knowing how to handle it. Sometimes you may understand perfectly well how come. So the question then is what do you do to help him, which is a separate matter from knowing what was cooking to begin with.

I want to give special warning here not to make aggression synonymous with violence. The two are not the same, although they are obviously related. There is a theme in violence that we can legitimately call aggression. On the other hand, not all violence comes from aggressive drives. The behavior is aggressive, but the basis may be quite different. Let me give a few illustrations of violence that does not spring from aggression.

Panic coping. A kid may get scared stiff, so scared that he doesn't know what to do anymore. So he does something violent; he tears something apart. The fact that the behavior is violent is important. But this child is not hyperaggressive; he is frightened and desperate.

The need to be heard. A frequent source of violence is the feeling that nobody listens. The child finally concludes that the only way to get someone to listen is to be violent enough. So when other avenues are blocked off, violence is a substitute for verbal and nonverbal communication.

The desire to display guts. If a kid is supposed to be tough, how can he show it? Who is going to believe it? "I'd better not let them know I'm scared. So I've got to find ways to show I'm brave." In order to do this in a peaceful life, he's got to create problems.

Demonstrating loyalty to the group code. This source of violence is not originally meant to be aggression for aggression's sake. ("If the rest of my gang thinks school is no good, I'd better show that I'm with them. So I put a thumbtack in the teacher's chair. I don't hate the teacher; too bad it's her rear that gets stung. But I'm a regular guy and I'm going to prove it.")

Risk taking—to study survival skills. For instance, how can a boy know if he can run fast enough to outrun the cop, unless he swipes something first? Or else picks a rat out of an ash can, swirls it by the tail, throws it in somebody's first-story window, and then hops over the garage roof fast before they can catch him? A kid has to know how good he is in handling a dangerous assignment.

The stink and the dust produced in the decay of group psychology. If a group suddenly gets anxious or panicky or wild or disorganized or elated or mad at each other, you get a lot of behavior that involves violence but that did not start as aggression. Although Joe and Jane may be doing something, they're not doing it as Joe and Jane but as members of a group.

Last on my list of violence that does not start with aggression but is secondary to it is, of course, *an invasion of societal turmoil from the outside.* Someone or something in the community ties a package of emotional TNT to the back of a kid and it blows up in the classroom. The kid responsible wasn't originally aggressive; he carries the whole load of community or neighborhood or subgroup aggression. As his teacher, you're just an innocent bystander. What he does has nothing to do with the way you taught him or whether you bawled him out or flunked him.

In short, there is some relationship between violence and aggression, but not a simple one. For teachers it's very important to begin to sense the difference between Joe's being loaded with personal anger at what you just did and the explosion that results when his TNT package goes off at a given time. They are different problems.

Now let me give a few abbreviated hints of what to do about various kinds of child behavior—hints that are not fancy enough to be written up much in books.

First, you sometimes need to get kids off the hook. The aggressive behavior is beginning but without having really been planned, and if you get pupils off the hook *now*, they don't have to continue. Another way of putting it is that you sometimes need to cut a contagion chain without making a big deal out of it. And in most cases knowing how to do this is very important in dealing with a normally well-behaved child as well as with a wild one.

Take Joe, for example. He's sitting over there shaking imaginary dice, and at the moment you're not too bothered. You catch his eye and he stops, but only momentarily. After a while everybody else gets interested. You want to cut that contagion chain now, because if you wait another five minutes, you'll have a mass problem on your hands.

If you interfere too early, everyone thinks you're a fusspot, a dope, or chicken, and you only aggravate things. If you don't interfere at the right time, you'll have trouble. Getting Joe off the hook at the right moment will stop his behavior without a big scene, and the rest of the group will not be too heavily afflicted. This skill of cutting contagion chains without making too much of a mess is, I think, one of the most important for anybody who deals with groups.

A second important technique for the practical handling of aggression in the classroom is signal interference. Signal interference in time saves nine. Very often teachers underestimate the possibility of stopping minor forms of misbehavior quite casually before the kid gets too carried away by it. They don't take the behavior seriously, because it isn't bothersome enough. So they wait until it does get bothersome enough, and by that time the situation is tense, the kid is already off his noodle, and anything they do now will have an explosive effect.

The big problem is that most teachers lack a good inventory of preaggression signals for their pupils. In some youngsters, the signals are easy to spot. Others apparently go aggressive all of a sudden from nowhere. That's because the teacher's radar doesn't pick up their signals. But if the teacher works at it, after a while he begins to get the messages from all around the room. One kid, for example, gets glassy-eyed and sits there quietly in a certain rigid position. If the teacher goes over and taps him on the shoulder, he'll go up like a rocket. Two minutes ago, if the teacher had gone around and said, "Come on, let's start working," that would have been fine.

A good many teachers—particularly those who are new to the class-room—do not know enough about the physiological and gestural signals that indicate the work-up to aggressive behavior. Everybody with experience understands them, but conveying this understanding to the other guy is hard. Apparently we don't think it's important because we don't have any fancy lingo for it, but if I were a beginning teacher, that's the kind of information I would like to have.

If you send me a kid with an unknown aggression work-up potential, I'd like to get to know that kid and figure out what he looks like before he goes off the handle. After that, I can tell at a glance that this is the moment to go over to him.

In observing classrooms and watching teachers with disturbed youngsters, I am constantly amazed at the terrific skill people with experience develop, and they can't ever explain it. What's more, they don't even mention it. They think it isn't worth discussing.

Let me describe one incident I observed:

A kid is sitting stiffly at his desk, obviously determined that he "ain't gonna do *nothing.*" The teacher walks over to him, pats him on the shoulder, and says: "Now, how about it? You don't feel so good, huh?" And he doesn't say anything. What does she do then? She says: "OK, I'll come back in a while. Maybe by then you'll be feeling better." That's all. She doesn't push him ("Why don't you. . .? What's the matter with you? What kind of family do you come from, anyway?")

She uses her judgment, and sooner or later he's over the hump. His face clears up; his posture is relaxed. Then she comes over and puts the pencil in his hand and he starts working.

Now, number three: Watch out for the choreography of the dare. In our present society we all have an insatiable, unquenchable thirst for tribal rituals. We still perform tribal dances. Take this scene:

We have what looks like a relatively normal classroom at·the moment. Here is Joe back there, who wishes I'd leave him alone. But he knows I'm a nice guy, that I've got to make a living, after all. And I'm pretty harmless, though a little crazy, maybe.

Still, somehow, the noise gets too loud, and I finally say: "Listen, you, you'd better stop that now." Then maybe things get worse, and maybe by this time I'm angry, too. So I say: "All right, now, if you can't be quiet here, why don't you go out and cool off?"

Let's assume I'm relatively lucky in my diagnosis, and the youngster gets up and moves to the door, but on the way he mumbles something under his breath. If I ask him what he said, he probably feels he has to lie—so I make a liar out of him. Or if he is decently honest, I have to send him to the principal.

The foregoing is one way the scene can be played. But it also can be played differently. If Joe is sensitive of his prestige in the group, and I happen to have adults looking over my shoulder, then both of us become involved in a tribal dance. He has to say, "Make me," and I have to say, "All right. I'll make you." So either I try to bounce him or I call the principal or whatnot. Then for three weeks, lots of procedures go on— all nonsensical and having nothing to do with the original issue. Joe's become a discipline case, almost.

What I've described here is a personal interaction, a limit-setting process of a very simple nature, really. Most of the time it works like a charm, but in the second instance it became a tribal dance. If I were a principal assigning teachers to study halls or other large groups, I would like to know how vulnerable they are to the tribal dance routine, because in a dare situation the pressure is terrific. If you send me a kid who is tough, I don't mind. But I would like to know how involved this kid is in a tribal dance.

You see, some kids who are plenty tough don't fall for that kind of nonsense. In fact, some of my best delinquents would never be so stupid as that. If I really challenged them, they would think: "All right, so let the guy have his little victory for a change. So what! So I go out. I'm tough enough. Nobody will think I gave in." If, however, the youngster isn't really tough enough, but has to pretend he is, then he has to do the tribal dance in order to impress the others with his plumage, or whatever.

This is a big danger. And many a teacher could avoid many a large discipline problem if he were able to recognize the first drum beats of a tribal dance. Very often we push relatively tough kids who mean well into tribal dances because we are unaware of the position they are in. At other times, we do not interfere when we should because we are too afraid we'll provoke a tribal dance when actually we wouldn't.

So the tribal dance is a whole phenomenon—separate from the usual problem of discipline—that is a rather deep psychological problem.

Number four: Watch out for the subsurface effect. Whatever I do also has a side effect, and it is not always visible right now. If we are aware of what else happens besides the immediate effect of what we do, we won't simply say, "Because I blamed him for being noisy or because I praised him for being quiet, everything is hunky-dory right now."

So it's important to look with one eye to the possible nonvisible side effect. I can do something about it afterwards, but only if I'm on the lookout for it. Like that boy we've been talking about. Let's say he leaves the room and doesn't start the tribal dance. In that case, I'll want to make sure we have a brief get-together afterwards to tell him that I appreciate his doing what I asked and that I'll defend his reputation with the rest of the kids. I'll say that there are no hard feelings; it was just that I couldn't let him get so loud in class. That's all; nothing more.

If you have to live with aggression, at least try not to breed it. We breed it, of course, by exposing even otherwise normal boys and girls to experiences, to space arrangements, to life situations that invariably produce inner frustration.

For instance, if I bore a youngster, I expose him to frustration. Or, if I have to delay giving help that is needed—say, a boy over there is stuck in the middle of a long division problem, and I can't get to him for a while because I have to be over here with the others. Sooner or later he's had it, and he gets mad.

Or I may breed aggression if I intervene with too little sympathy. If a youngster is doing something interesting, something he likes, do I say, "Get going this minute. Do you want to be late again?" when I could just as well say,

"Look, I'm sorry to have to break that up, but you know we've got to get out now."

One final point: Don't forget that from time to time, your own aggression will start showing. As you probably are aware, your hostile feelings and how you deal with them make a story no less complex and touchy than the one just presented. That your anger may be righteous and justified is not the only issue. You must ask yourself some questions: How does my anger make be behave in the classroom? Which (if any) of the behaviors it produces in me seem helpful in reducing youngsters' aggressive feelings, and which ones just make matters worse? Figuring this out requires clear thinking and real objectivity, but it is worth the effort. Your professional obligation is to handle your own aggression in such a way that the individual pupil or the class can manage the spillover effect.

Questions:

1. Which of the seven illustrations of violence that do no spring from aggression do you feel most prevents effective instruction and good classroom life?

2. Evaluate the technique used by the teacher on the kid who is sitting stiffly at his desk.

3. Which statements are facts and which are opinions in child behavior example number three regarding tribal dance?

CHARACTERISTICS ASSOCIATED WITH POPULARITY AMONG DIFFERENT RACIAL AND SOCIOECONOMIC GROUPS OF CHILDREN [1]

By RICHARD W. BROZOVICH[2]

ABSTRACT

A reputation test was used to discover the characteristics associated with popularity among children in sixth grade classrooms differing in SES and racial composition. The relationship of SES, race, sex of rater, and sex of ratee to the correlates of popularity was studied. Contrary to expectation, culturally deprived children showed higher associations between popularity and characteristics compatible with success in the school situation than did children not culturally deprived. Race and sex differences in the correlates of popularity were found. It was concluded that generalities about the norms and values of children from various SES groups may not reflect the prevalent norms and values among children from a specific SES level in a classroom setting.

PEER GROUPS exert a powerful influence on the behavior of individual members of a group[3, 8]. Classroom group pressure may foster behavior in harmony or in conflict with educational goals. Coleman[1] found that the socioeconomic level of high schools was a powerful factor in its association with the values and behavior prevailing at these schools. Sherif and Sherif[9] have also demonstrated how the behavior of children is related to the values of their peer group. Since peer groups exert a strong influence on student behavior, it is important for educators to be aware of the relation of such factors as race, sex, and socioeconomic status to the characteristics and behavior approved by classroom members.

Currently there is much interest in the problem of educating children from culturally deprived and minority groups. Passow[7] reviewed some of the educational programs being used in culturally deprived areas. His review illustrates the importance of peer group value systems in determining the success of an educational program.

The purpose of this study was to discover the social value of certain characteristics for children in sixth-grade classrooms differing in socioeconomic level and racial composition. It was assumed that the popularity of individuals seen by the group as possessing certain characteristics reflected the social value of these characteristics. Three general hypotheses were tested:

1. Culturally deprived children show higher associations between popularity and characteristics which conflict with conformity to and success in the school situation than do children not culturally deprived.

Reprinted with permission from the *Journal of Educational Research* (July-August 1970).

2. Negro and white children of similar socioeconomic background have differences in the characteristics they associate with popularity.

3. Boys and girls have differences in the characteristics they associate with popularity for members of their own and the opposite sex.

METHOD

Subjects. The twelve sixth-grade classrooms used in this study were located in the Nashville City Schools. The classrooms used were selected on the basis of SES, racial composition, size, and sex distribution.

Six classrooms were used in which the children were from upper-lower class and lower-middle class families. The SES level of this group of children approximated the level which Maas[6] has called the "core culture." The other six classrooms were from families living in housing projects in the poorest sections of Nashville. Most of these children would fall under the general classification, "culturally deprived." Classrooms were used only if the SES level was homogeneous within the classroom.

Median income of the families living in the areas served by each school was the major criterion used in matching classrooms for SES level. The median incomes in the four SES x race classroom groups were: culturally deprived white—$2,600, culturally deprived Negro—$2,133, core culture white—$4,400, and core culture Negro—$3,300. Negro and white SES levels were not closely matched in absolute income for several reasons. Some of the income difference was related to a wage differential between the races for similar occupations. More important, if Negro and white absolute income were equated for SES levels, one would be faced with differences between the relative positions of the groups in their own reference communities. Educators and others familiar with the community felt that the groups used in this study were representative of the culturally deprived and core culture groups in both races.

No integrated classrooms were used in the study in order to avoid confounding the race and SES variables. Three classrooms at each SES level contained all white pupils, and three at each SES level contained all Negro pupils.

Classroom size ranged from twenty-five to thirty-five, and sex distribution was balanced. Three classrooms were tested for each combination of SES and race. This resulted in a total number of 371 subjects, with a range of 86—100 subjects in each combination of SES and race. No schools in which ability or achievement was a primary basis for classroom grouping were used in the study. Such grouping might have produced biased results on the test instrument used in the study.

PROCEDURE

A reputation test was used to measure the popularity of each child and the degree to which each child was seen by his peers as having certain traits and characteristics. Hartshorne, May, and Maller[2] are believed to have made the first use of this type of instrument in their studies of the nature of character in young children.

The reputation test consisted of bi-polar items which were designed to describe opposite poles of each characteristic. The popularity item, for example, had the question "which children in the classroom are the most popular?"

followed by eight blank spaces—four for boy's names and four for girl's names. The subjects were encouraged to supply the names of at least two boys and two girls for every item. The opposite pole for this item read, "which children in the classroom aren't popular at all?" A child's name present on the odd numbered pole of each item was scored as +1, while the presence of his name on the even numbered pole was scored as -1. The algebraic sum of these scores for each item was the child's score on that item.

The reliability of the reputation test item pairs was measured by retesting a culturally deprived Negro classroom after an interval of two days, and retesting a core culture white classroom after an interval of five days. Test-retest reliability coefficients of each item pair were determined for four sex-of-rater x sex-of-ratee combinations. The median reliability coefficient for the item pairs ranged from .74 to .96.

A score on the Lorge-Thorndike Intelligence Test was obtained from the school records for each child who had taken the test the previous school year. These scores were not available for a small percentage of the children.

Each classroom was tested as a group in a single session. The testing was completed during a 2-week period in May. Classroom teachers were given prior knowledge about the nature of the study, but were requested to tell their students only that the writer was working on a project that required the help of the students. After the teacher introduced the writer, the tests were distributed, and instructions taken from Klaus's[4] study were read.

The writer told the children to read the instructions at the top of the test silently while he read them aloud. The writer was available during the testing to answer any questions the children had. Each child received a complete list of the names of all the children in his class to assist him in recalling the complete names of all his classmates.

RESULTS AND DISCUSSION

Out of a total of 371 subjects, 349 were present when the reputation tests were administered. The largest number missing from any single classroom was three. Scores for each child on the various reputation test variables were obtained with each sex considered separately as raters. The relation between these variables and popularity was analyzed for each sex as ratees. This resulted in four separate analyses within each group of classrooms: boys as rated by boys, girls as rated by boys, boys as rated by girls, and girls as rated by girls.

There was a total of sixteen variable scores for each child, except for some children whose intelligence test scores were not available. Fifteen of these variables were the child's scores on the reputation test item pairs. The sixteenth variable score, available for most children, was an intelligence test score. Table 1 shows the overall median correlation between popularity and each of the other fifteen variables. These are the medians of the forty-eight correlations obtained for each variable when each of the twelve classrooms was divided into four sex-of-rater x sex-of-ratee classifications for purposes of the analysis. Table 1 also gives an abbreviated description of the traits or characteristics included in the reputation test.

Equivalences of the relationships between popularity and the other fifteen variable scores in the four SES x race combinations, and over the four sex-of-rater x sex-of-ratee combinations, were tested through analysis of variance procedures. The correlations between popularity and the other fifteen variables were determined separately for each of the three classrooms within each of the sixteen SES x race x sex-of-rater x sex-of-ratee combinations. The obtained correlation coefficients were transformed to Fisher's z values to assure their meeting the assumptions for analysis of variance. Analysis was then conducted at the .05 level of significance. The basic design used for analysis was a replicated type III design[5].

TABLE 1.–OVERALL MEDIAN CORRELATIONS BETWEEN POPULARITY AND EACH OF FIFTEEN VARIABLES

Variable Number	Abbreviated Description of Variable	Overall Median Correlation with Popularity
I	Disturb class	.01
II	Athletic ability	.61
III	Answer questions	.56
IV	Fight and argue	−.04
V	Clean and neat	.75
VI	Sissy – Tomboy	−.38
VII	Laugh most	.27
VIII	Take big chances	.35
IX	Best schoolwork	.64
X	Act grown up	.53
XI	Best looking	.80
XII	Bossy	.07
XIII	Gregarious	.62
XIV	Like school	.45
XV	Popularity	---
XVI	Intelligent	.26

Table 2 lists all the variables showing significant differences in their relation to popularity between the two SES groups. It also shows whether these differences existed across all other factors or only for a specific race x sex-of-rater x sex-of-ratee combination.

Hypothesis I is not supported by the results of this study. The culturally deprived children in this study associated popularity more strongly than did core culture children with such characteristics as not disturbing the class, answering teacher's questions, being clean and neat, doing the best schoolwork, and liking school. All these traits conform to school-fostered values and should lead to successful classroom performance. The results of this study contradict the general belief that culturally deprived peer groups approve characteristics which conflict with school fostered standards. For this sample of culturally deprived children it appears that the approved characteristics are those conducive to adequate school performance. Thus, we cannot safely assume that values and group norms in culturally deprived groups can be used as partial explanations of the poorer school performance observed among the deprived.

TABLE 2.–VARIABLES SHOWING SIGNIFICANT DIFFERENCES IN THEIR RELATION TO POPULARITY BETWEEN CULTURALLY DEPRIVED AND CORE CULTURE GROUPS

	Median Correlation with Popularity		
Variable	Culturally Deprived Groups	Core Culture Groups	Race X sex-of-rater X sex-of-ratee combinations in which SES differences were significant
Disturb class	−.31	.23	for all factor combinations
Answer questions...	.73	.30	for Negro classrooms
Clean and neat	.81	.47	for Negro girl raters
Best schoolwork ...	.79	.42	for all factor combinations
Best looking.......	.81	.61	for Negro girl raters
Best looking.......	.74	.85	for white girl raters
Gregarious	.43	.74	for all factor combinations
Like school	.60	.20	for all factor combinations

Note: The median correlations reported for the variables in Tables 2 through 5 were calculated using data from only the factor combinations for which significant differences in the correlations were found. For example, consider Table 2. The extreme right column shows that disturb class had a significant difference in its correlations with popularity between SES levels across all factor combinations. This means the median correlations shown under each SES level for disturb class were calculated using data from all the race x sex-of-rater x sex-of-ratee combinations. For answer questions, the extreme right column indicates a significant difference in its correlation with popularity between SES levels among Negro classrooms only. This means the median correlation shown under each SES level was calculated using data from Negro classrooms only. This same form was used for Tables 2 through 5.

Table 3 lists all the variables showing significant differences in their relation to popularity between the two races.

This study does not contain evidence concerning the reasons why such differences exist among the groups studied. Further research will be necessary to determine the reasons for differences such as the greater relation of being gregarious to popularity among white classrooms. One hypothesis is that for this sample the Negro teachers are stricter in classroom control than white teachers. Perhaps among Negro schools, children who seek associations with other pupils are viewed as troublemakers, and their popularity is thereby reduced.

Table 4 lists all the variables showing significant differences in their relation to popularity where male and female raters are compared.

Table 5 lists all the variables showing significant differences in their relation to popularity where male and female ratees are compared.

**TABLE 3.–VARIABLES SHOWING SIGNIFICANT DIFFERENCES IN
THEIR RELATION TO POPULARITY BETWEEN
NEGRO AND WHITE GROUPS**

Variable	Median Correlation with Popularity		SES X sex-of-rater X sex-of-ratee combinations in which race differences were significant
	Negro Groups	White Groups	
Athletic ability......	.44	.67	for all factor combinations
Answer questions ...	.30	.62	for core culture classrooms
Best looking........	.61	.85	for core culture girl raters
Best looking........	.74	.87	for core culture classrooms
Gregarious	.53	.74	for all factor combinations
Intelligent	.16	.59	for girl ratees

Note: See note to Table 2.

The results show that boys and girls not only differ in their approval of certain traits as raters, but the approval they place on certain traits depends on the sex of the ratee. Variable V, clean and neat, illustrates these sex differences.

Table 4 shows that when core culture girls are the ratees, this variable is more strongly associated with popularity by male raters than by female raters. Table 5 shows, however, that the core culture male raters associate neatness and cleanliness more with popularity for girls than for boys. The core culture boys then, associate neatness and cleanliness in girls with popularity more than the girl raters, and they associate this variable with popularity more in girls than in boys. Cleanliness and neatness are associated more highly with popularity in

**TABLE 4.–VARIABLES SHOWING SIGNIFICANT DIFFERENCES IN
THEIR RELATION TO POPULARITY BETWEEN
MALE AND FEMALE RATERS**

Variable	Median Correlation with Popularity		SES X race X sex-of-ratee combinations in which sex of rater differences were significant
	Female Raters	Male Raters	
Clean and neat	.65	.82	for core culture girl ratees
Clean and neat	.47	.76	for core culture Negro classrooms
Laugh most	.30	.23	for all factor combinations
Best looking........	.76	.87	for girl ratees
Best looking........	.61	.83	for core culture Negro classrooms
Best looking........	.74	.89	for core culture classrooms

Note: See note to Table 2.

both sexes by core culture Negro boy raters than by core culture Negro girl raters.

Table 5 shows that boys' being sissies is more strongly rejected than girls' being tomboys. Variable VI, sissy-tomboy, is based on separate item-pairs for each sex in the reputation test. While this means that the boys and girls were not ratees on the same item-pair, we can still conclude that sex role is more narrowly defined for the boys.

TABLE 5.—VARIABLES SHOWING SIGNIFICANT DIFFERENCES IN THEIR RELATION TO POPULARITY BETWEEN MALE AND FEMALE RATEES

Variable	Median Correlation with Popularity		SES X race X sex-of-rater combinations in which sex of ratee differences were significant
	Female Ratees	Male Ratees	
Clean and neat	.82	.62	for core culture boy raters
Sissy—Tomboy . . . . —	.01	−.62	for all factor combinations
Best looking	.87	.75	for boy raters
Like school	.63	.26	for all factor combinations
Intelligent	.59	.18	for white classrooms

Note: See note to Table 2.

This study illustrates the feasibility of measuring peer approval or disapproval of the behavior and characteristics of their classmates. By using a reputation test, it is possible to infer what behaviors and characteristics have social value and are therefore being reinforced by the peer group. Since it is recognized that peer pressures are a powerful influence on the behavior of children, it is surprising that there has been little systematic study of peer pressures and the factors that influence which characteristics assume social value in various groups.

It was found in this study that culturally deprived children assign more social value to behaviors and characteristics fostered in school settings than do children not culturally deprived. This suggests that generalities about values and norms characteristic of large social groups may not apply to individual classroom situations.

The writer recognizes that factors not controlled in this study, such as individual student leaders, teachers, school climate, and community attitudes influence children's acceptance or nonacceptance of various behaviors and characteristics. The relation of these and other factors to peer pressures deserves increased attention if we are to gain understanding and partial control over the forces that often determine whether an educational program will be successful or

FOOTNOTES:

1. The research reported in this paper is based on the author's PhD dissertation in Psychology at George Peabody College for Teachers and was supported by the United States Office of Education, Department of Health, Education, and Welfare, Cooperative Research Program, Contract Number OE-5-10-028.
2. Now with Oakland Schools, Pontiac, Michigan.

REFERENCES:

1. Coleman, J. S., The Adolescent Society, Free Press of Glencoe, New York, 1961.
2. Hartshorne, H., May, M. A.; Maller, J. B., Studies in the Nature of Character: II. Studies in service and self-control.
3. Homans, G. C., The Human Group, Harcourt, Brace, New York, 1950.
4. Klaus, R. A., "Interrelationships of Attributes that Accepted and Rejected Children Ascribe to Their Peers," unpublished doctoral dissertation, George Peabody College for Teachers, 1959.
5. Lindquist, E. F., Design and Analysis of Experiments in Psychology and Education, Houghton-Mifflin, Boston, Massachusetts, 1953.
6. Maas, H. S., "Some Social Class Differences in the Family Systems and Group Relations of Pre- and Early Adolescents," Child Development, 22: 145-152, 1951.
7. Passow, H. A., "Education in Depressed Areas," in Passow, H. A., (ed.) Education in Depressed Areas, Bureau of Publications, Teachers College, Columbia University, New York, 1963.
8. Sherif, M., "Conformity-deviation, Norms, and Group Relations," in Berg, I., Bass, B. M. (eds.) Conformity and Deviation, Harper, New York, 1961.
9. Sherif, M.; Sherif, Carolyn W., Reference Groups. Exploring into Conformity and Deviation of Adolescents, Harper and Row, New York, 1964.

Questions:

1. What results on Tables 1-5 did you find to be unexpected? Explain.
2. If culturally deprived groups associate popularity with traits that should lead to successful classroom performance, then what about the studies that show culturally deprived children performing well in previously all-white schools because of the peer group relationships?
3. Do you feel that there is a positive relationship between popularity and academic achievement? Explain.

ANGER IN CHILDREN

By GEORGE V. SHEVIAKOV

In examining the characteristics of anger, two important considerations must be stressed.

1. *Anger and anxiety may or may not be consciously recognized by the sufferer.* More often, his feelings are repressed into his unconscious, and he is not aware of them. The indoctrination of children in our society against being angry or fearful is so strong that children deny to themselves their true inner feelings. Since the energy is still there, its outlets may take many different paths.

2. *A peculiar feature of anger is that it can accumulate in a manner similar to the accumulation of electricity in a battery that is being charged or steam pressure in a boiler.* This accumulated anger may not be visible at all, but it may express itself in round-about ways or in a sudden violent explosion. At least once a year we read about a "model" boy who has committed a shocking crime. We also see it in quiet, shy people who occasionally "explode" emotionally in response to a trivial provocation. Anger is taboo in our culture, but this does not extinguish the energy within the body.

Let us examine the various degrees of anger. This knowledge will help us to be more alert in detecting hidden anger, in understanding this complex phenomenon and in getting hunches concerning how to help the angry child. For instance, a child who expresses his anger freely and openly but who does not hurt anybody may not have a heavy burden of anger; whereas a "mousy" child or a nonlearner may have a heavy load of anger.

The *extremely hostile,* furious, and vicious child is a disturbed individual who is beyond the help of the school. Such a child needs 24-hour supervision and psychotherapy. Since he is too sick for the school, he does not profit from it and actually poses a danger to others in the class. Referal to a social agency is needed for a child with this much anger.

Indirectly expressed anger within a child is revealed in his perennially pessimistic view of life: "Well, I hope nothing happens to you on this auto trip." "Are you well? You look somewhat pale." "Yes, she is a wonderful girl, but isn't it too bad that she has buck teeth?" The list is endless. This sugarcoated hostility may be unconsciously directed toward a single person, it may express a high degree of hostility within the child in general, or it may be a form of atonement, which is not real atonement at all because the child frequently does express his hostility in other ways. Some children develop headaches or other genuine physical symptoms that are really meant to enslave the family or spoil its fun.

Reprinted with permission from *Today's Education* (September 1969).

With *Internalized hostility,* the target may be the child himself. Usually such reactions spring from punishment for expressions of anger or from great guilt feelings about one's hostile feelings, sometimes causing self-hate. The range of actual behaviors is very broad. Here are a few: Banging one's head against a hard object (an expression of impotent rage), cutting oneself, biting one's knuckles, managing to have "accidents," shying away from other children (thus becoming a recluse), having difficulty in talking to others (perhaps for fear of ridicule or inadvertently expressing one's hostility), avoiding competitive situations (because winning may mean an act of aggression, although entirely different feelings may be expressed through fear of competition, too), being apathetic or depressed, managing things so that other children dislike you, having an unconscious desire to fail, plus an endless list of psychosomatic symptoms, such as vomiting or stomachaches. All these may enter in the expression of anger. These are all complicated human reactions that may be caused by several factors and may have several meanings at the same time.

Projection of one's own hostility on others is another common phenomenon that expresses itself frequently in "Nobody likes me," "The teacher is picking on me," "Kids in this school are very unfriendly." We like to blame others for our troubles. It relieves us of guilt and responsibility.

Displacement of anger is another important phenomenon to realize. Many times a teacher may have trouble with a child because of the teacher who taught him in the previous period. I have known children who hated all their classmates as a displacement of their hatred of their brother or sister—a hatred often based on jealousy or envy. A number of children give their teacher a bad time one way or another based on their anger at their parents against whom they would not dare to express their anger. This works the other way also. A child who is "good" in school but who fears and hates his teacher may be a hellion at home. Parenthetically, this is one of the many reasons why it is important for parents and teachers to get to know each other.

Question:

1. Name the degree of anger that you feel most impedes the education of a student and give your reasons.

THE EXTRA COST OF BEING POOR[1]

By TRIENAH MEYERS

Some home economists consider the buying practices of poor families to be unwise and a major reason why the families remain at a poverty level of existence. However, Miss Meyers states from study and observation that it actually costs more to be poor—economically, educationally, psychologically, and physically. Rather than teaching "good money management practices," Miss Meyers recommends a three-pronged approach to help the poor—educational, economic, and psychological leverage.

IN ONE WAY, I'm a fine one to be talking to you about the extra costs of being poor. Like most of you, I sit at a reasonably comfortable rung on the economic ladder and the only times I miss meals are when my plane is late or misses connecting flights. When I was asked at the White House Conference on Food, Nutrition, and Health to limit myself to $2.50 a day for food as part of the demonstrations, I declined. I couldn't honestly do that without feeling like a hypocrite—playing at being poor for a few meals while attending meetings in one of the more elegant hotels in Washington.

On the other hand, if persons like you and me don't talk a little louder and considerably more frequently and coherently about poverty than we have in the past, there can be some dire consequences. For one thing, if we wait too long no one is going to be able to hear us above the growing roar at the bottom of the ladder. More important, though, the more people like us get ourselves involved, the more likely it is and sooner it will be that the national body will gain some real leverage on the problems of poverty.

The Economic Research Service (ERS) does get some exposure to conditions of the poor, the most recent of which is in the context of the evaluation of the U.S. Department of Agriculture's expanded food and nutrition education program. In this program, the Extension Service has over 5,000 indigenous aides, with special training and supervision provided through the land-grant colleges and universities, seeking out and teaching the culturally deprived on matters relating to nutrition. At last count, they were working with more than 150,000 poor families. Those who evaluated the program at the grassroots observed that this educational system is, appropriately, working two

Reprinted with permission from the *Journal of Home Economics*, June 1970, Volume 62, Number 6, pages 379-384.

ways. New insights and understandings about poverty indeed are seeping all the way up through the establishment (1).

On the basis of our most recent observations and reports, I would like to share with you some concepts about the cost of being poor that are not generally thought of, about the interactions among these costs, and about what promises to function best as leverage for change.

ECONOMIC COSTS

Franklin Roosevelt, in his memorable "four freedoms" speech to Congress on January 6, 1941, didn't mention "economic freedom" *per se,* but the nation's 30 million poor have infinitely less economic freedom than do their more affluent countrymen. Not only does the poor consumer have less money to spend but also his discretionary freedoms of time, place, quality, amount, and method of purchase are severely restricted. Let us look at each of these facets of consumer inflexibility for the poor.

Time of purchase. The time of purchase is an extremely important determinant of the cost of most items. The "thrifty" consumer can use fluctuations in prices to good advantage. End-of-season clothing sales are representative of the sort of saving which can be realized. The seasonal variations, even the weekly "specials," in food prices are another, particularly when the consumer has a home freezer. But the poor consumer can take little if any advantage of these possible savings. While the buying habits of the more affluent members of the buying public are determined at least partially by convenience, those of the poor are dictated almost exclusively by an existing need of the moment. Of what use is a sale on children's summer clothing in September if the seat has just given way in Johnnie's only pair of winter school pants? "Poor" is trying to keep expenditures as nearly even with income as possible, and there is very little flexibility in this situation. How quickly a good budget plan is destroyed when even a small emergency cannot be met—when there are no savings to absorb the "bumps," only present income!

Let me tell you about a recent case. Some of the expanded food and nutrition education program aides in a large Eastern Seaboard city became convinced that food retailers in their community were actually raising prices when welfare checks were distributed. Part of the aides' job is to help raise the nutritional level of their client families. Since increased prices would measurably affect their clients' nutritional intake, they advised families to delay buying food until a few days after the welfare checks were distributed. I am not going to debate the existence of this situation—and our research indicates it is not a problem of national scale. The crucial point is that the aides failed almost completely in their efforts to effect delays in food purchasing. This was *not* because of apathy on the part of the homemakers—they honestly believed that prices were being raised—but the families simply could not wait. Most of them had already been waiting—for a welfare check. In this instance, aides were suggesting only a few days' delay in buying. Can you imagine the effectiveness of telling a poor family that buying clothes a half-year ahead of time will save them money? "Poor" is buying *when* you can.

Place of purchase. Where one buys items also can have a distinct effect on how much items cost; and again, the poor consumer has little control over *where* he spends his money. Dr. Joseph Uhl at Purdue University, in reporting to economists on his studies of buying, commented recently that American education is producing scientific geniuses and illiterate consumers. Most people, particularly the affluent, know that prices on equivalent items often vary widely from store to store. Whether or not they make use of the information is up to them; at least they have the freedom to do so. The suburban purchaser can leave the children with a babysitter and take off in the car for whatever store has the best buy. She can classify her needs by purchase type—greens at one market, eggs at another, or draperies at one end of the city and appliances at the other. This is not the case for the poor. They have no babysitter, no car, no bus or taxi fare—in short, no freedom. They are somehow fenced by economic and psychological barriers into a small geographic purchasing area. This is particularly true of the rural poor, but it also applies in large metropolitan areas. "Poor" is *buying in the neighborhood* at whatever the prices happen to be.

The poor are particularly vulnerable to the door-to-door salesman. In a rural county in the South, for instance, nutrition aides reported on an enterprising appliance salesman who managed to sell home freezers to a number of poor families who had only recently obtained electricity for their houses. His primary selling point was that the families could prepare many foodstuffs for freezing and thus keep them throughout the months in which these foods were not grown or sold. The salesman was, of course, correct in this statement. But somehow the purchasers received the impression that the freezers could be used as substitutes for refrigerators. Their first experiences with trying to freeze such things as lettuce, cabbage, and butter were, needless to say, somewhat disappointing. It is not clear whether the salesman had deliberately tried to victimize the people, although the possibility must be admitted. Whatever his intentions, the results are clear—families who bought the freezers were saddled with payments plus the need for another major appliance.

Quality of purchase. Product quality is one of the most talked about areas in consumer-producer relations. We all are familiar with the growing outcry against the philosophy of planned obsolescence and shoddiness of manufacturing resulting in such problems as nontoasting toasters, cars which shed their parts like molting canaries, radios that go snap, crackle, and pop, and television sets that seem to be dependent on monthly visits by servicemen for their existence. Some of us can afford to buy insurance for repairs on major appliances; the poor cannot.

Another aspect of quality also has a bearing on the value of products to the consumer. I shall borrow a phrase from the military-industrial world and call this aspect "cost/effectiveness." If, for instance, a $4 pair of shoes lasts only two months and a $16 pair of shoes lasts 18 months, which is really cheaper? The answer is obvious. There is often, although by no means always, a positive relationship between the cost of an item and its relative quality. The discriminating consumer can learn to take advantage of this situation by buying items which are of sufficient quality to wear well but not so expensive that the benefit of buying them is outweighed by their cost. Again, however, this avenue is seldom open to the poor consumer. His lack of financial flexibility forces him to buy only what he can afford immediately. Even if he is aware of the advantage of buying a more expensive brand or item, he cannot take advantage of this knowledge. "Poor" is buying whatever quality shoes and trousers you can manage on your time payments.

Amount of purchase. Buying in bulk is another way to keep down household costs. Not only are many items discounted when purchased in comparatively large quantities, but taking advantage of sales by buying extra amounts of sale items is also an excellent way to decrease the amount spent on staples. We teach this constantly. The poor are not able to exploit the benefits of bulk buying. If a mother has to feed a family, she cannot forego buying milk in order to purchase five extra cans of beans which happen to be on sale at six for a dollar. So, "poor" is buying in amounts you can afford—usually one at a time—and not being able to take advantage of the "twofers and threefers." Many years ago a famous man expressed this quite effectively in a single sentence. He said, "The poor can't afford to be frugal."

Method of purchase. Generally, very poor people have almost no flexibility in the method by which they pay for their purchases. Without collateral and with the condition of poverty as a given, it is difficult, if not impossible, for many families to obtain credit. This closes the door on the possibility of using most of the avenues of cost/effective buying about which I have been talking. When they can get credit, it often works against them by enmeshing them in a financial web that they often do not understand and are powerless to control. Credit to the affluent is often a payday-to-payday convenience; to the poor, it is usually a long haul leading to a far higher cost per item than you or I would pay. "Poor" is paying more interest on credit terms because it takes longer to pay. And as an additional cost of credit, think how quick, easy, and inexpensive it is for us to pay our bills. If we keep a minimum balance in our checking account, the check costs nothing and it takes us very little time to pay our bills by mail. We sometimes even get the envelope free and just add a 6-cent stamp. Without this convenience, the poor must make a special trip to each store in which they have payments to make, spending bus fare and considerable time. They could send a money order, but that costs money and a trip to a post office which is not always close.

INADEQUATE CONSUMER EDUCATION AND FOOD PROGRAMS

The poor and, to a lesser extent the U.S. people in general, also are hampered by inadequate consumer education and sophistication. While the aspects of buying previously discussed comprise a considerable portion of consumer sophistication, there are other considerations. Through a lack of knowledge about merchandising and advertising techniques, the poor consumer often is led to purchase inappropriate merchandise. I noted earlier that the poor are particularly vulnerable to door-to-door salesmen. Salesmen rarely come in response to expressed needs of the consumer, and even less often in response to the real needs of the poor. For example, the evaluators of the food and nutrition education program observed in one county that a number of homes had the same gilt-framed picture of a martyred hero. Homemakers reported that they were paying a salesman $25 on time for a picture which the evaluators estimated might have cost $2.98 at a retail store. While the picture was probably a psychological necessity, the price was quite out of proportion to its worth. This episode might not have occurred if the purchasers had known more about buying and what was available in regular retail stores. Unfortunately, the people who are likely to be hurt most by a lack of knowledge are the very ones who are least likely to be able to acquire such knowledge. Because of their history of limited buying power, lack of consumer mobility, and inflexible finances, the poor have little opportunity to acquire the purchasing sophistication of more affluent consumers. And since poverty has in many cases become institutionalized, poor people are not likely to learn these skills from their families.

There are a multitude of agencies and programs set up to help the poor. Some of the most important are the various food assistance programs. When they work well, these programs accomplish a large portion of the desired outcome—improved nutrition for the poor and the release of a portion of their income for other kinds of expenditure. Yet even in these programs situations sometimes conspire to rob the poor of the advantages gained from participation. For example, in a rural area the nutrition aides reported an incident of a woman who was feeding the oatmeal from her commodity food program to her hogs. She said she didn't like oatmeal and didn't know any way to prepare it so that the family would eat it. Another family had painted their shed with a mixture of water and commodity powdered egg mix. No one in the family knew how to read well enough to decipher the instructions on the tin. The indigenous aides in the nutrition program have been particularly effective in situations like this because they generally can find the underlying causes for misuse or failure to use food assistance. The nutrition aides report that without special instruction and a chance to taste commodity items such as bulgur, poor people don't understand how to use unfamiliar foods. The fact that you and I pay 85 cents for bulgur under a different name doesn't mean a thing to them. For the thousands who aren't reached by the nutrition education aides, such problems can nullify the potential of food programs.

Up to this point, I have been talking only about economic matters. But there are other costs of being poor. Some of these are inextricably interwoven with the economic costs of poverty; some are indeed the result of poverty; but all are degrading. There is an entire spectrum of educational, psychological, and physical costs which may attend the condition of poverty.

EDUCATIONAL COSTS

The fact that a third of the adults in Marengo County, Alabama, failed to complete more than three years of education is a statistic that few people have on the tips of their tongues. (2). Its meaning in terms of the well-being of the people is known to even fewer. The coincidence of mass poverty and a low level of education marks ignorance as an added cost of being poor—all the prattling about equal education to the contrary.

The educational deficiencies of the poor are well known. In the inner cores of the nation's large cities where poverty is rampant, schools are notoriously poor. The report of the National Advisory Commission on Civil Disorders (3) takes note of the fact that ". . . ghetto schools have experienced overcrowding. Shortages of textbooks and supplies have developed. Double shifts are common; hallways and other nonclassroom space have been adopted for class instruction; and mobile classroom units are used." The report also mentions several instances of seemingly discriminatory educational practices, with overcrowding in schools being a much greater problem in areas with a high percentage of ghetto Negro enrollment than in white or predominantly white schools. Our society also spends less money educating ghetto children than children of suburban families. The teachers in schools attended by disadvantaged Negro children tend to be less experienced and qualified than those in schools attended by middle-class white children. The ghetto schools also tend to have fewer facilities than do those in more prosperous areas. This list of indictments of our educational practices and priorities could go on and on, but it tends toward overkill. Let's take a look at the results: The average black sixth-grader of a northeastern metropolitan area is, on the basis of standard achievement tests, 1.6 grades behind his white counterpart. By the twelfth grade, this gap has widened to 3.3 grades. The black student is almost four times as likely as the white to fail the Selective Service Mental Test and is three times as likely to drop out of school at ages 16 and 17. At least in urban areas, ghetto dwellers clearly are getting the short end of the stick (4).

PSYCHOLOGICAL COSTS

It has been estimated that as much as 60 percent of the nation's ghetto population may be emotionally unstable enough to require professional care. Eminent psychiatrists have pointed out that although the incidence of severe psychosis among some poverty groups is high, the treatment of poor psychotics has lagged far behind that of the more affluent members of society. Whereas the relatively well-to-do generally receive treatment by private psychiatrists or in clinics, the poor are treated in hospitals. In addition, poor people generally do not receive the individualized care that can be afforded by wealthier patients. They are much more likely to receive electroshock and drug therapy rather than the more costly individual psychotherapy. The reasons behind this condition are largely economic but not wholly so. It has been noted, for instance, that psychiatrists generally have failed to comprehend the kinds of problems and situations to which poor people are exposed. The psychiatrist attempts to treat mental aberration from his own socioeconomic point of view without developing the rapport and understanding necessary for effective therapy (5).

Perhaps a more basic issue than the lack of adequate psychiatric care for the poor is what makes ghetto dwellers develop mental and emotional aberrations in the first place. This is a difficult area to grapple with because interpretations of the causes are many and varied. Yet it does not take a great deal of insight to isolate a few potential causes—hopelessness, joblessness, fear, and frustration. I will leave specific interpretation to more qualified personnel. But surely a society which bombards its members with messages that cars, homes, electric ranges, hair dressings, and the "right" deodorant are all prerequisites for success and happiness, and then manages to exclude a significant number of its members from participating in the quest for these things, cannot expect only good to come from the situation. Can we rationally expect a housewife who is afraid to step out of her apartment door because of the gangs who roam the halls of many urban housing projects to have the same confidence and trust in society as does the suburban homemaker? I think not.

PHYSICAL COSTS

The extra costs of being poor also are physical. Many poor people exist under conditions which inexorably sap their energies and abilities to resist. Of the more than 2,000 homes on which our nutrition program evaluators collected data, roughly one-third did not have running water. Many of the poor families did not sit down together for meals because there was not sufficient room or furnishings. Can you imagine the energies that go into homemaking under those conditions? "Poor" isn't lazy; it is just very tired and often ill. The extra costs of being poor, then, are not only economic; they are also psychological, educational, and physical. Clearly these are not independent costs. In fact, there is an almost insidious interrelationship that creates an entrapment which might lead one to conclude that the *only* means of reducing the costs of being poor is to be rich. The recommendation made at the White House Conference on Food, Nutrition, and Health for a $5500 annual minimum income for a family of four was a thought in that direction; but that alone will not solve many of the problems that I have cited here, even if such federal expenditures were feasible.

When one looks in depth at the nature of the costs of being poor and looks across the effectiveness and ineffectiveness of poverty programs of the past few years, the importance of three separate types of leverage comes more clearly into focus.

LEVERAGE FOR CHANGE

The first and most far-reaching leverage is *educational* in nature. Education has long-term effects. It also has a multiplier effect. Aides in the nutrition education program have observed this multiplier effect of education among homemakers; they find that what was discussed in one household about low-cost meals sometimes is known to the lady down the block before the aide arrives at that home. Certainly education is generational within the family. What the mother learns about food preparation is learned by her children through example. The converse is undoubtedly true. What children learn in 4-H Clubs and in school is carried home and can influence parents. The same is true of all other facets of education of the poor. To educate one person in Marengo County beyond the fourth grade enhances the probability that several others will aspire to more than a fourth-grade education. And although the delivery costs of education are high, the maintenance costs are close to zero dollars. Once the concepts are incorporated by the learner, he has them at his disposal from that time on.

The second approach is through *economic* leverage, which has potential for what we might call positive regenerative feedback. That is, each dollar added to a poor person's income can reduce the added costs of being poor. The Food Stamp Program provides some of this type of leverage. Much more of this type of assistance is needed.

The third type of leverage is *psychological* or *motivational* in character. We have seen some of this leverage coming into play in the recent nutrition conference and more widely in the community action agencies throughout the country. The poor are becoming their own voice and the sound is penetrating the barriers of stereotyping, moralizing, and philosophizing that have separated the other two-thirds of the nation from them. Just to be heard is motivating.

On the optimistic side we do have hope—more importantly, they have hope. Let me share with you some findings of a recent ERS study. Identical questions were asked of 1,249 heads of households in the Mississippi Delta Region—some poor, some affluent. Researchers wanted to discover whether or not the poor were more pessimistic about their chances for bettering their lives than the affluent. It turned out that they were. Did this pessimism block them from attempting to escape their economic plight? Surprisingly, it didn't stop them from trying. They were asked about willingness to take special training, to change jobs, and to move to a distant city. Poverty status had no bearing on the response of the Delta residents to these questions. The persons most willing to take free training courses or make a 200-mile move were just as likely to be poor as affluent. But regardless of their financial status, these people were generally young rather than old, married more often than single, and Negro more frequently than white. Most were heads of rather small families and had at least a sixth-grade education. The persons who showed the greatest reluctance to alter their lives were Negro female family heads. Many of these women were poor, but it appeared that their family responsibilities hampered them more than poverty did.

People in poverty have not seemed to fit well into the mythical mold of "the American way of life." The larger portion of the American public has tended to see poor people as beings apart from themselves. They see and condemn the violence of the ghettos but do not seek to understand the causes of the violence. They berate the poor for their alleged laziness and lack of initiative, yet do not seem sensitive to the reasons for their joblessness. For the upper two-thirds of the population to really understand the lower third would be in itself a major psychological push forward.

I have the feeling that any one of these three approaches used alone won't work. Certainly the leverage gained by the three in unison will be far greater than the sum of the three used independently. Together they tend to nurture one another, to have a synergetic effort. Or, to put it in the language of the poor, that would really *bang* it.

REFERENCES:

[1]Economic Research Service Expanded Food and Nutrition Education Program Evaluation Report, U.S. Department of Agriculture, Subregional Conferences, Fall 1969.

[2]*Community Profile, Marengo County, Alabama.* Office of Economic Opportunity Information Center.

[3]*Report of the National Advisory Commission on Civil Disorders.* New York: Bantam Books, 1968.

[4]*Ibid.*

[5]Coles, R. Psychiatrists and the Poor. In *Man Against Poverty: World War III*, A. I. Blaustein and R. R. Woock (Editors). New York: Random House, 1968.

FOOTNOTES:

[1]This paper, which was presented at the National Agricultural Outlook Conference that was held in Washington, D. C. in February 1970, is based in large part on materials developed by Edna Jones, Senior Analyst, Datagraphics, Inc., Allison Park, Pennsylvania.

Questions:

1. Name three or four factors that you feel make various food assistance programs successful.

2. What approach would you use to encourage families to delay purchasing items for a day or two in order to save money?

3. Which of the three costs—educational, psychological, or physical—do you feel is most damaging to a ghetto dweller and why?

MALNUTRITION AND LEARNING

By RITA BAKAN

To paraphrase Hemingway's dialogue with Fitzgerald, the poor are different from us—they have less money.[1] They also have children who in general do poorly in school and on tests of intelligence. In part this is due to social and psychological factors, and such children have been called "culturally disadvantaged" or "socially deprived." But the poor also have a higher infant mortality rate, a higher incidence of infectious and chronic diseases, and a greater number of premature and low birth-weight infants.[2] All of these factors are in turn related to the disproportionate number of poor children who are mentally retarded.[3]

Data currently being developed indicate that malnutrition is the common denominator of all these ills. The characteristics of malnourished children bear a striking resemblance to a number of the known characteristics of "disadvantaged" children, e.g., apathy, irritability, sickliness, and a reduced attention span.

The combination of malnutrition and the other negative effects of poverty perpetuates a cycle of illness, educational failure, and more poverty. If the aim of compensatory education is to break this cycle, then it is imperative that social scientists and educators become aware of the negative impact of malnutrition on the development of the child. The purpose of this paper is to present some of the evidence, based on animal and human studies, linking malnutrition to the growth of the brain, the performance of various intellectual functions, and other developmental variables related to learning.

BRAIN DEVELOPMENT AND FUNCTION

Numerous investigations[4] of the effect of malnutrition on the weight of the brain of the rat and of the pig have reported similar results: Undernutrition from birth to 21 days produces a persistent and permanent reduction in brain weight. The earlier the malnutrition the more severe is the effect and the less likely is recovery. Undernutrition also results in specific degeneration within brain cells; again, the earlier the restriction, the more severe the damage.

Results of studies of malnutrition on cellular growth patterns indicate that early restriction of food interferes with cell division and that the animal is left with a deficit in the *number* of cells in all organs, even after adequate refeeding. Late malnutrition results in a decrease in cell size, with recovery on refeeding.

Reprinted with permission from *Phi Delta Kappan*, (June 1970).

While the extent and duration of undernutrition and rehabilitation are important, the age at which the undernutrition occurs appears to be the crucial variable.

There is also evidence of what may be term "double deprivation." The offspring of rats who are malnourished during pregnancy show a reduced number of brain cells. Even if they are fed normally after birth they do not recover and are left with a permanent deficit in brain cell number. The effects of postnatal malnutrition on animals who have already suffered prenatal malnutrition are more marked than effects of either prenatal or postnatal deprivation separately. It would seem that prenatal malnutrition made these animals more susceptible to postnatal undernutrition.

In general, the animal studies have shown that during the preweaning period in the rat an enormous amount of chemical change is taking place within the brain and that this is the time when the brain is most sensitive to the detrimental effects of undernutrition. The brain of the mature rat who was malnourished during this period is not only physically smaller but shows degenerative cell changes. If the deprivation occurs early in infancy, these changes are irreversible, while the effects of later deprivation may be reversed through proper feeding.

Behavioral changes were also evident as the result of malnutrition. After only four days on a restricted diet, rats began to develop spasmodic trembling of the head and forepaws, pigs exhibited various motor abnormalities, and puppies became hyperirritable.[5] A decrease in exploratory behavior was suffered by rats who were malnourished during the preweaning period.[6]

One of the most intriguing findings in this area is that poor nutrition of the infant female may affect the development of her offspring many years later.[5] On the basis of a number of studies, Cowley[7] suggests that the nutritional history of previous generations must be taken into consideration when studying the present generation. Whether the poorer test behavior of successive generations of animals fed deficient diets was due to enhanced nutritional deficiency in the young or to differences in the behavior of malnourished mothers toward their offspring is yet to be determined.

Available evidence from human studies reinforces the findings of experiments with animals and suggests that early infancy is a critical period for the development of the brain. This is also the time when the brain is extremely vulnerable to the effects of malnutrition.[8] Since direct measurement of brain growth in humans is not possible with living children, an indirect measure which has been widely employed is the rate of increase in head circumference. Malnutrition, especially during the first year of life, will curtail the normal rate of increase in head circumference.[9] This reduced head circumference of malnourished children, during the first six months of life, according to Winick,[10] accurately reflects the reduced number of cells present in their brains. Monckeberg[11] has demonstrated that the brain of a severely malnourished child may be even smaller than the head circumference would indicate. He has developed a "trans-illumination" test which reveals the presence of spinal fluid in the skull. The test is conducted by focusing a thousand-watt light on the top of the skull. As the light is diffused, the surrounding area glows. In normal children, this area is very small, but in the affected children the entire brain case glows, from the forehead to the back of the head. A fluid, similar to spinal fluid, fills the cavity between the brain and the skull.

What is the relationship of these changes in brain development to behavior and to intelligence?

The children in the Monckeberg study were restored to physical health, but follow-up intelligence tests showed that they achieved lower scores than children who had not suffered from malnutrition. Their greatest deficit was in the area of language development. Similarly, the malnourished children studied by Stoch and Smythe[12] who exhibited reduced head circumference had lower I.Q.'s even after long-term follow-up.

Using a wide battery of tests, Klein and Gilbert[13] studied the performance of malnourished and normally nourished children from the same social class. On tests where the test stimulus was only available for a short period of time, the malnourished children performed less well than the normally nourished. There was no difference in performance when the duration of the test stimulus was not controlled. The deficit which the malnourished children exhibited seems to involve speed of perception or of information processing and impairment of short-term memory.

A series of studies by Cravioto and his associates[14] in Mexico and Guatemala has shown that performance of children on psychological tests was related to nutritional factors, not to differences in personal hygiene, housing, cash income, or other social and economic variables. The performance of both pre-school and school children in Mexico on the Terman-Merrill, Gesell, and Goodenough draw-a-man tests was positively correlated with body weights and body heights. A similar positive relationship between size and performance was found in Guatemala. The tests used in this study provided measures of visual, haptic, and kinesthetic sensory integration. Children exposed to severe early malnutrition exhibited perceptual defects as well as smaller body size. The earlier the malnutrition, the more profound the psychological retardation. The most severe retardation occurred in children admitted to the hospital under six months of age and did not improve on serial testing even after 220 days of treatment. Admitted later, children with the same socioeconomic background and the same severe malnutrition but a different time of onset did recover after prolonged rehabilitation.

Cravioto *et al.* conclude that nutritional inadequacy may interfere with both the staging and the timing of development of the brain and of behavior. Their demonstration of delayed neuro-integrative development in children who have grown poorly because of malnutrition has important implications for more complex psychological functioning: "Evidence already exists that the lag in the development of certain varieties of intersensory integration has a high correlation with backwardness in learning to read. Studies of reading disability in British [and] American school children have shown that backwardness in reading is strongly associated with inadequacy in auditory-visual integration. Skill in visual-kinesthetic integration is found to be highly and significantly correlated with design copying in normal children. If it is recognized that such visual-motor control is essential in learning to write, it becomes apparent that inadequacy of intersensory organization can interfere with a second primary educational skill—learning to write.

"Thus, inadequacies of intersensory development can place the child at risk of failing to establish an ordinary normal background of conditioning in his pre-school years and at the risk of failing to profit from educational experience in the school years."

In addition to the negative impact of malnutrition on the growth rates and intersensory development of children, Cravioto found a relationship between these aspects of development and infection. Eichenwald[15] has shown that certain infections in malnourished children may produce severe and prolonged hypoglycemia, a condition which can by itself cause brain damage. In addition, various biochemical defects of children with malnutrition are accentuated by infection. There is the further possibility that many infectious diseases, or the treatment of these diseases, result in damage to the nervous system that is not necessarily evident during the acute stage of the illness. Eichenwald concludes by saying: "Infection and malnutrition thus act synergistically to produce a chronically and recurrently sick child less likely to react to sensory stimuli from his already inadequate social environment."

EFFECTS OF PRENATAL NUTRITION

Further evidence of the interrelationship of poverty, malnutrition, illness, and the development of the child is found in a study which identifies undernutrition of poor urban mothers as the cause of the low birth weight of their offspring.[16] Since it has been found that both low birth weight and a high infant mortality rate are more common in poor families, the finding that undernutrition appears to be the cause of prenatal growth retardation is an important one. In addition to being 15 percent smaller in body weight, the infants from poor families had multiple evidences, in terms of the relative weight of such organs as the thymus, spleen, liver, etc., of prenatal undernutrition. The biggest difference found was in the relative weight of the thymus. The offspring of non-poor families had a mean thymus weight which was 104 percent of the "normal" weight, while the poor infants had a mean thymus weight of only 66 percent of "normal." While the function of the thymus[17] is not yet completely understood, there is increasing evidence that it is involved in both growth and immunological functions.

Evidence that the nutrition of the mother is one of the important variables related to the intellectual performance of the child has also been increasing. Children whose mothers received a vitamin supplement during pregnancy had significantly higher I.Q.'s at three and four years of age than did children whose mothers received placebos.[18] Erickson,[19] on the basis of a later study, also found that "when vitamin supplementation was given to pregnant and lactating women with poor nutritional environment, the offspring at four years of age had an average I.Q. score eight points greater than the average score of the children of mothers given placebo over the same period." Kennedy's study of prenatal nutrition on the general measures of intellectual and physical health yielded similar results.[20]

NUTRITIONAL THERAPY AND I. Q.

A number of other studies have been done which have also demonstrated that nutritional therapy of the child may have a beneficial effect on intellectual performance. Kugelmass *et al.* [21] demonstrated an increase in the I.Q. of both retarded and mentally normal children as a result of prolonged nutritional rehabilitation. The children, ranging in age from 2 to 10, were divided into two groups, those who were malnourished and those who were well-nourished. Each of these groups included retarded and normal children. The *malnourished* retarded children showed a gain of 10 points and the normal children one of 18 points after a period of dietary improvement. In contrast, there was relatively little change in the scores of the *well-nourished* retarded and normal children.

Harrell[22] found that in closely matched groups of presumably normal orphanage children, the double-blind daily administration of a placebo versus a 2 m.g. thiamine tablet for one year produced a superior mental response in the vitamin group. Muecher and Gruenwald[23] demonstrated that improvement of intellectual functions can be extended even into the late teens. Students who received vitamin and mineral supplements showed a significant improvement in the performance of mental arithmetic as compared to students receiving a placebo.

Coursin[24] has shown that deficiencies in the B-complex vitamins and in vitamin C can produce abnormalities of nerve cell metabolism and function and can impair mental development. Vitamin therapy has effected improved mental functioning with such children.

MOTIVATION AND PERSONALITY CHANGES

In addition to the relatively direct effects of malnutrition and illness on learning, there are many more indirect effects which are difficult to isolate. It has often been observed that the malnourished child is more likely to be apathetic, irritable, and lack a long attention span. "One of the first effects of malnutrition is a reduction of the child's responsiveness to stimulation and the emergence of various degrees of apathy. Apathetic behavior in its turn can function to reduce the value of the child as a stimulus and to diminish the adults' responsiveness to him. Thus apathy can provoke apathy and so contribute to a cumulative pattern of reduced adult-child interaction. If this occurs it can have consequences for stimulation, for learning, for maturation, and for interpersonal relations, the end result being significant backwardness in the performance of later more complex learning tasks."[25]

There is an increasing amount of evidence which indicates that severe malnutrition of young infants produces significant brain damage. Mild malnutrition occurring prenatally or in the first six months of life may also produce negative effects on learning and growth. This is the beginning of a vicious cycle of illness, slow development of intellectual functions, and inhibited growth which in turn prevent the individual from being able to protect his own children from the ravages of poverty. The *time* at which malnutrition occurs is crucial to the further development of the child. The earlier the malnutrition the more severe the effects and the more likely that they cannot be reversed. There is evidence that if malnutrition occurs after a certain age its effects on learning are reversible. Though the exact nature of the timing is yet to be worked out, it is becoming clear that the prenatal period and the first six months of life are critical.

In view of these findings, what can be done to insure that every child in America has the same chance of being "created equal"? Obviously, those most at risk are pregnant women and infants. The school would hardly seem to be the ideal setting for reaching this part of the population. Consider, however, the enormous percentage of first babies born to teen-age mothers. If the vital importance of prenatal and early infant nutrition could be conveyed to these girls, not only would they spare themselves many of the complications of pregnancy and delivery[26,27] but they would also ensure the healthy development of their babies.

In addition, there are the benefits, both short- and long-range, of providing all school children, and pre-school children when possible, with high quality breakfasts and lunches. There is evidence that malnutrition is increasing regardless of social class,[28] and not only poor children would benefit from these meals. Finally, there is the effort which as citizens and consumers we can make to insure that key staple foods are upgraded by enrichment, that the nutritional knowledge of those purchasing food and planning meals is improved, and *that food is made more readily available to those in real need.*

The most noxious of poverty's effects is malnutrition and the most important of the causes of malnutrition is poverty. Until this cycle is broken, the success of all our other efforts, such as compensatory education or remedial education, will be limited if not doomed to failure. As Margaret Mead has so eloquently put it, "Human beings have maintained their dignity in incredibly bad conditions of housing and clothing, emerged triumphant from huts and log cabins, gone from ill-shod childhood to Wall Street or the Kremlin . . . but food affects not only man's dignity but the capacity of children to reach their full potential, and the capacity of adults to act from day to day. . . . It is true that the starving adult, his efficiency enormously impaired by lack of food, may usually be brought back again to his previous state of efficiency. But this is not true of children. What they lose is lost for good . . . deprivation during prenatal and postnatal growth can never be made up."[29]

REFERENCES

[1]Fitzgerald: "The rich are different from you and me." Hemingway: "Yeah, they have more money."

[2]C. U. Lowe, "Child Health and Public Policy," *Grover Powers Memorial Lecture.* New Haven, Conn.: Yale University Press. 1969, p. 16.

[3]A. Kushlick, "Assessing the Size of the Problem of Subnormality," in J.E. Meade and A. S. Parkes (eds.) *Genetic and Environmental Factors in Human Ability.* New York: Plenum Press, 1966. p. 121.

[4]M. Winick, "Malnutrition and Brain Development," *Journal of Pediatrics,* May, 1969, p. 667.

[5]B. S. Platt, C. R. C. Heard, and R. J. C. Stewart, "Experimental Protein-Calorie Deficiency," in H. N. Munro and J. B. Allison (eds.), *Mammalian Protein Metabolism,* Vol. 2. New York: Academic Press, Chap. 21.

[6]R. H. Barnes, A. U. Moore, I. M. Read, and W. G. Pond, "Effect of Food Deprivation on Behavioral Patterns," in N. S. Scrimshaw and J. E. Gordon (eds.), *Malnutrition, Learning, and Behavior.* Cambridge, Mass.: MIT Press, 1968, p. 168.

7J. J. Cowley, "Time, Place, and Nutrition: Some Observations from Animal Studies," in Scrimshaw and Gordon, *op. cit.,* p. 218.

8M. Winick, *op. cit.*

9M. B. Stoch and S. M. Smythe, "Undernutrition During Infancy, and Subsequent Brain Growth and Intellectual Development," in Scrimshaw and Gordon, *Op. Cit.,* p. 269.

10M. Winick and P. Rosso, "Head Circumference and Cellular Growth of the Brain in Normal and Marasmic Children," *Journal of Pediatrics,* May, 1969, p. 774.

11F. Monckeberg, "Nutrition and Mental Development," Paper presented at the Conference on Nutrition and Human Development, East Lansing, Mich., 1969.

12Stoch and Smythe, *op. cit.*

13R. E. Klein and O. Gilbert, "Malnutrition and Intellectual Development." Paper presented at the XI Inter-American Congress of Psychology, Mexico City, Mexico, 1967.

14J. Cravioto, E. R. DeLicardle, and H.G. Birch, "Nutrition, Growth, and Neuro-integrative Development: An Experimental and Ecologic Study," *Pediatrics Supplement,* Vol. 38, No. 2, Part II, 1966, p. 319.

15H. F. Eichenwald and P. C. Fry, "Nutrition and Learning." *Science,* February, 1969, p. 664.

16R. L. Naeye, M. M. Diener, W. S. Dellinger, and W. A. Blaine, "Urban Poverty: Effects of Prenatal Nutrition," *Science,* November, 1969, p. 1026.

17V. Defendi and D. Metcalf, *The Thymus.* Philadelphia: Wistar Institute Press, 1964.

18R. F. Harrell, E. R. Woodyard, and A. J. Gates. "Influence of Vitamin Supplementation of Diets of Pregnant and Lactating Women on the Intelligence of Their Offspring." *Metabolism,* September, 1956, p. 555.

19M. T. Erickson, "Intelligence: Prenatal and Preconception Environmental Influences," *Science,* September, 1967, p. 1210.

20W. A. Kennedy, addendum to "Intelligence: Prenatal and Preconception Environmental Influences," *Science,* September, 1967, p. 1210.

21I. N. Kugelmass, L. E. Poull, and E. L. Samuel, "Nutritional Improvement of Child Mentality," *American Journal of Medical Science,* November, 1944, p. 631.

22R. F. Harrell, "Mental Response to Added Thiamine," *Journal of Nutrition,* March, 1946, p. 283.

23H. Muecher and G. Gruenwald, "Pharmacologic Stimulation of Arithmetic Performance and Graphomotor Expansion," *Perceptual and Motor Skills,* August-December, 1962, p. 101.

24D. B. Coursin, "Effects on Central Nervous System Function," *Nutrition Review,* March, 1965, p. 65.

25J. Cravioto and B. Robles, "Evaluation of Adaptive and Motor Behavior During Rehabilitation from Kwashiorkor," *American Journal of Orthopsychiatry,* April, 1965, p. 449.

26R. H. J. Hamlin, "The Prevention of Eclampsia and Pre-Eclampsia," *Lancet,* January, 1952, p. 64.

27T. H. Brewer, *Metabolic Toxemia of Late Pregnancy: A Disease of Malnutrition.* Springfield, Ill.: Charles C. Thomas, 1966.

28N. Kotz, *Let Them Eat Promises.* Englewood Cliffs, N.J.: Prentice-Hall, 1969.

29M. Mead, "The Changing Significance of Food," *American Scientist,* March-April, 1970, p. 176.

Questions:

1. Which of the two, malnutrition or the other effects of poverty, do you consider to be more harmful to the educational life of the student? Explain.

2. Develop a school program in the area of nutrition that would effectively influence poor urban mothers.

3. Evaluate the need for a free or reduced price hot lunch program in the inner city in terms of achievement, cost, and community acceptance.

TEMPER TANTRUMS

By A. E. TRIESCHMAN

The cursing, fighting, wild anger of a child is an alarming sight to the adult in charge of him. If that adult is a classroom teacher, thoughts like, "What did I do to provoke this?" merge with alarm about "control of the class." The outburst not only upsets adults but demands that they take some action. Fear—even mild fear—and the need to take some action make a troublesome combination. It is in just such a situation that we tend to jump to hasty conclusions, which compound our difficulties.

"If only I hadn't insisted that he correct those mistakes" or "I'll ignore him; he just wants attention" or "If he wants a fight, I'll show him who's boss." Thoughts like these seldom can do much to help us face the awesome pounding and shouting of the child's tantrum. We may find brief solace in muttering to ourselves about "ego-defective children" or "displaced hostility." Or perhaps we quickly review the adequacy of the lesson plan, question the wisdom of the present seating arrangement, or feel doubtful about the child's placement in this grade. Often, however, the net result is bafflement.

Despite our best efforts and intentions, children occasionally have wild outbursts of temper. We have heard that "having some is normal," that we provoke them unconsciously, and that they are related to past incidents and learning in a child's life. This is all true, but it doesn't help much in understanding the events of the tantrum itself and is even less helpful in providing guidelines for what we might do.

In the process of working with seriously disturbed children at Walker Home, a residential school for young boys 7 to 12, we have encountered many temper tantrums. Our observations have suggested to us that the tantrum is not just one ugly disruptive event but a developing series of different crises in a child's functioning. By carefully observing the different stages and basing our management efforts on that understanding, we have been able to help the children master the crisis inherent in a tantrum. Over a period of time, we have learned how to intervene during the tantrum to teach the child alternative behavior that is less upsetting to him and to those around him.

Children with a long history of "emotional disturbance" are by no means the only children who have tantrums. Traumatic events, such as the death of a parent, betrayal of trust by a friend, or a severe and unexpected disappointment, may trigger a temper tantrum in a "normal" child. Because our study of

Reprinted with permission from *Today's Education* (September 1969).

disturbed children going through the states of a temper tantrum has given us insight into what is happening to the child in the throes of one and into when and how to intervene, we may be able to help the "normal" child substitute better behavior control than a tantrum as a means of dealing with his difficulties. In addition we may help him avoid becoming addicted to tantrums as a means of manipulating those around him when he is uptight.

We have thought of the typical temper tantrum as a sequence of six stages, which we have named for their characteristic behavior: Rumbling and Grumbling, Help-Help, Either-Or, No-No, Leave Me Alone, and Hangover. Of course no two tantrums are identical, and often a child can be helped out of his crisis before he has passed through all the stages.

RUMBLING AND GRUMBLING

In this first stage, the child often grumbles and looks grouchy. He dribbles hostility: He quietly marks up a desk, for example, or slams down a book. Occasionally, he will giggle and make some effort at comic relief. Nothing really satisfies him. He appears to be fighting himself and the teacher, but especially the growing panic within him.

This rumbling and grumbling seems to be the child's effort to manage his vague sense of mental discomfort, growing helplessness, and even near panic. For many children, the feeling of general anxiety may be so close to overwhelming that it does not serve as an effective signal to mobilize coping skills or behavior controls. The child's sense of self, or personal strength, may have been sapped by one of the normal crises of childhood, such as the loss of a beloved pet or the threat presented by the arrival of a new baby brother or sister.

The point here is that a child's growth and development is not a smooth ascendance to maturity. There are ups and downs in a child's sense of worthiness, in his feelings of being competent to deal with some difficulty and frustration. If anxiety hits at one of the low points, the child may fill the gap with a tantrum.

The rumbling and grumbling is the noise of the pretantrum discomfort. It occurs in the absence of a clear sense of what there is to be anxious about and in the presence of a lowered sense of personal competence. With only vague internal discomfort and a growing sense of helplessness, the child rumbles and grumbles until some external issue comes along to which he can attach importance. We all feel guilty if we happen to supply the issue (perhaps with a criticism we make or sometimes even a casual comment), because it is at this moment that the great roar of the tantrum bursts out.

Management Suggestions. Careful observations of the child are the crucial aspect of management in this first stage. Over a period of time, they give us knowledge about his particular vulnerabilities and about the issues, times, and places that are characteristic for him. We can begin to distinguish long-term rumblers from abbreviated rumblers; loud, open grumblers from quieter, less visible ones. Once we can see what is going on, we can often help the child package his issue in a more manageable size. We can help him verbalize his growing discomfort.

HELP-HELP

This next stage of the tantrum begins the really noisy engagement. The child manages to externalize his internal drama by dramatizing some event. His choice of an issue varies greatly: "You messed up my paper with your check marks" or "You know how I hate to be called 'Bob' " or "You lost my Yo-Yo" (the one you took from him six weeks ago and forgot about).

Once he has settled on an issue, the child usually signals his need for help with some deliberately iconoclastic act. He may curse loudly and vilely; he may attack another child or get himself attacked; he may break something—in short, he pointedly violates some generally accepted canon of behavior. He pushes one of the system's panic buttons by doing something he "knows" will alarm the teacher. The noise and activity he engages in usually cause the adult to move very close to the child in order to stop the forbidden act. At this point, the teacher often has to physically hold the child for the sake of his own and the child's safety.

The actions of the child at this Help-Help juncture indicate that he has given up the control of his own behavior. His pointed misbehavior operates to bring a restraining influence (the teacher) into the picture. He carries out *inter*personally (between himself and the teacher) what usually and in his better moments is carried out *intra*personally (within himself). Of course, the teacher or aide who responds to the child's Help-Help signal is not welcomed with open arms and a "Thank you." The child vents on the adult his rage and the sense of defeat he feels because he can't control himself.

Management Suggestions. The adult needs to provide the control that the child lacks and to do so in a way conducive to teaching the child some alternative way of signaling his distress and some skills of behavior control. Do not expect, however, that management at this point can be a calm, insight-promoting talk! The wild child struggling in your arms doesn't have enough control to manage his own body, much less to pay any attention to subtle comments from you about his problems.

Do not hesitate to give your directions to him loudly, clearly, and repeatedly. Hold the child no more firmly than is necessary, but give him the assurance that you are in charge and keeping things safe. Do not engage in discussion about the rules and the punishments for breaking them. Some children almost demand such a penance system. In reality, punishment is not a substitute for behavior control. You may want to mete out consequences later, but surely it is pointless to argue or threaten in the Help-Help, "out of control" stage of a tantrum.

EITHER-OR

With the adult pretty clearly in charge of him, the child now begins to express his rage in the form of impossible alternatives, threats, and insults: "Either you let me kill him or I'll kill you." "Find my Yo-Yo or I'll break a window." "You stole my Yo-Yo and I'm gonna steal something of yours." "You're dumb." "You're fat."

Ironically, we see in these wild threats and insults a primitive effort on the part of the child to feel some sense of competence. Robbed of his sense of bodily control, he proposes alternatives as if having some control of options were the essence of self. The child seems to attempt to compensate for his loss of control by exaggerating his sense of manipulating the environment.

Management Suggestions. Methodically attempting to deal with the child's proposals soon results in contradictions. The child gets pleasure from the adult's tormented struggle to maintain logic and consistency. Some adults become very uncomfortable with their own rising anger and take an overly passive attitude.

The adult's sullen protest to the child that "you can't make me angry" is unrealistic and often functions as an invitation to the child to escalate his behavior. The situation appears so boundless to the child that he becomes more agitated and more desperate.

On the other hand, it can be a helpful adult reaction to tell a child that you are angry and don't like what he is doing—sounding and looking appropriately stern as you say so. Reasonable anger is something a child can imitate more easily than boundless patience and complete impassivity in the face of fury.

Another possible intervention is seeking a legitimate Either-Or: "Perhaps we can find the Yo-Yo," for example, of "If you calm down, we can talk about the way I marked your paper." Usually it is advisable to indicate clearly the time and space bounds of the situation by saying something like, "You and I are staying right here until you are in better control. We'll get this straightened out before lunch."

If these techniques fail to stem the tantrum, it proceeds to the next stage—a more primitive effort by the child to maintain some sense of self, despite being overwhelmed by the tantrum.

NO-NO

In this stage, the child makes it clear that although it is not possible for him to propose alternatives or to cause effects, he most certainly is *not* doing what you ask. He tends to decrease his proposals for action and to increase his negations (in word and deed) of your words and actions. If you pull his arm in one direction, he yanks it the other way. If you try to help him get seated, he stands up or vice versa. If you suggest quiet, he shouts.

Unable to hold onto a sense of self as a proposer of threatening action, the child now seems to be defending his sense of self on the grounds that he is not you. He defines himself by negating or doing the opposite of what you wish for him. It is clear that he is still struggling to defend his sense of self even in this primitive way. It is interesting to note that the behavior in the No-No stage is similar to the negativism of two- or three-year-olds—something we have come to understand as early strivings for a sense of independence by the child. It seems quite natural that a process which helps build the foundations of self should be relied on later in life when much of the self has crumbled, as in the tantrum.

Management Suggestions. The primitive functioning involved in this stage of the tantrum makes it difficult to deal with the child. The No-No stage is not a good time to tell the child how much you want to help him ("No, you want to kill me"), how much you still like him ("You *hate* me"), or how he will feel better soon ("I'm never gonna stop hating you.") About the safest position for the adult to take is based on the premise that the child wants to regain some self-control. This idea is conveyed to the child by saying something like, "I want you to be your own boss again" or "You can be in charge of yourself when you can say NO to all this craziness and thrashing around."

If a rudimentary sense of self-control develops at this stage, it is often possible to push the tantrum back to the proposing-alternatives (Either-Or) stage. If no comfortable control develops during the No-No stage, the tantrum gradually runs down, nonetheless. The struggling diminishes, and depression begins to replace aggression. The child retreats from the interpersonal sphere and draws inward.

LEAVE ME ALONE

Gradually the movement and talk of the child become more perfunctory. Despite occasional bursts of negativism, the child seems more placid or sad. He may allow you to help him to get into a more comfortable position. Crying and yelling or taunting are replaced by a rather hollow distant-sounding voice. The adult who has stayed with the child has a peaceful moment and begins to notice the red face and red eyes of a tired child, who may accept an offer of water and a cool cloth.

Both the child's remarks and his movements suggest his desire to avoid—or at least curtail—interaction with the adult. He hangs his head, pulls his shirt over his eyes, blocks his ears. His acceptance of your help (the drink of water, etc.) is brief and is clearly not intended to reestablish a friendly conversation (and should not be exploited for this purpose by the adult). Your attempts at engagement with the child will usually be rebuffed with remarks like "Leave me alone," "Don't bug me," "Don't look at me." A mixture of relative calm, sadness, and a desire to minimize interaction seems to characterize this stage.

The child apparently suffers considerable inner defeat when neither his Either-Or's nor his No-No's produce any appreciable victory for his sense of self. The result seems to be a disengagement with the outside world. Energy seems directed inward, and the child pulls into his shell. He experiences a brief, poignant depression that should not be mistaken for the return of behavior control. Nothing terrible is happening, to be sure, but that does not mean that the child is really able to deal effectively with either your expectations or his own feelings. Don't return him too quickly to the classroom routine, or you may find him falling apart again.

Management Suggestions. It is important to respect the child's withdrawal during this stage. What you do say should be brief, quiet, and calm. The appropriate message is usually one of your availability, your concern for him, and your acknowledgement of his sadness. Don't ask searching questions or try to promote a responsive conversation. Indicating that the tantrum is over is often useful.

HANGOVER

This stage is really post-tantrum. Some children talk and look as if nothing had ever happened, except for showing a little fatigue and a slight redness of the .eyes or face. To all appearances, these children have "shot their wad," blown up, ventilated in the extreme, and now seem in their usual condition. Their anger outburst seems to have cleared the register for new transactions. By contrast, other children look hung over. Their post-upset time is marked by guilt, annoyance with self, even some self-reproach. The hung-over child's visible reactions may range from indirect expression of the leftover feelings to a direct self-reproach for his behavior.

When it comes to tantrums, let us be clear that we are in favor of hangovers because they make it much easier for the adult to teach the child some alternative to a tantrum. It is especially valuable for the child and adult to share descriptions of the behavior that occurs during the Rumble and Grumble stage. They may help the child to become aware of some feeling or piece of behavior that can function as an anxiety signal. He can come to recognize his vague "black mood" as anxiety for which he can seek help from an adult. The adult can then help the child understand and manage his feelings of helplessness with behavior that is more manageable than a tantrum.

We have presented a view of the temper tantrum as a sequence of crises in behavior control beginning with an apparently sudden loss of control, and proceeding through a series of compensatory efforts than can be discerned despite all the noise and shouting. Our management suggestions are no cure-all; they do, however, suggest a course that the adult can follow which provides for both management and understanding of the child. At a minimum, the stages of a temper tantrum help us bridge the gap between psychological theory and real-life encounters with youngsters. More hopefully, they help us keep open communication with troubled or difficult-to-manage children, even in uptight situations. At best, they aid the teacher in becoming an ally to the child in his struggle to deal with an emotional crisis. If we succeed, we have been able to help a child become more emotionally competent and more accessible to learning.

Questions:

1.   In the "Help-Help" stage, after the child has given up the control of his own behavior, what do you feel would be the child's reaction if you were to begin a discussion about rules and punishment?

2.   How is the leadership of the teacher with the class affected during the "Either-Or" stage when the child is making threatening statements?

3.   Should a child be allowed to remain in a classroom following the "Help-Help" stage? Justify your answer by preparing a pertinent statement for the "Either-Or", "No-No", "Leave Me Alone", and the "Hangover" stages.

PERSONALITY DIFFERENCES AMONG HIGH ABILITY UNDERACHIEVERS[1]

By LOUISE M. BACHTOLD[2]

ABSTRACT

Personality characteristics of achieving and underachieving bright fifth-grade students were studied with the Children's Personality Questionnaire. Underachievers were grouped on the basis of (1) low grades, (2) low achievement test scores, and (3) both low grades and low achievement scores. Credulity, self-confidence, and self-control were components in successful female achievement; emotional stability, seriousness and sensitivity were components in successful male achievement. Underachievers differed in personality factors according to type of underachievement. Underachieving female groups differed in credulity, self-confidence, self-control, and excitability. Underachieving male groups differed in emotional stability, cheerfulness, and sensitivity. Remediation should consider variation in need as related to sex and type of underachievement.

OF MAJOR concern to educators are the students whose scholastic achievement is below the expectancy for their level of ability. Such students have been identified in elementary, high school, and college classes. Although reports on the incidence, as well as the criteria of underachievement vary, the literature reports that nearly half of the more able students may not be attaining their potential scholastic rank.

Barrett (1) cautioned that only by a careful study of each individual can the reason for each underachievement be found. Passow and Goldberg (4) pointed to the need for investigating individual motivation, rationalization, and system of defenses. Frankel (2) reported that the onset of underachievement repeatedly lead to home and parents.

As desirable as the case study approach may be, information on shared characteristics of underachievers should contribute notably to planning remediation programs. Miller's (3) review of work undertaken in defining and identifying aspects of underachievement noted that the search for traits typical of underachievers had not been particularly fruitful. Investigation was recommended into personality characteristics which might foster different traits in different individuals depending on the circumstances. It was further suggested that a group of students selected as underachievers on the basis of school marks

Reprinted with permission from *Journal of Educational Research* (September 1969).

would differ in areas of personality from those selected on the basis of achievement test scores.

It therefore seemed profitable to explore the differences in personality characteristics among high ability students who were selected by different criteria of underachievement. Since the general pattern of scholastic underachievement has been shown to differ for males and females (6), grouping by sex was considered essential. The importance of such grouping was borne out in a recent study by Werner (7), who reported a personality profile for underachieving boys resembling that of conduct problems and delinquents, whereas the underachieving girls were more heedless, happy-go-lucky, and excitable than average girls.

METHOD

High ability fifth-grade students in the Rio Linda Union School District, California, were selected for study. Of a total population of 1,000 fifth-grade students, 227 scored in the top quartile of the School and College Ability Tests (SCAT). Scores on the Sequential Tests of Educational Progress (STEP), and report card grades were compared with SCAT scores on social studies, mathematics, reading, science, and writing for all students in the top quartile.

Underachieving group "A" was composed of those students whose centile band scores on three or more achievement tests fell below their centile band score on the ability measure. Nineteen girls and seventeen boys fell in this group with high report card grades, but low achievement test scores.

Underachieving group "B" was composed of those students who received poor report card grades although their STEP scores were satisfactory. To determine whether report card grades were significantly lower than grades of successful students, mean grade point averages (GPA) were compared by statistical test. The *z ratio* of 4.12 indicated significance beyond the .01 level of confidence. Group "B" included twelve girls and thirteen boys who were strong on achievement tests, but low on school marks.

Underachieving group "AB" was composed of those students whose STEP scores showed three or more achievement tests below their centile band on SCAT, and whose report card grades were significantly low. In group "AB" were six girls and nine boys.

The combined underachieving groups represented one-third of the students in the top quartile on SCAT, thirty-seven girls and thirty-nine boys.

To provide for comparisons of characteristics of achievers and underachievers, students from the top quartile on SCAT and STEP scores with high report card grades were matched by sex, ability level, and school to students who met one of the above criteria for underachievement. Thirty-eight boys and thirty-seven girls were obtained to represent successful students—"O" group.

The IPAT Children's Personality Questionnaire (CPQ) 1959, Form A was administered to all groups. For children eight to twelve years of age, the CPQ measures fourteen dimensions of personality described in Porter and Cattell's CPQ Handbook (5) as follows:

A—aloof, stiff versus sociable
B—less intelligent versus more intelligent
C—emotionally unstable versus emotionally mature

D—phlegmatic versus over-active
E—mild versus aggressive
F—serious versus cheerful
G—casual versus persistent
H—shy versus adventurous
I—tough-minded versus sensitive
J—group versus self-oriented
N—simple, credulous versus socially sophisticated
O—confident versus insecure
Q3—uncontrolled versus self-controlled
Q4—composed, relaxed versus tense, excitable

Analysis of variance and t-tests yielded nine factors that showed significant differences among achievers and different types of underachievers.

RESULTS AND DISCUSSION

No significant differences between groups were found on factors B, D, G, H, and J. The remaining nine factors revealed, at the .05 level of confidence or better, significant personality differences among the groups. These differences were not the same for female and male groups. Girls differed in credulity (N), self-confidence (O), self-control (Q3), and excitability (Q4). Boys differed in emotional stability (C), cheerfulness (F), and sensitivity (I). Sociability (A) and aggressiveness (E) indicated sex differences only.

Girls who were successful on the basis of standardized tests, but whose grades indicated poor progress presented greatest variability. They were less credulous (N), less confident (O), less self-controlled (Q3), and more excitable (Q4) than other girl groups. Girls low only on achievement test scores differed from other underachieving girls in the same characteristics as did the successful girls. In common, both groups received high report card grades and were more credulous, more confident, and less excitable than girls who had poor grades. Girls low on achievement scores and on grades showed greater self-control than did the girls low only on grades.

Greater emotional stability (C) was shown by boys who were underachieving on the basis of school marks than by boys who were identified as below ability level on achievement tests. It is probable that there is here indicated some relationship between emotional stability and high performance on standardized tests.

Boys whose school marks were high but who were weak on achievement tests were more serious (F) than both the successful male group and the boys who were low both on marks and tests. It might be wondered to what extent this introspective, sober, deliberate characteristic might influence teachers' grading practices.

Sensitivity (I), as noted in the CPQ Handbook, yields higher scores for females than for males. Further validation is offered in this study by the significantly higher scores for girls in each group. Although sensitivity did not appear as a discriminating characteristic in female underachievement, it did relate to male success. Boy groups who were succeeding on achievement tests, or on the basis of report card grades, or on both tests and grades, all revealed greater sensitivity than the group who were underachieving on both tests and grades. It appears that some degree of sensitivity is a component of scholastic achievement for boys.

Girls tended to be more sociable (A), and less aggressive (E) than the boys. Girls low on report card grades were significantly more sociable than their male counterparts, as were the successful girls. Boys low on achievement tests and report card grades were significantly more aggressive than their female counterparts, as were the successful boys.

CONCLUSIONS

Unless underachievers are studied according to type of underachievement, gross misconceptions may occur. Results of this investigation indicate that remediation for underachieving boys requires different approaches than for underachieving girls, and both sexes should be viewed in terms of the type of underachievement. For example, girls who are underachieving on the basis of GPA might be more successful if efforts were directed toward reducing their excitability, increasing their confidence, and helping them to be more credulous—more accepting of ideas. Since girls who were underachieving only on the basis of low achievement test scores differed from girls with low grades in the same direction as did the successful girls, it may be that assistance in techniques of taking tests would correct their difficulty. On the other hand, boys whose underachievement was based on achievement test scores showed less emotional stability than the boys whose test scores were satisfactory, but who had low grades. It would seem that counseling for increased emotional stability should be conducive to higher test performance for boys.

Characteristics of high ability, high achieving males as compared with underachievers were found to be emotional stability, seriousness, and sensitivity. Sensitivity as a characteristic of the successful males might well be further studied. A sex related factor, sensitivity as a component in male achievement at fifth grade level could be associated with the influence of teachers, who are usually women at the elementary level. There is also the possibility that the culture fosters sensitivity in academically oriented boys, and encourages the development of traits described as kindly, artistic, and imaginative (5).

Characteristics of high ability, high achieving females as compared with underachievers were found to be credulity, self-confidence, and self-control. An interesting area for further exploration is suggested by the finding that credulity, which implies dependency and acceptance of preconceived ideas, was a component in feminine scholastic success. Should this tendency persist at older levels, it might be wondered to what extent the culture imposes conformity in thinking as a price of feminine achievement.

FOOTNOTES:

[1]This paper is based on a doctoral dissertation presented in partial fulfillment of the Ed.D. requirement at the University of the Pacific. The author wishes to acknowledge her indebtedness to Jay W. Reeve, who served as adviser.

[2]Now at the University of California, Davis.

REFERENCES:

[1]Barrett, H.O. "An Intensive Study of 32 Gifted Children," *Personnel and Guidance Journal*, XXXVI (1957), pp. 192–194.

[2]Frankel, E. "Gifted Academic Underachievers," *Science Teacher*, XXVIII (1961), pp. 49–51.

[3]Miller, L.M. *Guidance for the Underachiever with Superior Ability* (Washington, D.C.: United States Department of Health, Education, and Welfare, Bulletin No. 25, OE25021, 1961).

[4]Passow, H.A. and Goldberg, Miriam. "Study of Underachieving Gifted," *Educational Leadership*, XVI (1958), pp. 121–125.

[5]Porter R.B. and Cattell, R.B. *Handbook for the IPAT Children's Personality Questionnaire* (Champaign, Illinois: Institute for Personality and Ability Testing, 1960).

[6]Shaw, M.C. and McCuen, J.T. "The Onset of Academic Underachievement in Bright Children," *Journal of Educational Psychology*, LI (1960), pp. 103–108.

[7]Werner, Emmy E. "CPQ Personality Factors of Talented and Underachieving Boys and Girls in Elementary School," *Journal of Clinical Psychology*, XXII (1966), pp. 461–464.

Questions:

1. What special assistance do you feel should be given to the classroom teacher to help girls reduce their excitability, increase their confidence, and become more credulous?

2. List the specifics which would aid an inner city teacher in helping high ability underachievers.

URBAN PRESCHOOL CHILDREN

By DORIS C. CHING

Who is the urban preschool child? What are his specific needs? What experiences will develop him?

Research[1] has shown that the quality of the child's experiences during his preschool years determines to a great extent his progress in education. It is the preschool teacher who will build the foundation upon which all future teachers will continue to build.

Within one classroom there are many different kinds of urban children with a variety of backgrounds. In order to help the urban child grow emotionally, socially and intellectually, the teacher must have a knowledge of the child's home background and its possible effects on him.

Let us find out about Jimmy, Maria and Johnny—all urban children from a preschool classroom.

Jimmy is a four-year-old Negro child, born in Nashville, Tennessee, who lives with his mother and eight brothers and sisters in a slum neighborhood. where others live who have also migrated from the South. His mother had two high-school years of education and is a domestic worker. She had moved West from Nashville, settled in Los Angeles with her family where she was able to get a steady job. Her husband had left to look for work one morning in Nashville and had not returned. The money she earns is needed for necessities of daily living, so there are few objects, toys, and in fact no books in the home. Jimmy's mother is too tired when she returns home from work to converse with him about his interests or activities. When his mother does speak to him, it usually is to give a command or reprimand him. His mother and the children with whom he plays all speak a dialect of English which varies considerably from standard English. The large number of children in the crowded quarters of the home makes it almost impossible to find a quiet corner. To keep the children occupied, the radio or television is turned on loudly. most of the day. In preschool Jimmy often does not comprehend what the teacher says to him and the other children. He doesn't seem to have the faintest notion of how to use toys or other objects in play; he competes for the teacher's attention and for toys in an aggressive and self-centered manner. He shows no interest in stories read to the class at story time.

Reprinted by permission of Doris C. Ching and the Association for Childhood Education International, 3615 Wisconsin Avenue, N.W., Washington D. C. Copyright © 1968 by the Association. (*Childhood Education*, September 1968, Vol. 45, No. 1)

In the same classroom is Maria.

Maria's parents were born in Los Angeles, California, the children of parents born in Mexico. The maternal grandparents live with Maria, her parents and six brothers and sisters. Maria's parents are able to speak English but are proud of their cultural heritage and often speak Spanish. The family is more comfortable and relaxed when conversing with one another in Spanish. Maria is shy and does not say much in school because she does not know the English words for objects and concepts and is not sure that she has the correct English words to express her thoughts and feelings. Because English is a second language and Spanish the primary language used in her home, Maria has difficulty when she enters school in understanding the teacher and in expressing herself in standard English. Differences in the pronunciation of sounds in Spanish and English often confuse her.

Johnny is a classmate of Jimmy and Maria.

Johnny lives with his parents and nine brothers and sisters in a depressed area. His father has been unable to find a steady job and frequently comes home in an alcoholic condition. His mother works in a factory and is the sole support of the family. Neither parent takes time to converse with Johnny about his experiences or interests. His father is absorbed with his problems and his mother too busy with her responsibilities when she returns home from work. There is a scarcity of objects, toys and books in the home and Johnny does not have opportunities to visit people and places outside the immediate neighborhood. In school Johnny is often inattentive and disinterested; in order to gain recognition from the teacher, he resorts to hitting and disturbing other children and making unnecessary noises.

Not all urban preschoolers are affected in the same manner by the deficits in their home environment. Various lacks within the home environment may bring about a variety of negative factors which may be present in varying degrees in children or, in some cases, not be present at all. It is important that the teacher of such children have a knowledge and understanding of the possible negative effects of the deficits in the home environment so she will be able to select appropriate experiences to meet their needs.

What are some of the deficits caused by home environments in Jimmy, Maria and Johnny?

LANGUAGE FACILITY

The first aspect of deficits is language facility. Because in Jimmy's home a dialect of English (not standard English) is spoken and in Maria's home Spanish is spoken, both children have been exposed to a different system of speech sounds and to a syntactical structure of considerable simplicity or one which may order words differently within a sentence.

When a sound with which they are not familiar is used, Jimmy and Maria tend to hear the sound inaccurately and reproduce it with its nearest equivalent in the sound system with which *they* are familiar. They sometimes confuse meanings of words because of confusion of sounds in the two languages or dialects. For example, when the teacher asks Maria to use the word *hot* in a sentence, she says: "I put the *hot* (hat) on my head" (*a* is pronounced *ah* in Spanish).

The word order and degree of complexity of the sentences which the teacher uses often overwhelm Jimmy, Maria and Johnny. Also, their vocabulary is woefully inadequate. Jimmy has learned labels which are unique within his culture for various concepts. Jimmy and Johnny have no labels for some concepts or objects because they lack experiences and opportunities to communicate much about them to anyone. Maria frequently knows the Spanish words but not English ones for various concepts.

The lack of practice in verbalizing in general by Jimmy and Johnny and the lack of practice in hearing and using standard English by Maria result in a negative effect on their language facility in school.

At New York Medical College scientists studying school failures in the first five grades discovered that the basic deficiency in these children was their inability to communicate. They had no defects of the nervous system, hearing or vision. Their problems were that they had seldom been spoken to at home; their family life was such that the use of language was not encouraged. Lack of communication with parents resulted in lack of ability to communicate in school.

SENSORY PERCEPTION

When Jimmy, Maria and Johnny enter school, their auditory and visual skills are likely to be less developed than those of their middle-class peers. The large number of people in the homes of Jimmy, Maria and Johnny gives them little opportunity for quiet, and thus they have learned inattention to their surroundings. Having learned inattention, they are less likely to be stimulated by and to respond to their surroundings.

Familiarity with a different system of speech sounds, particularly in Maria's case, has resulted in Maria and Jimmy being deficient in the auditory skills needed for understanding and eventually learning to read English.

Jimmy and Johnny are affected negatively to a greater degree than Maria in auditory and visual perception. Because they have not had opportunities to manipulate and organize various objects, their visual and tactile skills have not been developed to any extent. Lack of verbal interaction with adults and lack of corrective feedback in enunciation, pronunciation and grammar have resulted in their having poor auditory skills.

Thus, visual discrimination and auditory discrimination skills, both important to Jimmy, Maria and Johnny if they are to learn to read, have not been developed to the extent that will make it possible for them to succeed in school. Unless they are given help by the teacher in developing these skills during their preschool years, they will encounter much difficulty and frustration in school during their elementary years.

SELF-CONCEPT

A child's self-concept, what he thinks of himself, has an important influence on his ability to learn in the school situation. In Maria's case, because her family is proud of their cultural heritage, she will probably enter school with a positive self-concept. However, this may easily be reversed when she finds she is different from her classmates in culture, language and appearance—unless the teacher helps her and her classmates develop positive attitudes toward both the Mexican and the American cultures. Also, if her language background causes her to have difficulty in the school situation, she will develop an idea about herself as a person who cannot succeed in school.

Jimmy enters school with a negative self-concept because he has assimilated some of the reflected values of his culture through his mother and older brothers and sisters. Because of the absence of a father at home, Jimmy has had no experience with a successful male model. He has not developed the psychological feeling that effort can result in achievement. Since he does not understand, he is not succeeding in school and is not being stimulated, his negative self-concept is further developed, and he is acquiring a low evaluation of his individual competence. Jimmy may lose all motivation to do well and succeed in school unless the teacher is able to provide experiences and guide him to develop his self-concept in a positive direction.

Johnny has also had no experience with a successful male model. He too has not developed the feeling that effort can result in achievement. Because of his mother's fear that Johnny will grow up to be like his father, she pushes him to do well and, no matter what he does, she expects him to do better so that nothing he does ever pleases her. Unless the teacher can provide him with experiences in which he can succeed so that he can begin to develop a positive self-concept, Johnny will continue on his path to failure and frustration in school.

SOCIAL, EMOTIONAL, EXPERIENTIAL READINESS

Social, emotional and experiential factors play an important part in the child's ability to succeed in school. These factors have been interlaced in this article, but some points need focus.

Maria's shyness and Jimmy's and Johnny's aggressive behavior may hinder their school achievement. Maria's hesitancy in asking questions and Jimmy's and Johnny's inability to get along with their classmates may prevent them from learning as much as they could from the various experiences in which they participate in the classroom.

Jimmy's and Johnny's home experiences, in particular, have not helped them to develop positive attitudes toward learning and doing—to find pleasure in learning for its own sake. They have not been motivated by recognition for achieving and learning and, at most, probably enter school with neutral—if not negative—attitudes toward learning. Because Jimmy and Johnny have not been exposed to places and people outside their immediate home and family, they will need much teacher guidance in broadening their concepts and understandings to succeed in school.

One can readily see that Jimmy's and Johnny's needs are far greater than Maria's. If any child's needs are not seen and met by the teacher in his early years at school, he will have few success experiences and much failure and frustration in school and thus acquire a negative self-image as well as a negative attitude toward learning and school in general.

[1] See ACEI leaflet, *Review of Research Related to Advantages of Kindergarten,* by Mindess and Keliher, 1967.

Question:

1. Using the information presented in this article, write a composite picture of a typical urban preschool child.

WILL THE REAL MEXICAN AMERICAN PLEASE STAND UP

By PHILIP MONTEZ

The author is Western Regional Director, United States Commission on Civil Rights. The following is a revised version of a speech, originally delivered at The National Conference of Mexican American School Board Members held in Washington, D.C. and sponsored by the Scholarship, Education and Defense Fund and Southwest Council of La Raza, June 26-28, 1969.

When one examines the role of the Mexican American in education, one is also looking at the role of the Mexican American in the total society. For what happens to Mexican Americans in the schools will continue to be their role outside. It cannot continue to be the same role allotted to the Mexican American in the past. I refuse to accept that Mexican Americans can survive and graduate from our educational institutions only by having them become tanned Anglos. If we sincerely try to see what the Mexican American brings to schools and utilize that, we would be stimulating educational systems to create a new exciting person—the real Mexican American. A truly bilingual, bicultural person who epitomizes the best of two cultures. Who, incidentally, has existed since the coming of the gringo to the Southwest, not because of the system but in spite of it. As Harold Howe, past Commissioner of Education, said:

> *Mexican Americans are one of the few exceptions to this American rule of cultural elimination through cultural disdain. A distinctive Spanish-Indian-Mexican culture survives in the United States.*

We have to develop a frame of reference, a frame of mind, which takes in the total personality of the Mexican American. I, for one, am perturbed that I am constantly being tabbed as an immigrant. If we look at the history of the Southwest, the status of the Mexican American as an immigrant is unrealistic. The Southwest has been and will continue to be a cultural extension of our Latin neighbors to the south, especially Mexico. We are never going to eliminate that influence. Oh, I am sure that there are ways of doing it, if we took a big pair of scissors and cut Mexico off and sent it floating into the Pacific. Or we might build a fifty foot wall and everytime a Mexican tried to talk with somebody on the other side we might shoot him. Then we could begin to eliminate the cultural and linguistic influence of the people to the south of us. There are 260 million people south of the Mexican border, 260 million people who speak Spanish; and I have my doubts that if we went south and told them that English was the only language—nos iban a decir ha donde nos fueramos (they're going to tell us where we could go). This is not only historical reality, but cultural and linguistic reality, which will always exist. I repeat, that in spite of the system, the Mexico Americano in the Southwest will always be bilingual, bicultural

Reprinted with permission from *INTEGRATED EDUCATION: Race and Schools* (May-June 1970).

regardless of those of us who become assimilated, in spite of the system whose purpose seems to be the assimilation of everyone.

THE AGING SENOR MONTEZ

Several times I have heard students elaborate on the all important Mexicanismo of the Mexican American. I disagree with the youth movement today on one point—their interpretation of history—it may be a part of the generation gap because I am 22 and they are in their teens. But one thing which I found in researching the history of the Mexican American was the impact of the gringos. The inferior status which was given to the Mexican American was accepted by the Mexican American, forced to relinquish much of his overt Mexicanismo. Many of us today are grappling with that same status within our own personalities. Let us not forget that we are still dealing with the results of this historical event, trying to become Anglicized while at the same time, trying to retain our Mexicanismo. One thing which the students overlook is that the acceptance of this inferior status by those Mexican Americans was their way to survive in the Southwest. If they had fought that status, they would have been annihilated. Today, many of us could have been on reservations.

We don't have to kid ourselves about the past; we are all a product of it. When I recall the tears and sorrow which my parents felt as Mexicanos who couldn't understand the system; when I remember what they went through because they couldn't give me the necessary tools to deal with the society. I also remember that they encouraged me to try to get "in" (white liberal movements). I now remember their efforts, but for years, as many of us did, I rejected them—the older generation—not really understanding that the Mexicano did not want to accept the role which he was given; but he had no alternative if he wanted to survive. I think that this is important for us to understand, for in many ways the young people are stressing a philosophy which borders on cultural vacuum. This emphasis is an important step toward destroying the inferior status given Mexican Americans.

The young Mexican American wants to wipe out the experiences of his parents and grandparents.

This, I maintain, can't be done if we want to build on our Mexicanismo. To get where we're going we have to accept where we've been—no matter how degrading that past might have been.

Our greatest asset has been family cohesiveness. Why destroy it now with a so-called generation gap?

MEXICAN RAP BROWNS

Ironically, as I listen to many militants, and others in the community, I am not hearing Mexico Americanos; I am hearing Rap Browns and Stokely Carmichaels, who say that they are Mexicanos. For example, "Tio Tomas" in Spanish is a phrase of endearment, "Mi tio Tomas." You can't literally translate from Uncle Tom to Tio Tomas. It just doesn't have the impact. We see that even the young people speak with the vernacular of assimilated people while struggling for their Mexicanismo. But the real Mexican American is very different in many respects.

The ambivalence of these young people today reminds me of some of the strains I went through. I thought for a while that I was the only Mexican American attending the University of Southern California, and I began to develop an illusion—man, I said, I must be an exception to all the rules. I am making it. I recall when I graduated that the teacher placement office wanted to send me to a barrio school. I said wait a minute, man, I know I don't own the suit I have on, but I am going to own it in another six payments. I've been through the Mexican thing all my life, why do I have to keep doing it. Again, the conflicts of not knowing myself. I had a bachelor's degree and a general secondary credential and I was ready to become an Anglo. I thought I had all the credentials, but I had forgotten that I still looked like a Mexican.

IDENTITY DENIAL

There was another Chicano on the campus who became involved with a nice blonde, blue-eyed Anglo girl, and who for purposes of this meeting we will say that his name was Martinez. He made the terrible mistake of falling in love which was no problem until they confronted her father. The father said, wait a minute; I can go for the dating stuff, but you are a Mexican, so you can't marry my daughter. So it got to the point that the young man and the young girl said we are going to get married anyway. The father offered a compromise: "If you change your name you may marry; you don't really look like a Mexican, it's the name that bothers me. So the poor guy goes to court, goes through the whole ritual, and the judge says your name is now McKeever. He goes to the university and he and I were going all over the campus changing the records, gotta wipe it out. I remember one secretary that we spoke with while she was changing the record, and she said, "Martinez to What? McKeever!" It was a cultural shock for that gringa girl.

But one thing which always amazed me about Mr. Martinez McKeever, was that when he was married his parents couldn't even attend the wedding because they didn't speak English. They would have confronted the white world and blown my friend's illusion.

Despite the ritual of name changing, it is my contention, that today Mr. McKeever is still acting like a Mexicano. He changed his name and he did other superficial things, but I bet that gringa is saying how come you are acting so much like a Mexican?

That was the era when the system gave the Mexican no other way but to become assimilated. Now, with the student movement the pendulum has swung from one extreme—of the society demanding that we become assimilated—back to Mexican Americans demanding that they retain Mexicanismo. I see this step as a reflection of maturing democracy. But it is only a step. Neither extreme is going to do one bit of good, because the people who are talking about Mexicanismo articulate in English, act like assimilated Anglos, and make demands like Anglos. So consequently, that isn't our bag. We are not Mexicanos. If we travel to Mexico, we know that the educational system is as monolithic a structure as the Anglo system in this country. Only in a different language. On the other hand, is our answer total assimilation? No! Because total assimilation has tended to destroy the personality that we are—a combination of both—Mexican, American. We can not avoid that even in the barrios today. Families are speaking Spanish, comida de tamales, tortillas, frijoles, etc. But they leave that environment to go to the Anglo society to learn their tricks, and it is a very difficult psychological position for people. It can be self-destructive. Every Mexican American in this room must know what I am talking about because if you haven't gone through the process, brother, you've had it made.

When Dr. Jack Forbes testified before our Commission in San Antonio, Texas, he was asked the question by our General Counsel, "Why hasn't the Mexican American assimilated in the Southwest?" He answered, "Excuse me sir, but that is the wrong question. Why hasn't the Anglo assimilated?" That is what the problem is.

Just for now, I am not concerned with who assimilated with whom, but I would like to know why we haven't produced the educational programs which reflect an awareness of the bilingual, bicultural personality of the Mexican American. In a democracy, it is my contention that no person should have to become assimilated at the expense of his personality. It is self defeating. Mr. Howe has put this concept even more strongly:

> *[Our society] equates Anglo American origin and Anglo American ways with virtue, with goodness, even with political purity. Other cultures are not merely different; they are inferior. They must be wiped out, not only for the good of the country, but for the good of the child. Not only must he learn to speak English; he must stop speaking anything else.*

Is that democracy?

INADEQUATE SCHOOLS

Certainly, in this prevailing atmosphere, school districts in the Southwest are not attuned to educating Mexican Americans. We don't have to cite statistics on drop-outs and non-employables to know that. Some professionals with direct knowledge of the needs of Mexican Americans have looked at programs developed specifically for them. They say and I agree that the programs are superficial to say the least. Many of you as members of Boards of Education are continually plagued with finances. Since 1965, many new programs have been introduced to the schools, financed by the Federal and State governments to supplement and complement local resources, and especially to help minorities. Some of these programs have accomplished much, but a strange thing has happened. If money does not come from outside sources, these programs begin to diminish. If the program is really more than supplemental—actually reaching the students for the first time and producing results, it should be financed by all the resources so that it isn't discontinued if the Federal government says that there is no more money. That is the kind of local commitment which is presently lacking.

Today, when we analyze current research on Mexican Americans done by people who have an Anglo frame of reference we still see the abortive efforts to Anglicize Mexican Americans. Recently, a study was completed at UCLA (University of California at Los Angeles), the main focus of which was the low aspiration level of the Mexican American. And they proved that it was so. Now everybody is saying "up their aspiration level."

I have looked at other research by some leading scholars in the Southwest which also implies that I and people like me lack motivation. Yes, I lack motivation when it comes time to get up in the morning. But the crucial point for Mexican Americans is that no scholars have researched the psychology of what happens to a group when the predominant society spends 100 years degrading, kicking, segregating, and dehumanizing them. Consequently, they are not given equal educational opportunity. These things which the researchers "discover" such as lack of motivation, low aspirations are not Mexican cultural values. They are standards which occur when people have been degraded to the point that all they know is to isolate themselves and to separate themselves from a system which knows only how to hurt, y como duele (and how it hurts). Even the universities which produce our scholars in the Southwest have failed in attempting to know the Mexican American. They continue to place the cart before the horse. They look at motivation and aspiration before they know what society has done by us. By providing superficial programs, the society will never have to acknowledge what it has done to a people's culture in a supposedly democratic society. This indicates to me that in all the things we are trying to do for Mexican Americans nobody has accepted the fact that the system has done a lousy job and has given us a royal screwing. Nobody is willing to accept that.

The blame always ends up on my back. The blame always ends up on the backs of my mother and my father who lacked the motivation to send me to school. This is the biggest crock I have ever heard coming out of American research.

Let us look at the results of many of the programs now in the schools. What happens to Mexican Americans when they enter English as a Second Language bilingual program?

TRUE BILINGUALISM

They look around and once again the stereotype is perpetuated. Because the only people in that program are Mexicanos. And they go—ooh, otra vez (another time)—and they are caught in a tug-a-war, again. They say to themselves, "This can't be very important because it isn't for the other kids. It can't have too much status; how come only us Chicanos come here?" A true bilingual program is a program for all the citizens of this country, not a superficial one just for Mexicans.

The youth movement today has shown something to us and I hope that some of us who are a part of the generation gap have shown something to them. The students have shown us that the Mexican American personality can pull itself together enough to survive this devastating system which I have talked about. I contend to young and old, that the Mexican American because of his ability to be functional in two societies, the Hispanic as well as the Anglo, has the potential for being the class elite of the Southwest. That's what the Mexican American needs, a superiority complex to overcome the inferior status which was given to him. When this happens, we will be well on our way.

The young people are showing us that not as one person but as a group of people—just as we are gathered here as a group of Mexican American school board members—we can have a sense of self identity. That I, Felipe Montez, alias Philip Montez, can believe in a democratic society in which I was brought up, that I can be a Mexican American with dignity and self-respect. When we talk about educational programs I want to know what the Administration is willing to do to begin to learn what the Mexican counterpart of me and my children is. When will the schools finally acknowledge that I can't survive in that system if the only demands are that I become blonde, blue-eyed and Anglo. I have to beg and plead that I can't do it. I am happy like this, a little brown, but not too bad; I stayed out of the sun. But this is the only way I can be a total human being.

This acceptance of the Mexican part of me—by me and by others—is not nationalistic. It is a real day-to-day way of life for the people who live it. And this is the contribution to the educational institutions which the Mexican Americans extend with open arms. We bring our superior ability to schools not only for other Mexican Americans but for the total society. All peoples, black, brown, white, yellow, or whatever color, can share in the beauty of being bilingual and bicultural if they want. We are not going to force it down their throats. But we ask them, if they want a piece of it, aqui esta (here it is). If they don't, fine. Dr. Edmund Gordon warns us how difficult this interaction will be:

> *Few of us are really able to straddle cultures and to use knowledge of other cultures creatively. Even fewer of us have the capacity to adopt experiences from our own value systems to alien value systems without being patronizing.*

As difficult as this is, the Mexican American is willing to go half way.

ACCEPT DIVERSITY

It is my contention that every person who graduates from high school in the Southwest should speak Spanish and English. We have the natural resources to do it. Mr. Howe commented on this direction by saying:

> *Mexican American children offer their Anglo classmates a great natural teaching resource. It is time we stopped wasting that resource and instead enabled youngsters to move back and forth from one language to another without a sense of difficulty or strangeness.*

We saw a program in Webb County, Texas, outside of Laredo. The superintendent, an Anglo, said we have bilingual education for all students. It is not just because we have Mexican Americans in our district, but because we believe bilingual education is good for all young people. If you go to that district in Webb County, you see black, white, brown spending half a day speaking Spanish and half a day speaking English. The superintendent is developing truly bilingual, bicultural personalities in his district. It is the only real program I have seen.

What does this mean for the future? We as Mexican Americans are very responsible to the society in which we live. We always have been and we always will be. Mexican American is not a political term. America is a political term which means we owe our allegiance to this society; there is no need to go into our war record or anything else to illustrate our allegiance. Culturally, however, we are Mexican American. Will the society give the Mexican American a greater opportunity to make a contribution, in international politics, for example? If Latin America continues to develop the way it is, will the Mexican American who is bilingual and bicultural be able to make a contribution? Mr. Howe thinks that the Mexican American can, especially since the United States has taken on international responsibilities.

> *The notion of cultural superiority has seriously harmed the United States in this century in its dealings with other peoples. . . . In the middle of this century after nearly 150 years of largely ignoring the rest of the world, we have lumbered into the family of nations as an international force. A position of international responsibility was thrust upon us, and we were ill-prepared to assume it.*

We blew Cuba simply because we did not understand the Latin mind. Prior to the commitments of Castro to communism, we were ambivalent about our role in that revolution. So it was not a revolution of capitalism and free enterprise versus communism. It was a revolution of people who were hungry in a system that could not feed them. It was only after Castro came to the United States with his communism, that we cut the ties with Cuba. But we didn't know what was going on in Latin America.

So what does this all mean for Board Members and schools specifically? As we think about what is happening to the Mexican American in education, I repeat, that assimilation is not the answer. Mexicanismo all to itself is not the answer. The Mexican American can not survive trying to play both ends for the middle. It's impossible. We can't do it.

Young people today can not survive that way. This is the tug-a-war which has been going on for the Mexicano for over a hundred years. I don't think that in a democratic society anyone should have to become Anglicized or assimilated. We must accept the Mexican American as a functional personality who is bilingual, bicultural, who can take the best of two cultures and make a major contribution to this society.

We hope with the coming of young people to the colleges, with the help of the institutions (with or without their help), with the help of realistic programs in the public schools that we will see emerging the true Mexican American, the real Mexican American I mentioned in the beginning. Will the real Mexican Americans please stand up!

Questions:

1. To what extent do you feel that the Mexican-American in the urban community should be assimilated? Explain.

2. What are some questions to consider when discussing the need to raise the aspiration level of the Mexican-American?

3. Describe briefly the key points that you feel need to be considered in order for the Mexican-American to overcome an inferiority complex.

THE SLUM CHILD

By IMOGENE H. DRAPER

Last summer I was a member of a panel, a position not uncommon to those of us involved in the education of American youth. I was making a plea for a different approach to teaching English. As I asserted that the teacher must only provide stimulation through which each child may probe and discover himself and his world on an individual basis, I was forcibly interrupted by a middle-aged gentleman from a prominent, private, preparatory school who challenged, "Don't you teach any subject matter?" My quiet reply was, "I teach in the slums, Mr. X."

Subject matter to many a child in the slums is a nasty, nauseous dose administered by an innocent, well-meaning, cure-all agent: the teacher, with the following directions: Close your eyes. Open wide. Swallow quickly. Such directions are accompanied with a smile, a pat on the head, and the reassuring words, "It'll take a while, but that will do you good. Just wait and see."

The child too often gags, spits, spews and vomits it violently and even leaves uncured with a sickness for life. Could this be correlative to our society's rejection of him and his knowledge of this rejection?

The only meaningful learning takes place when motivation springs from within the learner and success is achieved upon the recognition of personal growth by an awareness of new gains in the control of the forces which directly affect his life. Opportunities to have a productive future for most of the children in the very heart of "Slum City, U.S.A." are still very limited. Those who are eventually able to establish productive lives for themselves will do so through traveling the economic route of semi-skilled and possibly skilled workers in America. Although the number is increasing, a relatively small number of the total will attend colleges and universities, and thereby enter the professions.

The teacher must face these facts realistically. If, at the beginning of the school year, the teacher conducts a survey among his students, he is likely to discover that each aspires to a productive, rewarding economic and social position in America. Ask, "What do you want to do with your life?" Replies such as the following may be expected: "I want to be a secretary, a nurse, a doctor, a teacher, a technician, a disc jockey, an entertainer." No one is likely to admit, "I want to be a failure," even if he has been socially promoted to the eleventh grade with a second grader's ability to read.

Parents' attitude is another consideration. Often parents in the slums are ignored or scorned. But parents echo the high aspirations of their children.

Reprinted with permission from *The Clearing House* (September 1970).

Contrary to the suspicions of the middle-class American taxpayer, who feels that he supplies the monthly welfare check, few parents in the slums are content with their plight of poverty, disease, and crime. They want a better life for their children.

I should like to offer some suggestions to English teachers for helping slum children set realistic goals and making learning a personal experience in the classroom.

First, use the beginning class periods in September as guidance sessions. Find out what each child wants to do with his life. Help him focus on how he can use the English class to his advantage. Avoid rushing in with your extensive reading lists and one-thousand-word essay assignments to show those kids what a tough teacher you are. Forget about your ambition to get through the English literature book by May this year. So your twelfth grade English teacher spent two months covering *Macbeth*. Perhaps you emerged with a new appreciation for the beauty of the language in Shakespeare. You were college bound. You needed that learning experience. Your students may not be college bound. Their needs are not your needs.

Throughout the year, spend most of your time in planning and guidance. Plan with the student—or better, let the student plan with you. What does he plan to do with his life? Guide him toward books which deal with subjects in his prospective field. Make use of his personal heroes in sports, entertainment, politics, world affairs. Must every poor, black boy read the biography of George Washington Carver? Why not Dick Gregory's *Nigger?*—Bill Russell's *Go Up for Glory?*—Richard Wright's *Black Boy?* Such books are apt to capture his interest and the spirit of his own personal struggle, which, unmistakenly, each black boy has. A small paperback library in the classroom facilitates the reading program greatly. The books are immediately at hand. Questions and comments may be shared with the teacher and classmates while the interest in a particular book is at its peak. There can be no waiting to go to the main school library. If you don't have a classroom library, harrass the department head, the principal, and the supervisor until you get it. In the meantime, you may have to invest a few of your own coins to begin one. I did; it was well worth it to see the eager response.

Let writing experiences grow out of practical needs. It is ridiculous to have a teenage mother in English 10 who spends weeks struggling through themes on *Julius Caesar,* while she never learns to write a legible note to her child's nursery school teacher. The writing journal is an effective way to provide for creative expression. For many students it becomes a possession of pride. They look forward to a few minutes each day to write. It is very revealing to the teacher, but it should be personal, and not be graded.

The only valuable study is independent study. The modern classroom sets a high premium on speed in learning. Not only must the student swallow big doses of "subject matter," but he must do it in gulps. We know that not all children learn at the same rate. Yet, in many high schools, we prescribe little blocks of time: a three-week unit, a six-week period, in which we demand that a measurable amount of learning take place. Let the student work toward his objectives at his own pace. Provisions can be made for this approach rather easily.

(1) Keep individual student folders for all work immediately accessible from the classroom file drawer.

(2) Maintain a wide variety of materials, such as newspapers, magazines, journals, and language drill kits.

(3) Keep a permanent place for displaying examples of improvement and special accomplishments.

(4) Arrange to have resource persons of diverse background come into the classroom for group discussions on contemporary topics.

(5) Plan field trips wisely, and often for just a small group of three to five students. Perhaps, take one, if there is a chance that his life will be enriched.

The teacher's role is simply to give guidance where it is needed. Check with the student to see how he is coming along in his daily work. Examine his folder regularly. Make comments and recommendations. Help him redefine his goals. Point him toward the most helpful resources. Finally, trust him to do his work after he has a clear view of his goals. This is a real challenge. The child in the slums is often perceived as a liar, a thief, and a cheat. What is worse, as a result of some forces in our society, this is likewise his perception of himself. Trust him. This may be his first experience at holding another person's trust. When he is convinced of your trust, he may surpass your greatest expectations in an effort to prove himself worthy of this newly found quality in a fellow human being.

What evaluation techniques may be used with an approach such as this one? Before making suggestions, I should like to emphasize that it is ironic that many a child in the slums is a repeated "failure" by the time he reaches high school. Realistically, he should not fail because he does not master what the teacher often calls "her" test. He should not fail because he does not accomplish what she expects him to accomplish. More importantly, he should not fail because he does not accomplish what she learned when she was his age. In such a context, the child's success or failure is entirely dependent upon the *teacher's* goals.

I suggest that evaluation should be conducted jointly by the student and the teacher. When the student's personal objectives direct the learning experience, these should serve as the basis of evaluation. One series of questions I ask students each time I am required to make out report cards is as follows:

How would you measure your growth this marking period?

What grade have you earned?

What reasons can you state in support of your receiving the grade?

No other writing assignment is more worthwhile. I have by this means received most forthright critical evaluations of self. Often, I have also received a forthright, critical evaluation of the teacher, which is seldom allowed for in the standard teacher-made test.

When oral or written tests are administered to the whole class, the phrasing of the questions must be done with care. Each question should be phrased to draw an evaluation of the lesson's personal significance to the student and his goals, independently of his classmates. Again, what does he plan to do? How can he make use of what he has learned in the future?

Through this approach, the high school English teacher of the child in the slum may rise to the call for relevance today. The goals are set by the student. The work is done by the student. The evaluation is conducted by the student. The role of the teacher is one of giving guidance when and where it is needed. The responsibility for learning rests with the learner. This is the personal approach to teaching and learning.

———————

Questions:

1. Describe the technique or method you would use to draw out from each student "What he wants to do with his life".

2. What do you feel would be the English consultant's reaction to the use of practical need themes as opposed to *Julius Caesar* themes?

3. Relate your feelings regarding the idea that student achievement is directly related to the interest and the trust expressed toward a student by the teacher.

BLACK POWER AND
ACHIEVEMENT MOTIVATION

By SAMUEL L. WOODARD

If I am not for myself, who will be?
If I am for myself alone, what am I?
If not now, when?

Ethics of the Fathers 1:14

Why was I, a black orphan at age six from a northern ghetto, sufficiently motivated to obtain an Ed.D. from the State University of New York? What have been major behavioral patterns of other black people who have overcome seemingly impossible odds to lead productive lives, even in the South? What is so intriguing and hopeful about the concept of Black Power? The answer to these questions revealed themselves over a period of years as I compared empirical facts of my struggle for survival to achievement motivation theory developed by a group of psychologists at Harvard University, most notably David McClelland.

Participation in an achievement motivation training weekend during the fall of 1967 while I was on the faculty of Temple University, and observation at the 1968 Black Power Conference in Philadelphia confirmed my thinking. In its highest sense Black Power is analogous to achievement motivation theory and practice.

I now make the assumption that any Afro-American who achieves above average amounts of education, income, and occupational status—in spite of a society which dehumanizes him—must exemplify Black Power on a micro-level. Although survival itself in such a hostile environment is quite an achievement, the stated criteria are preferable because they can be measured. Since the key to either survival or high achievement is how one reacts to the dilemmas and conflicts in values posed by a racist society, I shall discuss three responses which are prevalent. The black individual can accept none of the values, he can accept virtually all the values, or he can accept only certain pivotal values.

The first response is one of rebellion. Various activist groups and individuals advocate this course. Usually this type talks of destroying the system because it is so corrupt and unworthy of reform. His language, dress, hair style, and behavior are often in sharp contrast to the norm. Some have bushy hair called a natural, others shaven heads, but generally a deliberate effort is made to express an African ethos. Cryptic terms from Swahili are spoken and youth are encouraged to learn this language. The ultimate in rebellion, the final rejection of American values may take the form of involvement in the Black Power

Reprinted with permission from *Clearing House* (October 1969).

movement, demanding land for several separate black states, or plans for an exodus to another country.

The second response is antithetical to the first in that the individual is overly conforming. His major interest apparently is to be granted life membership in the cult of the average man. Since the average man in America is white, one must whiten himself in dress, hair style, language, and skin color. This person is likely to prefer being called Negro or colored rather than black or Afro-American; perhaps his greatest compliment is to be told by a white friend that he is not like other Negroes. Spirituals, blues, and "soul" food are less appealing than a home in the suburbs far from his own ethnic group. At best Black Power is misunderstood; at worst it is rejected outright. In spite of his skin color, this type is just as poor a choice to teach a course in Afro-American history and culture as an insensitive white.

The third response might be called creative individualism. This person, not unduly driven by rebellion or conformity, is capable of independently rejecting peripheral values while accepting pivotal ones. These latter values may be getting an education, getting ahead in life, rational-scientific approaches to changing American institutions through political action. Language, dress, and behavior stem from a need to fully develop his human potential with little desire to please others black or white. A pervasive need for self expression seems to provide the drive to overcome difficult challenges. Micro-level Black Power has been exemplified in his life, but he may not be interested or actively involved in the movement.

My purpose now is to describe the manner in which creative individualism can be encouraged within the framework of the Black Power-achievement motivation principles which I have listed. I assume that a self selection process occurs whereby those Afro-Americans who resist majority values are likely to find themselves interested or involved in the Black Power movement.

Creative individualism begins with the self, a sense of uneasiness, an unwillingness to accept things as they are. Indeed, such a person hears and marches to a distinctly different drum beat. An effort is made to recreate reality in one's own image, to put an idiosyncratic stamp on things. This can be the beginning of healthy self acceptance and respect based upon a well articulated value system, both vital preconditions for high achievement. Black Power offers support by teaching that one must define himself in terms of those values necessary to be one's unique self.

Self assertiveness is associated with achievement, but the historical fact is that Afro-Americans have been severely penalized whenever they were out of line. Lest we think it is strictly a matter of history, I almost did not receive my doctorate because I was considered too aggressive and threatening to certain white professors. This trained incapacity to be aggressive might be said to retard academic achievement at all levels. Black Power is a dynamic force here, because all racist values are summarily rejected. Aggressive behavior is seen as desirable as one redefines himself in terms of his need to survive as a black person. This is part of what the current campus agitation is all about.

Americans seem to have a pervasive need to be liked, to pursue conformity for the sake of popularity. Yet a desire for popularity can militate against achievement, because concentration and aloneness are frequently necessary for unusual accomplishments. What has been called a fear of success syndrome is discussed in *Black Rage,* a recent book by two Afro-American psychiatrists. Many bright black youth are simply following the ghetto norm in not wanting to surpass their peers. In short, the black high achiever finds himself in sharp dissonance with his sub-culture. Black Power advocates "doing your own thing" as opposed to seeking popularity. Thus a youth is given a cogent and sensible rationale for not lowering his level of aspirations to the usual ghetto norm.

Assuming that a strong self concept is developing, and one has begun to make certain essential value judgments, there is still the problem of deciding upon goals and what roles are necessary to attain them. Micro-level Black Power becomes a dynamic force encouraging achievement through planning strategy to overcome impediments. This endeavor is frequently on a pragmatic, empirical basis. Achievement motivation theory and practice offers a systematic approach to goal setting which can sharpen and strengthen Black Power efforts. Certain questions are asked:

(1) What personal shortcomings will keep me from achieving my goal?
(2) What obstacles exist in the world?
(3) What can I do about them?
(4) Who can help me achieve my goals and what will I ask of them?

Many black youth do very little thinking about such questions, especially who can help them and how.

Black pride and achievement are encouraged through an emphasis upon Afro-American history and culture. Thus the first two principles—self awareness and goal setting—are related to an achievement mystique. This adds fuel to the fires of creative individualism because one is linked with his brothers of another time and place. One learns to think, talk, and act like a person with a passion for achievement. A climate of opinion is created which gives the impression of being on the move overcoming obstacles, accomplishing things. In spite of a hostile world one can use one's brains and collective effort to solve the problems of living in it. This feeling of being at least to a degree in control of one's own destiny, of not being powerless, is essential for high achievement. We see an excellent example of such thinking on a winning athletic team. Rookies are quickly socialized into the proud winning tradition; they dare not think or talk of anything else.

Finally, creative individualism is fostered by an expansive sense of community or brotherhood. Efforts to achieve and be out of step are given solid group support. Since high achievement is not the usual norm among black youth, a new reference group with different norms is required. All members of the Black Power movement are brothers and sisters; one is not alone because an accepting attitude prevails. Individual changes in values and behavioral patterns are more likely to persevere when anchored in the group.

A broad political, social, economic movement develops for the masses. As a black psychiatrist explaining anger within the Negro personality put it: "The same hostility which is expressed in a disorganized way by a collection of people in a riot can be expressed in an organized way in a political movement. In this connection the Black Power movement is relevant." The highest level of creative individualism is attained as micro- and macro-level Black Power are synthesized. Differences in status and education are forgotten as everyone cooperates for the common good.

To return to a question raised at the beginning of this article, certain tentative conclusions seem clear. Why have there always been Afro-Americans who overcame seemingly impossible odds to lead productive lives? Black Power is a useful conceptual framework for understanding their high achievement because it is significantly related to achievement motivation theory and practice.

The key to survival for Afro-Americans is their reaction to racism, not the fact of its existence. Three response types were given in terms of pivotal values: rebellion, conformity, creative individualism. Creative individualism or acceptance of pivotal values while rejecting peripheral (racist) values was discussed within a Black Power-achievement motivation context. Theory and practice of the latter offers systematic ways of analyzing and controlling forces acting to retard Afro-American achievement. The desire to achieve has always existed. Now more efficacious efforts should be made to increase it in terms of the unique black experience.

Black Power

1. Self definition and determination of unique values: reject racism and other values retarding achievement.
2. Unite: lead own organizations, decide upon goals and what roles necessary to attain them.
3. Recognize cultural heritage: develop black consciousness, pride.
4. Build sense of community: call each other brother and sister; "soul" binds all regardless of differing education or status—"getting ourselves together."

Achievement Motivation

1. Cognitive supports: self-image; what is important and valuable in life?
2. Goal setting: life goal inventory, strategy for removal of obstacles to attainment; risk taking and responsibility for actions.
3. Language of achievement: social-psychological climate for achievement mystique.
4. Group support: achiever needs emotional as well as rational support in his attempts at self change; group leaders convey idea that—"whoever you are, we accept you as worthy of our respect."

Questions:

1. Explain how involvement in the Black Power movement affects a child's progress in school.

2. Black Power offers a student a chance to develop self-acceptance, a vital precondition for high achievement. How can the school help develop this self-acceptance through Black Power?

3. Explain the type of reaction to racism necessary for the Afro-American to survive.

BLACK LEADERS SPEAK OUT
ON BLACK EDUCATION

In preparing this special feature on black education, *Journal* editors invited black educators and other black leaders to react to the following questions:

1. What are the more fundamental reasons underlying the current intense discontent of blacks with the educational system at all levels?

2. What do you believe to be the legitimate demands of the black community in relation to the institutions of education—elementary, secondary, and higher education? What do you think, for example, of decentralization of the city school system? Of community control of schools? Of bussing students to get a racial mix? Of compensatory education for blacks?

3. In your opinion, is some form of black separatism—black dormitories, black studies programs open only to black students, etc.—part of the solution to black dissatisfaction with higher education?

4. What specific recommendations would you make to help solve the present disaffection between blacks and the educational community?

While each contributor was free to address himself to all or any of the questions, in some instances we requested that he react to a specific question. For example, we suggested to Nathan Hare and Roy Wilkins that we would be especially interested in their comments on question 3.

To some degree, each contributor reflects in his statement some aspects of each question. Their edited comments are given in alphabetical order.

Black Americans, like certain other ethnic groups, have seen too long the inequities in the established institutions of our country. Now the entire black community feels that it must take an interest and have an active voice in demanding that blacks get an education equal to any.

Black communities have inherited dilapidated school buildings, some 100-years-old, while the handsome new structures can be found in suburban areas. Blacks realize their schools need new buildings; fresh, dynamic curriculums; and new policies. Such changes are taking place, but at a frustratingly slow pace.

Parents of black children are painfully aware of the inequities in the school system and they no longer mean to be left out in shaping the destiny of their children. They are calling for decentralization and community control of the schools in our urban areas. Since it is physically impossible to maintain a school system of 200 or more schools from one central office, decentralization and community control are a must. If suggestions or complaints about the schools

Reprinted with permission from *Today's Education* (October 1969).

have to filter through a massive bureaucracy, parents and other interested citizens cannot always receive satisfaction from the system.

However, I don't believe that schools should be administered or classes taught by persons not in the field of education or by persons with no college background. They do more harm than good. Nor do I sanction the idea of local citizens demanding the removal of teachers other than on the grounds of immorality. I firmly believe that if parents are dissatisfied with a teacher, they should file a grievance, and then professional educators from within the system should take action.

Some citizens have called for the bussing of students to get a racial mix. While I believe bussing is equally damaging to blacks and whites, I do not think classroom space should go unused. If one school is overcrowded and another underused, bussing should be instituted to maintain a population balance.

Others have called for compensatory education to solve some of the problems of black children in our schools. Too many go through school with definite educational problems due mainly to a lack of adequate communication skills. If these deficiencies are detected and corrected early in childhood, the child's chances for a satisfactory school career will be enhanced.

Black students on our college campuses are calling for black history courses, which I believe should be a must for all college freshmen. The only way white students will get a deeper understanding of the causes of black unrest is through carefully designed courses in black history. These can be organized and taught by blacks who have the expertise to do so.

Today's black student is also calling for separate facilities on college campuses because he sees himself living under delusions. He must find himself. If this means that he and other blacks must band together for "soul searching" or to find amiable solutions to his problems, then so be it.

However, whatever the suggestions for improving the education of black students, it must be remembered that the problem is not really with the school in particular, but with our society in general. Black Americans what to be on the American scene—wherever the action is—with no denials of opportunity because of race.

> —William E. Adams, *classroom teacher, Franklin Elementary School,*
> *Baltimore; chairman, NEA Committee on Citizenship.*

For centuries, Negroes have tried to be a part of the white establishment, countrymen of these United States in every way. However, several factors have prohibited the Negro from complete participation in the land which he helped to build.

The white establishment asks, "What does the Negro want?" He does not want anything more than or different from what any other citizen wants. He wants neither to be denied opportunities nor to have things made easier for him because he is a Negro.

The Negro is trying to bring about change in the educational system by righting the wrongs of 300 years. Inferior teaching and token education are no longer acceptable. In the interest of their children, Negroes are demanding active participation on all educational levels. They want to be *sure* that Negro children are not shortchanged with poor teachers, inferior equipment, and lack of books and supplies; they want to be *sure* that each child gets an opportunity to succeed. The black community is trying to break off the shackles of slavery which have, in their minds, prevented their members from determining their destiny.

Our educational courses are built around what the majority group has done, but we cannot afford to forget, and must not ignore, what minority groups, particularly Negroes, have done to make this country great. The Negro has arrived at the point where he realizes that he, too, has a heritage; that he, too, has played an important role in our history.

All Negroes must be cognizant of the fact that what and how children are taught is very important. Curriculum must be carefully planned. We don't want high school seniors receiving diplomas with only a seventh grade education. We must prepare them with a program that will enable them to compete in the world—regardless of their color, origin, or religion.

Those of us who have taught Negro children have imparted to them the importance of education, of working to their fullest potential in order to achieve a place of worth and dignity in American society. However, we have not taught them about the obstacles they would encounter in trying to participate in this democratic society—obstacles of bias and prejudice because of skin color. How guilty did Negro teachers feel teaching the myth of equal opportunity for all to Negro children when they themselves were experiencing injustices and inequities because of race?

We have also taught these children to analyze, to criticize, and to try to improve themselves. We have, however, failed to teach them how to improve their environment in constructive ways, and when they heed our advice and attempt to correct abuses in our society by the only means they know, we beat them over the head and point the accusing finger.

We can now try to educate white people to accept the Negro as a human being with equal rights and to help the white man realize that a country and/or world built on white supremacy will crumble. Whites need to learn about the heritage and contributions of the Negro as much as the Negro does; whites need to rid themselves of racism; and both races need to learn to work and grow together. These changes are necessary to develop a great nation without inner strife, rebellion, or revolution.

 —Laura K. Campbell, *assistant principal, Stevenson Elementary School, Detroit.*

The American Revolution has finally been joined by black people. And we now intend to force America to make good its promises of being a melting pot where all are respected and honored. We must now ask that educators join the revolution and demand that institutions of education—the keepers of tradition—move on to the truly revolutionary task of radical mutation of the American national character.

We must ask that educators renounce curriculums and teachers who follow too closely the racist traditions of this country. We must finally get to the solution—we must from the beginning educate Americans to know and respect each other.

Educators must join the revolution by renouncing superpatriots who demand repression and yet have never responded to any demands, however mild, for change.

I wish that were some way I could offer a tranquilizer and say that change was not needed, but by doing so I would be untrue to my people and my profession. I wish that I could come to you as "a responsible Negro" and tell you that everything is going to be all right, but there are now few in our ranks who can honestly say to anyone that everything is going to be all right. There is an emergency in this land.

The institutions of education can align with oppressed people and ask for very specific things. We can ask that Brotherhood Week be changed to "Racial Confrontation Week." We must no longer dread the confrontation but push it, so that people can transform. The educational process must be shifted in school, so that every class at every grade level will discuss feelings, starting with feelings about race. We must make this nation one vast encounter group, dedicated and committed to immediate change, to a radical transformation of the national character. All schools including those where you work should devote an entire quarter to discussing nothing but race.

For there are no more psychological tricks blacks can play upon themselves to make it possible to exist in dreadful circumstances. No more lies can they tell themselves. No more dreams to fix on. No more opiates to dull the pain. No more patience. No more thought. No more reason. Only a welling tide risen out of all those terrible years of grief, now a tidal wave of fury and rage—and all black, black as night.

I am reminded of a great blues song:

"For unless man puts and end to this damnable sin,
Hate will put the world in a flame,
What a shame."

—Price Cobbs, M.D., *assistant clinical professor of psychiatry, University of California Medical Center, San Francisco. Dr. Cobbs spoke at greater length on this subject at the 53rd annual convention of the National Association of Secondary School Principals. His speech is carried at greater length in the May 1969 NASSP Bulletin. © Copyright 1969. Reprinted with permission.*

When students approach a subject for the first time and find that it is being presented in terms and concepts alien to their cultural experiences, they are likely to find the subject matter incoherent, and, should that problem be overcome, they are almost certain to find it irrelevant. The recurrent failure of educators to recognize and/or respond to that fact explains may of the problems currently besetting American education. For example, an elementary reader used in black schools in parts of the South describes the ubiquitous Dick and Jane having lunch on a veranda. This situation is one to which the poor, black child living in a tenement or a roadside shack could not possibly relate. The effectiveness of a text containing experiences so alien to his own must be minimal in helping a poor, black child learn to read. The level of reading skills of most ghetto children provides tragic evidence of that fact.

The "veranda" education that they received as elementary pupils remains fresh in the memory of most black college students today. That recollection, coupled with their acute desire to acquire an education relevant to the tasks they must perform in behalf of their still impoverished, still exploited community, is readily transformed into displeasure over their status in higher education.

Pleas for reform couched in traditional and "well-mannered" phrases usually meet with a massive wall of indifference thrown up by school administrators. In the face of such indifference, it is difficult to escape the conclusion that possibilities for reform within traditional avenues are exhausted. If legitimate requests produce no results, an inevitable and wholly predictable movement toward revolution develops.

The educational establishment should have foreseen the movement. Had it done so, it could easily have prevented it, for behind all the rhetoric lies a genuine desire, at least on the part of most students, to effect constructive changes in educational goals and techniques.

The reforms which we deem essential in education, however, are not limited to areas of curriculum and technique. Equally important is reform of the environment in which education is supposed to take place. Black people on university campuses do not seek separate facilities for the sake of preaching racial separatism or to create a new myth of black superiority and infallibility. They do so rather because they have too often found that the oppressive white environment (oppressive in ways which most white people even now cannot seem to comprehend) prevents them from accomplishing the tasks they feel they must be about—the improvement of the lot of black people in every dimension, in every particular. That task demands the commitment of a considerable amount of time and energy. To expect black people in the universities to make that kind of commitment and to accomplish something creative in the way of broadly based proposals for social reform in the face of their white colleagues' suspicion and overt hostility is to expect the impossible.

It should come as a surprise to no one that black people on campuses have learned and are applying the ancient lesson that there is no substitute for self-sufficiency. Black oases on university campuses should be viewed not as a threat to the principles of academic freedom and surely not a threat to the power of the educational establishment (except insofar as that power is derived from corrupt authority and justified on the basis of bankrupt principles), but simply as a means whereby black people seek to provide for themselves a position of security in social and academic affairs and to preserve their own intellectual integrity in the midst of a smug and condescending white majority.

—J. Otis Cochran, *chairman, Black Law Students' Union, Yale University, New Haven, Connecticut; national chairman, Black American Law Students' Association.*

Today, Americans of all colors, creeds, and national origins are no longer being told what to think, do, or believe. They are using their experiences and education to form their own opinions; they are basing their actions on what they believe to be best for strengthening their chances for survival in our society.

Who speaks for the black man? is a question of the past. Today's black man has no one leader. "To speak for the black man" is almost suicidal in our society. The opinions or actions of any individual or group cannot be construed as representing the thinking or action of the entire ethnic group involved.

Society has been forced to take a long, hard look at some practices that have caused blacks and other groups to become discontented with the educational system. In many cases, the "look" takes too long and results in little or no action to remedy the situation.

The black man is tired of waiting. He is making demands, and many of them are justified, including a meaningful education for his children, community control of big city schools, bussing in some instances, and compensatory education.

At present, the system allows for only a partial education of members of some ethnic groups. Therefore the product of such a system is lacking in the basic knowledge necessary to cope with the society for which he was supposed to have been trained. By ignoring the achievements of blacks and other ethnic groups, our educational system is saying that one must lose his identity, his individuality, his hopes for a better life.

Some changes to be considered in meeting the needs of a multi-ethnic educational system and society should include: (a) multi-ethnic textbooks and materials that depict, impartially, a true and complete picture of all groups; (b) fewer oral-aural experiences and more laboratory-type experiences; and (c) tests that all students, regardless of ethnic or cultural background, can understand.

Besides these changes in the school program itself, the community must be involved in running the schools—especially in our big cities, where schools will continue to be predominantly black because of housing patterns. Unless community members are involved, indifferent teachers and administrators, insensitive to problems of the community and the students, will deter the progress of the schools and the community they serve. One must remember, however, that community control must mean the best education for all groups concerned.

If a racially mixed school is the goal of the community, then, some bussing appears necessary. Bussing is now and has been a matter of fact to many Southern children—especially black children—in communities with dual school systems. Black and white children have ridden for miles—sometimes past a school for the other race—to get to their classroom.

And what of compensatory education for blacks? *All* who have not had the advantage of the best possible education need compensatory education. The opportunity to catch up, keep up, or climb further up should be made available to all who have been penalized in the educational process. The educational system itself, with public support, should assume the responsibility for training and retraining educators to teach according to the needs of all students instead of just those of a middle-class or affluent background.

 —Joseph C. Duncan, *principal, Jones Elementary School, Yanceyville, North Carolina.*

Confusion abounds these days on matters pertaining to black studies. The fallacies are too numerous and complex to treat well in brief fashion, but here are some corrections of a selected few:

1. Although two key functions of black studies courses are building ego-identity and ethnic confidence for the black student, white students should be eligible, as a general rule, for black studies courses. In fact, they need them—though black students, for converse reasons, may need them more.

Black studies courses are not merely courses of "Negro" content taught by a "Negro" teacher. Negro teachers have been fusing Negro content into ordinary courses for decades without success. No black studies courses are valid which do not emanate from a black perspective. (A black perspective, in current usage, is based on the ideology of revolutionary nationalism. A *Negro* is a person believed to have African ancestry who seeks assimilation, and hence conforms, to the oppressor. A *black* person is one who identifies with the black race and is reluctant to liquidate that category as a spurious prerequisite—he feels—to black liberation.)

Once in a blue moon, a white individual may be qualified (emotionally and ideologically) to teach a black studies course. However, this must be effected with extreme caution because of the need for black role-models, the natural climate of anti-racist racism among black students at this stage, the need for black assertion, and the great-white-father (mother) complex which pervades the white psyche.

2. Most students at the college level, let alone in secondary school, will not major in black studies. But anybody, especially those working in postgraduate life in the black community, will benefit from at least some black studies courses, as will the black community they aim to serve. It is my opinion that at least one course in black studies should be required for every student, white or black. Also, as effected at San Francisco State, students should be allowed to substitute approved black studies courses for their general electives.

3. Students who major in black studies can do anything anybody else with a liberal arts degree can do—teach, preach, go on to graduate or professional school. A major in black studies at San Francisco State is required to take only 36 units out of a minimum of 124. Someday soon, some will specialize in black studies at graduate school and they may earn Ph.D.'s and Ed.D.'s in black studies.

4. Far from restricting black students (even majors) to the study of their culture alone—and hence, further crippling them in acquiring the skills needed to overcome (or overthrow as may be their pleasure) their handicaps in a technological society—the major motivation of black studies is to entice black students (conditioned to exclusion) to greater involvement in the educational process. Black studies is, above all, a pedagogical device. That is why we have courses in black mathematics, black science, black radio and television, etc. this fall at San Francisco State. We intend to solve the problem of a black shortage in technical and scientific fields, not to aggravate it. This is probably one of the main reasons our efforts are resisted so.

The black student who is exposed to a "relevant" science course or a "relevant" mathematics course may be enticed to specialize, according to his interests, in an area which previously he detested. Probably the salient and most lasting contribution of black studies will be its impact on the entire cemetery of American education through student pressure and the self-reeducation of teachers who are struggling to be relevant.

—Nathan Hare, *former interim chairman, Department of Black Studies, San Francisco State College.*

It is very easy for us to relate what is happening in the cities, the public schools, and the universities today to blackness. Black reformation is the crisis, and no one seems to have any substantive solutions. People feel threatened.

In our haste to "get the crisis over with," we deal with the surface problems and fail to address ourselves to the underlying issues. Only when our nation is threatened from without (Sputnik is a case in point) are we quick to accept and implement practical solutions.

The current intense discontent of the black man with the educational system at all levels is a symptom of his intense discontent with all aspects of our society. He has focused on the schools simply because he perceives them to be one of the institutions that have been crippling his young, one that he can and must do something about.

Black people are not alone in their discontent. All those in minority groups who have suffered from inequality of opportunity and who have seen the extent of their poverty in the midst of affluence are discontented.

Since colonial times, schools have been our society's prime instrument for perpetuating our cultural heritage. Black people believe that society has used the schools to exclude them and members of other minorities from equal opportunities and reason that the only possible means of ending this exclusion is to gain control of the schools their children attend.

Suburban educators will attest to the fact that they are and have been subject to the pressures and demands of the community. This is as it should be. When communities, which are microcosms of society, do not influence their institutions of self-perpetuation, then society is destined to decay.

Black people and other minority groups have come to recognize the real meaning of power to control their destinies. It must begin with a knowledge of self and a realization of worth. The desire of black people today to acquire racial identity, separatism, pride, and self-esteem is similar to that of all other ethnic tribes in America. Why, then, are we so afraid of black identity?

Until we, as a nation, begin to deal with power equalization in a real sense, we shall always be putting out fires. Minorities are no longer content with patronizing and condescending responses, nor should they be. They wish to be a part of the system. They desire career opportunities in the education profession, for example. If our country hopes to avoid the holocaust from within, we must recognize and accept this fact. Unless we do this together *now,* we may be assured that the discontent of the black and the poor with our educational institutions will be only the beginning of even deeper troubles. Rather than reveling in the outdated concepts of the man who pulls himself up by his own bootstraps, the self-made man, or the myth of the rugged individualist, it is time we recognize that members of minority groups should have a legitimate share in our nation's wealth and power. Recognizing this may be our last hope for national greatness, if not for national survival!

—William L. Smith, *director, Division of School Programs, Bureau of Educational Personnel Development, U.S. Office of Education.*

Black and white people are like partners in a marriage that is about to break up. The black partner is saying, "You have brutalized me and degraded me. I believe we had better separate and take a good long look at this marriage, because I didn't enter it willingly anyway!"

But the white partner is reluctant to separate because community property is involved (e.g., America's land and wealth) in this forced marriage, and he fears having to share that property. The white partner is also reluctant to do what is necessary to have a humanistic marriage and is in effect saying to the black partner, "Forget the past and live with me even though I won't make the necessary changes to make this marriage work."

Those demands which come from the *various segments of the black community* are the only legitimate ones that white America needs to consider as it seeks solutions to problems which are truly black peoples' problems, i.e., poverty and survival as an ethnic group. White racism is not a black problem, thus white Americans must spend their time in the white ghettos humanizing white racists rather than attempting to "legitimize" black peoples' righteous demands. Too often, whites attempt to apply divide-and-conquer tactics to the various segments of the black community in an effort to maintain the status quo, and thereby legitimize their white perspective to the many problems confronting blacks.

In my opinion, some form of black separatism is not only part of the solution, but it is in many cases *the* only solution—especially with regard to decision-making power as it affects the daily lives of black people living in the ghettos. When we speak of black separatism, we're not talking about having such things as parallel highway systems. We'll still use the highways and public facilities paid for by our "first-class" taxes. What we're talking about is a separation from the white racist society, which dehumanizes our youngsters. Many "Negroes" have been programmed by the racist society to mess up, therefore we must have them separate into blackness in order to humanize their minds.

I would advise every white (and white-thinking) American to read Robert S. Browne's "The Case for Black Separatism" before condemning *our* method of solving *our* problem. With his permission, I used it to set a humanistic tone for my book, *The Black Curriculum: Developing a Program in Afro-American Studies.* I would also advise every white person to read my article, "Seven Proposals for Black-Directed Change," in the Spring 1969 issue of *College Board Review.*

—Sidney F. Walton, Jr., *principal, Martin Luther King School, Sausalito, California.*

To the dismay of at least 95 percent of the Negro-American population, many of the Negro college students to whom nearly everyone looked for new ideas on race advancement have come up with a theory of racial self-segregation.

For all the adult lives of every black American 40- to 60-years-old, the primary goal has been the abolition of obviously unjust racial segregation. No textbooks or philosophical theses are needed to drive this point home. The practical operation of the system is plain enough to a fourth grader. If one separates a minority from the majority culture (and the Negro-American is a distinct and relatively powerless minority), it is easy to build it into a deprived population.

Lily-white politics disfranchises blacks. The latter have no say in the election of men to office, in taxes, in legislation that literally affects their very lives. Lily-whiteism seals off the blacks' living quarters, their recreation, travel, employment, and schools. They are (and have been) ripe for exploitation. The white majority also administers the law and can fasten a criminal label on the black population through convictions and imprisonment.

Aided by the many tentacled communications media, the white majority can build an evil conception into racial policy almost overnight. Heavy tomes by "scholars," textbooks for millions of white children, picture books, tabloid and staid newspapers, magazines, opinion polls, and radio and television all can help create and maintain the net of public opinion that will hobble black people. If one adds the sermons and pastoral advice that can be given each week to, say, 50,000 congregations and parishes, he can envision and appreciate the enormous anti-Negro machinery.

Yet, in the face of these overwhelming facts, some of today's black college students have set up a singsong liturgy for black studies centers limited to black students and black faculty members. They want the universities just to give them the money—and go away. They will select the courses in the curriculum, hire and fire faculty, and generally run a separate black college within a college.

They have added to these demands one for separate dormitories arbitrarily established on a color basis, where all white students are barred and all Negro students are required to enter and live. There are tales of threats to hesitant or opposing black students by the minority of black activists. All this goes on despite the fact that the majority of Negro students seek an education for life in the real world of tough interracial competition and for rewards unencumbered by racial maneuvering.

The separatism called for by a highly vocal minority of Negro-Americans will harm the multiracial, pluralistic society America is seeking to perfect. It is certain to isolate the black population, to the joy of the white segregationist. With its unconcealed aspects of racial hatred and violence, especially its predilection for paramilitary strutting and boasts, it could foreshadow a tragedy in human relations comparable in concept, if smaller in scope, to the hateful Hitler dictatorship.

—Roy Wilkins, *executive director, National Association for the Advancement of Colored People.*

Questions:

1. For what reasons, educationally speaking, would black separatism be beneficial on the college level?

2. Evaluate the black community versus school community conflict in terms of trust.

3. Which of the demands of the black community would you consider to be valid?

ON TEACHING THE WORD "BLACK"

By ALBERT V. SCHWARTZ

The psychological potency of the word "black" in our culture is a focal point of formidable problems as today's classrooms reflect the social crises of our times. With its use, a multitude of conflicting feelings and emotional loadings may emerge which may be difficult to deal with in the classroom.

While politicians and sociologists are considering what is to be done, the teacher is forced to come to grips with the problem instantaneously. Children's demands are immediate and insistent. The purpose of this paper is to explore a few of the ramifications and dynamics of teaching the word "black" rather than to present answers or methods.

What teacher has not observed the disruptive qualities of the word among black as well as white students? It is invective — "You black, you!" or "Teacher, he's annoying me. He called me 'black.' " It is antisocial — "I don't want to hold her hand. She's too black." Indeed, these statements come from black as well as white students.

EMOTIONAL LOADING

Worse than these disruptive hostilities are some which may not surface as obviously as has been presented here. More tragic for the learner are the reactions of the child to whom the word "black" is a trigger for an inferior self-image. For this child, the word becomes his mental and emotional straitjacket which simultaneously lowers his self-esteem and blocks his learning capacity. Incapable of describing this to his teacher or his parents, he may sleep through the day. He may stare helplessly at the learning media, frozen in his immutable black vessel. He has no answer to why he did not do his work. Telling him to try or that he could do better has no meaning for him.

How often teachers have seen black children drawing white, blond people, sullenly rejecting the suggestion of even the slightest bit of color to the skin or hair. The white child too does this, even if his hair is black or brown. Both are building and projecting the blond-Nordic-super-beauty image.

Reprinted with permission of the Association for Supervision and Curriculum Development and Albert V. Schwartz. Copyright © 1969 by the Association for Supervision and Curriculum Development. *Educational Leadership* 27(3):225-28; December 1969.

TEACHER PERSPECTIVES

Certainly, the word "black" may be eliminated from spelling lists, from vocabulary development, and passed over lightly in stories. The surface discomfort will consequently be minimized for the teacher and perhaps the students. What teacher has not proceeded in this manner in other troubled areas? A strong disciplinarian may then be able to control the overt expression of the problem.

However, this will not remove the word from the vocabulary of the children any more than it will affect the society from which the child has come. The literature is replete with studies which insist that ignoring a problem is a temporary stopgap measure forcing the problem into other and sometimes more serious areas.

To proceed as if group differences do not exist is to ignore the cultural context in which children live, for society does not ignore differences. . . . A rule of silence about differences not only fails the child in not helping him to achieve a better understanding than he has of group factors, but the silence may also be perceived by the child as tacit agreement with societal prejudices.[1]

The worst case of which I know resulting from ignoring the potency of the word occurred in a junior high school in Brooklyn where the faculty, by and large, preferred to remain aloof from social issues. A newly arrived young girl from Greece called a child "black," which, in her native country, was not considered derogatory. However, it lit a fuse in the tension of another child and the girl was seriously gashed in the face. She needed four stitches.

A sorry way to find a refutation to the old folk saying, "Stick and stones will break my bones, but names . . . "

We see children who have to meet the problems of belonging to a minority race. The sociological frictions of this problem are of tremendous complexity. . . . In no part of the whole field of personality adjustment is the individual more helpless, and from no source are there more pressures. . . .[2]

BLACK IS BEAUTIFUL

Semantically the word "black" is related to evil or bad connotations—blackmail, blackguard, blacklist. Even a "white lie" is less onerous. Applied to humans, a black is a slave, a servant, or a primitive individual.

Kenneth Clark[3] and Mary Ellen Goodman[4] have demonstrated that in our country even preschool children are aware of the negative meanings of being black. Black is a term of inferiority and rejection, while white refers to superiority and acceptance.

There is a folk song that tells what blackness means to the individual who wants to partake in the American dream of opportunity.

> Now if you're white, you're right
> But if you're brown, hang around
> And if you're black, oh brother
> Git back, git back, git back, git back!

Is it any wonder that black power conferences are concerned about changing the meaning of the word black? Or perhaps "change" is the wrong word, adding a new dimension, a new point of view, is more accurate.

Sometimes, in order to avoid trouble, a teacher will deny that a particular child's skin color is black. She may hold up a piece of black construction paper in an attempt to disprove that skin is black. However, this is an over-simplification. It begs the question of whether or not the Negro or African -American child experiences prejudice and discrimination. It certainly does not remove sensitivities. No one need disprove that the so-called "white" child is white. Only when "black" and "white" are both equally acceptable will it be possible to eliminate both terms.

A word of precaution! I do not mean to imply that any child should now be called black. The negative connotations are still great at this point of history; the positive connotations are few. The intention is to introduce positive and new dimensions in order that a child may feel free to choose to be black with self-pride. A child should feel free to call himself Negro, colored, African-American, white, or American without fear of being downgraded. The teacher might conduct a discussion of terms, respecting all. Out of such discussion might come a genuinely meaningful lesson in spelling and vocabulary development.

However, a miracle of transformation could be set into motion by a teacher who presents a spelling list with a new dimension, defining the history of a word in a statement such as "Black is beautiful." Imagine what it would do for the inner life of the nervous eyes watching the black hands holding the yellow crayon.

The awakening learning capacity of the child might seem miraculous to an observer unacquainted with the hidden psychological dynamic; the teacher helped to remove the straitjacket of the negative self-image inherent in the word "black." A restored self-confidence is intimately entwined with the ability to learn.

NEW CONSIDERATIONS

For the child, the new meaning will require new thoughts, new values, new appraisals. The old cutting-edge and shame will be minimized. A search for a new self-respect will be set into motion. However, the mere introduction of a new theoretical framework does not imply acceptance. Concepts may have to be retold and restated many times. The new concepts will have to be redefined specifically and clearly.

The reactions of the children may not be smooth nor easy to cope with. A sore will have been opened; ugliness may come forth as well. For the child it might be like putting his tongue to a sensitive tooth which the dentist is working on. He may want to say the word, and other words, in a troublesome manner. The teacher should understand this phenomenon in developmental ways similar to what happens when children first explore other emotionally loaded words, for example, in toilet training.

Trust is an important element. The child may question in disbelief, "Teacher, did you say 'Black is beautiful'?" followed by an uncomfortable, self-conscious laugh. Underneath may be the incredulous, "That's not what *I* know." The definition may be challenged or disagreed with by both black and white students. The teacher will have to back up the statement to show that she means what she has said. What are the dimensions of the statement, "All children are beautiful," for the teacher?

THE TEACHER AND SENSITIVITY

Certainly teachers are not immune from the conflicted attitudes which beset the rest of the population in regard to race relations and desegregation.[5]

For the teacher there may be a sensitivity problem. A straightforward handling of a black-white issue might lead to insecure ground. The slight murmur among the children when controversial material is presented might frighten the teacher into avoiding discussion. Often the statement, "I treat all children alike," is the defense that prevents adequate focus upon a problem of treating children as individuals with particular needs.

A discussion with white and black teachers who are open to the implications of this issue would be an invaluable help in crystallizing feelings and concepts. The area of race relations in the United States is developing and progressing. Set ideas and attitudes or an avoidance of them will lead to a rigidity which is anathema to learning.

I have talked to teachers who feel that to say "black is beautiful" implies that "white is not beautiful." Some teachers are afraid that it will lead to a hate-white attitude. However, why should the concept that "you are beautiful" lead to hate? I have never seen a child turn upon me because I filled him with love and self-confidence. The concept that many different things are beautiful— that there is room for diversity in people as there is in nature and in art—does not have one face, one style, one color. The concept of white superiority should be examined as well as the concept of black inferiority and the history of where these attitudes have led our nation.

Once all colors are freely accepted for what they are—pigmentation—we can get to the deeper and more worthwhile values of human beings. Let us of the educational world move academia to the true criteria of judging a book.

OUTCOMES

Teaching words in a new, positive context is not a cure-all for the problems of the teacher. It will, nevertheless, help to create a more secure learning situation and serve to counteract the black child's introjection of racial inferiority feelings as well as the white child's false ideas of white superiority. A tool will be provided to probe classroom hostilities and alienation. Communication among the students and between the teacher and the class may be deepened. Further insights and sensitivities will be stimulated.

Pictures of "beautiful" men, women, and children of varied colors and ethnic origins might be used. Perhaps, on a "Beauty Shelf" in the corner of some classroom, a piece of ebony will lie side by side with a piece of white marble below a sign, "Black and white are beautiful."

REFERENCES:

[1]Marian Radke, Helen G. Trager, and Hadassah Davis. "Social Perceptions and Attitudes of Children." *Genetic Psychological Monographs* 40:444: 1949.

[2]James S. Plant. *Personality and the Cultural Pattern.* New York: The Commonwealth Fund, 1937, p. 157.

[3]Kenneth Clark. *Prejudice and Your Child.* Boston: Beacon Press. 1963.

[4]Mary Ellen Goodman. *Race Awareness in Young Children.* New York: The Macmillan Company, 1965.

[5]Group for the Advancement of Psychiatry. *Psychiatric Aspects of School Desegregation.* New York: GAP, 1957. p. 67.

Questions:

1. Do you feel that a teacher should hold open discussions regarding the meaning of the word "black"? Explain.

2. What are some of the things that can be done to remove the inherent negative meaning associated with the word "black"?

3. How do you perceive the role of the teacher regarding teaching the word "black"?

STRATEGIES FOR CHANGE: CONDITIONS FOR SCHOOL DESEGREGATION

By ARMIN BECK
ELIEZER KRUMBEIN
F. D. ERICKSON

To questions concerning school desegregation, black activists and scholars are responding more and more as Malcolm X did: "Desegregation as a concept is irrelevant. Every time we desegregate with the white man, we lose. Equality is what we're after." Is desegregation irrelevant? Can it be used as a vehicle for educational equality? This paper is an effort to answer those questions.

When the Coleman Report[1] and *Racial Isolation in the Public Schools*[2] were first published, they were heralded as answers to the motivation puzzle of underachieving minority-group children. *Racial Isolation* demonstrated that children from low-achieving backgrounds had higher rates of school achievement when, by the accidents of school and classroom assignment, they were placed in school environments which had been producing high-achievers. (In 1967-68 we were able to document such elevations in school achievement in several medium-sized cities in Illinois.) As a result, many school systems (Berkeley, Evanston, Urbana, White Plains, Syracuse, for example) moved with even more immediacy toward desegregation.

However, during the 18 months since *Racial Isolation* was published, the nation has become aware of the conflict that can develop when black and white students are placed together. Many schools with biracial student bodies have erupted in strife, and although the strife may not always be black against white, it does always have to do with aspects of black equality in the white setting. We understand better the following statement from the Coleman Report:[3]

As the proportion of white in the [biracial] school increases, the [black] child's sense of control of environment increases, and his self-concept decreases. This suggests the possibility that school integration has conflicting effects on attitudes of minority-group children: It increases their sense of control of the environment or their sense of opportunity, but decreases their self-concept.

Since equality is based on equal power, and since schools are basically creatures and extensions of the white middle class, how can equality of power be obtained by black students and parents in a white school?

We are not in a position to offer a comprehensive answer. However, we have had an opportunity to observe and analyze student, parent, faculty, and community responses in several communities. On the basis of these studies, we are suggesting, in the pages that follow, strategies for change. These are strategies which involve a number of conditions that should prevail in the school environment if the chemistry of race and class desegregation is to be given an oppor-

Reprinted with permission from *Phi Delta Kappan* (January 1969).

tunity to work. It is our observation that such conditions are typically absent in situations where biracialism in the schools results in strife and continued poor achievement by minority groups. We are not in a position to state definitively that such conditions exist broadly within high-achieving schools in which low-achieving students are experiencing accelerating rates of achievement.

The strategies and conditions which we present are based upon our preliminary investigation of schools and school systems where formerly low-achieving students are now successfully achieving. They are also based on our investigation of biracial schools and school systems where low achievement on the part of minority students still prevails. In both types of situation, however, racial and class unrest are evident. This paper includes findings from our investigations in Cincinnati and (from Illinois) in Champaign, Danville, Decatur, East St. Louis, Evanston, Joliet, Peoria, Proviso and Thornton Townships in Cook County, and Rockford.

Our investigations do not necessarily discredit school desegregation as a good potential route to educational equality among social class, ethnic, and racial groups. But they do demand a reconsideration of the process and content of desegregation. As a first step, desegregation should be carried out only after certain conditions are met. Without consideration of these conditions, the schools remain the domain of the white middle class, and other classes achieve success only to the extent that they are willing to deny their own heritage and adopt that of the white middle-class society. Perhaps if effective means can be found to assist both black and white members of the indigenous community to take principal roles in school organization, the newly desegregated school may be seen as relevant to both groups.

To achieve educational equality through desegrated schools, it is necessary for certain conditions to be present concurrently with, or in some cases prior to, physical desegregation of pupils and school facilities:

1. *Personnel Recruitment, Employment, and Training*—A first condition to be met is that adequate numbers of minority personnel be employed on each professional, paraprofessional, and subprofessional level. All levels are important, from the board of education to the rawest teacher recruits. Social class, racial, and ethnic groups must be assured of an effective voice in the determination of policy appropriate at each level. Since by white middle-class definition a large percentage of blacks are members of the lower class, a premium should be placed on identifying those black people and other people from a poverty background who have not forgotten their roots. It is important that black employees speak and act with strength concerning the unique educational needs of "their people." A criterion for their employment should be the ability to bring about the type of intellectual confrontation essential to good communication with their white colleagues. The same should be done for Southern white migrants, Indian Americans, Spanish-surnamed Americans, and other people who have different educational aspirations from those of the white middle class.[4]

Almost all biracial school systems have white personnel directors. Almost none have succeeded in recruiting large numbers of nonwhite personnel of the type described above. The directors go to the Negro colleges around their area and nationally, but results are disappointing. The excuse: "We try to recruit *them,* but *they* don't seem to want in." One school system has tried a different approach. This school's responsible officials asked the opinion of a black professor at a nearby university. He said, "Why should black college students believe *you* when you describe your school system and city?" He explained that white personnel directors don't understand the effects of white racism in their cities and cannot describe what life would be like for a black citizen in their school or community. He suggested that they hire black students and the few black teachers they have as personnel consultants, sending *them* to the black colleges and universities. When the school system goes to biracial colleges, biracial teams should be used, he said.

As a result of that conversation, the same city looked at its student teacher policies. It was then receiving from a far-away college about 15 student teachers per quarter, who moved into the community in one group with their professor. These 16 people lived in the city, in some cases together, for the whole quarter. Some of them were subsequently recruited as permanent teachers for the following school year. This had never been done with a black college, however. The school system is now in the process of trying to develop a large-scale student teaching arrangement with a black university in the South. It stands a good chance of success.

A word should be said here regarding the preservice education required for urban teachers. There is no institution in the country, according to a study recently completed by Robert L. Green of Michigan State University for the U.S. Commission on Civil Rights,[5] that is succeeding in its attempts to prepare students for teaching in urban society. Given the sorry state of much preservice teacher education, a crash program should be devised by the local universities in cooperation with the school system and the affected indigenous communities to devise many alternative models of teacher education. Such programs should be evaluated for their impact on students in terms of values, information, and skills for teaching in urban schools—black schools, biracial schools, and white schools.

At the same time, both intensive and extensive in-service training is required as an activity concurrent with attempts at school desegregation. Training workshops should deal with such topics as the racist nature of our society, both in the past[6] and today,[7] and its effect on the classroom; effective communication techniques with people whose culture and life style are at variance with those of the dominant white society; techniques of joint exercise of power with the community—which, after all, owns the schools; changing frames of reference toward understanding that people who are free to define others as "disadvantaged" thereby automatically set up a series of superior/inferior relationships, with themselves as the superiors and the "others" as the inferiors. This viewpoint, as Rosenthal and others[8] have demonstrated, frequently results in a self-fulfilling prophecy in which even students selected for special remedial training are "defeated" by teachers who unwittingly expect little from their students and so get little progress.

In sum, the first condition to desegregation is a radically different approach to personnel recruitment, employment, promotion, and training. An important element in this condition is that job qualifications be reassessed. Job qualifications should be based on "real" requirements, not those which have become traditionally and legally imbedded in the white school system's mores. They should be based on the reality that minority groups require the services of the school system and that minority-group members will never grow in dimension and skill unless they have a chance to be employed.

2. *Curriculum Revision*—A second condition for effective desegregation of schools is an examination and revision of the total curriculum to make it relevant to all classes and races of people served by the schools. The discussion here will include thoughts on the cognitive and psychomotor aspects of school life.

Urban America is multi-racial, multi-ethnic, and multi-cultural, despite the fact that urban schools are still, by and large, white middle-class oriented. The urban curriculum has been geared traditionally to prepare the student to take his place in white middle-class society. Those children whom the schools have not succeeded in preparing are described in today's educational world as being "disadvantaged," failures, stupid, or overaggressive. The reality of urban society, however, does not support these descriptions, except by white racist definitions. Current studies indicate that such students may not do well in tests of "middle-class" knowledge but are excellent learners when self-motivated.[9] For example, this is true of their ability to adapt themselves for survival in an often hostile world.

Therefore, concurrently with or prior to school desegregation, it is necessary to review the subject matter being taught, the ways in which it is taught, and the materials with which it is taught, toward the end of making it multi-cultural, multi-racial, and multi-ethnic. This is not done by brushing brown ink on pictures of children in a textbook but by revising the content in such a way that the books and materials, the major themes and curriculum emphases, are no longer "white." White history, white geography, white mathematics, white civics, white economics, and, on a different level, white sociology, anthropology, and psychology are no longer acceptable, if they ever were. As one student teacher observed, "The minority-group children are never heroes in the multi-cultural editions of the primers, perhaps because the publishers have to keep the 'story line' straight for their 'all-white' editions."

Thus history that omits the Negro, Jew, Catholic, and Italian and overdraws the WASP is distorted. Civics that omits racial and ethnic viewpoints and realities of survival and social change in the metropolis is tragic. Economics, sociology, and psychology which fail to reflect the omissions and racism of the affluent society are, at best, anti-scientific.

Vocational education which prepares minority-group children for non-existent jobs, or jobs they can never hold, is a tragic joke. Today, teaching such subject matter is described by minority groups as telling lies which their children are required to learn and reflect on examinations. As one black man reported to the white writers of this article, "The tools that I feel my children should have to be effective members of society are not necessarily the tools you think your children should have—but you control, and I am controlled."

Since urban society is multi-racial and multi-cultural, and each school system requires both special emphases to reflect its own population and multiple emphases to reflect the total complex of urban society, it is important for school personnel to seek the consultation of nonprofessional community personnel. This must include the poor and the disenfranchised, not merely the "representatives of the poor," so that a curriculum can be devised.

All children, including ghetto children, children of other minority groups, and suburban children, have the need to relate academic skills to action. "Better" schools, however, tend to emphasize cognitive learning almost exclusively. But children must learn to define their own values, to govern their own lives, on the basis of the realities of their present life and their future existence in the urban complex. This includes the need to learn nonintellective and psychomotor skills which are presently underemphasized in the schools. It is crucial that the knowledge system of the school be planned in conjunction with children and be relevant to them. The knowledge which is put into their minds and the experiences which are put into their "apperceptive mass" today become crucial in the decisions they will make regarding their future. "Relevance," at every level, must be the keynote in working with the adults of the future. Before mixing races and people of diverse ethnic and cultural backgrounds any further in the schools, broad-based community/professional discussions need to be held in each school system to bring subject matter into line with multi-cultural conceptions of honesty and value, something heretofore generally lacking in urban schools.

3. *Examination and Modification of the School Social System*—A third condition for desegregation is that educators, through use of the school social system, change the ethic of each school from that of white middle-classism to one which recognizes the "urbanness" of modern society. The culture of the school is transmitted through its social system. Questions regarding these issues need to be raised among teachers and principals: bulletin boards (black or white faces?); folk heroes (Tom Paine or Stokely Carmichael?); holidays (Lincoln's birthday or Frederick Douglass' birthday?); cheerleaders and prom queens (does the majority rule, in which case only exceptional Negroes will be nominated or elected?), and others. A merely desegregated school is not necessarily one which is rooted in racial equality. Such a school results from planning, not from the haphazard mixing of bodies. In planning for equality in the desegregated school it is useful to begin with a view of the school as a social system, a network of social relationships. The school as it is experienced by students, in contrast to the way it may appear on an organization chart, seems to consist largely of personal encounters. Many of the most significant encounters take place outside the classroom, outside the awareness of the school staff. Thus it is necessary to examine the school from the perspective of the student—what opportunities there are for him to interact with other students from the moment he enters the building in the morning until he leaves it in the afternoon. In addition, it is necessary to examine the power dimensions of the interactions which take place.

We identify three subsystems within the school social system as it is experienced by the student: the formal, the semiformal, and the informal. In the formal subsystem, the school board, the administration, and the faculty make most of the decisions that control interaction—determining classroom composition, scheduling, and tracking. In the semiformal subsystem, students and staff together determine interaction—the structure of student government and clubs, and the closeness of staff supervision of their activities. Generally, the school staff keeps its hands off the informal subsystem. As a result, the informal social relationships that take place in the hall and in the cafeteria, for example, are invisible. They only become visible when a "discipline problem" surfaces and reaches the attention of the teacher and administrator, who often wish that the informal subsystem did not exist. But it does exist and it cannot be ignored in planning, for it shapes reality for the student. It is at the informal level that the culture of the student body is carried and transmitted as a "hidden curriculum" from one generation of students to another.

This hidden curriculum has no lesson plan and no textbook. It is learned by students entirely by experience, a powerful mode of learning that we know is vivid and is retained for a long time. If changes are made only at the formal level of the school social system, the school will still not contain the elements of racial equality, for this is not possible without changes in the semiformal and informal subsystems as well. What the student learns at the formal level, the classroom experience, will be contradicted at the more powerful informal level in the hall and cafeteria experience. This is not only an inefficient organizational environment for learning, it is a breeding ground for interracial and inter-class conflict.

It is no longer acceptable to "treat all children alike." They are not all alike.[10] The schools must make conscious efforts to reorganize completely the school social system to provide an atmosphere where equality of inter-action may take place. An example of one way it could be done is to abolish all extracurricular and noncurricular activities, including the French club, inter-scholastic sports and their attendant activities, and the senior prom. The next step would be to set up a new coalition of power on which the whole social system could be re-devised. This coalition would be organized on a unit-of-power basis as distinct from the one-man, one-vote majority rule concept. If 75 percent of the student body is white, the tradition of majority rule demands that the whites always have exclusive power. Under a unit-of-power plan, a voting plan similar to that of the United States Senate can be devised. In this way, black vote would be equal to a white vote in importance and stature, regardless of the percentages of black and white students; a student vote would equal an adminis-trator vote, a parent vote would be equal to a teacher vote. Discussion would take place not on the basis of external status but on the basis of equal units of power. These units would be assigned to specific interest groups regardless of their numerical size so long as the outcomes have a specific bearing on these groups. To be elected to a school post, then, or to have a policy item considered, a person or organization would have to be responsive to everyone's interest; he would have to have minority support.

This third condition of appropriate modification of the school social sys-tem would help to assure that the culture of the urban school would be an urban culture, not one uniquely organized for the benefit of the white middle-class student or community.

Racial Isolation in the Public Schools makes clear that, taken on the basis of white achievement test scores, black children and lower-class children can raise their scores by being in desegregated school situations "in the proper pro-portions." There is more, however, to "equality of educational opportunity."

Experiences in some biracial schools during the past school year have been duplicated all over the nation: Racial antipathy and violence can result from the kind of desegregation that results in the creation of merely biracial schools. Such schools retain a white middle-class ethic to the exclusion of the values, the knowledge system, and the expressive needs of other races and cultures.

School desegregation should not be undertaken unless conditions such as those described above are implemented by the total community on the broadest of all possible fronts. Voices in the country need to be heard that have hereto-fore not been permitted to be heard in public.

REFERENCES:

1. James P. Coleman, Equality of Educational Opportunity. Washington, D.C. U.S. Goverment Printing Office, 1966.
2. U.S. Commission on Civil Rights, Racial Isolation in the Public Schools, Washington , D.C.: U.S. Government Printing Office, 1967.
3. Coleman, op. cit., pp. 323-24.
4. Figures supplied by one large Midwestern city reveal a marked disparity between the percentage of Negro pupils in the school system, estimated at about 42 percent, and the percentage of Negro professionals serving their educational needs, estimated at 21.8 percent. The disparity is greatest on the administrative level, where decisions are generally made. Of the administrators, 8.1 percent are Negro; 8.5 percent of the supervisors are Negro; 10.7 percent of the principals are Negro; and 24.3 percent of the assistant principals are Negro. Just as important as the small percentages in these categories is their placement. Negroes are generally placed in all-black schools; very few are in biracial schools. To be effective as spokesmen for "their people," they should be hired in large numbers and placed in white, biracial, and black schools, in this way white children and teachers can receive instruction with a "black" value orientation and vice versa. Such instruction tends to modify words, views, attitudes, and behaviors.
5. Robert L. Green, "Crisis in American Education: A Racial Dilemma," a paper presented before the National Conference on Equal Educational Opportunity in America's Cities, sponsored by the U.S. Commission on Civil Rights, Washington, D.C., November 1967.
6. Winthrop D. Jordan, White Over Black. Chapel Hill: University of North Carolina Press, 1968.
7. Report of the National Advisory Committee on Civil Disorders. New York: Bantam Books, 1968.
8. Robert Rosenthal and Lenore Jacobson, Pygmalion in the Classroom. New York: Holt, Rinehart and Winston, 1968.
9. B.J. Chandler and Frederick D. Erickson, Sounds of Society: A Demonstration in Group Inquiry, Final Report, Project No. 6-0244, U.S. Department of Health, Education, and Welfare, Office of Education, Bureau of Research, 1968.
10. Benjamin Bloom, in his longitudinal study of children from various subcultures, indicates that there are many discernible differences in children which have been mediated by their early childhood environments and which are clear by the time children are presented for enrollment in kindergarten or first grade. The other side of the coin is that even if children were "alike" when they enrolled in school, there is ample evidence from Rosenthal, the Racial Isolation study, and the Report of the National Advisory Commission on Civil Disorders that children from different backgrounds cannot, in schools as we know them today, be treated "alike." This is true because teachers and other controllers of education are also products of this society and respond in racist fashion to their life challenges.

Questions:

1. What do you feel are the advantages and disadvantages of the "peer group" concept for placement of students?
2. Describe the method that you feel would be most successful in the recruitment of minority group school personnel.
3. List the personnel you would include on a curriculum committee whose task would be to make the curriculum relevant for minority-group children.

URBAN EDUCATION
STRATIFICATION, SEGREGATION, AND
CHILDREN IN THE INNER-CITY SCHOOL

By DANIEL U. LEVINE

That the Nation's cities are in a state of tragic crisis is recognized by almost every American. Were the crisis not focused on youth in the inner core sections of our big cities, we could view our situation with some optimism and perhaps even wait for urban problems to work themselves out as a new generation grows to maturity. Unfortunately, however, urban disorder is being fueled by discontent among young people who, rather than acquiring the attitudes and skills needed to succeed in our society, are demonstrating an increasing tendency to behave in a self-destructive and socially destructive manner. From this point of view, the problem is getting worse rather than better.

To understand why this is so, it is necessary to recognize that there are a variety of forces which determine how well and whether youngsters will succeed in our society. In the language of the social scientist, these are the "socializing" institutions which should operate to prepare young people for positive personal adjustment and for social mobility. The most important of these institutions are the church, the school, community agencies which serve families and children, the adults and peers who provide "models" of behavior for the child to emulate, and, above all, the family—particularly the nuclear family which consists of both parents and their children living separately from all or most of their relatives and other people.

Living in the modern world, it is hard for us to realize that through most of history the typical family arrangement has been one in which many individuals related by blood or by close social ties live together in extended units. Until only a few hundred years ago, as Philippe Ariès has shown in his *Centuries of Childhood: A Social History of Family Life,* "Life . . . was lived in public . . . privacy scarcely ever existed . . . [and] people lived on top of one another, masters and servants, children and adults, in houses open at all hours to the indiscretion of callers." Without privacy, and with many adults perpetually present, it was difficult to prevent children from seeking adult satisfactions and from copying the behavior of the adults around them rather than postponing adult goals and pleasures in order to acquire the self-control and the special knowledge needed for success in the emerging post-feudal economy.

As Aries shows, it was not until many youngsters were removed at least temporarily from the "public world" to be educated in a variety of special school settings that childhood in the western world began to be conceived as a special period of life during which a child slowly learned specialized roles he

Reprinted with permission from *School and Society* (February 1970).

would be called on to perform as an adult. This process was circular, because it was particularly the youngsters who were socialized according to the new pattern who were encouraged to form nuclear family units in which they better could control the socialization of their own children in order to provide them with the habits and values needed for success in modern society.

Having recognized the crucial importance of the parents' ability to shield children from forces that make it difficult to socialize them for success in a modern society, it is instructive to take note of the changes that have occurred in the "socializing environment" which now exists in the heart of American cities. The inner core of the city served for at least a century-and-a-half as the "port of entry" for migrants from rural areas and for immigrants from other lands. What happened in America's cities between 1800 and 1940 must be counted among the most glorious achievements in all of human history, for surely there was a unique beauty to the process wherein millions of people sought to build a more prosperous way of life for themselves and their children by exchanging one set of traditional customs and behaviors for a new set more suited to a free people and to an industrial economy. The family, the school, the church, the community agencies, and other institutions as well were knit together in a way that helped individuals acquire the skills and attitudes which equipped them to move out of the inner core and to prosper in the wider society. Low-income youngsters growing to maturity in the inner city could see this happening all around them, making it relatively easy to persuade them to adopt behavioral patterns which obviously had led to success for other people much like themselves.

Millions of our fellow middle-class citizens either grew up in poverty or are but one generation removed from ancestors who started in poverty or semi-poverty, but worked successfully to attain an improved station in life. For these millions, the "American Dream" was not so much a dream as a reality. Today, however, youngsters growing up in the inner core areas of our big cities live in a much different world than did their counterparts as recently as 30 or 40 years ago. Where low-income parents once were aided in raising their children by a whole web of reinforcing social institutions, conditions in the inner city have changed in many important respects, so that the social forces in the low-income sections of the big city now conspire to mire many youngsters ever deeper in despair and poverty.

Most of these changes are related very closely to the fact that urban areas in the U.S. have become more socially stratified and segregated in the past 20 or 25 years. The term "socially stratified" is one which social scientists use to describe a pattern wherein middle- and low-income citizens live geographically apart from one another, while the term segregation is used most often in describing a residential pattern wherein whites and Negroes live in separate communities. Because many of the newcomers to the cities since World War II have been Negroes, the increasing tendency toward stratification and segregation so characteristic of our metropolitan areas typically has been manifested in residential patterns wherein low-income Negroes live in older parts of the city which are surrounded by middle-income, white neighborhoods in the outlying parts of the city and suburbs. Some of the resulting changes with respect to the socialization of youngsters in the low-income areas are as follows:

1. No longer is there the highly motivating example set by large numbers of friends, relatives, and acquaintances who give up the habits of low-income life, acquire the skills of middle-income life, and move out into the wider society to compete on an equal basis with other Americans. It is very much harder today for the low-income individual, no matter how hard he may work, to make a meaningful career for himself. Automation and mechanization have done away with most of the unskilled jobs which traditionally enabled the poor to get a good start in life. Even where still available, unskilled and semi-skilled work generally represents a dead-end in life, a fact which is recognized quickly by young people. To make matters even worse, fields of work which enable a person to rise on the social ladder almost universally have come to require a better educational background than is being provided in schools in the inner core parts of the big cities.

2. The school, the church, and other social institutions no longer are able to exert as positive an influence in the low-income neighborhood as they did 30 or 40 years ago. In the case of the school, stratification has meant that middle-income students who set an example of good school behavior no longer are available to provide this needed stimulus. In the case of the church and the family agencies, stratification has meant that the financial support for these institutions, and often even their professional personnel, have moved far out to the suburbs, thus leaving community institutions in the inner city to struggle weakly along as best they can.

3. The family unit in the inner core parts of our big cities is less frequently of the nuclear family type than was true years ago, primarily because the black family was broken up systematically during the time of slavery and because the efforts of Negro adults to establish a nuclear pattern since then have been thwarted tragically by discrimination in employment and by government policies which have discouraged attempts to build strong nuclear ties.[1] In some low-income sections of the big cities, as a result, as many as three-quarters of the young people are growing up without the full support of family resources which most sociologists believe could help protect them from the negative influences in a socially and economically depressed community.

4. Today, the population of the inner-city ghetto consists in large part of a discriminated-against black minority. One result of this discrimination is that even those low-income citizens who do acquire middle-class habits and skills have been prevented from moving out to live and work wherever they prefer and from enjoying all the fruits of their hard-won success. This effectively destroys the influence of parents attempting to socialize their youngsters by arguing that "You can succeed and move out in the world if only you work hard and follow the advice of adults who have your best interests at heart."

5. Even if they had been able to exercise the full range of choices open to the white middle class, middle-class Negroes would not have been able to provide a sufficiently effective model for the black child merely because they belong to a group which historically was kept quite small by limiting the opportunities available to Negroes and which, therefore, was recognized—and thereby discredited—as being dependent on the favors of more powerful white groups. Since even the presidents of Negro colleges had to bow and scrape and practice uttering a properly servile "Yassuh, Yassuh," middle-class blacks were and are

viewed by many low-income youth not as models to imitate, but as individuals who have gained their success by "selling out" their own people.

6. Since urban areas contain more people and are more stratified than was true years ago, the slum itself is naturally both larger and denser than it used to be. The low-income child, therefore, no longer lives in a low-income tenement or block which occasionally brings him into personal contact with alternate social environments; instead, the only universe which he knows at first hand is the world of the defeated and alienated.

7. To make matters still worse, the modern slum now is used explicitly as the "dumping ground" for society's misfits. In earlier times, "skid row" was a separate area clearly set apart from other parts of the community, but today "nice people" no longer are willing to tolerate having attention fixed on the disgusting behavior of its hopeless inhabitants. The skid row areas, as a result, are being demolished to make room for urban renewal projects, and the derelicts, perverts, and addicts who once lived there in exile are shifted to the nearby ghetto. Parents in the ghetto, in this situation, rightly feel that they have become "everybody's doormat," and their children are exposed still more pervasively to the example of social failures in order that youngsters in middle-income areas may be shielded completely from this harmful influence.

8. Forty or 50 years ago, inner-city parents striving to persuade their children to work hard to attain long-range goals in school and society were aided by newspapers, magazines, books, and other mass media which told the child to save for the future, to renounce worldly pleasures in favor of spiritual ones, and to view the satisfaction of many of his impulses as sinful and paganistic. Does anyone believe that this is still the case? Today the messages communicated to children by the mass media tell them to "buy now, pay later" and to regard the satisfaction of worldly desires as the most glorious and personally fulfilling of all human pursuits. These messages are directed, of course, at middle-class as well as low-income children, but it is the lower-class child who is victimized most by them because the inner-city environment does not, and at the present time can not, provide him with the alternate social support available to the middle-income child.

Considering all these changes together, it seems almost as if our society is determined to establish and maintain two nations at once, one of them the genteel and child-nurturing world of the middle-income suburb, but the other the medieval child-destroying world of the big city core. Is it any wonder that parents in big city ghettos throughout the U.S. are complaining bitterly that "I can't control my children"? Or that thousands of parents literally try to lock their children in confined quarters in a last-ditch, but seldom-successful, effort to protect them from the unwholesome environments into which so large a proportion of the black population—whether low-income or not—has been squeezed systematically? Or that we have produced a generation of youngsters in our big cities inclined to strike back violently and indiscriminately against a society which has condemned them to stand forever at the bottom of the social ladder? The anguish typical of parents striving desperately, but unsuccessfully, to protect their children against the hostile environment in the heart of the big city ghetto has been expressed forcefully by one bitter mother who attempted to describe the insuperable odds she faces every day in trying to raise her children:

I live on the ninth floor of Wayne Miner [a large housing project in Kansas City] and I think it's a concentration camp. When you're up there you can look down and see children of all ages without room enough to play so they have to fight. . . . [My youngest son is 17 and] won't work and won't go to school. When I ask him what he wants to do he says, "I want to die. What else?" . . . It's too late for me but my grandchildren must have a chance. I don't want to sit back and take it any longer. I'd rather die standing up in the street fighting for a chance for my grandchildren.[2]

One need not look beyond the inner core part of the nearest large city to see what happens when large numbers of low-income citizens are massed together involuntarily to bear the twin brunts of pervasive racial discrimination and poverty in the midst of a modern economy. Thus, special Federal censuses conducted in Cleveland and Los Angeles, for example, have shown that:

Outside of the poor neighborhoods in Cleveland, Negro families made major gains between 1960 and 1965. Average incomes rose, the incidence of poverty and the number of broken families were reduced.

But in the poorest neighborhoods, all of the social indicators showed decline. In Hough, which is one of the worst of the poor neighborhoods, the incidence of poverty increased, the proportion of broken homes increased, and the male unemployment rate was virtually unchanged. A similar study was made in various neighborhoods in South Los Angeles after the riot in Watts several years ago, and showed much the same pattern. Despite the general improvements in the conditions of life for Negroes nationally, conditions have grown worse in places like Hough and Watts. As Negro families succeed, they tend to move out of these economically and socially depressed areas to better neighborhoods where they and their children have the opportunity to lead a better life. They leave behind increasing problems of deprivation in the heart of our cities.[3]

Described neutrally, the crisis can be enumerated primarily in impersonal statistics which tell us, for example, that in September of 1967 there were 56,000 unemployed citizens seeking jobs in Detroit, and that 70,000 others had dropped out of the labor force entirely;[4] that employment among young adults in the Woodlawn section of Chicago has held steady at 30-35% throughout a period of enormous increase in the gross national product;[5] or that researchers making an intensive study of the 640 households on a single block in Spanish Harlem found that half the residents heading households were unemployed and another third were working at jobs paying less than $60 a week.[6] Described more personally and meaningfully, what Lyford calls the "tidal fact" in the inner city is the "waste and loss of human life" and "the destruction of children" brought about among the unfortunate masses of people who have been condemned to live there.[7]

Most Americans are aware of the fact that poverty and social disorganization are widespread in the inner city. All too often, however, this awareness tends to be shallow and unidimensional. Have we really understood, one might ask, what it means to grow up or live in the inner city? Do we really understand how seriously stratification and segregation inhibit the operation of educational programs in settings where—to enumerate some particularly glaring examples— adult basic education classes are poorly attended because large numbers of clients who would like to take advantage of such opportunities may be afraid to leave their homes to go to evening classes?[8] Have we really recognized the plight of parents and children striving to improve their lot in life in environments in which one-third of the teenagers interviewed in a 1965 study had become heroin addicts by 1968, and in which these addicted youngsters tended to be drawn disproportionately from those families with *more* rather than *less* "economic and social stability . . . perhaps . . . because the kids from the stronger families are better able to see the world they will never succeed in."[9] Do we really appreciate the situation in elementary schools where serious troubles requiring almost daily police action have culminated in the type of "educational" environment to which one frightened principal has drawn attention in describing how:

Two boys opened an attache case, pulled out a sawed-off shotgun and began firing away on the playground. You should have seen that sight. You would have thought you were in Vietnam. . . . [as the bullets were flying] youngsters were diving for cover. . . . I have police in the building and they responded immediately. They came out firing,too. It is by the grace of God that nobody was hurt.[10]

At the present time, observers disagree on what must be done so that children who are the victims of poverty and discrimination can grow to maturity with mind and soul whole and undestroyed. Some believe that giving the poor the power to make decisions which determine their future will enable them to build a community favorable for socializing the young. Others believe that inhabitants of the ghetto can seize control of their community only if roused by emotional appeals to "Black Power" and only after taking "therapeutic" revenge against the wider society. Still others believe that the more constructive course of action—and possibly the only effective one—would be to eliminate the forces of stratification and segregation which result in the psychological murder of young people in the inner city.

No one can say for sure which of these alternatives, if any, can solve the crisis in our cities. One thing, however, is certain: those who would do nothing but conduct small anti-poverty programs in the inner city while righteously telling its inhabitants that they will have to "shape up" and redouble their already desperate efforts to educate their children are prescribing a remedy appropriate to a world which no longer exists, and to follow this course of action may result in disasters far greater than any we yet have imagined. Stratification, segregation, and other changes in our society have made the world of the inner city a qualitatively different place from what it was years ago. It is no more realistic to expect the child condemned to live in the new world of the inner city to "pull himself up by his bootstraps" than it would have been to expect most corner grocery stores to have competed successfully with the A&P or other giant food retailers. In this context, for a citizen to write off the problem of growing up in the inner city as it now exists by reiterating the statement that "My people did it and so can you" constitutes little more than blind rationalization for the pattern of stratification and segregation which has come to dominate our national existence.

Implications for the educator concerned with the inner-city school should be immediately obvious. The most important of these implications is that efforts to raise the achievement of disadvantaged students in the inner city must be far more wide-ranging and comprehensive than those we have tended to focus on in the past. On the one hand, educational programs designed to compensate for the inner-city child's particular problems in the school must be intensified to a level which will require the expenditure of many billions of dollars per year. Smaller classes, more suitable curricular materials and instructional methods, new school buildings, pre-kindergarten classes emphasizing the development of cognitive skills, tutoring, sophisticated new equipment and technology such as the Edison Response Environment or other multimedia educational systems, more and better-trained counselors, teacher training programs, pupil assignment policies which take account of the damage done to children growing up in the inner city,[11] and a variety of compensatory services and actions must be expanded greatly if they are to have much impact on the learning performance of students in the inner-city school.

In a very real sense, however, compensatory education represents little more than the educator's equivalent of the "bootstraps" philosophy inasmuch as, taken by itself, it does nothing to attack or modify the root problems of stratification and segregation which have made the inner city a horribly damaging environment in which to raise or educate children. Unless we address our solutions more directly to these root causes, we may find that all our efforts and money will continue to produce little more than bitterness and frustration among every party—student, teacher, parent, etc.—concerned with improving educational performance in the inner city.

A comprehensive program which recognizes stratification and segregation as a primary source of the educational disadvantage of low-income children in the inner city should be visualized as centering on two conceptually distant dimensions. One of these dimensions is concerned with reducing the existence of segregation and stratification to whatever extent this can be achieved. Components under this dimension should include the following:

1. Vigorous efforts to place as many inner-city students as possible in classrooms which are neither socioeconomically stratified nor racially segregated.

2. Strong actions to reduce stratification and segregation in the residential and employment patterns of the metropolitan area. In some cases, these actions should include a refusal to build new schools for predominantly middle-income or white student bodies as well as new schools in the inner city. In general, educators should work closely with many other groups to enforce open housing and other anti-discrimination laws and to build cities in which neither housing nor schools would be stratified or segregated.

The second dimension in a comprehensive program to provide an effective education for disadvantaged students involves efforts to overcome the out-of-school effects of stratification and segregation in every way possible. Components under this dimension should comprise the following: support for community and group development movements variously referred to under such headings as "Black Power," "Chicano Power," "Power of the Poor," etc., which are aimed at achieving the political, social, and cultural unity needed to develop viable communities in the inner city; initiation of community school programs incorporating adult literacy, recreational, home-making, and other services in the inner-city school; decentralization plans which give parents in the inner city sufficient voice in educational decision-making to enable them to hold administrators and teachers accountable for any glaring failures in the implementation of instructional programs in the classroom; systematic programs to help parents in the inner city learn how to provide more effective educational environments in their own homes; active and vigorous support—including lobbying and other forms of political pressure—for programs of the Office of Economic Opportunity or other anti-poverty organizations, particularly those which focus on the creation of well-paying jobs or on other approaches to reduce the economic powerlessness of the inhabitants of the inner city.

The basic argument of this essay is that the low-income child in the inner city—and particularly the low-income black child—is a victim of underlying social processes which place him in an environment even less conducive to academic achievement than was true in previous historical eras and that educators must take this very explicitly into account in framing programs to help children residing and attending school in the poverty core of the big city ghetto. It is difficult to make this argument without being misunderstood. For one thing, the argument of this paper is not that all or even most youngsters in the inner city have succumbed irretrievably to the negative forces set in motion by stratification and segregation. In a way, the argument is just the opposite: the number of clearly deviant youngsters and adults is sufficiently large so as to constitute a "critical mass" which defeats the efforts of the objectively larger numbers striving desperately to survive against the social forces and traditions that have placed them in today's big city ghetto. Second, it also must be noted that many teachers are only too ready to acknowledge how difficult it is to educate a child whose family or neighborhood background has not prepared him well for success in the school—but to acknowledge this primarily in a superficial way, without taking steps to help change or improve the child's environment while doing everything possible to improve instruction in the classroom. Starting from a shallow recognition of this sort, some teachers who have experienced frustration in the difficult task of teaching the inner-city child sit back and blame the child or his parents and conclude that the inner-city child can not be expected to learn very much in the school. Understandable though this reaction may be, it is neither justified nor constructive. To say that most inner-city students are not learning in the big city school districts as they presently are organized and operated is not to say that they are incapable of performing at an adequate level in the school. Indeed, educational researchers are providing data which suggest that inner-city students who possess the particular kinds of abilities and behavioral orientations which happen to be favored in the school do fairly well there, but little has been done to tap the divergent abilities and build on high aspirations of low-income pupils;[12] that the way teachers respond to pupils can help generate a process wherein students internalize the negative expectations held for them by others; and that in some cases progress is being made in counteracting the well-known pattern according to which low-income pupils fall progressively further behind national achievement norms with every year they remain in school.[13]

Certainly we must recognize how destructive the inner-city environment often is for children who grow up and go to school there, but a logical and professional response based on this understanding is not to conclude that inner-city students are unable to learn very much, but rather to bend every effort to help change the psychological, sociological, and physical environments in which inner-city students function both inside and outside the school. On the one hand, this means that the inner-city educator stands ready to give up any instructional or curricular approach which is not working in favor of approaches which possibly might be more effective. On the other hand, it means that he perceives all of a child's experiences as having an effect on mental and emotional development, and, therefore, that he does not withhold vigorous support for the anti-poverty program, the Black Power movement, school integration plans, or other possible attacks on segregation and stratification on the fallacious grounds that these activities have little or nothing to do with education in the classroom.

REFERENCES:

[1] Jessie Bernard, *Marriage and Family Life Among Negroes* (Englewood Cliffs, N.J.: Prentice-Hall, 1966).

[2] Patricia DeZutter, "Life in the K. C. Ghetto." *The New People,* April 26, 1968, p. 5A.

[3] *Social and Economic Conditions of Negroes in the United States,* Current Population Reports, Series P-23, No. 24, p. XI (Washington: U.S. Government Printing Office, October, 1967).

[4] Sar A. Levitan and Garth L. Mangum, "Programs and Priorities," *The Reporter,* Sept. 7, 1967, p. 21.

[5] Julian Levi, "The Greatest Domestic Challenge", *Chicago Today,* 5:3, Summer, 1968.

[6] David Burnham, "Heroin Traps 33 Per Cent on Harlem 'Addict Block,' " *The New York Times,* Oct. 13, 1968.

[7] Joseph Lyford, *The Airtight Cage* (New York: Harper & Row, 1966), p. 344.

[8] Peter Deuel, "Street Terror Blocks Training of Reliefers-County Aid Boss," *Chicago Daily News,* Sept. 19, 1966.

[9] Burnham, *loc. cit.*

[10] Basil Talbott, Jr., "Principal Describes His Playground: A Viet Battlefield," *Chicago Sun-Times,* Jan. 11, 1968.

[11] As Foster pointed out in a recent issue of the *Phi Delta Kappan,* unless we make teacher education more realistic and ". . . Until we admit to the incidents that do take place in our schools, perform action research, and devise methods of excluding but educating the disruptive disturbed pupil minority so that those who may want to learn may do so, we will compound our failures with the disadvantaged school population." Herbert L. Foster, "The Inner-City Teacher and Violence Suggestions for Action Research," *Phi Delta Kappan,* November, 1968, p. 175.

[12] Helen H. Davidson and Judith W. Greenberg, *School Achievers from a Deprived Background* (New York: City College of the City University of N.Y., 1967), processed.

[13] Title I/Year II: The Second Annual Report of Title I of the Elementary and Secondary Education Act of 1965. School Year 1966-67 (Washington: U.S. Government Printing Office, 1968).

Questions:

1. Fields of work which enable a person to rise on the social ladder almost universally have come to require a better educational background than is being provided in schools in the inner core of the big cities. What is your reaction to this statement?

2.   Do you feel that bussing inner-core students to suburbs would have a positive effect regarding stratification? Explain.

3.   What impact do you feel Head Start has on lessening the psychological murder of young people in the inner city?

PRECONDITIONED PANIC RESPONSES
TO BLACK MILITANCY

By GLORIA D. REEVES

The new black identity challenges the traditional image of the passive, subservient Negro bound to the white man for survival. So-called black militants now challenge existing white institutions and their neglect of the needs of black people. Because of a revolutionary ideology and hostile, aggressive rhetoric, black militants have stirred up panic responses in white people to imagined aggression and retaliation by blacks. The long history of victimization within a white racist society has created the black militant.

Barbara E. Shannon, in a perceptive paper on white racism, concludes:

. . . most whites — including social workers — believe that the current aggression of so-called militant blacks is destructive and inappropriate. . . . responsible Negroes . . . [are] those who agree *to behave white* and *to think white.* When a black person deviates from this expectation, he immediately tends to be thrust into the role of a militant with all the anxiety-producing characteristics that white people have assigned to this role.[1]

Consequently, the black militant, whose revolutionary and angry rhetoric is both alarming and frightening to white people, triggers racist preconditioned responses in white people that interfere with reality testing and impede adequate judgment and appropriate interpretation of the behavior of militant blacks. Generally, reactions of white people are extreme and far out of proportion to the actual physical danger posed by such groups.

This article will examine panic responses observed among predominantly white staff members of a black inner-city parochial school where a free breakfast program was started by a black militant group for neighborhood youngsters, many of whom were coming to school unfed. The panic responses in the white staff members have validity in terms of the preconditioned response concept because the staff members had not had contact with black militants prior to the breakfast program, could not document any incidents of actual violence perpetrated by the black group, and stated that their only knowledge of the group came from the news media.

Although admittedly the news media have emphasized the aggressive ideological rhetoric of the militants, the responses of white people are too automatic to be attributed solely to the influence of the media. A long legacy of white superiority has conditioned the white man's responses to militancy in blacks. The black militant does not fit the white man's image of a "Negro."

Reprinted with permission from *Social Casework* (January 1971).

Keith E. Baird writes that the term Negro was taken into the English language at the time of the slave trade and was used "to designate those Africans who were enslaved or who it was deemed could be enslaved."[2] Angry black militants are determined to be free of white control even at the risk of violent retaliation.

The manner in which white responses to the militant group were manifested can be examined by focusing on (1) conditions under which the breakfast program was implemented, (2) precipitating factors that aroused panic, (3) individual responses in staff members, (4) an analysis of their responses, (5) the role of the social worker in relating to emotionalism, (6) the black versus white perspective of militancy, and (7) implications for a new white identity.

IMPLEMENTATION OF THE PROGRAM

Black militants were granted permission by a white priest to operate a free breakfast program in the parish community center for youngsters living in a black inner-city ghetto. The center functions as an extension of the parochial school across the street and is used for recreational and community activities. There is a public elementary school in the next block and a public junior high school is located two blocks away.

The administrator and the staff at the parochial school had been informed that the black group would offer its program to youngsters in the neighborhood. Initially they showed no resistance. During the early phase of the program, several teachers took youngsters to eat at the center, and one teacher permitted her picture to be taken with a group of children. The picture appeared on a flyer distributed by the black militants to advertise their program throughout the community and to solicit community support and donations. Students from the public schools as well as from the parochial schools came to eat. The program had the potential of reaching children within a broader spectrum because a widespread publicity campaign was under way and the support of merchants had been solicited.

PRECIPITATING FACTORS LEADING TO PANIC

Although the population of the school is predominantly black, there is a small minority of white youngsters, some of whom reportedly showed up for the breakfast program and were turned away by the black militants. Rumors began to spread among white parents, who panicked and started telephoning the school.

One report stated that children were being snatched from school buses by "men in black" and forcibly taken to the community center. Several irate white parents believed that their children were in imminent danger and withdrew them from school. The principal was verbally abused and accused of permitting the militants to "take over the school."

The crucial breakdown for teachers came when several teachers complained that the children involved in the program returned to the classroom chanting antiwhite slogans. The teachers stated that they would refuse to teach if this situation persisted. They viewed the children's behavior as insulting and disrespectful.

INDIVIDUAL REACTIONS OF STAFF MEMBERS

During an emergency staff meeting that was called to discuss the breakfast program, the majority of the school staff decided to issue an ultimatum to the principal, stating that classes would be boycotted the next day if the black militants did not vacate the premises immediately. It must be noted that two white teachers were aligned with the only two black teachers on the faculty in vocalizing the need for "someone" to assume responsibility for feeding hungry children. They expressed concern about disrupting the educational program for youngsters who already showed a learning deficit.

The principal, after receiving the ultimatum from staff members, met with the parish priest in an attempt to have him retract permission for the black militants to use the center. This effort was not successful.

The responses of individual staff members became more personalized, anxiety increased, and irrational behavior became evident. The teachers, whose conversations were dominated by talk of the militants, expressed overt fear that the militants might take aggressive action against white people. One staff member, who had a history of mental disturbance, became hysterical at the lunch table and gave a rambling, incoherent account of her personal problems. A male teacher, who formerly had taught in an all-white school but came to the innercity to help "poor, unfortunate black children," volunteered to "padlock the community center doors." It must be pointed out that individual responses were not always related to the degree of experience staff members had with black people. A staff member who spoke with authority about his experiences in Harlem where he worked with poverty-stricken black children became the spokesman for the teachers who were threatening to boycott classes.

ANALYSIS OF REACTIONS

The panic responses of white people to imagined aggression by the black militants were based on emotionalism rather than on any real threat of physical danger. Objective data showed that all activity related to the breakfast program was confined to the center. There was no evidence of coercion in trying to have youngsters participate in the program. In fact, a spokesman for the group had visited the school and explained the program to the staff; teachers had been encouraged to bring children to the center to eat; and flyers were circulated throughout the community advertising the free meals.

It should be noted that the pupils identified by staff members as those who chanted the militant, antiwhite slogans were children already known to school personnel as disciplinary problems. Their chanting appeared to be an additional tool in their ongoing effort to resist control by authority figures rather than revolutionary rhetoric.

Reality factors do not support the overreaction of white people to black militancy. Their preconditioning, however, has instilled in white people the image of a powerless and invisible black person. Irrational panic responses occur when there is an imagined threat to white control and superiority over black people. Thus, the necessity to reassert white supremacy leads to arbitrary and repressive actions against black people who are perceived as a threat to white power and authority.

It is coincidental, yet significant, that the school situation described was occurring simultaneously with publicity given to a black militant group in Chicago. One staff member acknowledged that he had known nothing about black militants until he read about them in the newspaper.

There exists within white people an emotional image of black militants that stirs up fear of retaliation for white racist practices. The white man's response to black persons is an automatic preconditioned response that can be discussed strictly in behavioral terms rather than in terms that presuppose feelings of guilt. The syndrome of white superiority has built-in defenses against any guilt feelings that might arise.

Much has been written about the dehumanization of black people by personal and institutional racism. In the dehumanization process, they are projected as perpetrators of unrelenting violence on white people if they are given the opportunity. As a consequence, white people's panic reactions to imagined aggression from black persons influence their attitudes toward black militants. Black people, for the duration of their long history in this country, have endured such name-calling as "nigger," "coon," "heathen," "savage," "culturally deprived," "colored," and "Negro," a word that deprived the black man of identification with his heritage. Black youngsters courageously survived the name-calling by angry white mobs in the South and the North during attempts at school integration.

By no means is this article suggesting that black militants will *not* resort to violent tactics to arouse a society to their disillusion with the "American dream." Social workers are well aware of the brink to which poverty, despair, and second-class citizenship can push an individual. One should be careful, however, to discriminate between what represents actual physical danger to white people and what is merely their own projection of imagined threats of aggression to justify mobilization to repress black persons. A real threat of the new militancy in black people is to white supremacy and racism because the protection of a system of inequality for black people is what racism and repression are all about. An angry, aggressive, vocal black man must elicit a response, even if it is a negative one. Traditionally, white people have been conditioned to the invisible black man.

RESPONSE TO EMOTIONALISM

In the application of traditional clinical social work methods, any severe disturbance in reality testing is viewed as pathological and becomes part of the treatment focus. Social workers in the past have not responded to racism in clients—possibly because of some countertransference—but any social work model used with black or white people in a predominantly black setting must be relevant to the black experience and adaptable to the reality problems of black people. As Kurt Spitzer and Betty Welsh point out:

> It is necessary for the social worker to have no special commitment to a particular method. He is thereby in a position to see the possible use of a variety of interventive methods, procedures, or tasks as they seem most applicable in the light of his assessment of the problem.[3]

Whether relating to the individual, group, or the broader community, the social worker is nonjudgmental and problem focused. Having no alignment, he is an objective respondent who is able to place issues in the proper perspective without distortion of reality. In relating to the panic responses of staff members to black militants, the school social worker intervened in the small group discussions among staff members and enabled certain individuals to become cognizant of their purely emotional responses to black militancy.

The principal had written a highly emotional letter to parents in which he pointed out that verbal attacks on white people "would not be tolerated" and threatened to close down the school. The social worker challenged the principal on the content of this letter by pointing out that the black parents to whom it was addressed had become so conditioned to name-calling that they had become desensitized. The administrator was asked whether name-calling was adequate justification for stopping a program that fed hungry children and for interrupting their education. The social worker raised the issue of the commitment of white staff members to teaching black children and suggested that individuals examine their own responsibility in this matter.

As emotionalism decreased, there emerged some concrete concerns about the operation of the program. Staff members asked why the administrator had not given parents whose youngsters were involved information about the program before the program began. Because the school in loco parentis was responsible for the welfare of the youngsters, the staff felt that certain requirements should be met by the program. Children who wanted to eat breakfast arrived at school early, but there were no provisions for crossing guards at corners. The fact that the people handling the food did not adhere to the sanitation code raised a health issue. The principal regarded the concerns of staff as administrative issues and responded accordingly. He followed the suggestion of the social worker and requested a meeting with parents to let the black parents decide what they wanted for their children.

The social worker helped to facilitate meetings among parents, school staff, and the militants in order to establish lines of communication that would provide each group with an opportunity to express opinions. He challenged attitudes in white staff members that implied that black people are intellectually and experientially incapable of sharing in the resolution of their problems. Such attitudes have traditionally enabled white people to decide which programs are appropriate for black communities and even to censor programs set up by black people in their communities. The fact that some staff members were initially apprehensive about meeting with parents and militants because they were afraid that black parents would support the militants and decide to keep the program illustrates the racist attitude that the opinions of black people must be controlled.

BLACK VERSUS WHITE PERSPECTIVE

An examination of the responses of black parents to the breakfast program supports the thesis that black parents have been thoroughly acculturated by the established normative values regarding children. As a group, they are undoubtedly as conservative as white people on many issues. Many blacks are still afraid of retaliation by the white people in power and black parents have the same concerns for their children as do white parents.

The black parents did not react to the militants along ideological lines. They did, however, express concern about the fact that they did not know the people who were feeding their children—the identification with "blackness" as a common brotherhood did not remove the status of "stranger" to these parents. The black parents emphasized their right to be in control of the ideas to be transmitted to their children, which they said was consistent with their right to teach philosophy and religion in the home. Although several parents expressed their support of black militancy, they did not want their children involved in the struggle. Others held attitudes similar to those of the white parents toward the black militant group and expressed the same fears.

The social worker was instrumental in enabling parents to deal with the fear of a face-to-face confrontation with the militant group by emphasizing the humanitarian effort of the breakfast program that could not be overlooked. Thus, stress was placed on giving the militants an opportunity to explain their program and philosophy to the community and on the community's right to decide whether the program was to continue. White staff members who had anticipated that black parents would want the militant group to continue their program in the center expressed surprise when parents volunteered their services to operate a program that would utilize federal funds and community resources.

The few white parents responded as staff members had responded—with anger, panic, and shouts of "padlock the doors." Their panic reactions created a crisis atmosphere. In addition, the police appeared at the meeting and reported that they had been called by someone who expected trouble. Nevertheless, despite the preconditioned fear of the white staff members and parents and despite the rhetoric of the black militants, parents and militants were able to engage in a meaningful dialogue. An agreement was reached that the group would withdraw its program from the center and the school would set up its own program.

The black militant group, through its breakfast program, served as a catalyst against apathy and indifference to hungry black children within the school and community. As Whitney Young points out, "It was not Rap Brown who built the ghettos of this country; it was not Rap Brown who caused the unemployment we have in this country. We had the ghettos and the unemployment before the Stokely Carmichaels and the Rap Browns."[4] Militant blacks did not create hungry children, but an insensitive society tolerates hunger.

THE NEED FOR A NEW WHITE IDENTITY

The new militancy in blacks has stimulated the latent, preconditioned fear among whites that blacks will retaliate for "white racism" and are no longer willing to "turn the other cheek." Howard E. Mitchell points out that "the white man, who finds himself in a confused and ambiguous position" in confronting the more militant blacks, "must himself seek a new identity."[5] White people need to become aware of their own racism and how it conditions the behavior of black people. Without self-awareness and empathy, they will never respond realistically to the "black experience."

Barbara E. Shannon states that there is:

> . . . *an acceptable, conditioned response which has been strengthened by gross, negative, dehumanizing generalizations and stereotypes and*

maintained by conditioned fear of strong group reprisal if the prohibition against socialization with the black man is broken.[6]
Therefore, the fundamental aim of a new white identity is a greater responsiveness in white people to the societal problems created by racism that underlie the angry, violent rhetoric of the more militant black person.

What does this hostile rhetoric coming from black persons mean for white individuals who choose to work in a predominantly black community? Obviously, a white person in a black setting can anticipate some racial slurs, such as those that isolated black individuals in white settings have experienced for years. However, as black persons have become desensitized to name-calling and the projected hostility of white people, the white man also can become desensitized as a result of his new identity, which would stress fair play for black and white people alike. Thus, this new identity becomes the antithesis of white racism. Black militancy must be examined within the context of the frustrated attempts of a race to attain complete viability in a rejecting, white racist society.

REFERENCES:

[1] Barbara E. Shannon, Implications of White Racism for Social Work Practice, *Social Casework,* 51:275 (May 1970).

[2] Keith E. Baird, Semantics and Afro-American Liberation, *Social Casework,* 51:266 (May 1970).

[3] Kurt Spitzer and Betty Welsh, A Problem Focused Model of Practice, *Social Casework,* 50:325-26 (June 1969).

[4] Whitney M. Young, Jr., Tell It Like It Is, *Social Casework,* 49:210 (April 1968).

[5] Howard E. Mitchell, The Urban Crisis and the Search for Identity, *Social Casework,* 50:10 (January 1969).

[6] Shannon, Implications of White Racism, p. 273.

Questions:

1. Evaluate, according to your own insights, the real deep feelings of the teacher who came to help poor unfortunate black children and yet volunteered to "padlock the community center doors."

2. What type of activity would you as an administrator initiate to resolve the problems brought about by the breakfast program?

3. How can a white teacher who has a racist nature be reconditioned to obtain a new white identity?

THE IMPACTED GHETTO

By DAN BLACKBURN

When he put his name to the $24-billion Elementary and Secondary Education Act authorization, Mr. Nixon described the spending in the three-year extension measure as both "excessive and misdirected." And he said the bill calls for an "unrealistic level of appropriations." Public attention focused on the battle over language in the bill affecting school desegregation, but the sleeper which the Administration spotted is an amendment sharply expanding aid to federally impacted school districts. The beneficiaries, hitherto untouched, would include the children of the ghetto.

The impacted aid program began as a temporary measure to ease the strain on school districts over-crowded by the surge of workers to federal installations during the Korean War. The money goes to rich and poor districts alike and critics delight in pointing to such areas as wealthy Montgomery County in Maryland, which draws impacted aid because of the federal employees, including members of Congress who live there. Conservatives normally oppose federal aid programs but they like impacted aid because it brings in money at home without calling for local tax hikes and because a large block of the aid goes to the South, which enjoys the biggest share of federal installations.

The amendment, sponsored by Sen. Thomas F. Eagleton (D., Mo.) and now signed into law, extends impacted aid to a new category—federally financed public housing. It adds about $236 million annually to the cost and broadens the scope to cover an additional 1.2 million school children, largely those who now get inadequate education in the big city schools. More than half the federally financed public housing units are located in the forty-six largest cities. Into this housing flock countless refugees from rural poverty, while industry, business and middle- and upper-income taxpayers move steadily out. The tax base shrinks as the burden grows. "Those school districts," says Eagleton, "are just as much impacted as a military base and this plan is a logical extension and improvement of the present program."

The Administration doesn't see it quite that way. HEW officials contend that the plan gives erratic benefits across the country, with a bias favoring the older Eastern cities rather than the newer Western cities. Further, they argue that some public housing has tended to alleviate school problems. But when the Administration tried to kill the plan on the Senate floor, the measure survived by a healthy 43-to-32 vote. Not only did several Republicans vote to support the Eagleton approach but so too did Sen. Richard B. Russell (D., Ga.), who leads

Reprinted with permission from *The Nation* (May 4, 1970).

the conservative Southern bloc and chairs the powerful Appropriations Committee. However, the two types of impacted aid—federal installations and public housing—were separated for funding purposes. This means that the money for the Eagleton plan will certainly be the target of a special drive in the Appropriations Committee. The support of Senator Russell and several other members of the panel, including Education Subcommittee Chairman Sen. Warren Magnuson (D., Wash.), is thus important.

The plan provides that the local school districts would be reimbursed for roughly one-half of the cost of educating each public-housing pupil. Supporters admit the plan doesn't cure the ills of the present program, but they argue that it would get needed aid to ailing school districts. Some legislators are looking further ahead. "All we have to find," said one of the plan's backers, "is a way to include poor rural and suburban districts and we'll have a little something for everyone."

Question:

1. Devise an expansion to the Eagleton Plan which would include poor rural and suburban districts in the public housing impacted aid program.

WHY GHETTO SCHOOLS FAIL

By HENRY M. LEVIN

Urban schools have been failing disadvantaged students for a long time. This failure has been a fact despite its not having been widely recognized by a society that acknowledges Southern problems but not those found in the cities of the North. We are now facing a problem that is complex, pervasive, and of longstanding duration. Not only does the present method of financing place most large-city school districts at a severe disadvantage in supporting needed services, but the distributions of those finances systematically shortchange those children drawn from poor and powerless constituencies. But, most importantly, much of the money that finally filters down to schools attended by the urban disadvantaged is wasted on traditional approaches that are not appropriate for inner-city schools.

The inequities of the present system of financing schools through local property taxes and state aid constitute a by now familiar litany. Greater pupil needs, higher costs, municipal overburden, and smaller resources to draw upon mean that the present system of financing schools places a city at a severe disadvantage relative to its suburbs. It is more difficult for a city to raise equal dollars; equal dollars do not buy equal educational services because of higher costs in the city, and the educational services that a city must provide are far more massive than those that must be provided by suburban neighbors.

At the same time, there is evidence that many cities receive fewer dollars from the state for each pupil than do their wealthier suburbs. Although some states provide additional financial support to their cities for educating children from low-income families, the supplemental aid is so nominal that the pattern does not change appreciably. Even the effect of federal aid for schooling the disadvantaged, such as that allocated under Title I of the Elementary and Secondary Education Act of 1965, makes but a small alteration in the basic system of support, which is unequal to begin with.

But the financial stringencies faced by the large-city school districts are not the only such factors hindering the improvement of inner-city schools. The school districts themselves systematically shortchange those schools attended by disadvantaged populations. Few school superintendents or other high officials will admit that such disparities exist since to do so would be politically dangerous. Nevertheless, internal audit studies of the school-by-school funding patterns within cities have consistently found that fewer dollars are spent in schools educating poor children and black children than in schools attended by their white middle-class counterparts. Not only have these differences been tolerated (and perhaps promoted in the past), but it appears that even the monies for compensatory education are often used to support district-wide services instead of being applied to the disadvantaged populations for whom they were intended. If the inner-city schools are shortchanged under the existing distribution of funds, there is no reason to believe that funds from higher levels of government for the disadvantaged will reach their mark. Traditional administrative devices, an accounting system that masks school-by-school discrepancies, and uneven distribution of political power all augur the financial shortchanging of schools attended by the disadvantaged.

But perhaps the greatest tragedy in the financial chain is that, when additional dollars finally filter down to the inner-city schools, they are often squandered on traditional approaches that have consistently failed the inner-city youngster. The record of spending on compensatory education is an outstanding testimony to the futility of doing more of the same things that have not worked in the past.

Indeed, the inability of compensatory education programs to produce significant results is traceable directly to the questionable ideology on which they are tacitly based. Inherent in compensatory education programs is the condescending view that the urban minority child is somehow inferior to the middle-class child. The schools assume that his cultural differences represent inferiorities that must be eliminated. "Remediation" is considered the key to the minority child's emancipation. Inherent in this approach is a total disregard for the cultures and experiences of black and other minority children. Yet, to a minority youngster, his experience is certainly as valid as that of his white counterpart.

There is no reason that he must deny or deprecate his background in order to "learn." Indeed, such forced self-denunciation can only guarantee the development of a serious and widening breach between the school and the child. Unfortunately, the large urban school systems have shown themselves to be incapable of building educational programs that will capitalize on the cultural attributes of minority children. This fact becomes quite clear when one examines the way in which so-called compensatory education programs have been formulated. Most money has been spent on such traditional routes as reducing class size, increasing the number of counselors and remedial specialists, and buying more library volumes. That is, more money has been spent on the same remedies that have not worked well in the past. The inevitable result is that a larger budget purchasing more of the same ingredients will make a larger version of the same dismal cake. There must be qualitative changes in the recipe in order to improve the quality of education for minority children.

Comparing dollar inputs between schools attended by minority students and those attended by middle-class whites is an erroneous way of measuring school resource endowments between races. To the degree that money is spent in both cases on teachers, curriculum, and other inputs that are more effective for white children than for black or Spanish-speaking students, dollar expenditures tend to overstate vastly the relative resources available to the latter groups. Rather, nominal resources devoted to the two groups of schools must be weighed by their effectiveness in order to ascertain their true value.

The ludicrous nature of comparing schools attended by majority and minority children on the basis of physical checklists of characteristics or on dollar expenditures is reflected in the following illustration. If black schools and white schools have the same number of teachers with the same preparation and experience, the two sets of schools are considered to be equal according to conventional criteria. Now what if all of the teachers have white racists views? Clearly, if black schools and white schools have equal numbers of white racist teachers, the two sets of schools are not equal even though the actual numbers of teachers are. This example raises additional questions about the present definition of remediation and compensatory education. If we double the number of white racist teachers in black schools, class size will be reduced by 50 per cent; yet, it is difficult to argue that healthy increases in educational output will take place. Such a situation, however, is perfectly consistent with the conventional arithmetic of spending on compensatory education. Attention is heavily focused on the amount of traditional resources available to minority children with almost no consideration of the appropriateness or the efficacy of those resources.

It follows that such a simple cure as merely obtaining more money for the cities will hardly guarantee solving all or even most of the infirmities of urban education. Rather, the solution requires a tripartite response. First, how can we increase the financial resources available to large-city school districts? Second, how can we assure that an appropriately large share of the additional resources will be devoted to inner-city schools? And finally, how can we increase the probability that this support will be used on educational programs that will produce results?

Strangely enough, obtaining more dollars for the large-city school districts is the problem most likely to be solved in the near future, because present financing arrangements for schools appear to violate the "equal protection" clause of the Fourteenth Amendment of the U.S. Constitution. Simply stated, the states are responsible for financing the schools. Whether school taxes are collected by the state or by local school districts, they are considered to be state taxes; and if disparities exist in the revenue resources available to school districts, then such differences exist as a consequence of the state's discretion. By basing school support for any student on such fortuitous circumstances as where he lives, the wealth of his community, or the community's concern for education, it is contended that the states are not granting equal protection of the law to all residents.

On this premise many cities have begun to sue their respective states with the goal of requiring the states to foster a true measure of equality of educational opportunity. While some of the suits argue for equal expenditures among schools, others assert that equal protection under the law requires unequal expenditures based upon the higher costs and greater student needs in urban schools. In practical terms, the states would be required to undertake a far larger share of the educational burden, one that would shift substantial financial resources to the city schools.

Unfortunately, more money for the city schools will not be enough in itself to overcome the particular problems of the inner-city schools. Under the present accounting system, where school-by-school expenditures are not reported, the central school administration can continue to discriminate against inner-city schools with virtual impunity. The states can make a salutary move towards ensuring that cities make fair allocations to the inner-city schools by requiring school-by-school reporting of budgetary allocations. That is, each state should require expenditure information for individual schools from all of its school districts. The visibility of school-by-school budgets would provide a relatively simple method of seeing that monies for compensatory education are spent in the schools for which they were intended.

The reporting of expenditures and other information by cities on a school-by-school basis would have additional advantages. Since aid from higher levels of government is often given according to the socio-economic level (degree of disadvantage) of the student population, it is easiest to assess this criterion for each school. In a feasibility study for New York State, it was found that a measure of educational need for disadvantaged children could be constructed from information provided by school principals. Using various combinations of data on student race and social class—generally available for each school—a useful measure of need for resources could be computed. The authors of this study also suggested ways in which a measure of school resource need could be woven into the state school finance formula. Accounting for expenditures on a school-by-school basis is mandatory, if we are to obtain equity for the inner-city schools.

Obtaining more money for city school districts and ensuring that inner-city schools receive adequate shares of those finances requires fairly specific mechanical changes in any state's finance and accounting procedures. Given the recommended changes that we have specified in these two areas, the impact of the new arrangements is fairly predictable, and both goals can be achieved with rather straightfoward departures from existing state policies. The third problem, that of spending dollars more effectively in the inner-city schools, is more elusive, for, although financial and accounting arrangements can be mandated, school effectiveness cannot. Indeed, this is the weakest link in the financial chain, for it is the one over which the bankers of the public schools have the least measure of control.

The basic flaw that characterizes an educational system (as well as most public enterprises) is that there are no incentives built into the system to satisfy social goals. If students are not learning to read in a particular school, there are no direct incentives to change the situation. Principals and teachers get pay increases on schedule, whether they fail or succeed. A teacher has only to live long enough to rise to the top of the salary scale. Nowhere in the present organization of schools do we have financial or nonfinancial incentives for making schools succeed. The reward structure is systematically divorced from educational effectiveness.

This fundamental weakness of the schools must be remedied by an approach that rewards success and penalizes failure, just as other organizations do. The kinds of appropriate incentives appear to be ones that would reward educational responsiveness in terms of the needs of the students and families served. Two kinds of models have been posited that would pursue these goals: the market approach to schooling and the political or community control approach.

The market approach is based upon a plan suggested by Professor Milton Friedman of the University of Chicago. Schools are essentially monopolistic in that they provide services for a captive audience. Since most children and their parents have little choice but to attend their local schools—no matter how poor the performance of such instutitions—the students are locked into a system which does not have to satisfy their educational needs. The proponents of the market approach believe that by giving students and their families a choice of schools, and by requiring schools to compete for students, substantial increases in educational effectiveness would result. For, if schools had to compete for students in order to survive, they would likely be much more responsive to the particular needs of their potential clientele.

What are the mechanics of such an arrangement? The state would provide tuition vouchers to parents for a specified maximum sum per year for each child. Parents would be free to use these vouchers at any approved institution of their choice. Institutions would be encouraged to enter the marketplace to compete for students, and any school that met minimal requirements in such areas as curriculum and personnel would be eligible to participate. Thus, a system of nonpublic schools would compete with the public ones for students.

Data on school costs, programs, strategies, effectiveness, and student populations might be required of all approved schools in order to keep parents and potential educational sellers informed of available alternatives. Such an arrangement would induce innovation and experimentation in that each school would try to obtain competitive advantages over the others. Only those public schools that would be responsive to the needs of their students could survive such competition; so a healthy infusion of nonpublic schools into the market would also tend to keep the remaining public schools on their toes.

In addition to the basic Friedman plan, there are many other ways of using an educational marketplace to fulfill the social goals set for inner-city schools. In an excellent discussion on the subject, Anthony Downs has suggested that the cities merge several existing attendance areas so that all students within a given section of the city can attend any of a number of schools within that boundary. Schools within the merged area would compete for students, and teachers and other resources would be shifted from the less successful schools – those whose enrollments decline – to those attracting new enrollments. Portable classrooms could also be added to the latter schools, if necessary. Thus, principals would have an incentive to maximize the important educational outputs desired by the residents of the merged attendance areas, or face a loss of clientele and resources.

In a similar vein, James S. Coleman, author of the Office of Education's report *Equality of Educational Opportunity,* has suggested contracting out such services as reading and arithmetic, and paying educational contractors only on the basis of their students' results on standardized tests. There are many ways to create competition within the inner-city schools, and virtually all of them would provide market-type incentives for utilizing educational resources far more effectively than they have been in the past.

Yet, the market schema is not the only means of providing incentives for ensuring that schools in the inner city will fulfill the needs of their clientele. It is also possible to redirect the efforts of such institutions through revamping the political processes by which decisions are made. Good educational strategies are made on the basis of the particular characteristics and needs of the children being served. They cannot be set out at a highly centralized, abstract, and depersonalized level just to satisfy an administrative compulsion for order.

Decentralized school districts could be formed in the inner city based upon proximity and commonality of needs among schools. Each decentralized or community school district would elect a representative school board to govern its constituent schools. Financial accounts and accountability would remain in the hands of the central school authority, but the actual disbursements for each school would be authorized only by the local governing board for that school. On the basis of this decision-making power, the local governing boards, in conjunction with administrators and teachers (and perhaps student representatives), would construct their programs and purchase the necessary components to implement them — a course of action not permitted under existing regulations. Political decentralization would then enable schools to reflect more closely the educational needs of their constituents. The inner-city schools would be pressured to break out of the pattern of ineptitude fostered by the mindless universalism of traditional big-city school administration.

Both political and market incentives could be combined to make the inner-city schools more effective. Under a system of decentralized schools, students should be given a choice of attending a school in their own community or in any other community. Morevoer, the central school board would continue to operate a few schools as alternatives open both to individual students and parents via market choice, and to groups of students and parents via political action within the community.

Further, the decentralized school districts might find it desirable to purchase some services from private contractors. The community school board would plan its educational requirements and compare these with its capabilities. The school board would then solicit bids from industry, universities, and nonprofit groups for fulfilling objectives in those areas where the local district had the least proficiencies. Educational contractors would compete for the particular services the community wished to buy, and remuneration might be based on the success of the programs.

All these suggestions are possibilities for the reform of inner-city schools. The point is that it is imperative to recognize that an increase in city, state, or federal dollars will make little difference to the inner-city school if nothing is done to improve educational effectiveness. Some system must be adopted that will reward schools that are excelling while penalizing those that are failing, differences that are ignored by present financial arrangements. The use of market and political incentives both show promise in this respect. Without substantial moves in this direction, much of the additional financial support for the inner-city schools will be wasted through the same inept and insensitive schooling processes that have not worked in the past.

Question:

1.   List several ways in which educational programs can capitalize on the cultural attributes of minority children.

THE GHETTO DROPOUT:
ANALYSIS AND PARTIAL SOLUTION

By STEWART COHEN

A south side Chicago shopkeeper dispenses rock and roll records to the denizens of his business community for good report cards. Impoverished Kansas City youngsters earn tokens for academic behaviors which may be subsequently exchanged for commodities such as candy and toys. A Los Angeles psychologist pays potential dropouts negotiated monetary rewards for school achievement.

THE DROPOUT PROBLEM

A major problem confronting the secondary school is the dropout, a term typically employed to indicate premature departure from school attendance. While figures indicating the severity of this problem vary from community to community, its pervasiveness is ever apparent to the potential employer, as well as civic and national leaders. One particular facet of the problem that has gained increasing attention is the acute economic and racial imbalance in the composition of the dropout population. (4) A vast preponderance of dropouts are recruited from the lower socioeconomic strata, specifically, the lower-class Negro community, those who can least afford academic deprivation.

While the above picture is clearly an ominous one, it represents only a partial facet of the problem of academic under-achievement among ghetto youths. Somewhat less apparent, or subject to statistical placement, but nevertheless related to the problem, is the psychological precursor of potential sociological data. Specifically, for every youngster who physically leaves school, there remains a "psychological dropout," an individual who for miscellaneous and sundry reasons maintains physical proximity to the school, yet for all practical purposes achieves little or advances only slightly in terms of intellectual growth.

This represents a critical educational dilemma. Moreover, the priority and need for solution to this enigma is scarcely more warranted than at the present, where increasingly greater knowledge and the development of relevant skills are required for social and economic achievement. Obviously, as most educators would contend, more interesting and meaningful programs that will attract and motivate the potential dropout are mandatory; greater emphasis need be placed in teacher training programs on the understanding of psychological and sociological factors contributory to this problem so that teachers may be more capable in anticipating and acting with respect to the potential dropout, and

Reprinted with permission from *The Clearing House* (October 1969).

stronger guidance programs designed to counteract this waste in human resources must be developed. Yet, before advocating the creation of multi-faceted solutions, we need to look more closely at the problem and ask ourselves whether more appropriate and parsimonious answers exist.

ACHIEVEMENT AND UNDERACHIEVEMENT

Of critical import to our problem is the question of why the school experience, in spite of repeated pronouncements of the need for educational skills, is incapable of sustaining interest and relevancy among lower-class youths. One answer lies in the examination of achievement attitudes among the varied social segments of our population. Research findings suggest that achievement attitudes, attitudes conducive to intellectual and, specifically, educational advancement, attitudes that are critical for scholastic attainment, are essentially part of the middle- and upper-class value system. Moreover, we find that achievement attitudes are imposed through a long history of reinforcement for intellectual accomplishment, and as such, support educational goals in children of middle- and upper-class membership, whether or not the school experience does. Yet, similar attitudes are either lacking or arrested in the case of the economically impoverished. (6, 7, 8)

The middle-class youngster is neither inherently motivated to achieve scholastically, nor acquires achievement attitudes without exposure to, and experience of, reinforcement contingencies encountered in his social environment. Initial interest in learning may be evoked through the environment's provision of novel and stimulating cultural products. However, it is through the judicious control of reinforcement that initial motivation is sustained and related to academic goals. In essence, the middle- and upper-class child enters the school with the knowledge that his acceptance of academic goals and his display of related accomplishments will be rewarded as similar behaviors have been in the past. For these youngsters the system pays off.

The composite picture confronting the child of lower-class membership is essentially less supportive of achievement attitudes requisite to educational accomplishment. Initially, the lower-class youth is subject to fewer and less qualitative intellectual growth experiences. As a child, he will have played with a limited number of stimulating toys; have looked at few, if any, books; will have never attended a museum, theater, or concert; and, in a large number of cases, he will have never even ventured out of his immediate community. (10)

Furthermore, not only are fewer attempts to foster intellectual curiosity initiated by his environment, but self-intiated exploratory tendencies are often unrewarded, inconsistently rewarded, and, in some cases, negatively sanctioned. In essence, the social heritage of the ghetto youth, initially and subsequently, is less supportive of intellectual growth experiences and achievement attitudes which may be actualized through educational advancement.

A PARTIAL SOLUTION

Two areas of social impoverishment contributory to premature school departure and academic underachievement among ghetto youths have been cited. The analysis suggests that the extra-school environment of the disadvantaged youth is initially deficient in stimulating intellectual curiosity, and subsequently nonsupportive of behavior directed toward the realization of intellectual growth. Moreover, these deficiencies are most apparent in the ghetto child's failure to develop achievement attitudes necessary for educational accomplishment. The question that suggests itself at this point is in what way can the school supplement the experiences of the ghetto youth in the development of achievement attitudes which serve as precursors of educational attainment.

Creative teaching and the implementation of programs stressing the motivational antecedents of educational success need be encouraged. Yet, such solutions alone are insufficient in combating a career characterized by educational neglect. What appears to be needed is some method which will supplement the enhancement of intellectual curiosity, a method that is subject to precise control, on the one hand, and that is capable of sustaining accomplishment over time, on the other.

The literature on the differential value systems of middle and lower socioeconomic groups indicates a disparity in values related to educational achievement. Achievement attitudes are enhanced in the middle-class child through the use of reinforcement contingencies. However, this is not the case for the lower-class youngster. Hence, in order to compensate for initial impoverishment in the social learning heritage of the ghetto youth, the initiation of a basic system of rewards similar to that experienced by the middle-class child appears warranted. In specific terms, a program of remuneration in which students receive some form of reward congruent with the development and maintenance of scholastic behavior should be established. As exemplified in the passage preceding this paper, provision of monetary or token reinforcement to ghetto youths in order to foster attitudes necessary for educational accomplishment should be considered.

This proposal is hardly new. (9) Behavioral science research has demonstrated the efficacy of utilizing principles of reinforcement in a variety of situations. (11) Moreover, these principles have met with initial success in educational settings regarding the treatment of behavior problems (1, 3, 5), and the development of achievement attitudes in young children. (5)

At present we have few definitive programs concerning the use of reinforcement principles with adolescents. Yet, the success of research efforts in producing behavior change over a variety of seemingly insurmountable conditions has been dramatic. Moreover, as initial efforts in application of these principles in school settings have demonstrated, the plausibility of extending our knowledge to the problem of underachievement in ghetto youths is evident.

ETHICAL, PSYCHOLOGICAL, AND ECONOMIC CONTINGENCIES

Several queries involving the ethical, psychological, and economic feasibility of the proposal suggest themselves. Of primary concern, the first issue, the question of morally sanctioning direct payment to the student, is of critical importance. Polemics aside, the idea of remuneration is historically justifiable and morally consonant with our system of education and economic enterprise. From an historical frame of reference, it may be noted that economic considerations have long pervaded educational practices. Decisions ranging from the length of our school calendar to provisions for vocational and technical training programs represent economic interests.

In our form of enterprise people are paid to produce a product or perform a service. Moreover, monetary considerations do not only serve as payment but as incentives to competence. What is suggested here is an extension of this system to a rudimentary level. At present we have cooperative economic plans where students work and attend school jointly. The cooperative program, however, is only feasible insofar as the student perceives the school experience as meaningfully related to vocational aspirations, a situation which unfortunately is not the case for the potential dropout or academic underachiever.

The psychological feasibility of this proposal is called to attention by the question of whether pupils will continue to learn when reinforcement is decreased or removed. In other words, will students become so "conditioned" or dependent upon immediate reinforcement that they will only learn under provision of payoff. This issue is partially answered by psychological experimentation. In general, research findings on the effects of reinforcement support the use of continuous reward for the establishment of initial behavior patterns. However, as Bijou and Baer (2) report, "Once a response has been strengthened by continuous or nearly continuous reinforcement, the schedule may then shift through a series of increasing ratios or increasing intervals, to the point where an extremely powerful, stable, or durable response exists, maintained by a minimal amount of reinforcement."

By way of illustration, one surprising finding of research studies utilizing token reinforcement with children is that after the establishment of performance criteria, subjects soon spontaneously increase their work load in order to acquire rewards previously earned for less output. By extension, it may be hypothesized that as learning is perceived to have personal and vocational consequences, direct payment as an incentive will diminish in importance.

The economic feasibility of providing remuneration for educational achievement is an important issue. We may argue that direct payment to students is base, as well as economically prohibitive. Looking at the first argument, we find little to substantiate the view that remuneration for scholasticism is reprehensible. Actually, the reverse appears to be the case if we examine accepted practice. Students are awarded scholarships and stipends for educational accomplishment. Moreover, the continuance of monetary support is contingent upon acceptable levels of performance. We find that a fellowship or grant is not only acceptable in educational circles, but accords its recipient high esteem in the eyes of his colleagues. During the middle ages it became an established practice to support artistic endeavors. Since then, subsidization has been extended to include a variety of professional and semi-professional needs, including those of education. (It is interesting to note that federal subsidization in the form of tax credits is extended to individuals attending school so that they may advance within their professions.)

The second half of our question asks whether the cost of the proposal is economically acceptable. While it is difficult to place a monetary value on human achievement, the consequences of human failure are self evident. (4) The uneducated ghetto youth is destined to live a menial existence. His access to better jobs, his chances of success, are limited. Moreover, the culture of poverty personifies a vicious cycle that not only perpetuates itself from one generation to the next, but with each succeeding generation tends to become less subject to amelioration.

REFERENCES:

(1) Becker, W. C., C. H. Madsen, C. R. Arnold, and D. R. Thomas, "The Contingent Use of Teacher Attention and Praise in Reducing Classroom Behavior Problems," *Journal of Special Education,* 1:287-307 (1967).

(2) Bijou, S. W. and D. W. Baer, *Child Development,* Vol. 1. New York: Appleton-Century-Crofts, 1961.

(3) Carlson, C. S., C. R. Arnold, W. C. Becker, and C. H. Madsen, *"The Elimination of Tantrum Behavior of a Child in an Elementary Classroom."* Unpublished manuscript, University of Illinois, 1967.

(4) Clark, K. B., *Dark Ghetto.* New York: Harper & Row, 1967.

(5) Hamblin, R. L., D. Buckholdt, D. Busell, D. Ellis, and D. Ferriton, "Changing the Game from 'Get the Teacher' to 'Learn,'" *Trans-action,* 6:20-31 (1969).

(6) Hyman, H. H., "The Value System of Different Classes," in R. Bendix and M. Lipset (eds.), *Class, Status and Power.* Glencoe, Ill.: Free Press, 1953, pp. 426-442.

(7) Rosen, B. C., "The Achievement Syndrome: A Psychocultural Dimension of Social Stratification," *American Sociological Review,* 21:203-211 (1956).

(8) Sewell, W. H., A. O. Haller, and M. A. Strauss, "Social Status and Educational and Occupational Aspiration," *American Sociological Review,* 22:67-73 (1957).

(9) Skinner, B. F., *Science and Human Behavior.* New York: The Macmillan Co., 1953.

(10) Stendler-Lavatelli, C.B., "Environmental Intervention in Infancy and Early Childhood," in M. Deutsch, I. Katz, and A.R. Jensen (eds.), *Social Class, Race, and Psychological Development.* New York: Holt, Rinehart & Winston, 1968, pp. 347-380.

(11) Ullman, L. P. and L. Krasner, *Case Studies in Behavior Modification.* New York: Holt, Rinehart & Winston, 1965.

Questions:

1. Discuss the advantages and disadvantages of stressing middle class values.

2. Design a compensatory program at the high school level which you feel would effectively lower the dropout rate.

3. Develop a remuneration plan at either the elementary, junior high, or senior high level which would provide incentive for learning to potential dropouts.

POOR EDUCATION

By JOSEPH FEATHERSTONE

The President's long-awaited March 3 pronouncement on education turned out to be a mousy document. There will be a Commission on School Finance which will spend two years finding out why public and parochial education is going broke, which we already know: schools, especially big city schools, need more money for classrooms and teachers, and the only taxing authority that can supply it in sufficient quantity is the federal government. Nevertheless, the federal share in school expenses will be reduced from 8 percent in fiscal '68 to 6.6 percent in fiscal '70. Mr. Nixon endorses Commissioner of Education Allen's "Right to Read" program and recommends a network of experimental centers to discover what works best in early childhood education. No one has said what the "Right to Read" means, but whatever is made of it, the President wants it to have $84 million, money that will have to be taken from some other part of the budget. The "Early Learning" program ($52 million) will involve only poor children, and here too it is not known which existing or planned programs will be robbed to pay for it. Meanwhile, the country is starved for preschool and day care facilities. The Public Broadcast Corporation will be kept alive, the President hopes, but it will have to raise private money to match the federal funds it gets. A National Institute of Education is proposed, somewhat along the lines of the National Institutes of Health, to do more research, particularly on compensatory education, which Mr. Nixon judges a failure.

Underlying the President's case for not spending more on schools now are a number of reports made over the years casting doubt on the efficacy of Head Start or of programs under Title I of the Elementary and Secondary Education Act. Yet many of these programs were never designed simply to "improve education." They were intended to give cities some temporary relief, to buy peace in the ghettos, to persuade the poor that society cared about their children, to demonstrate a federal responsibility for education. There are no strict criteria by which *all* these different goals can be evaluated. We do, as the President says, need to know more about learning. But we do already know some elemental truths which Mr. Nixon barely mentions: hungry children don't learn; they don't learn much in understaffed and overcrowded classes; and city school systems that lurch from one financial crisis to another can't plan or provide a good education. And the irony of the President's calling for yet more expert studies of school needs is that he had on his desk at the time a document which told him what those needs are — an "Urban Education Task Force

Report" prepared by an advisory committee appointed by HEW Secretary Robert Finch and chaired by Wilson Riles, deputy superintendent of public instruction for California. The Administration had commissioned but not seen fit to release it publicly. However, a copy was leaked to Rep. Jeffery Cohelan, who had it inserted in the January 19th and 20th *Congressional Record.* It is an excellent statement of what's wrong with urban public education and how to begin setting things right.

Parts of the Riles Report are familiar: the cities are losing the affluent middle class, while their decaying centers fill up with the poor who need costly social services. But it also explains things many people don't understand: why big city schools are more expensive to run than schools elsewhere; how archaic state aid formulas, written in the days when city schools were disproportionately wealthy, discriminate against the cities by giving them less aid per capita than suburbs; how the high cost of urban social programs like welfare leaves cities proportionately less money for schools than the suburbs; and how the collapse of the parochial schools adds to city burdens. It draws a stark picture of decay and deterioration, with worse to come, as city voters turn down bond issue after bond issue and the poor rise up against the institutions that fail their youngsters. In Philadelphia, for instance, the '68-'69 school budget was slashed to the bone; only emergency funds provided by the state prevented the system from closing down May 1. The '68-'69 school year in Detroit ended with the schools $5 million in the red, even after severe budget cuts; school officials talk of deficits this year running $30- to $35-million. Defeat of tax and bond issues left a shortage of $32 million in the Los Angeles budget. In smaller cities the story is the same: deficits, bond issues turned down, degeneration of facilities and programs, the flight of good teachers who are fed up with these working conditions—all at a time when demands on schools are unprecedently heavy.

The President should have paid attention to the Riles Report's caution on "evaluations" of federal programs to date: we simply don't know what difference they might make if they were adequately funded over a long enough period. For example, Congress authorized $9 billion under Title I of the Elementary and Secondary Education Act for "disadvantaged children," but no more than $3 billion has been spent. Between the '67-'68 and the '68-'69 school years, federal cutbacks of $68 million, combined with growing costs, meant there was actually $400 million less for poor children under Title I than in the first year of the program. Nationally, the increase in eligible children has meant there has been less and less money per capita to go around. By last spring in New York State, Title I funds per pupil had declined from $366 to $200. A number of reports on Title I from different sources have indicated that aid has been spread too thin or given to the wrong children, raising grave doubts as to the good faith and competence of local and state educational authorities. Even if it were all administered honestly and wisely, Title I doesn't amount to that much; the average per pupil expenditure is $95, not an impressive sum when measured against the national average per pupil expenditure of $700. And Title I is the only federal program that even nominally gives city children a fair share; all other federal aid to schools goes in disproportionate amounts to the suburbs.

The whole structure of education works against the interests of the cities. That structure includes the US Office of Education, whose benign neglect of cities and the poor in general is a major barrier to reform. The Riles Report recommends creating a Bureau of Urban Education to shepherd all the programs dealing with the cities, and suggests incentives to states that properly serve their urban populations. Clearly more money spent the same old way is not going to be enough; equally, there has to be more money. City schools should have top priority, the Riles Report says; we should start spending $471 million on them for a start, building up to appropriations of $7- to $14-billion (depending on the aid formula) by 1974. Title I should be fully funded. And while the committee favors the President's welfare proposals — though pointing out they would make little difference to big cities — it said that only education, not subsidy payments, stands a chance of providing a long-term solution to the welfare problem.

Rightly, the Report is critical of plans for sharing federal revenue with the states — which habitually cheat the cities. Moreover, it argues that reform of the schools should aim at transforming the entire curriculum and teaching practices, and not just focus on one subject like reading. It recommends cutting class size anywhere from 4 to 10 students per class. It insists on the necessity for integration — which the Nixon message barely touched on — and defends the eventual compatibility of the movement for community control of schools with integration. The Riles Report shows an awareness — rare in official documents on education — that ghetto schools need to build on the real strengths of their children, instead of treating them as "disadvantaged" deviants from some suburban norm.

The battle to save the city schools has two fronts: the fight for more money; and the fight to break educational rotten boroughs, old, rusty bureaucratic machinery remote from the people it was intended to serve. The Riles Report links the fight for the city schools to a larger urban battle whose outcome will determine whether or not America becomes two separate, hostile nations. The President's March 3 message suggests that, for the schools, at least, the cities will be fighting on their own.

Questions:

1. What would you do to provide a better education for the poor (ghetto children, slum kids, educationally disadvantaged, culturally deprived) if you were President?
2. Develop a way to effectively evaluate the ghetto children in terms of their real strengths instead of using the standardized tests to evaluate them.
3. Draw up a plan for a more equitable distribution of federal money to provide urban areas with necessary funds for quality education.

RACISM: VECTOR OF GHETTO EDUCATION

By RAYMOND L. JERREMS

Racism is an ugly word. White educators, like most other educated whites, usually assume that a racist is an Alabama farmer with a pick handle in one hand and a whiskey bottle in the other who goes around saying "nigger" and "boy." The reality is, however, that a teacher in the black ghetto who does not expect children to achieve up to the level of white children is just as racist and is doing more harm to black people than a field full of southern farmers in white sheets. The racist in our schools drinks his whiskey from a glass (on the rocks) and, instead of a pick handle, he hits black children with "standardized tests." He does not say "nigger" or "boy"; his epithets are "culturally different" and "slow learner."

The evidence of racism in our schools has been documented so many times it seems incredible that we should try to pretend that it does not exist and have an effect. Consider the miniscule number of black administrators in white or integrated school systems. Consider, too, the large proportion of black administrators who have "black" jobs such as "Assistant Superintendent in Charge of Human Relations" or "Director of Federal Programs." Consider the ratio of black students to white students in any school system as compared to the black-white ratio of teachers or other staff. Consider the racial make-up of school boards, teacher training institutions, publishers of educational materials, or other school oriented business. Consider the tests, the curriculum materials— not those being developed on a crash basis, but those actually being used. And search to find how much of this new curriculum material is being used in all-white schools where it is essential if we are not to raise a new generation as racist as its parents. The only place where blacks have any significant influence in education is in all-black schools and even there they seldom have a controlling influence.

One might well compare epidemic malaria to ghetto education. Malaria is endemic in an area where a balance has been struck between the number of people who are susceptible and the number of carrier mosquitoes within striking distance. A degree of immunity has developed with the population and the disease is in a stable state—and swatting mosquitoes can help to make endemic malaria more tolerable. An epidemic occurs when one of the variables changes. It may be that colonial development increases the population of susceptible humans manifold; it may be that changes in rainfall or land management increase

Reprinted with permission from *Integrated Education: RACE AND SCHOOLS* (July-August 1970).

the breeding places for mosquitoes, or it may be that a new strain of malaria is imported or developed by mutation.

Ghetto education has become epidemic after a long period of being endemic. The change has resulted from the influx of poor whites and blacks from southern rural areas to cities, and from environmental changes with respect to automation, and job opportunities. Such an analysis is, of course, over-simplified, but it is accurate enough for this discussion.

POINTS OF INTERVENTION

When seeking a point of intervention to control an epidemic, one analyzes the whole cycle and looks for points at which the cycle is vulnerable, then the various vulnerable points are assessed with respect to the feasibility and economics of attack. Many such points were found in the malaria cycle in addition to the swatting of mosquitoes on the victim. Let me list a few of them: screens to keep mosquitoes out of buildings, especially sleeping quarters; chemical repellents to keep them away from people; draining and covering still water where mosquitoes breed; putting fish or poison in ponds to destroy the larvae; flushing still water with running water; use of insecticides on adult mosquitoes; perfecting drugs to disable the plasmodium parasite in the human bloodstream. This represents the present state of the art of malaria control, but new ways are still being sought. There is optimism that new ways of interfering with the reproductive cycle of mosquitoes by sterilization may be found. Developing genetic immunity in man is also conceivable. Thus, many activities have been more effective in reducing malaria than swatting mosquitoes. There are certainly as many points of intervention for improving ghetto education. It would be surprising if some of them were not more efficient and effective than trying to improve the teacher-pupil exchange directly.

THOSE WHO INTERVENE

To continue the malaria analogy it is worth noting that different lines of attack were developed by different kinds of people. We might translate this as "everyone does his own thing." Swamp draining was done by engineers, mosquitoes destroyed by entymologists, redistribution of population by politicians, attacks on the disease in the human bloodstream by physicians, protective housing built by architects, and mosquito repellents concocted by chemists. These specialists often work on the problem from a distance. Their involvement is on an abstract level and they may never see a mosquito or an infected patient. The person out in the field, where the action is, can do little to solve the problem except to swat mosquitoes. Even this is not possible until he learns enough to know that mosquitoes rather than vapors from the swamp or evil spirits cause malaria. In his physical and emotional involvement with the real problems of his real world, he may look askance at an expert who insists that he divert his energy to draining swamps or raising fish. "Here I am up to my ears in mosquitoes with sickness all around and you ask me to dig ditches!"

The important point is that the malaria cycle is understood. When malaria breaks out a public health worker can assess the problem and choose a strategic point of intervention. He knows how to treat the victims and how to provide immediate protection for those in the area while working on the long-range solution. It is important, too, that society understands the cause and effect of malaria and supports the public health worker's efforts as legitimate.

We are accustomed to the idea that urban ghettoes are focal points of disease. Although they may not be at epidemic levels, there is a high incidence of infant mortality, tuberculosis, lead poisoning, and, of course, wide spread malnutrition. In addition to these physical ills we know, too, that ghetto residents suffer from assorted diseases of the mind and spirit. Examples of these are high crime rates, illegitimacy, unemployment, and poor education. I believe that the social ills are societal and environmental in nature in the same ways that the physical diseases are. There are those who claim that a woman who has illegitimate children has only herself to blame and that when her child dies from lead poisoning after eating paint in a slum apartment it is her fault for not preventing it. This is equivalent to blaming the malaria patient for permitting the mosquito to bite him, which is irrelevant because we know that diseases are curbed by controlling the environment and developing immunization techniques, not by exhorting individuals to avoid the infection.

A CASE STUDY

Let us look at the disease of "ghetto education" as it develops in a black child as he grows from five to fifteen in an urban ghetto. Let us consider his behavior as if it were indeed symptomatic of a disease and try to relate these symptoms to the environment, thus avoiding the trap of judgments which mask the etiology of the disease under a blanket of recriminations against the child and his family.

When a black child from the ghetto arrives in kindergarten at the age of five he is vulnerable to the disease of ghetto education. Although he may not yet be infected, his resistance is low. He has physical, mental, and emotional disabilities as a result of his five years in the ghetto. He may have several of the following: one or more dietary deficiencies, carious teeth or other dental problems, minor but undiagnosed congenital defects, limited vocabulary, inability to communicate ideas as complete thoughts, inability to respond to verbal instructions, and limited ability to relate to large groups of people. The school program is designed to identify and work with these deficiencies, but it usually fails to do the job. Physical problems may be identified (programs for giving physical examinations are improving), but in most cases this merely results in notification of parents, and perhaps a preliminary referral. Usually, the defects are not corrected. The lack of communication skills is attacked assiduously by kindergarten teachers. The children are guided through carefully devised experience in language and pushed to develop vocabulary and verbal skills. Emotional problems arising from the need to relate to large groups of children and to adapt to the new norms of the school and to its different values are usually dealt with by authoritarian methods and because of the size and strength of the teacher the children comply.

As the child lives through his first two or three years in school, symptoms of the disease of ghetto education begin to appear. For some, the symptoms appear almost immediately, for others the onset is delayed. The earliest are usually poor attendance and tardiness accompanied by a rapid decrease of effective communication between school and parents in efforts to remedy it. Next to develop is the child's failure to come prepared for school activities. This lack may take the form of less appropriate and less well cared for clothing or not having notes for field trips, crayons, or other things needed from home. Again this is accompanied by reduced effectiveness of communication between teachers and parents.

Another set of symptoms which begins to develop in the early grades is related to distractability. As school activities become more structured and more abstract the child begins to tune them out. He loses interest in the word and number tasks assigned and begins to experiment with other behaviors. He opts for coloring, working with clay and blocks, and listening to music instead of dealing with the more structured tasks assigned by the teacher. As this happens, and as the teacher begins to make the child's access to the clay and blocks contingent on prior completion of the less desired tasks, a new set of symptoms begin to develop. School personnel usually call them discipline problems.

The child whom we are following in our observation of the development of the disease of ghetto education has reached this stage in the second grade. He is now seven years old. His conflict over the choice between school tasks he does not understand and does not wish to engage in and those other tasks which he does like is easily resolved by the teacher. She is able to impose her will rather easily since she is so much bigger, stronger, and wiser. He does comply, after a fashion, and produces the paper products which she demands. They are covered with numbers, or words, or "x" marked squares, but the child's mind has been unimpressed, or perhaps even reinforced in its resentment.

A year later, in third grade, he is "tested" to determine his level of accomplishment in verbal and number skills, and it is discovered that he is below grade level in these areas. This is not a surprise to his teacher, to his mother or to the child himself. The teacher has been evaluating his work and telling him (and his mother if they are still in contact) that he is not doing as well as he should, and that he needs to "try harder." Now, on the basis of the official documentation of the standardized test, he and his parents are informed that he has "failed" to achieve the goals set for the third grade and that he must be retained in that grade for the next year. He now has another symptom of the disease of ghetto education. He is overage for his grade.

As this overage child moves through grades four and five, the symptoms which the school calls discipline problems become aggravated. The child begins to experiment with a variety of ways to avoid the kinds of school activities he dislikes and does not understand and to engage in other activities which he sees as more productive or more enjoyable. These may be surreptitious, but as he gets older he is likely to do them openly and to challenge the authority of the school to compel him to do otherwise. Now, in addition to a distaste for school tasks, he has developed a dislike for school personnel. In addition to challenging the school program he begins more and more to reject the behavior norms set by the school. In his milieu, disputes are settled by physical force and power politics. The school insists that disputes be settled by verbal activity and by politics of negotiation; or failing in these efforts they will be settled by fiat and sanction enforced by the power of the institution. As he grows older the alienation increases.

We find our sample child in the eighth grade, at the age of fifteen, stricken by the disease of ghetto education. Test scores indicate that he reads at the fourth grade level, but such scores are meaningless numbers. This boy does not read at all for any useful purpose. All his verbal communication is oral. He may communicate well orally, but not according to the standards set by the school. He is at a similar level in mathematics skills. He can deal with numbers in his own life, but not at all in the abstract ways required for further educational advancement. His knowledge and skills in the other curricular areas such as science, and social studies are near zero. He hates school as an abstract idea and hates a great number of the people who control it. He sees no hope of its ever making any contribution to his future and longs for the time (now only a few years away) when he can leave it forever.

EDUCATORS DO THEIR THING

The cycle which perpetuates ghetto education is not well understood and no one can say which is the strategic point of intervention. Most efforts by educators have been directed toward treating the patient. Each educator tries to decide what he can do and comes up with "his own thing."

Classroom teachers develop remedial programs and new motivational techniques; curriculum specialists develop new textbooks and syllabi; special education experts build programs for "slow learners" and "the culturally different"; administrators propose new organizational plans for tighter control and more discipline; early childhood educators develop programs for four and five year olds; social welfare workers work out new arrangements for assisting parents and children; physicians propose health programs; linguists look for new ways to teach language and to teach English as a foreign language—the list is endless. To it could be added programs developed by athletic directors, outdoor educators, lawyers, psychologists, businessmen, religious leaders, musicians, college professors—and on and on. I do not intend to disparage these activities, but only to illustrate that in our efforts to confront ghetto education each one swats the mosquitoes which he sees on the victim. Few look at the total problem. Sadly, everyone is not even swatting mosquitoes. Some are swatting flies, some are combatting the vapors from the swamps, and some are inveighing against "evil spirits."

It is inevitable that such efforts are wasted; some may be in conflict, some may be misunderstood, and many are aimed at symptoms rather than at causes. Here is one example: there are programs designed to contact school dropouts and give them counseling and other help so that they will return to school. Dropping out of school is seen by the designers of such programs as a cause of the teenager's lack of skills and abilities. It is clearly not the cause; it is the result. We may look at the issue of dropouts another way. When we try to measure the effectiveness of urban educational efforts we use dropout rate as an indicator; it is a way to quantify the results of educational programs. High dropout rates may be seen as an indication of the failure of such programs. Therefore a simplistic way to improve education is to lower the dropout rate by exerting influence on the dropouts not to do it. To return to our malaria analogy, this would be like measuring the effectiveness of a malaria control effort by counting the number of hospital patients and then proposing to make improvements by advising patients who were not too feverish to leave the hospital and thus improve the score. A more sophisticated effort might be developed from this which would urge patients to keep their temperatures down and not to shiver when they had chills.

UNDERSTANDING THE DISEASE

Perhaps we can apply the techniques of epidemiology to the problems of ghetto education. To do this we must look at the disease from a distance. We must consider the disease as it affects each individual—how he is infected, what the symptoms are, what the effects are, and what remedies or cures are available. Next we need to discover how the disease is transmitted—to identify the carriers. To understand the cycle of infection we must study the environment: Where is the disease most virulent? What environmental factors favor its spread? What is the mosquito which carries the infection?

The last question is key. We can use our knowledge about where the disease of ghetto education is most virulent and what conditions appear to ameliorate it to give us clues to the identity of the "mosquito" which transmits the disease. Epidemiologists refer to the insect or other animal which carries a disease from one victim to another as a "vector." The question then is: "What is the vector of ghetto education?"

The answer to this question is still uncertain in the eyes of many educators and sociologists, but to others it is crystal clear. *The vector of ghetto education is racism.*

Racism is the mosquito which is responsible for the disease, and it breeds, not in the ghetto, but in white communities and white institutions, one of which is public education. If this is true then it is easy to understand why the disease of ghetto education is at epidemic levels. We bring the child at an early age into an institution where mosquitoes are bred and compel him to remain there for at least eleven years. If he had not succumbed to the disease by then, we try to make him remain even longer. If he is able to develop an immunity or a tolerance for the racism he may get an education. It appears that as many as twenty-five or thirty per cent of the students in ghetto schools may learn enough to justify giving them high school diplomas. A higher percentage than that survived malaria before any preventive measures were discovered.

If our racist educators—and by this I mean the vast majority of all educators—are indeed the vector, the carriers, of the disease of ghetto education we must abandon the malaria analogy and seek solutions elsewhere. If mosquitoes had been in control of the government and economy of our country, how successful would we have been in draining swamps and developing insecticides? Mosquito legislators would certainly have said, "I am a decent insect and it isn't my fault that some of my constituents may carry the malaria parasite in their bodies." Mosquitoes in control of the economy might, under pressure of impending revolt, have provided money for the treatment of malaria victims and the building of hospitals, but certainly nothing which might diminish their control.

So with ghetto education. Efforts are aimed at treating the victims, not at attacking the cause of the disease. Our children in ghetto schools do need help, immediate help, in massive doses. But, every day thousands of black children are being born who will become infected by this same disease. Racism is the cause. Its parasite is carried in the hearts and minds of a preponderance of our educators.

IF THE SEGREGATION DOESN'T GET YOU, THE AIR POLLUTION WILL: CHICAGO, 1969

The Department of Air Pollution Control, City of Chicago, maintains air monitoring stations at public schools throughout the city. In 1969, the pattern of pollution followed the pattern of racial segregation in the schools. The numerical measure below refers to suspended particulate concentration, micrograms per cubic meter.

Four predominantly white high schools:

Taft	85
Steinmetz	100
Lake View	112
Kelly	122

Average micrograms per cubic meter   105

Four predominantly black high schools:

Cooley	150
Crane	143
Hyde Park	158
Carver	144

Average micrograms per cubic meter   146

On January 28, 1970, the Air Pollution Control Board, State of Illinois recommended a standard of air quality for suspended particulate concentration. Under this standard, to be achieved by January 1, 1972, the *maximum* annual geometric mean concentration would be 75 micrograms per cubic meter.

———————

Questions:

1. In an urban school system of 50,000 pupils with a 42% non-white population, what professional staff do you feel would be needed to provide a satisfactory racial make-up?

2. At what point do you feel that an attack on the disease of "Ghetto Education" would be most effective; pre-school, primary, upper elementary, junior high school, or senior high school? Explain.

3. What ideas or plans do you feel would effectively eliminate racism: vector of ghetto education?

THE URBAN TEACHER:
SAINT, SINNER, OR SUCKER?

By SEYMOUR METZNER

Every year Hollywood awards an Oscar for best actor to the second best actor in the United States. By right, on the basis of sheer acting skill, this award should go to any high school graduation speaker who can perform his duties without bursting into laughter or showers of tears. The impulse to laugh arises from the speaker's realization that the main wish of his audience is for him to get finished so they can get on with the business of living and learning, while the tears might spring from his knowledge of how dismally prepared some of them are for either living or learning. In any school serving urban poverty areas one can be absolutely certain that many of the graduates have reading and mathematical skills anywhere from two to three years lower than would be expected on the basis of their graduate status.

The American public, especially as represented by parents and other interested community members such as professional social reformers and jazz critics, have been searching for the causes of pupil underachievement and believe they have come up with the main culprit — the teacher. Among the terms used in recent literature to describe teachers in deprived areas are "awful people," "tyrants," "malicious," "perverse," and "case studies in abnormal psychology." The most virulent denunciations tend to come from professors of sociology or psychology who have little or no experience in public school teaching anywhere — let alone in deprived areas — and from sweet young things (either male or female and preferably from Ivy League institutions) who do a one- or two-year stint of slumming in the public schools and then race away to write a book exposing all those nasty people who have taught there for 15 or 20 years without being smart enough to leave and become authors.

Rather than follow the usual technique of citing case studies and individual anecdotes to buttress biases for or against teachers, let's examine the main charges against teachers which might be relevant to pupil learning and look at the research in the field to see how much truth there is in these charges.

Charge: The teachers haven't been adequately prepared to teach in disadvantaged schools.

Evidence: If we define "adequate preparation" in terms of productive pupil achievement, which is not an unreasonable thing to do, then it is quite obvious that teachers are not prepared to teach in ghetto schools. However, considering that not a single teacher education program in any college or university in the United States can show that its graduates are teaching any more

Reprinted with permission from *Phi Delta Kappan* (May 1970).

successfully in disadvantaged schools than graduates of any other college or university, can we blame the individual teacher for failing? She can't deliver what hasn't been invented.

We are faced with the spectacle of soldiers who haven't been trained to fight a battle but are nevertheless staying and fighting it, however poorly, being attacked by those who were never in the front line or else left shortly after seeing how difficult the fighting was.

Charge: The teachers are reluctant to abandon old methods and adopt innovative and individualized techniques.

Evidence: There is little doubt that teachers have been reluctant to adopt innovative, creative, or individualized practices. James I. Mason,[1] in studying teaching practices in recommended "good" school districts in non-disadvantaged areas of Pennsylvania, found that in almost all cases the more flexible, open-ended, and individualized a particular teaching practice was, the less it was used. Similar findings were reported from places as far apart as Utah[2] and New York State.[3] The urban teacher is no exception to this nationwide finding of a lack of individualized instruction.

Why, then, doesn't the teacher get on the ball and do something about individualizing instruction? This question must be supplanted by the more basic question, "Considering the fact that the average teacher is a middle-aged housewife with family responsibilities and limited time and energy at her disposal, how much can she realistically be expected to accomplish in individualizing or meaningfully differentiating the curriculum and instruction for 25 to 30 children in at least a half-dozen different learning areas?" This question is particularly pertinent when we realize that efforts to individualize instruction have met with very limited success at such institutions as Stanford University and the University of Pittsburgh, despite the work of a corps of subject matter specialists, professional educators, and clerical help, and millions of dollars in federal funds, not to mention the support of private foundations. Little of this high-powered professional help is offered the overworked woman teaching in the classroom, and the only foundation support she might be lucky to get is from the girdle manufacturers.

Charge: The teachers expect little academic achievement from their pupils, and the children sense this and respond as expected.

Evidence: There is little reason to doubt that teachers in deprived areas have lower academic achievement expectations for their pupils than do teachers in affluent neighborhoods. This is unfortunate, since psychologists believe that individuals or groups who feel that much is expected of them tend to do better than similar individuals or groups from whom little is expected. The problem here is that of the chicken and the egg — which came first? Do the children achieve less because they feel less is expected of them, or do the teachers expect less because they are continually disappointed when they expect more, while those teachers who can't adjust their standards to lower expectations leave the profession or go to other schools? This is a question we must answer before casting the teachers as the villains in this tragic situation. Much has been made of an experiment by Robert Rosenthal[4] on the West Coast, in which teacher expectations of the academic potential of particular students seemed to result in greater than expected test gains for these children. Not only is Rosenthal's research suspect, the relevance of his findings for ghetto education would be clouded anyway because of the fact that the experiment was carried out in a less deprived area than exists in many urban centers, and also by the fact that the children who made the greatest gains were those already operating at a moderate level of performance, while the basic problem in ghetto areas is the consistently low-level performance of most children.

It is wrong for any teacher to give up looking for new, different, or more effective means of teaching deprived children because of a belief that all such efforts are doomed due to the pupils' crippled learning capacity. This can be a handy device for taking the easy way out, but to a truly professional teacher, knowledge of pupil learning handicaps should be an even greater spur to discover procedures which will be as effective as possible. Teachers must not equate "difficult to teach" with "unable to learn."

It might be appropriate to place in fluorescent letters across the desk top of every teacher in a ghetto area the following quotation from Quintilian: "Those who are dull and unteachable are as abnormal as prodigious births and monstrosities, and are but few in number."

Charge: The subjects taught and the methods used by the teachers relate to other times and other school populations and don't reflect the needs and learning style of children in poverty areas.

Evidence: The curriculum taught is geared to middle-class standards, as is the moralistic value structure invoked by the teachers in class. And this is true not only for teachers in urban districts; a study of teacher behavior in the Southwest concluded that, in teaching Indian and Spanish-American pupils, teachers showed a lack of sensitivity to motivational patterns differing from their own and generally followed an undifferentiated curriculum based on middle-class values.[5]

The degree to which we damn the teachers for imposing middle-class values on others will depend on our answer to the following question: In a technological civilization in which middle-class values and behavior patterns are almost essential to the material prerequisites of success, what is the function of the teacher when faced with a subculture whose mores and behavioral patterns are often inimical to success in this society?

We must recognize that the function of the public school in American life has *not* been to administer to the psychological, social, or emotional needs of children but rather to develop the skills and life style necessary for them to achieve their full potential within the framework of the American society and economy. Since this economy is predominantly a technological one, the problem is not to meet some vague, unspecified "needs" of disadvantaged children but rather to discover means for helping them meet the needs (or demands) of this economy. If we do this successfully, these same disadvantaged children may eventually be influential in shaping the future of the society, and their children will be better equipped to meet new demands of a better society.

Charge: Teachers are unsympathetic and racially prejudiced, and they lack understanding where lower-class children are concerned — especially when these children are also Negro or Puerto Rican. Some people feel the children react to to this attitude by purposely not learning, as the only way they can "get back" at these teachers.

Evidence: It is, of course, almost impossible to investigate why a child does or doesn't do something, since he himself may not be aware of subconscious motivations. It is, however, possible to study teacher attitudes toward these children.

The charge that middle-class white teachers exhibit racial prejudice and lack of sympathy and understanding toward children of minority and lower social class groups is one that is difficult either to refute or establish. No studies have been made which contradict the overall finding that teachers act negatively toward lower-class children; but there is a definite possibility that this action is not a function of class or racial prejudice. If we take into account a study by Hart,[6] we find that *all* teachers, regardless of their own class backgrounds, act negatively toward lower-class children. Indeed, this study found that lower socioeconomic-class teachers behaved less sympathetically toward the lower-class children than did teachers of higher-class origin.

A more tenable theory than race or class prejudice to explain teacher reactions to pupils of different class levels is that teachers tend to act positively toward *all* pupils who adopt teacher-conforming behavior and exhibit high achievement, which the teacher interprets as a credit to her teaching ability. Since conforming behavior and high achievement patterns are characteristic of middle-class rather than lower-class children, the middle-class children would naturally be favored. For this theory to be acceptable, it would be necessary to find that the teacher's favorable disposition toward achieving pupils declines as their grades decline, despite pupil social-class status. This is precisely what was found in a study by Davidson and Lang.[7] We would also expect to find that although the favorable disposition declines with low grades in spite of social status, the teachers would react more favorably toward middle-class children — rather than lower-class children of similar achievement — because of the higher degree of conforming behavior from middle-class children. Davidson and Lang found this, also, to be true. Therefore, teacher reaction to children in deprived areas can most simply and adequately be explained as a generalized response to pupil behavior and achievement, rather than a reflection of basic class or racial prejudices.

It is logically impossible to show that teachers do not, to some extent, possess racial prejudice. Moreover, there is a definite possibility that all people have, in varying degrees, some type of prejudice against those who are noticeably unlike them in one respect or another. Nevertheless, the little evidence available indicates that teachers tend, if anything, to be less prejudiced than the average person. In a study of prospective teachers in upstate New York, Dodd[8] used the Minnesota Multiphasic Personality Inventory to determine the degree of prejudice among them and found that it was well below the average for the populace in general.

We can acknowledge that teachers have been markedly unsuccessful in solving pupil learning problems in disadvantaged areas; it is equally necessary to acknowledge that teachers are not the basic source of these learning problems. What, then, is the primary source, if indeed one source may be considered more important than any of several others?

Probably the most important and consistent finding in the search for the underlying causes of poor achievement concerns the relationship between sensory stimulation during early childhood and learning efficiency during school years. Research studies and analyses by Martin Deutsch[9] and Benjamin Bloom[10] strongly underline the importance of the child's early environment to his later intellectual development. The further removed a child is from the values, living patterns, and activities of a typical middle-class childhood, the more difficult it is for him to adjust to the demands and expectations of middle-class-oriented schools. This is particularly true where verbal skills are involved.

All studies have shown significant differences in child-rearing practices, home environment, and language usage between middle-class and lower-class families. School achievement studies inevitably illustrate the advantage enjoyed by middle-class children in middle-class schools. Lower-class Indian, Negro, and Puerto Rican children are even further removed from white middle-class practices and values than are lower-class white children and might, therefore, be expected to achieve at a still lower level — and they do.

Those who are unwilling to accept the theory that children in disadvantaged neighborhoods start school with an initial handicap point to the nearly normal achievement of these children in the early grades and contrast it with the massive retardation which is increasingly apparent from third and fourth grade onward. They see the contrast as proof that these children start as equals, but thereafter poor school practices cripple their learning capacity. However, this phenomenon is better explained by noting that early-grade achievement tests are so restricted in the range of achievement tested that little more than regular class attendance is required to master the content, while the more abstract concepts and complex skills tested in later grades are heavily dependent on previous environmental experiences. This explanation is also more logical in view of the considerably higher scores achieved by middle-class children, even in early grades, when wider-range aptitude tests are used.

Teachers are not the cause of educational deprivation but rather the legatees of a social situation which puts limitations on their classroom effectiveness. Although their greater effort with the disadvantaged should result in greater degrees of success, it still would be out of proportion to the success to be expected from similar efforts in middle-class neighborhoods.

Given the unanimity of research evidence regarding the tremendous handicap to learning imposed by inhibitory early childhood experiential patterns, it is obvious that fiddling around with teacher training programs or in-service education programs is likely to be as unproductive and disappointing as have been the provision of compensatory education, cultural enrichment, or supplementary facilities and personnel. Several studies by the Center for Urban Education and the most extensive and best-documented study extant, *Racial Isolation in the Public Schools,*[11] fully revealed the failure of the "Let's take them to a concert" philosophy, along with the "All we need to do is lower class size" group and the "We need more guidance and remedial services" advocates. All have had their turn at bat and all have struck out. A realistic appraisal leads to the inevitable conclusion that simply doing more of the same will be like applying mercurochrome to a cancer: We get a psychological satisfaction from doing *something,* but the malady continues unchecked.

In order to overcome educational deprivation there will have to be a complete restructuring of the social environment of the child and his family — not just some minor school readjustments. A stimulating educational environment will have to surround the child by the time he is two or three years old at the latest.

This has not been done.

His parents will have to be drawn into the school on a decently paid basis to aid in a carefully planned program of relevant educational experiences.

This has not been done.

There should be, at least through the primary grades, a ratio of one community aide or paraprofessional for every three to five pupils. The professional teacher should supervise them in a carefully planned and strongly structured educational program based upon individualized learning materials which have been pre-tested for effectiveness.

This has not been done.

These materials should be well enough organized to be effectively administered by a paraprofessional with a minimum of training.

This has not been done.

This program should not be just for the traditional three to six hours daily. In one form or another, it should go on all day with special evening programs for particular needs. Variations of this program should be continued during much of the summer.

This has not been done.

All these are basic prerequisites for equalizing opportunity in American society.

They must be done.

The tremendous financial outlay involved would be more than repaid by the diminution of social and welfare services in disadvantaged areas, and the nation could benefit from the greater productivity of the graduates of these schools.

It is time to stop attacking the teachers and start attacking the problem.

REFERENCES:

[1] James Ira Mason, *Preferred Practices in Elementary Education Applied to Selected School Districts to Determine the Extent of Use and the Factors Involved.* Unpublished doctoral dissertation, University of Pittsburgh, 1957.

[2] Millie Almy, "Intellectual Mastery and Mental Health," *Teachers College Record,* March, 1962, pp. 468-78.

[3] Anthony Milanovich, *A Critical Study of the Experience Unit in Elementary Education with Special Reference to the Elementary Schools of Erie County, New York.* Unpublished doctoral dissertation, Ohio State University, 1952.

[4] Robert Rosenthal and Lenore Jacobson, *Pygmalion in the Classroom.* New York: Holt, Rinehart and Winston, 1968.

[5] Horacio Ulibarri, *Teacher Awareness of Socio-Cultural Differences in Multi-Cultural Classrooms.* Unpublished doctoral dissertation, University of New Mexico, 1960.

[6] Joe W. Hart, "Socially Mobile Teachers and Classroom Atmosphere," *Journal of Educational Research,* December, 1965, pp. 166-68.

[7] Helen Davidson and Gerhard Lang, "Children's Perceptions of Their Teachers' Feelings Toward Them Related to Self-Perception, School Achievement, and Behavior," *Journal of Experimental Education,* December, 1960, pp. 107-18.

[8] John M. Dodd and Harold Strang, "A Comparison of Prejudiced and Nonprejudiced Freshmen Elementary Education Women," *Journal of Educational Research,* May-June, 1966, pp. 424-26.

[9] Martin Deutsch, *et al., The Disadvantaged Child.* New York: Basic Books, Inc., 1967.

10Benjamin Bloom. *Stability and Change in Human Characteristics.* New York: John Wiley & Sons, 1964.

11U. S. Commission on Civil Rights, *Racial Isolation in the Public Schools.* Washington, D.C.: U. S. Government Printing Office, 1967.

Questions:

1. Do you feel that a teacher can write an authoritative book on slum schools after a one- or two-year teaching experience in the inner city? Explain.

2. The charge has been made that teachers are reluctant to use individualized techniques. Which group of teachers—inner city or outer city—do you feel would be less likely to individualize instruction? Explain.

3. For what reasons would you favor or be opposed to the teaching of middle-class values and standards to slum area children?

INNER-CITY TEACHING - FRUSTRATING, EXCITING AND REWARDING

By BARRY E. HERMAN

Teaching inner-city children is not a job for a lazy, weak, unimaginative or placid teacher. The very best teacher is needed to do the job. This person must have the patience of a saint, the warmth of ten mothers, the wisdom of Solomon, the strength of Hercules and the endurance of an astronaut. A teacher of these children will face days of frustration and hard work and days of excitement and satisfaction.

Many inner-city children suffer from poverty unknown to middle-class children. Inner-city children have been given many labels. A few include: culturally deprived, disadvantaged, slum children, culturally different, under-privileged, educationally handicapped and transients.

Some of the characteristics of inner-city children may include:

1. Lack of response to conventional classroom approaches
2. Inadequate performance in communication skills
3. Socially unacceptable behavior
4. Indifference to responsibility
5. Physical defects and poor health habits
6. Exaggerated importance of status symbols

Further study of inner-city children reveal:

1. Overage for the grade
2. Poor school attendance
3. High rate of failure
4. High drop-out rate
5. Low aspiration level
6. No kindergarten, or nursery experience
7. Low achievement in reading and arithmetic
8. Limited cultural and enrichment experiences
9. Potential appears to exceed what test data shows
10. Crowded living conditions at home

Goff (1) wrote that many children work below their capacity because of distracting, often soul-breaking experiences for which no relief has been granted. She illustrated this statement by relating an incident in the life of a fifteen-year-old girl. . . . "stuffed into a third-grade seat, whose drunken father the night before had kicked her pregnant mother to death and then attempted to

---

Reprinted with permission from *Education,* P.O. Box 5504, Milwaukee, Wisconsin 53211 (Vol. 90, November-December 1969).

rape the girl on the front porch in the morning. The teacher went blithely on with abstract subject matter."

How does one succeed as a teacher of inner-city children? There is no secret formula for success. A love of children, a sense of humor, fairness, firmness, dedication, hard work and a sincere desire to teach are a few basic ingredients that will help. An inner-city teacher must be sensitive to the needs of his children. He should learn what words act as triggers to set off feelings of hostility. He should talk to children in order to make them feel they are wanted, needed and belong. Such children can easily spot a phony! An inner-city teacher should be sincere in dealing with children. He should try to say something nice about a different child each day. Comment on Mary's new dress, Jim's neat paper, or Ann's new baby sister. Teachers must realize that these children have not been imbued with the same values they hold so dearly. Values regarding honesty, family, ambition and cleanliness will not always be identical to the values they know. The inner-city child wants respect and not sympathy from his teacher. The teacher and child should learn to build on mutual respect for each other's values and ideas.

Lessons should be carefully planned. All activities should be well organized, structured and basic to the needs of the children being taught. Variety, innovation and experimentation are three points that will help break through the inner-city "curtain". The teacher should be an actor using every theatrical technique imaginable to gain and keep the attention of his pupils. Lessons and units should relate to life needs, issues and problems involving family life, economic concepts, human relations, and problems affecting urban living. Teaching should be more child- and life-centered rather than subject-matter centered.

The inner-city teacher should borrow the best from both traditional and progressive school philosophies. Riessman (2) reported that the traditional approach contributes rules, discipline, authority, rote, organization, order and strong demands for achievement. The progressive idea places an emphasis on motivation, learning by doing, and child-centered experiences. A teacher must learn how to bridge the gap between theory and practice. Children should be encouraged to help in the planning of field trips and room projects; in the solving of some class problems; and in arranging physical aspects of the classroom.

Some successful teaching ideas and activities based on experiences in working with inner-city children are as follows:

Attractive Classroom Surroundings. Children will respond to a classroom that has pleasant bulletin boards, interesting centers of interest, plants, an independent activity corner, and examples of the children's own work hung up. The effectiveness of any display or exhibit is measured by the length of time it is up. When the pupils no longer notice a display, it should be taken down.

Be Alert At All Times. The teacher should keep an "eye" on the entire room so that disturbances can be resolved before they get out of hand. A veteran teacher once said: "A teacher has to be deaf, dumb and blind at times." The successful teacher does not make a major issue out of a minor episode. Teachers should use their eyes or a shake of the head at times instead of their voice. A sharp glance can be just the thing to give a would be troublemaker the hint that he better stop what he is doing. To prevent frustration make sure each pupil has the information and the skills needed to complete an assignment. Frustration leads to misbehavior, resentment or restlessness and these elements often trigger serious trouble.

Involve Parents. Encourage parents to come to school when the class has prepared a little skit or a special activity. Ask parents to accompany the class on field trips and with class parties. The inner-city teacher should make home visits when it is deemed necessary. Many inner-city teachers in the course of a school year visit the homes of all their students even when there is no problem. In this way, the parent gets to know the teacher and feels that the teacher is sincerely interested in her child. The teacher will then gain the parent's support and cooperation if and when a problem with a student should develop.

Masculinize The Reading. In the female dominated elementary school, boys usually get into more trouble than girls. Boys usually dislike reading. The inner-city teacher should plan the reading program so that the boys will become interested. Girls will enjoy stories intended for boys, but boys will reject reading if they are "fed" pallid fiction and fairy tales that are far removed from their lives. To motivate children to read, the teacher should introduce his students to action, sports, adventure and science fiction stories; simple biographies of vigorous people; and stories that deal with real life situations.

Teacher's Pet For The Day. Give each child in the class a chance to be the teacher's personal messenger for the day. Even though each classroom may have class helpers on a weekly or monthly rotating basis, this job should be on a daily basis. The teacher should start from the first seat in the first row and go right down the line, a different child each day, leaving no one out. Every child will enjoy being "teacher's pet" for the day. Good rapport will be built with all the pupils and each child will feel that the teacher trusts him. Even the "problem child" will respond to this display of trust.

Develop Multi-ethnic Picture Files. Each teacher should develop picture files showing multi-ethnic faces and different types of people. It is important to include different racial groups in bulletin board displays. Leading Negro magazines as well as sports and movie magazines can furnish the teacher with plenty of material.

Cheyney (3) reported that teachers who teach in an inner-city school shouldn't feel sorry for themselves. A few years ago these teachers were looked upon by their friends as being intellectually incompetent or "You must be dumb or flunked basket weaving in college to get into schools like these." This picture is changing because teachers in schools located in inner-city communities are now being looked upon with increasing professional respect. Cheyney felt: "If there is any place to be in the fore-front of educational thought and experimentation, it is in the disadvantaged neighborhood school. These teachers should be increasingly aware of their position and the deep responsibility they bear to children and to the teaching profession."

REFERENCES:

[1]Goff, Regina M. "Negro Education in America", *Sixteenth Yearbook of the John Dewey Society.* New York: Harper & Row, 1962.

[2]Riessman, Frank. *The Culturally Deprived Child.* New York: Harper & Row, 1962.

[3]Cheyney, Arnold B. *Teaching Culturally Disadvantaged in the Elementary School.* Columbus, Ohio: Charles E. Merrill Books, Inc., 1967.

Questions:

1. Comment on the following statement, "A teacher has to be deaf, dumb and blind at times." Be specific.

2. List what you consider are the eight most important characteristics of a good inner-city teacher.

3. What do you feel would be the three most frustrating aspects of being an inner-city teacher?

HOW CAN I TEACH BLACK CHILDREN?

By FRANCES K. HEUSSENSTAMM
MINTA PALMER-BROWN

Whether you are a beginning teacher or an experienced one, you can be sure that wherever you teach, you will sooner or later be teaching black children. Most of you are concerned; some of you are afraid. The questions from teachers in training replied to here by Professors Heussenstamm and Palmer-Brown reflect the concerns and fears of many teachers about the children, about the black community, and about the best way to function as teachers in this new situation.

Do black children feel "different" from white schoolmates? If so, how does it affect their education?

Reaction If one is black in America, it means one is almost continually aware of that blackness. As Cobbs and Grier point out in *Black Rage* to be black is also to be paranoid. When a black person is denied a basic right, he knows whether the opportunity does not in fact exist, or whether the right has been denied because of his color. Certainly this awareness affects his development as a human being. But in the long run, it is his attitude toward being black that makes the real difference. This is where the teacher has considerable responsibility—to develop black consciousness and racial pride. A white teacher can do this only if he is comfortable with black students.

Reaction Black children have the same range of emotions as white children. If they feel different, it is from having a mirror held up to them that reflects them as different from other people in the society. People who are victims of prejudice often internalize the message of their alleged inferiority. The child develops his self-concept as he encounters others in the larger community, and when the self-concepts are negative, he simply cannot develop into a fully functioning adult. If, however, he feels that his teacher respects him, invests him with dignity, has confidence that he can perform satisfactorily—if his teacher provides support, materials, and encouragement, and rewards achievement—some of his paranoia may be countered. A teacher may gain insight from accounts, both autobiographical and fictional, which report the pain of coming of age as a black in America.

What effect has black militancy had on the relationship between white teachers and black students?

Reaction One effect of black militancy has been to make some white teachers fearful of their black students—especially teachers who have not been doing an adequate job and are now being called to account. Where white

Reprinted from *INSTRUCTOR,* © August/September 1970, The Instructor Publications, Inc. Dansville, New York.

teachers have expressed strong concern for black children, the relationship between black and white is often closer, more supportive, and more reciprocal than ever. Of course, black teachers are sometimes no more able than white teachers to teach black children—it depends on what they are as individuals and on the circumstances.

Reaction Obviously, black militancy has tended to alienate white teachers and black students. One of the reasons is that black militancy means different things to them. The majority of black students think of militancy as an opportunity to manifest hostilities they have long suppressed. This includes, for many, hatred of white authority. On the other hand, many white teachers are angered by the increasing willingness of black students to question the relevancy of their schooling and its relationship to the community. Black militancy leads them to rationalize and express the fears and uncomfortable attitudes they have been suppressing.

What are your suggestions for discipline in a classroom of black children?

Reaction What most teachers mean by discipline is control. I am not willing to assume responsibility for controlling the behavior of any other human being. As teachers, shouldn't we want young people to become increasingly responsible for their own behavior and actions? When boys and girls have the opportunity to experience consequences for their behavior in a consistent manner and make choices based on those consequences, they tend increasingly to make choices that provide for optimum learning. Current experiments in open-structure schools where children are free to choose their activities have proved effective outlets for the aggression and hostility which racial discrimination creates. Such curricula, supported by Glasser's Reality Therapy or the class-meeting technique, have allowed children the opportunity to discover the effectiveness of problem solving through other than physical means.

Reaction Regardless of ethnicity, children in some families are raised by being punished quickly and physically for transgressions. Middle-class teachers may be shocked when a parent says, "If my child doesn't mind, give him a good swat." But the child, though he may not like it, feels perfectly comfortable with this response and understands it. When control is entirely verbal, he may find it difficult to know the teacher really means business when he gives directions. It is important to talk this over with the children, then make a detailed plan of dealing with conflict so the children will know what to expect from the teacher in response to misbehavior. Herbert Kohl makes useful suggestions in *Teaching the Unteachable,* as do others reporting ghetto school experiences.

To what extent should a teacher compromise his own middle-class values with those practiced and understood by black children?

Reaction A teacher should never feel it necessary to compromise his own values. However, neither should he try to impose his values on his students. The music, the dances, the speech, even the facial and body expressions of black children are too often rejected by the school. To have one's dialect frequently corrected is to be told that one's language is not beautiful. To have one's taste in books or reading materials rejected is to suggest that one is inferior. To be rejected for solving problems in an aggressive manner rather than being shown another way to solve them is to find out that the teacher considers one's values unimportant or inadequate. If the dull, dreary, chalk-and-talk blackboard jungle could become a creative learning laboratory in a truly democratic environment, the teacher would not try to inflict his own values.

Reaction This question implies that the black child's standards are "inferior" to the teacher's, an inadequate description of cultural differences based on life experiences. No teacher, white or black, should compromise his professional standards. A teacher who is genuinely teaching cannot in fact compromise his standards except by doing something less than an adequate job. His behavioral objectives should be the same for all children; the challenge lies in how these objectives are to be attained. When students cannot meet the traditional standards of a school, lowering standards is not the answer, but rather reexamination of the means by which achievement is attained.

Is the response of a black child to black teachers any different or better than to white teachers?

Reaction I am convinced that children respond to teachers who are competent, whatever their color. The fear of rejection common to beginning teachers is what makes them say things like, "No white teacher can be accepted in the black community." This is simply not true. White teachers are acceptable in terms of their own professional skills and personal authenticity. The criterion is how well they do their jobs. They cannot provide the insights into the black experience that a black teacher may. But what they *can* provide is sensitivity and well planned, relevant instruction.

Reaction I am convinced that black children respond better to black teachers—IF those teachers are similar to them in background, and IF they have a commitment to the black movement. With the increased participation of community groups in the black movement, children at increasingly younger ages are aware of their differences and are concerned about them. Black teachers, traditionally members of the black bourgeoisie trying to create black imitations of middle-class white children, are becoming more aware of the needs of the black community, and are developing ways for black children to prepare themselves to remedy their community problems. Inherent in the black movement is the commitment of black people to remain where they are needed until equality of opportunity is available for all blacks in their country. A black child would find some difficulty in accepting such a challenge from a white person, especially a white person who is not answering the same challenge in his own community.

Why isn't there any motivation or encouragement in the home of the black ghetto child?

Reaction All people have motivation; it is the teacher's responsibility to find out toward what. The family of a black child encourages him to obtain the education necessary for his survival. Teachers, especially those in black ghetto schools, should analyze the kinds of irrelevant activities to which black children are subjected daily. School begins with a "sharing" period during which children are not allowed to talk about the realities of ghetto life. It proceeds to a social studies lesson about families, neighborhoods, and communities that the children cannot recognize. They read about Dick, Jane, and Spot, and work on long columns of numbers whose use in their daily lives has never been explained. Why should a black mother encourage her child to persist in such irrelevant activities? As a teacher, I find such patterns of education irresponsible.

Reaction It is simply not true that there is not motivation and encouragement in the homes of black children. A teacher who finds a child is not learning should not jump to such a conclusion. A more fruitful point of view would be to assume that parents generally want their children to do well, not only in school but in later life. To get parental support, the teacher has to convince the parents that he also wishes the child to succeed, by going to the home to talk with them if necessary. It's true that many black people feel that even if their children get an education, they won't have equal opportunities to find jobs, and often they are right. But it is a gross act of irresponsibility to suggest that such parents don't motivate or encourage their children. Poverty parents may not be able to give an individual child as much attention as the teacher feels would benefit him. However, it then becomes the teacher's responsibility to devise tutoring strategies and alternative support for the child.

How welcome is a white teacher in the home of a black family?

Reaction Black parents, just like white parents, are usually happy to welcome a friendly adult who demonstrates genuine concern about their children. If the teacher has any doubt about it, his best avenue might be to make home visits accompanied by a black teacher aide, a school-community aide, or someone from the parent support group, if his school has one. The quality of the reception accorded to a white teacher will depend on who the teacher is, what he is, and how he demonstrates his interest in the children.

Reaction This is a question that only the black family could answer. It seems to me, however, that a white teacher who needed to ask this question would probably exhibit his fear and uncomfortable attitude, and had better forego the visit. When a teacher has a genuine reason for visiting the home, most parents are grateful for the teacher's interest. Of course, the traditional pattern has been that the school contacts the family only when something is wrong. When the family is poor, every contact with traditional institutions is suspect—any family eventually wearies of negative contacts. A teacher might be able to change the picture by setting up a pattern of frequent positive contacts.

What is the most important change that must take place in our school system to give blacks equal education?

Reaction The most critical change needed is for teachers and administrators to develop an awareness of the impact of racism on human beings, white as well as black, and a will to attempt to alter attitudes which reflect prejudice. Whites in all walks of life must examine themselves on these issues, and all must assume responsibility for bringing about change. We may then be able to devise real solutions to the problems, and provide alternative ways of organizing the curriculum so equality will be more than a shibboleth. One major criticism of our society is the lack of congruence between practice and preachment. Hypocrisy must be replaced with educated concern and a commitment to improved human relations.

Reaction For change to take place, educators must first be willing to admit that something is wrong. No effective educational program can be developed as long as prejudiced professionals continue to dominate the American school system. The retraining of teachers is essential. It cannot be expected that a teacher who accepts the system that has destroyed the minds of black people for generations will easily admit that the system has been so wrong. Teachers and administrators should be required to live in the community, in ghettos and barrios, as the National Teacher Corps requires of its recruits. Those who do not speak the language, who are unaware of the culture, who are disapproving of the styles of dress and the mode and tenor of the community, should not be allowed to work with the children. A professional of the 1970's who still believes his job is to pass along a body of information to his students is an anachronism. The teachers who believe they have as much to learn from children as they have to give will be the effective teachers of the schools of the future.

Questions:

1. Whom do you feel is most effective in developing black consciousness and racial pride, the teacher or the parents? Explain.

2. For what reasons would you favor the use of competent black teachers instead of competent white teachers in an inner city school?

3. Which statements are facts and which are opinions in the section, "Why isn't there any motivation or encouragement in the home of the black ghetto child?"

EDUCATIONAL UNCLE TOMISM

By JOHN R. SCUDDER, JR.

Naom Chomsky chided the philosophers at the Western Division of the American Philosophical Association meeting in St. Louis for not using their analytical ability to criticize procedures and policies used by our government and social institutions. When asked for examples, he suggested investigation of the philosophy that underlies our programs for educating the disadvantaged. Chomsky's challenge struck me full force, not only because I am a professor of philosophy and education, but because I had recently taught in a black high school, and I am now teaching in an MAT program designed to prepare teachers of disadvantaged children.

Chomsky's suggestion could be approached in at least two ways. First, one could analyze and appraise the presuppositions of the stated practices and policies of programs for the disadvantaged. Second, one could become involved in teaching the disadvantaged and make his analysis and appraisal from inside the classroom. This paper will use the testimonial approach.

The success of Herbert Kohl's *36 Children* and Jonathan Kozol's *Death at an Early Age* suggests the possibilities of the testimonial approach. On the other hand, the unwarranted conclusions often drawn from their testimony indicates the danger of this approach. Testimony as to how one experienced and appraised a particular situation cannot be used as empirical proof that these conditions exist in similar situations. Instead, testimony should evoke analysis and interpretation of other situations in a manner that will increase understanding of them.

In utilizing testimony, it is necessary to know the perspective from which the testimony is given. Three factors are essential to understanding the perspective from which the testimony in this article is given. First, I was one of a number of white teachers who began the integration of faculty of the pre-dominantly black schools of Eastern North Carolina—a region with a high ratio of blacks to whites and with a heritage of using blacks to harvest the tobacco crop. Second, I was a philosopher of education with extensive academic background in the teaching of history. Third, I was there to gain experience in teaching history in the public schools rather than to prove or test any theory about the education of the disadvantaged. For this reason, my attention was focused on teaching world history to black students in two grade ten classes. This article is the result of reflection on the meaning of that experience.

Reprinted from *Educational Forum* (May 1970) by permission of Kappa Delta Pi, An Honor Society in Education, owners of the copyright.

My experience contradicted what I had been led to expect by the literature on teaching the disadvantaged. Reading this material as a prospective
teacher rather than as a scholar surveying the literature, I gathered that the
primary deficiency of the disadvantaged was lack of verbal and reading skills.
Presumably, what was needed was to develop verbal skills by improving technique in their use.

My students were far more competent in this area than I expected. In fact,
the college students who occasionally taught with me reported after doing
student teaching that my black students read as well as most white students in
county high schools in which they taught. Also, I expected my students to need
much remedial work in writing and in speech. Again, their speech and writing
were not significantly different from that in neighboring county schools. In
short, the differences in verbal skill development was not significant enough to
say that the black students were "disadvantaged" in comparison to the white
students.

The main difference between the Negroes we taught and the white
students in both the city and county high schools where my student teachers
taught was not in skills but in understanding the basic concepts and values of
western culture. For example, I attempted to give my students more adequate
understanding of place concepts by getting them to think in terms of global
space relationships. I hoped to eliminate the false conceptions of space they had
acquired from previous instruction with maps. If I had succeeded, they would
have understood such concepts as east being the direction in which the earth
turns and not the right hand side of a map. To my amazement, they seemed to
have fewer wrong ideas about space relationships than other young people I had
taught. In addition, some of them had undergone teaching which was based on
global rather than map concepts of space. Consequently, my students seemed to
make rapid progress.

I was completely unprepared for their total failure on my first test. Later,
I discovered that they had really no functional knowledge of continents, oceans,
nations, and their relationships. This deficiency became apparent to me through
a conversation between my third-grade son and sixth-grade daughter
immediately after a frustrating failure to teach space concepts to my students.
My son heard on the radio that there had been trouble in Israel. He asked my
daughter where Israel was. My daughter said she did not know exactly, but it
was somewhere near Egypt. My son responded. "Oh, I see." Very few of my
high school students could have participated meaningfully in this conversation.
These students had been exposed to more schooling dealing with continents,
oceans, and places than my children. Their minds had more fully matured than
my children's minds. If my children had been put in competition with my
students, the latter would for the most part perform much better. However, my
students were completely unable to use space concepts functionally.

A second example of the lack of understanding of the concepts and values
of western culture concerned their inadequate grasp of civil rights. Although
they could define civil rights adequately, they had absolutely no understanding
of the values and ideas that underlie civil rights. For instance, we listened to a
recording of the portion of Sophocles' play, *Antigone,* in which Creon and his
son quarrel about the rights and duty of a ruler. Creon takes the position that
because he is king whatever he demands is just. His son argues that even the king

is bound by the principle of justice. Most of my students thought that the position argued by Creon was the right one. Ironically, this same argument was being used by the white majority to deny blacks their civil rights.

Certainly a good course in history should remedy this lack of understanding. But the teacher is plagued by the lack of concepts on which to build. When students are completely unfamiliar with the basic concepts underlying our constitutional government and its processes, how does one develop adequate understanding of civil rights? If they cannot locate such places as Africa, how does one develop a meaningful understanding of spatial relationships in the world? If they have no conception of the cultures of the Egyptians, Hebrews, Greeks, Romans, how does one begin a high school course in world history which develops understanding of how our ideas, institutions, and values were formed? When a functional understanding even of the elementary concepts and values of the west is lacking, it is extremely difficult to teach history so as to prepare students to live meaningfully and well in the modern world.

Of course, these understandings are lacking to a disturbing degree among the slowest students in all high schools. Also, they are lacking to a large degree in white high schools in slums and in such areas as Appalachia. Disadvantaged blacks differ from whites in one important respect, however. Most white children are raised in slums because their parents have not succeeded in American society. Most Negro children are raised in slums because they are born black. This difference should mean that there is far more academic potential in an all-black ghetto high school than in an all-white one. With these potentially talented students, disadvantagement in education is most apparent. There was great difference in understanding of both the basic concepts and values of the west between the talented black students whom I was teaching and the talented white students whom my college students taught. Negroes who had the potential to attend college and become teachers, professors, doctors, lawyers and businessmen lacked the fundamental knowledge of their civilization necessary to compete for and to acquire the education required to develop their potential.

The concept of being disadvantaged which developed from this experience is that one is disadvantaged when he is not adequately exposed to the culture of which he is a part. The lack of adequate exposure to culture is most evident in a course such as world history. This does not mean, however, that the disadvantaged need more courses in world history. They need an understanding of what in the broadest sense is termed humane learning.

The type of humanistic learning needed by the disadvantaged should not be confused with the useless information that wins quiz contests or makes an impression in a women's circle. My students seem to have had an overexposure to this kind of artificial education. Its primary effect had been to immunize them against serious humane learning. The other block to learning was their overexposure to verbal skills divorced from content. My students were able to organize and present a formal debate more adequately than the white students in surrounding schools. They were able to locate the answers to questions in the textbooks quite well. But they lacked the understandings necessary to read meaningfully or take part in serious class discussion.

When we studied Socrates it became obvious that my students had participated in little serious conversation. They were very fascinated by his dialogical method of teaching. To my amazement they did extremely well on difficult test items concerning Socrates. When I asked why they were so interested in Socrates, they responded that they had been unable to understand what I was doing until we discussed Socrates.

Conversation or dialogue on their level with people who really understand the cultural heritage and its meaning is the one thing these students need most. They apparently had been over-taught by persons who had familiarized themselves with the knowledge of western culture in order to teach it so that it could be memorized. They had been given the forms of learning so that they could locate information, read orally, and present speeches and debates. The net result of this experience was skills devoid of any content or understanding. Even worse, they had unconsciously come to believe that this empty formalism was real learning. What they needed was a functional understanding of the values and concepts of our culture. This one acquires best in conversation with those who are well initiated into the culture.

Working on this assumption, I assigned the college students in my teaching of history class to small discussion groups. The success of these groups, of course, was varied. But when lively college students who knew something of western culture were put in small groups with these students the results were outstanding. For instance, I placed an imaginative, lively, soft-spoken, and mild-mannered young lady with a group of girls who were the troublemakers in my class. Most of these students had good minds but poor performance records. I wanted to find out if this young lady, who had all the qualities needed for this group work except the ability to enforce strict discipline, could succeed. Discipline improved, test scores went up, and a warm relationship was established between the students and the group leader. In fact, the students actually saved their own money in order to present her with a gift when the semester was over. Incidentally, after graduation this young lady took a teaching position in a predominantly Negro junior high school.

Given the climate of contemporary debate about race, the disadvantaged, and education, the contention that persons who know their culture should initiate the disadvantaged more fully into our common culture could be misconstrued as fostering Uncle Tomism. Actually, educational Uncle Tomism is the exact opposite. The students whom I taught were victims of educational Uncle Tomism. They had been introduced to the forms and skills of the culture without its substance. The nature of their education had been dictated by propriety rather than the desire to free them through understanding and mastery of their culture.

The concepts needed to describe this form of educational Uncle Tomism came to me from Melville J. Herskovitz's distinction between enculturation and socialization. Socialization is concerned with learning to live with other persons through the patterns of relationships and social roles of a given society. Enculturation includes socialization but it stresses learning the traditional and new skills, ideas, and ideals of a culture. It focuses on the portion of human experience peculiar to man as distinguished from other social animals. It fosters individual expression as well as social adjustment and change as well as conformity.[1] When enculturation is subordinated to socialization, the result is educational Uncle Tomism. Children are taught *only* those skills, ideals, and ideas which will prepare them for the role assigned them by society. The groups (WASP [White, Anglo-Saxon, Protestant] or other) which control society restrict enculturation to prepare persons belonging to minority subcultures for "their place." This "practical" approach to education determined that blacks would not be taught to read and write during slavery, that they would learn practical subjects like brick laying and table waiting between emancipation and 1954, and that they would be given "proper" and extensive instruction in verbal skills in recent years.

W.E.B. Dubois argued against restricting enculturation to fit a particular societal role in his famous debates over education with Booker T. Washington. Although Washington's position was more complex than restricting enculturation to fit a particular social role, many of his disciples, white and black, held this limited view. Against this "practical" position, Dubois rightly argued for full enculturation for black students.

The culture to which black students should be enculturated is our culture! Throughout this article "our culture" has been used deliberately and explicitly. In our course in world history my black students and I traced the development of the civilization which produced our culture. They were amused that my German ancestors lived in such primitive conditions that their enculturation almost destroyed western civilization. We speculated about what would have happened had the Sahara desert been between Italy and Germany rather than between North Africa and the rest of Africa. Would my ancestors have been slaves of their ancestors? One thing they seemed to grasp was that our culture is a product of western civilization. This fact is usually overlooked by persons who speak of "WASP" culture and "black" culture. Failure to recognize this has created the WASP culture myth with Dick, Jane, and the rest. White children as well as black have suffered from the attempt to initiate them into a culture that does not exist. Changing the WASP myth into a black one will not improve the situation. It will simply misdirect our efforts from initiating our children, black and white, into the culture in which they will live.

Practical programs for the full enculturation of black students, the relationships of the various subcultures in our society, and the value of our culture and civilization are all beyond the scope of this paper. I am simply contending that living in our culture requires mastery of its skills, ideas, and ideals. Indeed, without this mastery supplied by our mass educational system our society would collapse. Good education must perpetuate the cultural heritage. In our country, this ought to include the ability to criticize our culture and transform or reject it. But, to advocate its neglect is to deprive children of the skills, ideas, and values necessary to decide intelligently whether or not to attempt to succeed in it, to improve it, to withdraw from it, to reform it, or to revolt against it.

The view of education presupposed by this argument is advocated in the teaching of history by William Cartwright and in general education by the cultural realism of Harry S. Broudy. It can be labelled "conservative" only if "conservative" merely means that education should transmit the cultural heritage from generation to generation. Certainly, the heritage can be transmitted in a manner that seeks to preserve the status quo. But it can also be perpetuated in a way that attempts to transform or radically reform society. Certainly in a democratic society criticism and reform ought to be built into the process of transmission.

Education should involve maximum enculturation. Full enculturation breaks the bounds of class and societal restrictions. One student in my class was an excellent example of this process at work. He began the class as one of the better students. By the end of the course, although he was only a sophomore in high school, he was doing work comparable to that of students in western civilization in our college. He suffered not only from the disadvantagement resulting from his race, but also from the fact that he came from the wrong side of the tracks in the Negro community. Indeed, while most of my fellow teachers in the high school knew my other outstanding students, few, if any, knew this particular student. His ability was most clearly evident on "Teacher Appreciation Day" when he delivered the lectures to my classes. We agreed that he would review space understandings. He discussed oceans, continents, nations, and their relationships to each other on the map and on the globe. He did very well, but like most beginning teachers he ran out of information half way through the class. He then requested that I show him what I was planning to do in the next session. I showed him a very complicated map which showed the cultures (East, West, Near East, or primitive) of the various areas of the world, their major religion, and the degree of their technological development. After looking over the map for five minutes, he lectured to the students on these rather advanced concepts. Why was he able to do this? There were several students in the class who could read better than he could, more who could write better, and several who could deliver prepared speeches more effectively and clearly. The difference between this student and his colleagues was that he really had a functional understanding of space concepts and of culture. For instance, he explained western culture by pointing out similarities between our life style and that of Europe. Although the understanding of our culture which made it possible for him to converse intelligently about it certainly did not result primarily from being in my particular class, it was in this class that he began to focus these understandings to the point that he could actually use them in conversation.

This young man was acquiring the understanding of our culture which could free him. Free him to what end? It is his privilege and right to choose whether he will attempt to succeed in the establishment, improve our society, radically reform it, or withdraw from it. To attempt to determine his role in society, whether it be as shoe shine boy or militant black nationalist, is to engage in educational Uncle Tomism. Rather than creating Uncle Toms, white or black, by restricting enculturation, our responsibility as teachers is to free through the maximum possible enculturation.

FOOTNOTES:

[1]Melville Jean Herskovitz, *Cultural Anthropology* (New York: Knopf, 1955), pp. 325-329.

Question:

1. Defend the position that the main educational weakness of the Negroes in your community lies in the area of understanding the basic concepts and values of western culture and not in the basic academic skills.

DISCIPLINE: A MAJOR FUNCTION
IN TEACHING THE DISADVANTAGED

By ALLAN C. ORNSTEIN

In this paper the word discipline refers to the degree of order and control established in a group. This paper is written, with full awareness that what is said is general, and can be modified for any group, but with the hope that some of the suggestions may be particularly useful for the teacher of the disadvantaged. It is written with the understanding that discipline is not the major task, but rather a necessary function of teaching and continuously reinforced by treating it as part of the teaching process.

In the slum school, we usually judge the teacher's success by the way he handles or disciplines a class. Since the problem of discipline is perhaps the number one problem for most slum-school teachers, its function often replaces teaching as the major task. For example, according to Deutsch's findings in a study of urban school classrooms, the time devoted to discipline takes up as much as 80% of the teacher's time. It is no surprise, then, that if the teacher is unprepared or unable to maintain good discipline, each day is likely to end in emotional exhaustion, compounded with resentment and fear of the students, anxiety, and the ruin of his self-ego. This is usually what drives the teacher out of the school. That a great many slum-school teachers request transfers to another school indicates that they are unhappy with their disciplinary prowess and are undergoing emotional strain; therefore, some suggestions along the lines of discipline might prove worthwhile.

Without detailing the methods, six general guidelines for developing classroom order and control are outlined. The teacher should have: (1) an understanding of the disadvantaged child's values and behavior; (2) the ability to size up, analyze, and anticipate situations; (3) the ability to appraise realistically his own personality; (4) an understanding of good rules and routine; (5) the ability to keep calm and emotionally controlled; (6) the ability to develop a group spirit among the disadvantaged.

1. The teacher should have a basic understanding of the psychological and cultural patterns and problems and learning process of the disadvantaged. These children often see themselves as victims in many of their life situations, particularly in school and with their teachers. The disadvantaged child often feels his teachers pick on him and seldom give him a fair chance. Consequently, he is less apt to feel guilty, lacks inner-control, is quick to defend himself against criticism, and is more direct in expressing hostility. Even when the approach is sincere, the teacher is sometimes greeted with what is to him unwarranted

Reprinted by permission from *IMPROVING COLLEGE AND UNIVERSITY TEACHING*, Spring 1970.

cynicism. Constant questions, interviews, advice from social workers, police, and even other teachers have helped to create a feeling of suspicion on the part of the child.

Despair and hopelessness also afflict the disadvantaged child. You cannot remain in a slum area and not feel it in the air: young men and old "hanging out" on street corners or on stoops or near the local liquor store, of which there are many, with nothing but time on their hands. Perhaps his father, if he knows his father, or an older brother, is one of them. This is what he has to look forward to; furthermore, he is forced by the law to enter a school which neither abides nor understands his behavior. At school he is forced to fit a mold which does not fit him and which he does not need to prepare him for the life which he envisions for himself. He feels surrounded on all sides by authorities who castigate and further reject him for failing to appreciate what it has done for him.

To help the child, the teacher should avoid harsh criticism and censure, since this reaffirms the child's belief that the world is to blame for his failure; likewise, it merely perpetuates his negative self-concept. Ideally, the teacher accepts the child as an individual; he recognizes the child's overlooked positive qualities, without romanticizing or creating a false image too far on the other side. He encourages and gives honest praise, careful not to overpraise, for praise becomes ineffective if the child feels it means nothing.

On the other hand, some Negro children have newly gained confidence, as expressed in the social revolution sweeping across the country. Some see themselves as leaders, and not helpless, inferior youngsters. This new pride is evidenced by their tendency to challenge authority. The teacher should expect, encourage, and channel this energy toward contructive goals. Rather than avoid the concept of Black Power, for example, it might be worthwhile to enlarge the idea in the classroom, to give the Negro child a spark, some intrinsic motivation for him to work in class and succeed.

2. When control is gone the teacher must analyze the causes and consider what effect his own behavior has had on the individual or group, and consider what steps can be taken to alleviate the causes and regain control. Ideally, the teacher is aware of undercurrents of behavior. He reserves part of his attention while instructing for watching, looking, and listening. He does not become so absorbed in the lesson that he losès audience contact. He does not fix his eyes on the child who is reciting. He takes note of everyone's work. If he feels the lesson is becoming boring, he makes the necessary changes. He looks at facial expressions; he feels the pulse beat of the class; he senses when the children are confused.

Most important, the teacher learns to avoid trouble by anticipating what is going to happen. This should become ingrained by his being in the actual situation, doing something wrong, realizing what happened, and knowing the next time that he will anticipate and will not make the same mistake. For example, the teacher sees a strange child open the door and poke his head in the classroom. The teacher says, "Please close the door," and the child slams it. The next time, while managing to conduct the lesson, the teacher might walk across the room and quietly say to the child, "Please leave," and then close the door himself. Or, on the first day of school, say six children come to class unprepared, some accidentally and some intentionally. Of course, it is permissible for one child to borrow pencil and paper from a classmate, but when six children have to ask six others, and perhaps walk around the room to obtain them, control weakens. Anticipating this situation, the teacher has paper and sharpened pencil on hand.

Disadvantaged children will continuously test the teacher until they are convinced of his worth as a person. The teacher should be aware of what is happening, and be swift to use such incidents to his advantage. He can be honest with the child and inform him that he senses what he is trying to do. He can inform the class, too, what the child is trying to do, and together with the class joke about and show the wit of it.

When the teacher is exposed to ridicule or looks foolish, he should admit it and laugh with the class; in fact, confirm that he looked foolish. False dignity, vanity, and excessive pride cause more disciplinary problems. Similarly, when the teacher makes a mistake, he admits it, but avoids lengthy explanations, since they have a defensive ring. When the teacher has to account for the reasons why he did something, the explanation is clear and brief, too. An effective procedure is to make clear the position of the teacher, and/or to ask what the child or children would do if they were the teacher.

3-4. Knowing one's own personality and establishing good rules and routine are related and therefore discussed together. Teachers must be willing to assess their own weaknesses and strengths and to adapt realistic teaching styles appropriate to their own personalities. Disadvantaged children are quite astute and quick in manipulating their environment and judging the worth of a person. They know what will upset teachers, often better than their teachers know; they sense what they can and cannot do with a particular teacher; they know just when to stop before it becomes unsafe or before the teacher gets angry; they "play the game," meaning they learn the educational clichés about themselves and often answer or behave in the manner they are expected to say or do.

A teacher who unrealistically evaluates his strengths and limitations is at a great handicap with these children, and eventually makes a number of mistakes and particularly idle threats, which in turn weaken his authority and control in the classroom. Once this happens, these children will progress to criticism of his personality, commenting on his clothes, looks, etc.

No matter if the style is strong and loud or quiet and patient, effective teachers generally have the same "ground rules." While rules and routine should be clearly defined, fixed with boundaries and limitations, and established with a minimum of explanation, the procedures for implementing them varies in light of the individual's personality. The fact that "it works" for one teacher is meaningless unless one knows his own personality. Although the best advice sometimes does the most harm, it can be used if adapted to one's personality and teaching style. What the teacher should do, then, is learn the basic rules and routine for a foundation or reference point and subjoin them to his own style of teaching in accordance with his own personality.

5. Disadvantaged children easily become excited in groups and lose control; therefore, the teacher needs to be calm and emotionally controlled. He applies restraint and does not react to the behavior of the children with his own emotion or mood. Also, by remaining calm, the ideal attributes of an effective teacher come into view; namely, decisiveness, firmness, fairness, flexibility, etc. On the other hand, a hostile or emotional teacher works the child or class up to the point where they cannot save face or where they have no control and cannot

help themselves; audience situations occur and hostility is created in the children toward the teacher.

In order to help himself remain composed, the teacher should expect and be able to cope with rejection and hostility without showing anger or returning it. He realizes that sometimes the child needs to hate him, that the child expresses anger easily, that he resents authority figures, and that his language is vocal and expressive. This means that misconduct is not construed as being directed toward the teacher or that it is a sign of one's inadequacy. Teachers often feel guilty and feel their ego is threatened because they are not succeeding or because the class is noisy; they become anxious, involved, and as the students say, "they lose their cool." We may induce this guilt when we raise the point that problems would never arise if the teacher was effective.

If the situation becomes so bad as to make one feel helpless or frightened, and the teacher has done his best (by conversations with the parents and guidance counselor, referrals to the dean or department head), then he should adopt a detached attitude with the class. Indeed, it is easy for people from the outside, the so-called "experts," to say teachers do not care or try (in fact, this is the new vogue), but they are not teaching these students. The teacher should try to remain as calm and unemotional as possible, not feel threatened or at fault; otherwise, he will be less effective with his other classes since his feelings will carry over in the other classes.

6. Classroom discipline is enhanced by an "esprit de corps," a group loyalty and group morale, with the intention that each student has a significant part to play for the satisfaction and good of the group. Not only is self-confidence augmented when each youngster feels he is contributing to the group endeavor, but the youngster is reluctant to misbehave and spoil it for the group. In this connection, rules and routine are structured around the viewpoint that the teacher and the class are working together, and that any discord is a breach of this mutual endeavor, as well as a waste of time.

Peer group approval or condemnation becomes an effective tool for dealing with surface behavior. Says the teacher, "John, you're ruining it for the class." Positive alternatives are suggested. "Your idea has merit, but let's see if we can think of another way to do it." If the child needs to be disciplined, the teacher acts in relation to the group's values. A punitive climate is avoided, since it is damaging to group spirit. In the same vein, it is wrong to mistake good discipline for fear. Students stop caring, do not fight the teacher's efforts any more, but they despise him and have no interest in the subject.

Group sessions, whenever deemed necessary, are helpful for reminding students of their role and their need for cooperation. It is also effective for helping youngsters understand themselves, and to cope with their personal and environmental problems. Just as many disadvantaged youth need assistance in their academic work, many need help in gaining insights into their behavior, so that they can look at it more realistically. They need to distinguish right from wrong in class and outside of class, and to learn to cooperate.

All work stops during a group session. Each child is encouraged to contribute to the discussion, and to respect the values and opinions of others. The teacher directs the discussion. The students arrive at their own solutions. They ask questions and comment about each other's work and behavior. They know who the "cut-ups" are, and want, but rarely have a chance, to express their viewpoint. The child who does little work is reminded by his own classmates that he is failing himself. The child may contend that he does not understand the work, with the result that someone volunteers to explain it after school. The child who misbehaves is reminded about group codes. Hopefully, the youngsters accept their responsibility in class for both themselves and others; they accept the learning situation, the role of the teacher, and modify their behavior according to the suggestions of the group.

The ideas set forth in this paper have been acquired mainly through experience with teaching the disadvantaged. In no way should they be considered as the end-all for developing classroom order and control, but rather as suggestions which perhaps may be used as guidelines for slum-school teachers.

REFERENCES:

Crow, Lester D.; Murray, Walter I.; Smythe, Hugh H., *Educating the Culturally Disadvantaged Child,* New York: David McKay Company, Inc., 1966.

Deutsch, Martin, *Minority Group and Class Status as Related to Social and Personality Factors in Scholastic Achievement,* Ithaca, New York: Society for Applied Anthropology, Monograph No. 2, 1960.

Ornstein, Allan C., "A Strategy for Preparing and Assisting Teachers of Disadvantaged Youth," *Teachers College Journal,* October 1967, pp. 38-42.

Ornstein, Allan C., "Teaching the Disadvantaged," *Educational Forum,* January 1967, pp. 215-223.

Ornstein, Allan C., "Techniques and Fundamentals for Teaching the Disadvantaged," *Journal of Negro Education,* Spring 1967, pp. 136-145.

Riessman, Frank, *The Culturally Deprived Child,* New York: Harper & Row, Publishers, 1962.

Sheviakov, George V.; Redl, Fritz, *Discipline for Today's Children and Youth,* Washington, D.C.: National Education Association, 1956.

Strom, Robert D., (ed.) *The Inner-City Classroom: Teacher Behaviors,* Columbus, Ohio: Charles E. Merrill Books, Inc., 1966.

Strom, Robert D., *Teaching in the Slum School,* Columbus, Ohio: Charles E. Merrill Books, Inc., 1965.

Questions:

1. What steps would you take to regain control if your classroom became unmanageable?
2. How can a teacher show the class that he is truly interested in them as individuals?
3. Evaluate any three of the six general guidelines for developing classroom order and control in terms of being practical.

THE DISADVANTAGED—
THE NATURE OF URBAN EDUCATION

By EUGENE KRUSZYNSKI

Urban education, a recent entry in the educational glossary, already has outlived its usefulness. This is not to deny its legitimate value as a descriptive concept serving to focus attention on the contemporary problems of big-city schooling, but to caution against its possible development into a definition as a kind of education, which it is not.

In this connection, I am reminded of the statement once made to me by the late Prof. Harvey Eby of UCLA, who had taught courses in rural education for two decades at the University of California: "Gene," he stated earnestly, "there is no such thing as Rural Education." Was I to understand from this apparent contradiction that professional maturity disturbingly had revealed an academic lifetime misspent in teaching a hoax? Certainly not. He simply was indicating that the problems which faced his future teachers of farm youth in the 1920's and 1930's were, in the final analysis, educational (teaching) problems; their context was rural. These courses merely prepared the teacher to understand the cultural and social setting as a sort of language in which his students could be expected to express their problems, problems which the teacher then had to translate into educational terms. For these teachers, the educational task was not the training of successful husbandmen in some special content, but the teaching of standard school subjects to future citizens of a complex society, some of whom, to be sure, might choose agricultural pursuits. In other words, rural education differed from education anywhere only in its setting—rural America.

A people's most sophisticated formal education takes place in its population centers as a result of cultural determinants and demands. There, the temple, marketplace, school, and university initiate future participants into the life of the tribe and nation. So long as these rudimentary educational institutions were primarily urban and drew their students from the immediate area, few unusual problems were encountered. In the U.S., the rapid growth of industrialization, technology, and urbanization, coupled with the extension of political and social democracy, soon forced expansion of educational opportunities into the countryside. Primitive rural schools, traditionally staffed with their own graduates, proved unequal to the new legislative, curricular, and societal demands, and professional reform accelerated. However, the rather rapid qualitative improvement sought via increased appropriations and an upgraded

Reprinted with permission from *School and Society* (March 1970).

teacher corps fell short of expectations, so attention was directed to the relation of the classroom problems of this "new" teacher and his professional preparation.

In brief, there emerged strong indications that teacher training was geared largely to the production of teachers who were "effective" in teaching that proportion of the urban population which remained in school—students who resembled their teachers in many crucial attitudes and habits, all based upon urban drives and expectations. Teachers trained to adjust to the problems inherent in taking the typical city dweller through the standard curriculum could not cope easily with the "backwardness" of farm youth seeking the same diploma. It was the recognition that rural youth differed from their city cousins in educationally significant factors related to environment that prompted the development of rural education courses for teachers entering that field of endeavor.

The differences between teaching urban and rural youth, which previously had focussed professional concern on rural education, have their parallel in our time, except that the disparate groups now exist side-by-side. Both groups today are urban, seeking an education within a single school district, and not infrequently attending the same school. Who are these groups of neighbors, only one of which is apparently in need of urban education?

The positively defined city-dwelling group, and the one which establishes the norm, needs but brief elaboration: teachers not only identify it readily, most identify with it as successful alumni. Its latest arrivals to academia are representatives of the group for whom schools always have existed. Western history marks the steady extension of educational opportunities to groups which see themselves as hard-working, responsible, conforming, ambitious, and virtuous bearers of what has become known as "the contemporary wisdom"—the middle class. Its youth adjust readily to schooling, since it is but an extension of home and all its values; they understand it, and it understands them. Their variations in behavior are familiar, seldom exceed well-established limits, and are within the teachers' expectations. It is for them that the curriculum was selected and for the learning of which their teachers have developed traditional methodologies. The situation is stable, predictable, and, on the whole, satisfying. What they experience is called education—not urban education—as they move confidently toward graduation.

Accompanying these pupils in the urban school setting is another group, composed of those originally thought to be culturally deprived, but now more accurately described as being culturally different, or educationally disadvantaged. They are the late arrivals: Negroes, poor whites, Mexican-Americans, and other minority groups seeking membership in the defining group—the middle class. They arrived late not only to the city and to participation in its life and culture, but, more significantly, they are the latest group to seek education beyond the rudiments. Near-universal compulsory education, among other factors, has determined their continuing presence through secondary education, where their differences increasingly become magnified. They are identified quickly by teachers as being "difficult to teach," and from then on find themselves defined negatively.

It was the evident inability of the disadvantaged to amalgamate easily with their middle-class schoolmates without necessitating significant instructional modifications that led to the apparent need for urban education. Their unfamiliar attitudes, values, habits, and responses were upsetting to established teaching methods, though not enough to encourage much variation. Evidence that teaching still was taking place was available in that those who always had learned still were learning; only the late arrivals were not—they merely failed. But, as the teachers took credit for the one, they did not take the blame for the latter, citing superficial sociological analysis as indicating that the fault lay with the pupils. The situation intensified as various minority groups supplanted the suburb-bound middle class in its old city neighborhoods, and the proportion of ill-prepared youth increased alarmingly. The very magnitude of the problem now supported the rationale which discouraged instructional innovation, as the pedagogical consensus seemed to indicate a different kind of education for the disadvantaged—Urban Education.

Urban education is based on the theory that the teacher must be familiar with the culture of the taught, especially to the degree it differs significantly from his own. Armed with this knowledge—family background and traditions, self-concept, value system, and expectations—he better is able to make the vital psychological contact required to lead the pupil intellectually through the subject matter. The function of the teacher everywhere is that of intermediary between the pupil's experience and course objectives, as he alone commands a view of both. For middle-class pupils, the task is familiar, since course objectives, textbooks, and appropriate activities are based on long-established assumptions about their experiences, both in and out of school. Now this is what effective teachers always have done, except that inertia and institutional practices in middle-class education have transferred much of this burden to the members of the relatively homogeneous student body. The successful pupil soon learns to learn the teacher, since there is less teaching of individuals than there is of classes. Teachers, therefore, have reasons for developing rigidity in their procedures, since comparatively few pupils fail to measure up and give cause for any serious professional self-evaluation. Such security, however, does not exist in teaching the disadvantaged, where the standard assumptions are distinctly less valid for pupils whose scholastic disabilities are the result of an environment which can not find expression in the curriculum easily. Unfortunately, hurriedly mobilized teachers of the disadvantaged perform as though their sole purpose in learning the pupils' culture is to be able to recognize it when it rears its ugly head and then teach "around" it.

The true urban educator must be willing not only to learn this other culture, but to relearn his specialty in its terms in order to design classroom activities which will result in understanding, *i.e.,* learning. After all, it is the quality of what pupils do that results in learning. The teacher either will seek to teach his subject matter in terms of the pupil's culture—a difficult task for the teacher; or he may require that the pupil deny his own past and accept the teacher's along with the content—a difficult task for the pupil. The former alone constitutes teaching and is in keeping with the ideals of urban education, while the latter becomes a pseudo-remedial process which negates both as it deteriorates to busy-work and the keeping of order. Such teaching will produce memorization at best and, at worst, confusion, hostility, and failure. Superficial success here would be an indication of mechanical rather than thoughtful learning, equivalent to the remedial work considered valid for middle-class pupils. With the truly disadvantaged, such memoriter-based progress will be devoid of the experiential involvement so necessary to understanding, and of no value as a basis for further intellectual growth. Pupils so taught never will "catch up," though they may lead that class; their very accomplishments would tend to mask the deeper problem as they continue to require remedial instruction year-after-year. Effective teaching of the disadvantaged can be measured best by a decreasing demand or need for its services.

Now, has anything been stated here which applies to teaching disadvantaged youth, but not to teaching the advantaged middle class? Is it not true that every principle of education found to be effective in the instruction of the former is as valid for the latter? If so, then urban education as a kind of education indeed does not exist; it is merely a matter of the application of that degree of pedagogical expertise necessary to produce desired changes in disadvantaged, *i.e.,* non-middle-class youth. Furthermore, it is a matter of instructional involvement and intensity equally applicable in classrooms on both sides of the tracks.

In other words, urban education is but education conducted under certain conditions—in the slum, the ghetto, the inner city—much as rural education was education for farm folk. And, as such, it operates under the same principles, seeks solutions to the same kinds of problems, and pursues the same goal: the reduction of ignorance.

Questions:

1. "Urban Education differs from education anywhere in the United States only in its setting—urban America." Take a stand on the previous statement, and defend your position.

2. What are some of the things that a teacher can do in order to teach his subject matter in terms of the pupils' culture?

3. A large portion of the federal programs for disadvantaged children is in the area of remediation. Explain why the author would probably have serious doubts about the effectiveness of this type of education.

A UNIQUE APPROACH TO
INNER-CITY TEACHER EDUCATION

By MANOUCHEHR PEDRAM

Almost every inner-city school today is faced with the problems of teacher turnover—resignation or desire to transfer to a more attractive school. While many experienced teachers do leave the inner-city, there has been deepening concern about those who remain, hampered by their difficulty in understanding the cultural, environmental background as well as behavioral patterns of inner-city children. The upgrading and revitalizing of inner-city teacher education programs is badly needed, if we are to minimize the teacher turnover problem, improve the climate of inner-city teaching, and "keep dedicated teachers who have know-how, insight, and commitment to extend educational opportunities to disadvantaged children." [1]

To meet this need and prepare teachers who can function effectively in such a situation, the Cooperative Urban Teacher Education (CUTE) project has begun a unique and experimental teacher education program. The project is based on the assumption that teachers competent so far as instructional skills are concerned, and who are enthusiastic and possess a useable knowledge of the community in which they plan to teach, will provide the qualities crucial to success in the inner-city schools. The program hopes to improve the *quality* of teachers who plan to become employed and remain teaching in these schools.

As a project of the Mid-Continent Regional Educational Laboratory (McREL), the project is in its third year of operation in Kansas City, Missouri, and is being field-tested in Wichita, Kansas and Oklahoma City, Oklahoma. A most unique aspect of CUTE is the cooperation and participation of a number of liberal arts colleges and two state universities (18 in the Kansas City program, 12 in Wichita, and 7 in Oklahoma City), as well as public school systems of the three cities, with each contributing a share to its success.

The program implements the college preparation of participating students with a one semester (16 weeks) full-time field experience. Students receive credit from their home colleges or universities in the area of urban sociology, psychology, student teaching, and related educational subjects. What motivates these students to participate in this field experience program is unknown for the most part, and a great deal of research is yet to be done. It is clear, however, that they recognize the great need for effective teachers of disadvantaged students. They have the desire and willingness to examine their values, and they want to play a role in one of the major problems of their generation. This is evidenced in the course of the program as the students involve themselves in constant

---

Reprinted with permission from *The Clearing House* (January 1971).

struggles, adjustments, self-evaluation, and perception changes. The following quotation is a typical (though perhaps biased) reaction of a CUTE graduate.

At times it seemed one's whole past life had been lived with blinders on. The things I had seen daily for the majority of my life, now became focal points of observation. It was as if I had been granted a new pair of eyes much more in tune with living as it existed in real life and not in textbooks and college classrooms. All at once, it seemed imperative to recognize and acknowledge the condition and people of the community in which one is teaching.

The CUTE project has developed a rugged academic and field experience program aimed at shock-proofing the prospective teachers before they enter inner-city schools through exposure to sociological, psychological, and educational factors relevant to the problem. The curriculum was designed with three basic assumptions in mind in order to help the prospective teachers become skilled in methods and strategies unique and essential to the inner-city school system.

. . . a prospective teacher would be better prepared if he (a) understood both his own and his pupils' attitudes, insecurities, anxieties, and prejudices; (b) understood both his own and his pupils' environment and culture, (c) was knowledgeable of and competent in reflective teaching methods for inner-city learners. [2]

Based on these assumptions, prospective teachers are encouraged to explore and experience first-hand the social and cultural variations of the inner-city by residing, mingling, and participating in the community in which they plan to teach. To insure that exposure to the community is real and not superficial, CUTE students participate in such activities as tutoring inner-city children, working in neighborhood centers, store front churches, local hangouts, and experience a weekend live-in where the white students are placed in low-socio-economic black homes and vice-versa. All community activities are selected on the basis of their relevance and importance in promoting understanding and insight into better relations of inner-cultural significance.

A psychiatrist is available for analyzing student teachers' problems and frustrations, scrutinizing individual feelings developed in the cultural-shock process, and interpreting situations that have evolved from classroom participation.

The teacher education component (both elementary and secondary) includes philosophical, psychological and pedagogical viewpoints as well as consideration of the relative effectiveness of various classroom methods in coping with inner-city problems. Emphasis is placed on methodology of teaching and psychology of learning. Several micro-teaching sessions provide grounds for teaching experience on a smaller scale; here students apply methodological approach discussed in seminars, and are given the opportunity to see and analyze their strengths and weaknesses.

Eight weeks of student teaching in inner-city schools under the supervision of a well-qualified teacher gives the prospective teachers a realistic preparatory experience. Throughout the program, student teachers have the opportunity periodically to discuss their problems, frustrations, and fears with each of the faculty members. They also get advice and suggestions on handling a variety of problems and on improving their teaching styles to meet the need of the inner-city youngsters.

Since a majority of the students come from the middle or upper-middle class, there is no doubt that a long soul-searching process is needed to develop the social understanding required of teachers in the inner-city. To evaluate a participant's attitude and knowledge of the inner-city, a number of professionals working in the inner-city agencies and residents of the area interview each student at the end of the eight-week participation in the program. In addition, a quantity of information has been collected in the last two and one-half years, in order to evaluate the CUTE program and its influence upon prospective teachers. The research in general and particularly the use of the Dogmatism Scale (Rokeach, 1960), Teaching Situation Reaction Test (TSRT, Duncan and Hough, 1966), The Minnesota Teacher Attitude Inventory (MTAI, Cook, Leeds, Callis, 1951) and Cultural Attitude Inventory (CAI, Skeel, 1966) has indicated a significant change in the attitudes of students participating in the CUTE program contrasted with the comparison group. McREL Interaction Analysis (MIA, modified version of Amidon and Flanders, 1967), in regard to classroom teaching behavior, showed that CUTE students made significant changes and became more indirect in classroom control in their 16-weeks training than did their comparison group.

The effectiveness of the program is reflected in the increasing number of CUTE graduates accepting a teaching position in the inner-city schools of several metropolitan areas. As one of the CUTE graduates wrote: "As an individual my values were challenged, which caused me to sit and ask myself, why? As an individual, I have allowed myself to grow and broaden my knowledge, and now I am ready."

REFERENCES:

[1] Harry A. Passow, "Diminishing Teacher Prejudice," in Robert D. Strom (ed.), *The Inner-City Classroom: Teacher Behavior.* Columbus, Ohio: Charles E. Merrill, 1966, p. 107.

[2] Mid-Continent Regional Educational Laboratory, *Innovation in the Inner-City.* Kansas City, Missouri: McREL, 1969, p. 12.

Questions:

1. For what reasons would you favor this approach to training potential inner-city teachers?
2. Evaluate the idea of residing, mingling, and participating in the inner city in terms of community acceptance.
3. Which of the three basic assumptions (A, B, or C) would you consider to be of greatest value?

WHAT'S GONE WRONG IN OUR BIG-CITY SCHOOLS?

Angry parents . . . picketing teachers . . . broken school windows . . . dropouts . . . embattled school boards . . . violence in the classroom. Day by day, newspapers tell the grim story of turmoil in our city schools.

A dozen years ago all the talk about education seemed to focus on the suburbs. Parents complained that local schools weren't doing enough to prepare their kids for getting into college. Magazines and newspapers ran story after story about "new math," foreign languages in elementary school, new teaching techniques, modern science courses. Hardly anyone, it appeared, was much concerned about education in the cities, particularly the "inner cities" where the poor were concentrated. Yet it was there—because they got so little national attention—that some of the country's most explosive educational problems were brewing. Now almost every major city faces the consequences: a massive school crisis.

THE TRANSFORMATION OF THE CITIES

Look at the dramatic change in city populations and you begin to understand the core of the problem. For years hundreds of thousands of poor people, especially Negroes, poured from rural areas, mostly in the South, into the large cities. At the same time, white families (and recently black middle-class families) have been leaving the central cities. Result: Though a majority of Americans now live in metropolitan areas, the inner cities are gradually becoming inhabited mostly by the black poor. As a consequence black enrollment in the public schools is rapidly rising, too. Some examples:

Baltimore	64%	St. Louis	63%
Philadelphia	58%	Indianapolis	33%
New York (+ about		Boston	26%
22% Puerto Rican)	30%	Cincinnati	42%
Detroit	58%	Newark	71%
Chicago	52%	Pittsburgh	38%
Cleveland	56%	Buffalo	35%
Dist. of Columbia	92%	Rochester	27%

Reprinted by permission from *Changing Times,* the Kiplinger Magazine, (July 1969 issue). Copyright 1969 by The Kiplinger Washington Editors, Inc. 1729 H. Street, N.W., Washington, D.C. 20006.

What these children inherit aś they take over city schools are conditions that seem designed to throttle education:

• *Almost total segregation.* A survey of 75 cities revealed that three out of four black elementary pupils attend schools that are 90% or more Negro. This means that they spend most of their time with disadvantaged children who, like themselves, are poorly prepared for school.

• *Severe overcrowding.* Example: In the District of Columbia a couple of years ago the one predominantly white school operated at lower than top capacity while Negro high schools were running at well over full capacity.

• *Old buildings and obsolete equipment.* "Inner-city schools," said the National Advisory Commission on Civil Disorders (Kerner Commission) last year, "are not only overcorwded; they also tend to be the oldest and most poorly equipped." According to another study of a typical big-city school system, 30% of the children in the lower economic half of the city go to schools that are at least 50 years old. None in the upper income half attend schools that old.

• *Lack of money.* With the middle class in their exodus to the suburbs went the tax dollar. Taxable property valuation, the most common basis for school financing, failed to keep pace with city needs. Besides, new highways, bridges, federal and state buildings, and slum clearance programs—all non tax-paying— have been eating up city space that might have yielded revenues for the schools. "Our society," said the Commission on Civil Disorders, "spends less money educating ghetto children than children of suburban families." The need, as many educators see it, is exactly the reverse.

• *Inexperienced teachers.* Qualified teachers shy away from the rough conditions of the inner city. A survey in Chicago a few years ago revealed that in the ten schools at the lowest economic level only slightly over 60% of the teachers were fully certified. In the ten schools at the highest economic level, 90% were. The Kerner report noted that many teachers, with no special training for work with disadvantaged students, often begin with negative attitudes toward the students, and become more and more dissatisfied with their jobs. Teachers who don't expect much from their students, as the report says, don't get much out of them.

• *Scanty materials, irrelevant courses.* City kids aren't given the wide variety of classroom materials—magazines, paperback books, filmstrips, recordings—that many suburban youngsters are accustomed to. The materials and courses they do get are aimed at middle-class students and don't have much connection with their own experiences. To the poor Negro child, school, like the white world outside his ghetto, seems alien.

The effects of these conditions are obvious: "For the children of the racial ghetto," says the commission, "the schools have failed to provide the educational experience which could help overcome the effects of discrimination and deprivation." And the report adds, "The bleak record of public education for ghetto children is getting worse."

In the essential skills—verbal and reading ability—inner-city children fall steadily behind. The average Negro first-grader in a northeastern city gets somewhat lower test scores on standard achievement tests than a white pupil. By the sixth grade he is 1.6 grades behind; by the twelfth, he's 3.3 grades behind the white student. But by then thousands have quit.

Smoldering resentment is the end product. "The typical riot participant," said the Commission on Civil Disorders, "was a high school dropout." Ghetto adults as well as ghetto youth are aflame with anger against the schools. And it's this feeling that is now at the core of the school crisis in the cities.

WHAT'S TO BE DONE?

As the facts about city schools emerged in report after report, certain remedies seemed obvious, and many cities, supported by the federal government, moved to put them into effect. Yet the crisis grew worse and is now more acute than ever. What happened? What is the answer?

Desegregation. One of the first things that had to be done, it seemed clear, was to desegregate the schools. Back in 1954 the Supreme Court had ruled that segregated education was unequal education. Many studies subsequently showed that minority children do lag when they are educated in segregated schools. Most educators believe the reason is not race but poverty—poor children perform better in schools with more affluent children than they do in schools where most kids are poor. That's because achievement is affected more by the background and aspirations of other students than by the quality of the school's facilities or even of its teachers. And most Negroes are poor. Only 25% are middle class, that is, have a white-collar occupation, a high school education or a middle-class income, compared with 60% of whites.

The problem, then, was how to achieve a mix. Many experiments have been tried, with varied success. New Haven "paired" some elementary schools and redistricted a couple of junior high schools to change racial balance. Pasadena redistricted its high schools and adopted an open enrollment plan. Evanston began to reduce racial imbalance substantially in its elementary schools. In Berkeley, where the school population is about 41% black, elementary schools have been mixed to reflect this percentage. This required moving 2,000 white and 2,000 black children. According to one report, predictions that teachers would resign and white families move away did not come true. Right now, intensive teacher training and community relations programs are under way to make the plan work.

One of the most controversial methods being used to mix children of different races is "busing." Nearly a thousand students from Boston's black ghetto are bused to schools in 20 surrounding areas. Rochester transports some 10% of its black children to outer communities. New Haven, Waterbury and Hartford move Negro and Puerto Rican students to a couple of dozen suburbs.

The Nixon administration has said that it will enforce the provisions of the Civil Rights Act of 1964 that help schools desegregate and cut off funds from those that should but don't. Some states—New York, California, Massachusetts, Washington—have gone further than the federal government in outlawing racial imbalance in schools.

Still, desegregation has been extremely slow. One reason is bitter white resistance. Lawsuits by individuals against busing are under way in several communities. The heavy concentration of black families in large cities also makes racial balance difficult to achieve. As a result, schools are now more segregated than ever.

The push toward racial balance will continue, but it certainly offers no immediate solution. Black families are resentful about its failure, many say they don't want to depend on the tolerance of whites to make it work and most now demand that more be done to improve inner-city schools.

Compensatory education. Most cities, using federal aid, are trying to give special attention to poor children to help them catch up with the rest of the population. At least 20,000 programs around the country offer remedial help in reading, arithmetic, speaking, vocabulary development and so on. In Milwaukee, poor children who showed a lack of speaking ability received intensive training by speech therapists. In Detroit, remedial reading centers were established. Flint has a program involving parents directed at raising the level of underachieving Negro pupils. One of the best-known projects is the More Effective Schools Program in New York City. It provides about 20,000 disadvantaged children with small classes, specialists and a variety of extra services and materials.

There's much argument about the effectiveness of compensatory programs. The New York City effort appears to help youngsters who are continuously exposed to it. Many of the other programs around the country, according to the Office of Education, have shown positive results. But there's not much evidence that improvement has been substantial or lasting, and certainly it hasn't been great enough to wipe out the gap between poor and nonpoor students. Compensatory education, says one influential critic, is a "Band-aid approach" to the problem, not a cure.

Many other approaches are being tried—"adoption" of ghetto schools by colleges for experimental projects, student-to-student tutoring, home visits by specialists, concentration of multiple services—educational, health, job training—on small groups of young people. The greatest gains occur when everything that seems to block achievement is taken into account—hunger, a broken home, lack of motivation, poor health.

A crucial problem in the ghetto is the lack of specially trained teachers, particularly young men who can understand and identify with poor children. The Teacher Corps tries to deal with this but is too small. That's the trouble with most approaches so far. Well-intentioned as they may be, they barely scratch the surface of the problem.

THE LOCAL-CONTROL RUCKUS

Everyone who looks into ghetto problems agrees on at least one thing: If there is to be any real improvement in the schools, local citizens, especially parents, must become involved in the education of their kids. Now ghetto parents are getting involved and the result is violent controversy over local control of schools.

Bitter at white resistance to desegregation and the failure of the city to educate their children, Negro parents declare: Now we'll tell the schools what we want for our kids just as middle-class white people do in the suburbs and small towns all over America.

"Many of you now accuse us of . . .'separating ourselves' from the mainstream of the nation," says Dr. Norman Johnson, a Negro professor at the University of Pittsburgh. "The hard bitter truth . . . is that we have never . . . , regardless of personal success, been in the mainstream of American life ... We feel our responsibility now is to our community alone. ... We have determined that we will take over the direction and control of our children's schools.

"We may make some mistakes. However, these mistakes can hardly be more serious than the ones being made at present. They certainly will not be as long-standing. Because we, holding the welfare of the children as our only criterion, will effect change as soon as we ... deem it to be necessary ... When people have an opportunity to be really involved ... , when they know that they can be part of making decisions that have meaning, we will not have to worry about parental apathy or student disinterest. When members of the school board know that they are *accountable* to all the people whose children they serve, and *to the students themselves,* they will [respond] ... to the needs and desires of these groups."

Opponents argue that decentralization plays into the hands of local pressure groups. Teachers say it undercuts tenure and the criteria for teacher selection. We've spent years, they argue, taking education out of city politics in order to improve professional standards; decentralization throws it right back into politics.

Local boards, goes another objection, cannot provide a wide enough range of programs or sufficient financial support. What's needed is the opposite of decentralization–a broader base of support, more metropolitan, more state, more federal commitment. All that local control will do is turn anger away from the city board, says the president of the New York City teachers union. "It gives people the trappings of power and local control without really giving them the ability to do anything." And he predicts increased conflict.

Last year's upheaval in New York City revealed the depth of the bitterness behind the controversy. The clash between the teachers union and a local school board in Brooklyn produced strikes that paralyzed the city schools, affecting over a million children. Other clashes occurred this year and more may be ahead.

Despite the controversy, many cities are talking about local control; some are trying it. Washington, D.C.,'s Morgan community school has a locally elected board that decides how funds will be spent, what kind of staff and what curriculum changes are needed. In Los Angeles, 13 schools have "critical authority" over their own budgets. St. Louis involves local citizens in planning through "Parent Congresses." Chicago is trying out a four-school subdistrict. In Boston several schools are run by a local board supported by state funds.

Though evidence is scanty, the effects of decentralization for the moment look promising. A *Wall Street Journal* report on Brooklyn's Ocean Hill-Brownsville district, scene of last year's trouble, says that under local control student interest is high, discipline has improved, suspensions and vandalism have declined. A new individualized reading program has "turned on" children who once resisted reading. Chief reasons for progress: involvement of residents as "community liaison workers" and · classroom aides; imaginative teaching; determined young teachers (most of whom happen to be white) who believe in local control.

There's no longer any real argument about whether inner-city residents ought to have a voice in the operation of their schools. The only question is how much actual control they should have. "The day has passed," said President Nixon's task force on education, "when external agencies ... can tell the black man, the Puerto Rican . . . in the ghetto what is good for him. His ideas and his resources must form the basis of any new approaches."

Actually, much of the argument about control is semantic. Not many parents, according to a 13-city study for the Urban Coalition, really want to operate their schools. What they're after is "accountability," the right to see that the schools do their job. "What we are talking about is not parents . . . becoming teachers and principals," says one of the most militant local-control supporters. ". . . We are not telling [professionals] to get out . . . We are saying that we want to be in there to see that [they] do the job of educating our children."

IT ALL COMES DOWN TO MONEY

The arguments about local control will spread. The push toward desegregation will continue. New compensatory education experiments will be tried. However, most experts now agree that nothing will really make a dent in the problem until ghetto schools get a much bigger chunk of the education dollar. But the outlook for more money is bleak.

Cities are going broke. As pointed out earlier, middle-class families moving to the suburbs take their taxes with them. In Baltimore the tax dollar behind each pupil dropped 19% in five years; at the same time it rose by over 10% in Maryland's rural and suburban areas. Cleveland suffered a 10% erosion of the tax base while noncity areas of the state gained almost 5%.

Another pressure on cities: They have to spend more on nonschool services—health, welfare, safety. On the average they can allocate only about a third of local taxes to education. Suburbs can give two-thirds of their income. In many places the difference is much greater.

State aid is off balance. State legislatures have traditionally favored rural areas over the cities. In the past noncity schools needed the help more; now the situation is reversed. Today city kids· often get proportionately less aid from state funds than rural and suburban kids. In New York the discrepancy is over $100 per child. In some cities—Chicago, Detroit, Los Angeles, San Antonio—court suits have been filed to try to change unfair state allocations.

Even if some cities and states do manage to raise additional dollars, they can hardly produce enough to close the gap between the suburbs and the cities. A study of the 37 largest cities showed that $449 is spent per student compared with $573 in their suburbs, and the difference is widening.

Will the federal government produce the needed funds? The National School Boards Association, which not long ago opposed federal aid, says it should. The new Commissioner of Education, Dr. James E. Allen, Jr., has said that he favors a program of "massive" federal aid to city schools. He plans to develop and present to Congress an "urban education act" that would focus on big-city problems. (See article by Dr. James E. Allen, Jr.)

Meantime, nothing big enough is in the works right now. According to the National School Boards Association, as many as 30 of the largest cities may not have enough money to open their schools on time next autumn. Those that do open face continual crisis and turbulence. Time is running short.

Question:

1. What arguments have opponents of decentralization used to support their position?

CRISIS IN CITY SCHOOLS

INTERVIEW WITH JAMES E. ALLEN, JR.,
U. S. Commissioner of Education

Reprinted from U.S. News & World Report (June 30, 1969).

Big changes are coming in U.S. schools, if ideas of the new Commissioner of Education are followed. Dr. James E. Allen, Jr., came to the conference room of "U.S. News & World Report" to tell in this exclusive interview what he recommends to meet "a very real crisis." He suggests new types of schools, new teaching methods, more-effective integration—and more money.

Q Dr. Allen, what kind of job are American schools doing today—good or bad?

A I think the American schools, by and large, are doing a very good job. When you compare school achievement statistically, you find:

A generation ago, the average length of time that a person went to school was only eight years, and now it is 12 years. The number of Americans who go on to college has more than tripled since 1946. Only about 1 in 5 persons of college age was in college in 1946; today it's 1 in 2. A generation ago, only about 50 per cent of our teachers had bachelor's degrees; today, virtually all of them do—about 96 per cent, I believe.

Also, looking at the intellectual and social interests and activities of our young people, the questions they are raising and so on—these, in my judgment, are indications that the schools are doing a good job.

Now, obviously, the expectations of society for education are far greater today than they were a generation ago. We are now trying to educate everybody, to reject no one. And we're finding that for many young people, the traditional educational system does not do a good job.

To this degree, there would appear to be some substantial failures. But I look upon this not so much as a failure of the educational system as a failure of our society to provide adequate educational opportunities for large numbers who have been neglected or have suffered deprivations or discrimination of various kinds.

In terms of the dimensions of the task that we have to do, I would say that the American schools are doing a good job.

Q Better than in the past, do you think?

A It's difficult to compare it with past years, because we have a different society today. I recall a few years ago in New York State we gave that year's graduating class the Regents' examinations that had been given 50 years

---

ago—and the students of that year did much better on those same examinations than the students of 50 years back.

In other words, schools today are doing better at teaching the kind of knowledge that was expected 50 years ago.

But, again, if you make your comparison in terms of what the people expect of the schools today, we have a long way to go to do as good a job as needs to be done.

Q What, most of all, needs to be done to improve schools?

A I think that many things need to be done:

One is that we need to develop a kind of nationwide strategy for the improvement of education. We need more money for research to find out how to teach children better. In business, you set aside 10 per cent or more for research and development. I'm told that less than one half of 1 per cent of the 60 billion dollars we spend annually for education in this country goes for research and development. And education is big business.

We need to bring together in a better way than we do now the information we already have about better ways of education, and to disseminate that information more widely through our educational system. Furthering research in education and disseminating information are things in which I think the U.S. Office of Education could be very helpful.

Also, I think we need to enlist more outside help in education—business help, for example. I don't think we've begun to tap the potential of business enterprise for help in making our educational system more effective.

We need to do a better job of training and retraining teachers—particularly retraining. A large proportion of our teachers were prepared for a kind of school system that is quite different from that in which they now find themselves. This is especially true with respect to dealing with new approaches and concepts related to the needs of the disadvantaged.

We also need to make better use of the technology that is available today—technology that can enable us to learn much more about a student through computers and other measurement systems and to apply the school programs more effectively to meet the needs of each individual.

What we really need to do, to sum it all up, is to make our advanced methods more available to all our schools.

Q Is this going to require the setting of federal standards for education?

A No, I don't think it is at all. If you mean uniform standards laid down at the federal level, I would not like to see that.

I do believe, however, that the Federal Government has the obligation to insist upon high standards, and to encourage and help every State and locality to maintain them. The setting of standards and their enforcement, however, is a State and local responsibility, and it is up to the people to hold their school officials accountable for achieving high standards.

Q Will federal aid have to be increased substantially to solve our school problems?

A Well, more money is part of the problem—a large part. There is no question that in many parts of our country we are about reaching the limit of the property tax—and this is the major base of support for most of public education.

passed by Congress. And, unless those are changed, I see no reason to change the guidelines.

Q Is the Federal Government now turning more toward the problem of integrating Northern schools?

A There is evidence that some segregation in the North is the result of discrimination, and therefore a violation of the Civil Rights Act. In such cases the Federal Government has just as much obligation to act as it does in the South.

Q What about the so-called *de facto* segregation in the North—the kind that results from housing patterns and neighborhood schools, rather than from discrimination? Do you regard *de facto* segregation as unconstitutional?

A No. I just think it's bad education and bad socially—bad for the children, bad for our country. However, it seems to me that the primary responsibility for action in eliminating *de facto* segregation rests with the States and communities, rather than with the Federal Government, unless discrimination is clearly established.

Q In 1963, when you were State commissioner of education in New York, you called upon local schools to report "any problem of racial imbalance" and said: "For the purpose of this report, a racially imbalanced school is defined as one having 50 per cent or more Negro pupils." That directive also said: "There must be corrective action in each community where such imbalance exists." Did you mean to hold that any school over half Negro is illegally segregated?

A No. This has always been very much misunderstood. I put out a request to every school system in the State asking them to let me know what schools had more than 50 per cent black students. The reason I wanted that information was because we knew that once a school gets up around 40 or 50 per cent black, it is likely to move rapidly right on up to 90 per cent—so if you are going to do something about the problem, you should become concerned at about that 50 per cent point.

This doesn't mean seeking a 50-50 balance, because, in the first place, that is impossible in most communities. A percentage balance is not the goal. But we wanted information on which to begin a program for helping communities to avoid, or where necessary, to eliminate serious *de facto* segregation.

Q What did you do when you found such segregation?

A The commissioner of education in New York plays a quasi-judicial role. Anybody who feels himself aggrieved by the action of a local school authority may appeal to the commissioner. Under this judicial function, I had cases asking me to order a local school system to desegregate its schools. In each case I examined the facts and made a decision which had the force of law.

Two famous cases I ruled on were in Malvern and in Mount Vernon, N.Y.

Q What did you order in those cases?

A I ordered them to correct the segregated situation.

Q Did you order busing of pupils to get integration?

A I didn't order busing per se. But, in the case of Mount Vernon, school officials there claimed the only way they could desegregate in the manner ordered was to provide some busing.

You know, it isn't busing that people get concerned about. We bus 16 million children to school every day in this country. What concerns some people is cross-busing.

REAL VALUE OF BUSING—

Q By cross-busing, do you mean busing black children into predominantly white schools and white children into predominantly black schools? Do you favor cross-busing for integration?

A Busing is a means to an end, and the end is a better education for all children. The only real justification for busing is to get a child safely to a better education than the one he otherwise might have. I happen to believe that an integrated situation is part of a good education. So I would say that if busing were the only way to bring about a good, integrated situation, then I would bus.

Q What is the educational advantage of having a mixture of black and white children in a school?

A It seems to me to be very important that children learn how to live together, respect each other, and not feel that they are in a particular school simply because they happen to be black or white.

Q If you cross-bus, aren't you sending a black child to a certain school because he is black, and a white child to another school because he is white? Isn't this actually assignment of pupils on a racial basis?

A Only as an incident of a larger purpose. Basically, you are making the assignment to overcome educational deficiencies that result from racial discrimination.

If a child is in a "ghetto" school where the neighborhood is all black and run-down, and the child knows that his chances in life are limited because of that situation, his motivation in school is going to be greatly impaired. If he gets into a school where he feels on a par with all other children, then I think his motivation for learning is going to be much greater.

Q What about the so-called neighborhood school, where children attend the school nearby—in their own neighborhood? Is this kind of school on the way out?

A I'm for the neighborhood school, believe me. But if the neighborhood school can't produce good education, if it is considered as exclusive for one race or creed, then I think that particular neighborhood-school area ought to be enlarged or changed to correct that situation.

Q When you were commissioner of education in the State of New York, didn't you suggest enlarging city districts to include the predominantly white suburbs in order to get more integration?

A I think the people in the suburbs—many of whom left the cities and helped to create the problems in the cities—have an obligation to help the cities find answers to their problems.

Q How could suburbs be compelled to do this?

A I would hope it could be done through a change in attitude, through more understanding. But if some people are not willing to face up to this kind of educational problem, then somebody must seek to protect the educational well-being of the children. And it seems to me it has to be the State.

The constitution of the State of New York, for example, says that the State shall provide equal educational opportunities for every boy and girl. And

Also, many Governors and State legislators will tell you that many of the States are reaching the point where it's difficult to tax further without destroying their competitive positions.

I'm not at all sure that the best answer to more federal aid is a general aid formula. It may be a question of returning to States a larger part of the tax dollar now collected at the federal level—of sharing the taxes, or some other such arrangement. But I am certain that the present pattern of supporting schools in many of our States and localities has reached a point of great strain, and is going to have to be changed considerably. And I believe that this will mean a substantially larger proportion of school support coming from federally collected taxes.

We need a major national study of educational finance—new approaches are called for.

Q What about the immediate future? Are big increases in federal spending for education being planned by the Nixon Administration for this session of Congress?

A There are lots of studies being made and proposals being considered. We have been listening to school boards from many cities—Baltimore, Philadelphia and others—who tell us that they are up against a very serious financial situation. But no plan has yet been settled on by the Administration.

Q As Commissioner of Education, where would you propose increases in federal aid?

A I'm not ready to say. I have been on the job here only a few weeks, and I have not had an opportunity yet to put forth my own proposals in a considered way.

All I can say is this: I think the urban school situation is in a very real crisis, and one of the things we're looking at is how to get more money into those school systems.

"THE BASIC CHALLENGE" —

Q Would you say that urban education is the most urgent problem confronting you in your new job?

A Well, the basic challenge is to raise the quality of education for all children. But there is particular urgency for those who are seriously behind in achievement, primarily the disadvantaged. We have these in rural areas and among Mexican Americans, Indians and Eskimos, but it happens that the largest proportion of those most difficult to educate are in the large cities.

Q One hears a lot of criticism about big-city schools. Are they really worse than rural schools?

A Some of the best schools we have are in the cities. New York City, for example, has some outstanding schools—though New York schools vary.

But the problem is not solely the quality of the school. It's the students they have to educate. If students come to school from home well prepared, it's much easier for the school to teach them. But if they come from families—or from lack of families—where they do not have the advantages of home preparation for schools, then the problem of teaching them is more difficult.

Many of our children who are behind in reading come from homes where education was not regarded as important, or at least where the parents were not

A We need changes to make our schooling more relevant—to use a word that is too much used these days.

A great part of our educational system—and this is true especially at the college level, as the students are reminding us—seems to give both young people and society a feeling that the schools are really preparing students for the world of the past more than for the world of the future.

So I think we need changes in programs as well as in techniques in many school systems. But you have to leave this to the local community, by and large, and then make the resources available to them so that they can make changes. I believe very strongly that you get better schools by a diversified approach. It is important for all communities to experiment, to evaluate their schools in terms of the quality and the relevance of their efforts.

Q In many cities we find a growing demand for what is called decentralization of schools—breaking up the citywide system into smaller districts under "local" or neighborhood school boards. Is this a part of the change that you are suggesting?

A In some cases, it may well be. I have been active, as you know, in seeking decentralization in New York City. I believe that this is a proper approach to problems there. I am not ready to say that this should be the pattern for every other city—not developed in the same way, at any rate.

But I am convinced that the best schools are those where parents and other local people can have and take a real interest in what is being taught, and how.

In a school system as large as New York City's, with more than a million pupils, this lack of a say by parents is one of the things that have brought about so much unrest. Parents see their children coming home unable to read, but they find it very difficult to make any change in the system in order to correct such a deficiency, because they have to go through a large, bureaucratic organization where everything is handled at the center.

WHAT CITY PARENTS CAN DO—

Q Aren't those parents who send their children to school unprepared for education the same parents who would be given control over the neighborhood schools by a system of decentralization?

A I am not speaking of control in the sense of turning the whole system over to them. They shouldn't have power to assume professional duties. And I think protection has to be provided to insure that the teachers who are employed are the best available for the children to be taught.

But city parents should have authority to make some decisions—as people do in suburban communities—about what things the school should teach and how they should be operated and managed.

When I say that some parents don't prepare their children for school, I don't mean that it's a case of the parents not wanting to do so. In many cases the parents simply cannot, because of circumstances. I believe that inner-city parents who have not had the kind of advantages that suburban parents have had would nonetheless accept responsibility for helping to direct their schools if given the chance. They want good schools. They want their children to learn.

Q Is there a problem in finding the right kinds of teachers for schools in "ghetto" areas?

A There is that problem. Some teachers in "ghetto" schools are really not prepared to teach the kind of student who attends those schools. Most teachers have middle-class backgrounds. They often don't understand the culture of the community. Some do not really believe that poor children or black children can learn. Of course, the child quickly becomes aware of this, as do the parents, and the child loses his motivation. We all know that when the teacher has faith in the child's ability to learn, and lets the child know this, the child is far more likely to learn.

STARTING RIGHT, AND EARLY—

Q How effective are programs of compensatory education for disadvantaged children?

A In general, I think they are necessary and helpful. Despite some well-founded criticism, Head Start, for example—the preschool training of small children—is an excellent program. Other good compensatory programs include the "More Effective Schools" in several of our cities. Ineffectiveness in such programs is usually due to poor planning and lack of adequately prepared teachers.

I think these compensatory programs should be enlarged. But, more importantly, I think we need to improve the quality of education from the very beginning—from early childhood—and then continue that improvement all the way through the educational system so that it will become unnecessary to have these large programs of remedial action.

Q When you say from early childhood, do you mean as early as age 2 or 3?

A That's right. This is being done in some communities now. And we know that young people at a very early age can learn a lot more than we once thought they could.

Q As Commissioner of Education, what role do you play in policing the desegregation of schools in the South?

A The Office of Education no longer plays any direct role in the compliance part—enforcing Title VI of the Civil Rights Act, which authorizes withholding federal money from school districts that discriminate. That has been placed under the Office for Civil Rights in the Department of Health, Education and Welfare. And I am delighted with this change, so that I can now work not as a policeman, but as an educator.

This does not mean that I do not very strongly support the court decisions and the laws that require that discrimination be eliminated everywhere. I feel that it is essential to move strongly against discrimination wherever it is practiced.

Q Do you favor any changes in the so-called guidelines that the Department of Health, Education and Welfare has laid down for desegregation of Southern schools?

A No, I don't see that any are needed. It is my understanding that the guidelines were established to comply with court orders and the Civil Rights Act if it is true, as the courts and educators have said, that equal educational opportunity cannot be provided in separate setups, then the State has an obligation to try to correct this situation.

Q Dr. Allen, how long can unrest on college campuses go on without damaging the quality of education?

A I don't think it can go on very long. It will be tragic if the kind of disruptions and violence that we've been experiencing this past year continues very long.

Q How do you think the situation can be remedied?

A I think if we would give as much attention in the universities and the Government to the causes of the unrest as we are giving to the manifestations of it, then we would begin to get somewhere.

I think the institutions—the students, the faculty and the administrators—must get together and begin to make the kinds of changes that ought to be made to recognize the legitimate demands of our young people—and do it fast.

Q Do you favor withholding federal aid, such as loans and scholarships, from students who break laws?

A Where students are found, through due process of law, to have committed a crime, then the university has an obligation to take appropriate disciplinary action—and under present law federal assistance to such students must be withheld. But I am strongly opposed to legislation at any level that takes money away from the institutions for this reason. I think that disciplinary action should be confined to the individual who commits the crime.

GIVING THE YOUNG A VOICE—

Q Recently you were quoted as saying that the Office of Education is preparing to give students a larger voice in shaping federal educational policies that affect colleges. How are you preparing to do this?

A The Office of Education administers some 80 programs of various kinds, and we have many advisory committees. I'm asking our staff to look over these advisory committees to see to what extent the young are represented or can be represented where these programs directly affect young people. Also, I have appointed on my staff a special assistant for youth affairs, a young fellow, to help me find ways in which we can listen better to the views of young people and act on their legitimate concerns.

Q Parochial schools are reported to be having increasing difficulty financing their operations. Is there anything the Federal Government can do to help them? Or should public schools be prepared to absorb the pupils from parochial schools that are forced to close?

A This is a very serious problem for the parochial schools, and it could be very serious for the public schools in terms of the added cost of educating these additional youngsters.

I think we need an extensive study of the financial problems of the nonpublic schools to determine the causes of their difficulties and to try to ascertain the effect of these difficulties on the future of both the parochial and the public schools.

Questions:

1.   List four or five key points that you feel should be covered in an effective
     teacher retraining program.

2.   What educational opportunities do you feel should be provided culturally
     deprived children in order to compensate for disadvantages?

3.   Discuss the advantages you feel would result from the busing of white
     children to predominately black schools.

STOP SHORTCHANGING
INNER-CITY SCHOOLS

By LOUISE H. TAYLOR

Teachers, school administrators, and business organizations can no longer afford to simply pay lip service to students who attend inner-city schools. There is an urgent need that must be met without further delay. We write about, we talk about, and we plan for inner-city schools, but unfortunately, far too often we do nothing beyond writing, talking, and planning. As a result, students who attend inner-city schools continue to drop out at an alarming rate, and far too many of those who are graduated find themselves without any salable skills.

This situation developed primarily from poor curriculum planning. Other contributing factors include lack of adequate counseling, the launching of Sputnik (which resulted in greater concentrations in science and mathematics), and over-emphasis on achievement and IQ scores. In many inner-city schools (as well as some not in the inner city), students average or above average in ability (based on test results) were persuaded *not* to take vocational courses, while on the other hand, students with low ability were *required* to take whatever vocational courses were offered. As a result, vocational education became a program primarily for slow learners.

The Vocational Education Act of 1963 made specific provisions for persons with special needs, along with provisions for many other vocational programs including training in merchandising, office occupations, industrial education, home economics, and so forth. An enormous increase in vocational programs, especially in middle class city schools and suburban schools, resulted.

The growth of vocational programs in inner-city schools was not so rapid. There were too many obstacles such as the inability of inner-city students to meet the standards required for participation; the unwillingness of employers to participate in cooperative programs involving inner-city schools; the lack of cooperation among local administrators, teachers, and central office personnel; and, perhaps most important, the rejection of vocational programs by inner-city students themselves whose older brothers, sisters, or cousins had been forced to take shop, clothing, or foods and had hated it. These students perceived such courses as the kind from which they wanted most to escape. This has been our dilemma. We are unable to gain acceptance by inner-city youngsters for the vocational programs which would provide them with salable skills. Some progress is being made, but much more needs to be done.

Reprinted from *Business Education Forum* 24:6-7, April 1970, by permission of the National Business Education Association.

The inner-city school is a creation of our society—not a deliberate one perhaps, but our creation nevertheless. It emerged as a result of several factors: the transition from a rural to an urban society, the pattern of segregation including the separate but unequal school system, the high rate of unemployment, poor housing, and many other sociological, political, economical, and educational factors. Instead of a massive, determined effort to cope with these conditions, society has maintained an attitude of complacency or made inept attempts to do *something*.

As the number of inner-city schools increased, the number of competent teachers and administrators in these schools decreased, and schools became seriously over-crowded. The quantity and quality of textbooks, teaching materials, supplies, and equipment (inadequate to begin with) became even more scarce. Inner-city schools became undesirable, unattractive, and unwanted by teachers, administrators, and students. Those who had aspirations of "upward mobility" used every means available to transfer to better schools. (However, it must be emphasized that many excellent teachers, administrators, and students remained in inner-city schools and continue to work against almost insurmountable obstacles. They must cope with an influx of inexperienced teachers, inadequate counseling, inadequate facilities, and large classes.)

There has been the additional problem of the typical middle class teacher trying to relate to the student in the inner-city school. Their cultural backgrounds differ greatly, but those who teach must learn to understand and accept their students' culture in order to teach effectively. To say that a student cannot read often means that he is unable to relate to textbooks which have been prepared by middle class authors for middle class students and prescribed by middle class curriculum developers. Inner-city school students are painfully aware that they are being short-changed. The resulting frustrations are often exhibited in such unacceptable behavior patterns as absenteeism, tardiness, physical destruction of property, and verbal and physical abuse of teachers.

Education in this country has to a large degree been one-sided. This is not to say that those students who have the desire, aspiration, and ability should not be urged to go into the professions or government. But, we educators should expose students to various occupations and emphasize that it is important for the student to make his own decision. To ignore the possibility of economic competency in vocational occupations is to shortchange the student. A chef, for example, is considered one of the most important persons, occupationally, in France. In this country, bricklayers, carpenters, and plumbers, have erected buildings which are still standing after more than 100 years. This is of particular significance to black students whose great-grandparents built many of the magnificent mansions and government buildings still standing.

While this is but one field of vocational education, it is interesting to note that those whose ancestors were the original construction workers in this country have been systematically denied the opportunity to follow "like father, like son." Even those who studied a trade in a vocational school found little or no opportunity to follow that trade once they were graduated. The vocational school open to inner-city students was poorly equipped when compared with other city vocational schools, and the public trade school excluded inner-city students. Thus they were locked in the inner-city school with little hope of being graduated with competitive skills.

My first teaching experience was in an inner-city school on the west side of Chicago where I spent six years serving in various capacities. In that time the school grew from 400 to 2200, all seventh and eighth grade pupils. Approximately 80 percent were over the age for these grade levels and were what we call today the "disadvantaged" or "culturally deprived." They were labeled slow learners, using the same devices that were used to determine the level of ability of middle class students. As a matter of fact, many of these students learned very quickly. An inner-city youngster is often forced to fend for himself at an early age and, as a result, acquires a certain degree of autonomy and independence. In other words, he learns to survive by his wits. He usually enters school with a qualitatively different preparation for the demands of the learning process and behavioral requirements than does the middle class student. Chances are strong that he will experience failure and eventually become a school dropout. Motivation has most likely been reduced by a history that includes lack of expectation of rewards, verbal or tangible, for performance of and successful completion of tasks.

I spent an equal number of years teaching in a middle class school where everything which typifies it was in evidence: self-motivation, a large number of above-average students, interested parents, a stable community, large enrollment in college prep programs, and stable faculty. The contrast is so obvious as to require no further comment.

Inner-city schools can be and must be made quality schools. To do this will take more than desire. It will require the determination of those responsible for all schools to provide: (a) competent teachers and administrators who are not stifled by procedural requirements, (b) qualified counselors, (c) smaller classes, (d) a curriculum developed in accordance with the needs of the community, (e) realistic textbooks, (f) adequate supplies and equipment, (g) intense concentration on the needs and aspirations of the students, and (h) an atmosphere conducive to acceptance of a cultural, racial, and ethnic background which may be atypical.

In-service training, workshops, summer institutes, and college-level courses are now being offered to prepare teachers for inner-city teaching assignments. But, can a seminar, workshop, institute, or classroom prepare the teacher to be warm and accepting instead of resentful and frightened? To be fair yet firm instead of permissive and selective? To be mother, father, counselor, and friend instead of a missionary? To teach respect for and obedience to rules and regulations? The key to success (measured by the success of the students) in inner-city schools is dedicated, competent, and experienced teachers who are selected with great care by the school administrator.

Vocational education is not the answer to the problems facing inner-city schools. However, it can be one of the answers if it is explored and utilized to its fullest potential. To do this we must take advantage of one of the most important aspects of our economy—advertising. Any good product, if it is to earn a profit, must get into the hands of the consumer. Vocational education is a good product and should be advertised so that it can earn a profit for its "owner," the school. To do this it must get into the hands of the "consumer," the student. Often businessmen accept new products based on advertising, and as a result, the product usually sells itself once it gets into the store. The same is true of vocational education. Sufficient advertising will sell the product before it reaches the employer. Those prospective employers must be shown that participation in cooperative vocational programs is profitable. Not only does the prospective employer have to be sold on vocational education, but so do teachers, counselors, administrators, students, and labor unions. If we recall how mathematics and science were sold following the launching of Sputnik, we can realize that selling vocational education is not an impossible task.

Vocational programs in inner-city schools must be oriented to the needs of the seventies. Students want to learn telephone installation, business machine repair, computer programming, television maintenance, and other relevant subjects instead of being limited to woodshop, metal shop, and automotive repair. Retailing provides more jobs than any other industry except manufacturing and farming, and yet many schools exclude course offerings in salesmanship, retailing, or marketing.

Absenteeism and tardiness are patterns which inner-city students have developed over a lifetime in the ghetto and as a result of being *pushed through* rather than *trained in* school. The employer must work with the school in order to develop in the student work habits, initiative, and the ability to get along with others.

School administrators who measure their success by the number of students in college preparatory programs are failing in their obligation to the majority of students who either do not go to college or who drop out during the first semester or year. Counselors who concern themselves with only the top 10 percent of a graduating class are failing to provide for the remaining 90 percent. Students who attend school only two or three days per week should be encouraged to go into vocational programs which have been set up to provide job training at the freshman and sophomore levels. Inasmuch as the greatest dropout rate is at the sophomore level, more job training programs should be developed for these students. Labor unions whose doors have been closed to black apprentices must accept their share of responsibility and, more to the point, open the doors!

Inner-city school students have often been characterized as lazy, shiftless, destructive, and dishonest. All elements of society must provide the opportunity for them to prove otherwise.

Questions:

1. Why has the growth of vocational programs in inner-city schools been slow?

2. How is the inner-city a creation of our society?

3. What elements are necessary to produce a quality school?

4. What is the key to success in inner-city schools?

BUSING: WRONG PRESCRIPTION
FOR DISCRIMINATION ILLS

By CALVIN GRIEDER

Although I am a lifelong "Roosevelt Democrat," I applaud President Nixon's support of the neighborhood school and his administration's deceleration of compulsory busing of pupils to achieve "racially balanced" schools. Neighborhood schools are chiefly of importance at the elementary and preschool levels. In most cities and towns, secondary schools serve attendance areas much larger than neighborhoods. So my observations pertain to early childhood and elementary education.

IMPORTANT DISCLAIMERS

In self defense, this position requires some explanation as protection against the slings and arrows of those who go all out for busing. Party affiliation has nothing to do with it, and I mentioned it above merely to illuminate the point.

I also am opposed to all forms of unfair or injurious distinctions based on differences of race, national origin, religion, sex, social class, economic status, or political belief. With these avowals and disclaimers, stated in good faith, I will try to explain my stand.

If there were clear-cut and incontrovertible evidence on the advantages to pupils of busing, opposition to it could be explained only by prejudice. But the evidence is not clear, and a lot of dispassionate scientific investigation remains to be done to settle the issue.

Other considerations, in addition to the lack of evidence, compel me to support neighborhood schools for young children. I don't have evidence to support these convictions either, but there is a modicum of logic and sense on their side.

First, I believe that busing pupils is treating the symptoms rather than the disease of social and economic discrimination. The two main manifestations of our society's sickness (in relation to minority groups) are job discrimination and housing discrimination, which, in spite of constitutional and statutory prohibitions, are widely practiced, openly or covertly.

Thus a vicious cycle is perpetuated. If you are a kid in a poor minority group, you live in a part of town with poor housing, poor schooling, and poor job prospects.

Reprinted with permission, from *Nation's Schools,* June 1970. Copyright 1970, McGraw-Hill, Inc., Chicago. All rights reserved.

I also oppose busing because I believe the money spent for bus purchase and operation should be spent on improving education in substandard neighborhoods. This money would not be anywhere near enough, but it would help.

Schools in deprived neighborhoods have a more inclusive educational task to work at than do schools in more favored parts of town. In the former, supplementation of the home vastly exceeds what is needed in the latter. Then, too, in two-way busing when children are taken from a good school situation to a poor one, they lose out. You can never improve a child's education by sending him to a poorer school.

I further believe that children of nursery school and elementary school ages should not be far removed from their home neighborhood and should not be in transit too long, or too early or too late in the day.

CHILDREN EXPLOITED

And finally, I oppose busing as a means of desegregating schools because I do not believe that children should be used to treat social and economic problems for which they have no responsibility whatever. We have all seen pictures and read reports of attacks on little children, buses overturned, schoolhouses burned; of boys and girls ostracized and victimized by classmates who resent their coming to the school — all the worse because the kids who are bused, and their parents, have no choice in the matter. Nor do even the boards of education.

Pupil busing is supported, I believe, by those looking for an easy way out, and unwilling to tackle the real, the fundamental problems of social and economic injustice. So the kids become the victims of a society not ready to face up to its problems and to work out the drastic remedies that are required.

Questions:

1. Which statements are facts and which are opinions in this article?

2. Develop a plan to desegregate schools other than by overcoming job and housing discrimination.

REACHING FOR THE DREAM:
AN EXPERIMENT IN TWO-WAY BUSING

By NORMAN N. GROSS

I have a dream that my little children will one day live in a nation where they will not be judged by the color of their skin, but by the content of their character,—Martin Luther King, Jr., at the March on Washington, August 28, 1963.

One of the greatest obstacles to realization of Dr. King's dream is de facto segregation in the schools of our metropolitan areas. As long as white children and black children do not have an opportunity to meet naturally in the course of their day-to-day lives, they run the risk of growing up to see each other as racial stereotypes rather than as people.

Dr. King's dream is becoming a reality, however, in some parts of Rochester, N.Y., most particularly at the Clara Barton School. Each morning during the past school year in this innercity public school, 240 white children from all parts of the city began the day with about 1,300 black children. Before the program to bring the white children to Clara Barton was started, the school was nearly 98 percent black. Today the white percentage would be even greater than its present 16 percent if the many white children on the waiting list could be accommodated. Families from all over the city are asking to send their children to Clara Barton for one or both of two reasons: (1) the school is known for its record of high academic achievement, and (2) the parents wish to have their children participate in a racially integrated educational experience.

Busing schoolchildren is a two-way proposition in Rochester and is carried out entirely on a voluntary basis. It began in 1963 in the more common one-way direction. At that time in response to pressure from parents, the New York Board of Regents, and the U.S. Civil Rights Commission for the city to end de facto segregation in the schools, the local school board adopted an open enrollment policy. To encourage transfers the superintendent of schools sent letters to the parents of children in the seven predominantly black innercity schools, offering to transport their children to schools on the city's outer rim. The board received 1,500 requests from the parents of children in six innercity elementary schools for the 513 places open in the 18 outercity elementary receiving schools. Of the 513 children selected, 495 completed the school year in the schools to which they had been assigned. Of these 480 returned the following year along with 195 new transfers. In the fall of 1969 these 18 schools in the city's white rim increased to 23 schools containing 1,237 children from

Reprinted with permission from *CHILDREN* (July-August 1970).

the inner city. In addition, there were some 321 youngsters from one innercity secondary school traveling to three outercity secondary schools.

The success of this experiment led some suburban school districts where the schools had few if any blacks to open their facilities to children from the inner city with the announced purpose of overcoming the isolation of the white children. The first to do so was the school system of West Irondequoit. This school system has been taking in 25 first-graders from the inner city each year since 1965, with the goal of eventually having about 300 innercity children in the school system at one time. Before the program began, West Irondequoit had only four black children in its school system's total enrollment of 5,800. During 1969–70 it had 87.

Four other suburbs eventually followed West Irondequoit's lead. The city provides transportation and pays tuition for the innercity children who attend these suburban schools.

BUSING IN REVERSE

Busing in reverse—from outer- to inner-city areas—however, did not begin until the fall of 1967.

In following the school board's direction for a voluntary enrollment policy, the superintendent of schools had announced that two of the newer inner-city elementary schools were also open to pupils from any part of the city and that transportation would be provided for children who lived outside the school's normal boundaries. One was the new Public School Number 2, the Clara Barton School, and the other Public School Number 6, which covers only kindergarten through the second grade. When there was no response to this offer, some members of the black community who had been working for greater school desegregation began to express resentment that the black children had to do all the moving.

Many people in Rochester said that white parents—even those who had been clamoring for desegregation—would not send their children to a predominantly black school in the inner city. At first they seemed to be right. Early in 1967 the superintendent's office sent out 28,000 brochures to parents of elementary school children in the white outer rim of the city, urging them to send their children to the "beautiful new Number 2 School." Only four responses pledging unqualified support of this policy were received from this mailing.

The superintendent did not give up. Armed with slides and a well-prepared statement of the educational advantages of a racially integrated school experience, he and members of his staff met with groups of white parents. Parents who showed interest were asked to gather others. Coffee hours to discuss the plan were held in homes in all the white areas of the city. Applications from white parents for transfer of their children to the Clara Barton School began pouring in to the superintendent's office.

This courting of white parents, however, almost proved to be a disastrous mistake. Black parents who lived in the school's neighborhood expressed resentment at not being accorded similar attention. After all, they pointed out, if white children were to be admitted to the Clara Barton School, some black parents would have to volunteer to send their children elsewhere. Since these criticisms were valid, the superintendent and his staff began enlisting the support of the black community for making the Clara Barton program a success.

In September 1967, 140 white children from 30 schools in the outer parts of the city began attending the Clara Barton School in the heart of the city. Among them were the children of doctors, lawyers, and prominent community leaders, including the city manager.

Parent involvement was a crucial factor in the success of the program. The Clara Barton School had a black parents' organization, unaffiliated with the traditional PTA. White parents who attended their meetings soon discovered that there was no lack of black neighborhood leadership. After several months of cautious testing by black parents and white parents alike, a truly integrated parents' group emerged. Apparently judging each other "not by the color of skin, but by the content of character," black parents and white parents worked together to bring improvements to the school. Among their achievements was a successful demand that officials provide the school with a hot lunch program.

There were numerous irritations during the first year. Buses would arrive late and leave late. Teachers and parents had to supervise the bused-in children at lunch time. Led by a deeply committed principal, the school's staff accepted the difficulties with grace. The teachers seemed to respond to the new mix of pupils in their classes with a revitalized interest in teaching.

The untimely death of Martin Luther King, Jr., resulted in an even more vigorous effort to expand this reverse open enrollment program. The Committee for Expanded School Integration, a racially integrated group of parents and teachers from the Clara Barton School, gave this renewed effort energetic support. This time the appeal for voluntary enrollment of children in other than their neighborhood schools was made to black parents and white parents alike.

The new Virgil I. Grissom School, Public School Number 7, in the city's white rim, was paired with the Clara Barton School for a voluntary exchange of pupils. Both schools received some of the same enrichment programs, such as special instruction in mathematics and science, remedial reading, a French program, and a Far Eastern Studies program. In addition, Project Beacon, a black studies program designed to develop self-esteem in black youngsters, was offered to all children at the Clara Barton School. It was found that white children were as interested as black children in this program.

To make certain the message reached the parents, the children of each school carried home a brochure that their fathers could assemble into a model Saturn rocket. Most of the brochures reached home. The responses were encouraging. Informational meetings were held in various places in the city, including private homes. This time experienced parents, both black and white, their children, and teachers from the Clara Barton School fielded the questions from other parents of both races.

Some 192 white children from all parts of Rochester attended the Clara Barton School in 1968-69. In 1969-70 the white enrollment had increased to 240, with a waiting list of 170 white children.

Today campaigns are no longer needed to recruit white children for the Clara Barton School. In fact, several white families have moved into Rochester in an effort to have their children admitted there. Other suburban parents have also sought to have their children admittted to the school, with no success. Some white parents have asked to have space reserved at the school for their preschool children. In addition, the formerly all black Number 6 School, which has not received the same kind of concentrated attention, now has 24 white pupils enrolled.

The lack of available space has become the major obstacle to further integration of the Clara Barton School. The school has such a reputation for achievement and such esprit de corps among parents, teachers, and children that neighborhood parents are reluctant to transfer their children elsewhere, even though they are assured of an equally good school. Consequently only 19 of the school's 38 classes are integrated. To spread the 16 percent of the white children throughout the school would result in a truly integrated experience for nobody.

ACADEMIC ACHIEVEMENT

More than 3,000 pupils have been involved in Rochester's open enrollment program. In the beginning there were dire predictions from some quarters that the presence of the innercity children in classes with white children would slow up the academic program and result in lessening the white children's achievement. Such has not been the case. In fact, in some instances the results have been the opposite—the mixed classes seem to have been a spur to achievement to white children and black children alike. Studies of children's achievement records show, for example, that—

• In the West Irondequoit school the white children in the integrated classes are doing better than the white children in the nonintegrated classes. The black children in that school are doing as well as or better than the children in the same grades at the schools from which they transferred.

• In the Clara Barton School the achievement record of the entire school has risen since the white children have come in. The black children in the integrated classes are doing about the same as the black children in the nonintegrated classes, but the achievement of the black children in both types of classes has risen. The white children are doing as well as the white children in the schools from which they transferred.

• In the Rochester area as a whole the black children who transferred to predominantly white schools are doing as well as or better than they were in their former schools, and the white children in the integrated classes are doing as well as they were before.

THE FUTURE

True racial integration in the schools is still a distant goal in Rochester. In spite of the auspicious beginning, most of the children in the public schools still see only members of their own race in their classes. Moreover, each movement made toward desegregation has met with some resistance from segments of the local community.

New moves toward further integration are to be made in the fall of 1970. A new program will put less emphasis on busing, on the theory that—all else being equal—it is more desirable for children to go to schools near their homes. The two-way transfer program will, however, be continued.

Under the new program two school zones will be expanded to include both predominantly black and predominantly white neighborhoods. Each of the neighborhood schools in these zones will be reorganized to include only specific grades. For example, in one zone, which contains three elementary schools, two schools will include only kindergarten through the third grade, while the other school will serve the fourth through the sixth grades. Since each school will draw its enrollment from throughout the zone, each school will be integrated. Yet most of the children who attend them will live near enough to walk to school.

This plan, too, will meet with some resistance. But, like the two-way busing program, it stems from a resolution adopted by the Rochester School Board in 1963. In this resolution the Board expressed the belief that "the function of the schools is to prepare children for life in a democratic society" and that "the fulfillment of this function depends in part on the degree to which children have opportunities during their public school careers to become acquainted with children from a variety of cultures."

The experience of the two-way transfer program suggests that such opportunities help children to academic achievement. They may also lead to the fulfillment of Dr. King's dream.

———————

Questions:

1. Prepare a list of objections that parents would give regarding "busing in reverse" in your community.

2. Organize a bulletin or newsletter that you would send to the parents in Rochester initially explaining your experimental program in two-way busing.

3. Explain either the strengths or the flaws in this program, using the information from this article as well as your own insights.

DESIGN FOR REGENERATING A CITY

By WILLIAM W. CHASE

Inside Pontiac, Mich., in the old neighborhoods that shoulder against the dying commercial center, stand a half dozen or so elementary schools: McConnell, 69 years old; Baldwin, 67 years old; Central, 75 years old; Wilson—but you get the picture. So did the leaders of this industrial city that lies just beyond reach of Detroit's megalopolitan sprawl. They recognized the symptoms of the urban sickness that beset their community, and they felt that an improved and extended educational program was a first step in restoring it to health.

It would be natural, of course, to replace these old schools with modern new buildings on the same sites. But Dana P. Whitmer, superintendent of Pontiac's schools, had a different thought.

"The replacement of these schools should do more than provide warm, attractive housing for school children in segregated neighborhoods," he says. "Two schools were predominantly black, the other four were all white. If we can bring white and black parents and their children together in one setting with fully enriched educational, social, and recreational programs, there should be a potential environment to improve the total living of residents in that quadrant of the inner city."

The Pontiac board of education picked up this lead and expanded it into an idea for a human resources center. They viewed their concept as a kind of education park set down in one of the city parks.

Then David Lewis, an urban planner and architectural consultant from Pittsburgh, asked a revealing question: "Wouldn't such an education park simply be an isolated elementary school on a larger scale and one that most likely would become completely segregated?"

Lewis agreed that Pontiac's ailment indeed went beyond that which could be remedied by the replacement of a few broken-down school-houses. There were blighted and isolated neighborhoods to nurse back to life. The decay of the central business section had to be checked and the area revived, and there certainly was integration to be considered. He also suggested that the education park concept contradicted the total city development.

In Pittsburgh, Lewis and his co-workers at Urban Design Associates had demonstrated how education could be used to catalyze large-scale inner-city renewal. They felt that education should not be conducted from an isolated facility but should be part of the urban processes for which the young are being trained.

Reprinted from *American Education* (March 1970), by permission of Department of Health, Education and Welfare, Washington, D.C. 20202.

The urban designers saw the human resources center as much more than a place to provide education for approximately 2,300 elementary school children drawn from different racial, cultural, and economic backgrounds. It would have adult education facilities and house community services for health, welfare, social and recreational needs, and family counseling. It would also serve as a destructive force to smash Pontiac's traditional neighborhood isolationism, and as a constructive force to stimulate a revival of the deteriorated inner business and residential sections. Finally, it would "serve as a focal point for activities to improve the life changes of citizens of all ages."

From the board of education's original concept and the turn the urban designers gave it came Pontiac's present planning for a human resources center.

Pontiac needs a concept of total city redevelopment to protect its future as the focus of its surroundings. Its citizens know that Pontiac's singular identity as an independent industrial city cannot long endure, that the population front advances irresistibly northward from Detroit. In three more decades 1.5 million people will swarm over the Pontiac area. The city can be the axis of their activities, their promise of a quality life, the marketplace where they receive the things they want in exchange for their energies and talents. Or it can sit in apathy and let the human tide wash it into oblivion in favor of new or more active communities. Pontiac has already made its choice.

"We believe that the problems of our urban centers have become so complex, the importance of solving the problems so urgent, that we can no longer rely upon piecemeal, independent action, or inaction, by segments of our community, public or private, to achieve the level of coordinated developmental planning which is required now." This passage from the organizing preamble of the Pontiac Area Planning Council, an advisory group of 35 widely representative individuals joined to revitalize Greater Pontiac, sets the tone of the city's determination to be a vitally functioning part of 21st century life. Considering the problems, now is not too soon to start.

An aerial view of the city shows its central core as a hub from which highways and railways radiate like spokes, connecting commerce and residents with lakes, woodlands, and other natural recreational resources. Its radial structure clearly marks Pontiac as the focal point of the area.

If, however, this urban pattern has placed Pontiac in an ascendant position, it has also figured chiefly in the decay of its central core. The arterial spokes brought shopping centers to bloom along their edges out where the city begins to thin. Other businesses and industries sprang up helter-skelter to line the traffic channels. This growth pulled middle-income whites from the old and tired inside neighborhoods out to the city's bright, clean—and often higher priced—skirts. The exodus further depressed an already downhill central business community and abandoned the shabby nuclear residential sections that were built in the early 1900's to overcrowding by poorer families, physical neglect, and the encroachment of industries that were incompatible with the area—dry-cleaning and cement manufacturing plants with their heavy truck traffic.

Another of Pontiac's urban ills traceable to its radial layout is its neighborhood isolation. The same avenues that give access to and from the city's center also slice the residential areas into wedges, each segment becoming almost an entity in itself with its own school, churches, neighborhood groups, and service businesses. Such a neighborhood was acceptable in the past, but today these tight little enclaves nurture racial and economic segregation; their boundaries quarantine them against fresh and progressive ideas. How can such an insulated neighborhood be rescued once it loses its vitality and begins to slide? How can the black and Spanish-speaking minorities be integrated through its invisible walls? To break down these walls is one of Pontiac's major problems, and it has launched the attack.

The human resources center will be a prime force in bringing its part of Pontiac back to sound urban health and may mold a pattern for other sections of the city, and even for other cities. It, of course, has just entered the fruition stage; construction began in January. However, the partnership of all the different agencies needed to make the center a reality has already been working for several years. The Pontiac board of education approved a feasibility study on the proposed center and shortly afterward the city commission passed a resolution endorsing city involvement in the study. Then the Mott Institute for Community Improvement, a private foundation, provided a grant of $10,000 to begin the study.

The idea for a human resource center was given wide circulation. More than 30 citywide service and professional organizations were asked for their reactions; all the city departments that had anything at all to do with services to people—police, health, library, public works, recreation—were asked to comment on the project; the directors of the United Fund agencies were presented with the idea and the possibility of eventually bringing their services to the center. Oakland County agencies made known their interest in the center.

The public got wind of it through various community club meetings and through a newspaper that supported the project and covered its development. Parents and other area residents were attracted by the new concept and many sought active participation. "We at Wilson feel that it will be a great uplifting of the whole community if the center can become a realization. Therefore I hope we can be included in the planning as much as possible," wrote Barbara Hoover, PTA president at one of the elementary schools. Many residents were included and, working with school and city officials, helped identify some of the needs that the center is now designed to fill.

Despite the variety of services the center will offer and the functions it is expected to perform, it is still basically an educational facility. It is not surprising, therefore, that Oakland University and Oakland Community College have thrown in their support with offers to conduct extension and college credit classes there. The Michigan State department of education came on the scene with many helpful suggestions and assistance in developing a proposal for a Title III ESEA study grant from the Federal Government.

Federal help was also sought last summer when the planners called on the U.S. Office of Education for advice in raising necessary funds. OE's Office of Construction Service arranged a meeting with officials from the Department of Housing and Urban Development to determine whether a portion of the center could be funded as a community facility. It was decided that the theater of the center qualified for HUD construction funds. Upon application, Pontiac would be eligible to receive the cost of building the theater portion of the project, which amounts to approximately one-fifth of the estimated $5 million total cost of the center. This effort established a landmark for HUD: a departmental first for financing a portion of a school-oriented facility.

There was, however still a pitfall in this particular path. It was learned that Michigan law prohibits a local district from accepting Federal funds for construction of a portion of a building. But the State, too, was cooperating with Pontiac. Last fall the legislature passed a special bill permitting the city to accept the HUD grant, and the governor signed it just before Christmas.

And so the center, which will occupy 14 acres, moves toward its completion target date in mid-1971. As Dr. Whitmer puts it: "Human beings have an almost unlimited potential for growth, for learning, and for self-improvement throughout most of their lives. It is to assist in this life-long development of human talent and human potential that the human resources center concept was born."

With that birth, Pontiac's chances of gaining a more conspicuous dot on the map that will be dated A.D. 2000 are eminently increased.

Questions:

1. What efforts have Pontiac made to meet the challenge of the future in education?

2. Describe Pontiac's human resource center.

3. Explain how a human resource center of this type would or would not fit into your community.

SCHOOL TERRORISM

By SEYMOUR METZNER

The issue of violence in the public schools has assumed dimensions unheard of a decade ago. Historically, violence in high schools or elementary schools has been a matter of local concern exclusively, and seldom involved more than sporadic vandalism, isolated fist fights, and occasional group melees after supercharged football or basketball games.

Now, violent disruptive behavior has become a national issue, with a swelling tide of felonious violence, widespread vandalism, and planned disruption aimed at the school as an institution and teachers as its representatives, rather than emotional, unpremeditated outbreaks.

Serious educational conflict is manifested country-wide in many forms. In New York City, a junior-high school principal is beaten in his office by three men (5) and an elementary-school principal is threatened with the rape of his daughter (12). A St. Louis elementary-school teacher is stabbed by a 14-year-old girl, causing other teachers to flee from the building in terror (18). In staid Boston, a junior-high-school principal resigns after six weeks because of inability to control pupil disorderliness which erupts into mini-riots (9); while San Francisco hosted 180 pupil assaults in elementary schools during the first three months of the 1968 school year (17).

The trend in violence and vandalism is sharply upward. School arson and vandalism cost New York City $1.95 million in 1967, compared to $1.5 million in 1966, a rise of almost one-third (6). The Riot Data Clearinghouse of the Lemberg Center for the Study of Violence reported that 17 percent of incidents in 1967 involved schools, while in the first four months of 1968, this rose to 44 percent (7). The report noted that this trend was strong even after allowing for the violence following the Martin Luther King assassination. In New York City, there were 271 assaults on teachers in 1964 (17), compared to 60 assaults in 1962 (2). A Chicago board of education attorney noted a rise of 1,000 percent in assaults on teachers from 1962 to 1964 (1). This lends a note of unwholesome reality to teacher perceptions which leads to claims that 415 teachers rejected teaching posts in Philadelphia in 1965 due to fear of pupil attacks (3), while 317 Los Angeles teachers asked for transfers to other schools because of fear of driving through troubled areas (4).

A study of the New York Times Index for the years from 1940 to 1968 validates the accelerated tempo and importance of school unrest and violence. Before 1960, the "student activities" section had very few items and these were

Reprinted from the Spring, 1969, issue of *CHANGING EDUCATION,* official publication of the American Federation of Teachers.

generally about ongoing programs or inventories of student beliefs. From 1960, there were increasing signs of interest in student activities with six to 12 items a year involving problems of fraternity hazing, student-publication censorship, and violations of school-dress and appearance rules.

The year 1964 heralded the current emphasis on teacher assaults with elements of racial unrest. The major change in the student activities section occurred in 1967, which listed 56 items, compared to nine in 1966. This trend continued with the first six months of 1968 listing 42 reports. The 1967 and 1968 incidents were particularly notable because of a large incidence of group actions as opposed to previous individual activities, and almost all items had racial overtones, either explicitly or implicitly *(16)*.

Although the trend of school violence is clear enough that documentation of it runs the risk of elaboration of the obvious, the possible reasons for this violence are much less clear.

One reason is that the schools may be an all-too-faithful mirror of society and are not insulated from it. Why should school violence decline while violent crime, nationwide, is up 21 percent from the first nine months of 1967 to a similar period in 1968, with rates in urban "transition" areas, such as Newark, N.J., having double the national-rate increase*(13)*? Why should the lower educational echelons have less disruption while the first six months of 1968 resound to 221 major demonstrations at 101 colleges and universities *(8)*? How can a school expect to be exempt when even the monastic sanctuary of a library is violated enough to close it *(14)*?

There is also the development of a power vacuum in many educational relationships. The simple certainty no longer holds that pupils are in school to learn what is taught, teachers are to teach, and administrators are to administer, while parents make happy, encouraging noises to their offspring.

Now, the roles are much less-defined and tensions are generated by the various groups scrambling for a bigger piece of the action. This is particularly true of the urban areas in the Northeast, Midwest, and Far West. Role change is less advanced in the South, where tradition is stronger and dissident elements have migrated out to climates more responsive to their aspirations. This helps explain the comparative lack of turmoil in Southern schools.

The Civil-rights movement is undoubtedly a major element in the present series of school crises. It was highly visible in almost all secondary-school incidents while, in colleges, issues of race relationships were the major reasons for 97 student demonstrations compared to 50 demonstrations for "student power" and 26 protesting the Vietnam War *(8)*.

The worldwide demand for self-determinism among previously subjugated people in underdeveloped areas finds a sympathetic echo from American minorities which have never been granted equal opportunity in any aspect of American life. This demand for equal opportunity inevitably must focus on the schools as a major source of friction because economic and social advancement has been traditionally linked to schools as the escalator to success in American life, while technological advances reinforce this avenue as the *sine qua non* for advancement in American civilization.

There is no doubt that American schools have been notably unsuccessful in helping some minority groups, such as blacks, Puerto Ricans, and Indians, attain the knowledge and skills necessary for success. In the past, the reasons for this failure were believed to mainly hinge upon social and environmental weaknesses in the social structure of these groups, and many people within these groups concurred in this belief.

New currents of thought, gaining wide credence among minority people themselves, hold that the basic reason for lack of success was the unresponsiveness of the educational structure to the needs, aspirations, and learning styles of ethnic minorities which were culturally different from the majority of the American school population. A portion of the current unrest and disorderliness stems from a combination of rancor at these past wrongs combined with frustration with the slowness with which change is occurring to remedy these wrongs.

The self-deterministic aspect of this struggle is readily seen in the demands of the black students for more black teachers, greater voice in the hiring and firing of the teachers, and a share in the decision-making policies regarding what is to be taught.

Another element in school disruption is the lack of administrative foresight in recognizing potential problems, no clear pattern of successful strategy to follow to disarm this time bomb, and Hamlet-like vacillation when the situation explodes. Lacking the framework of clearcut guidelines, the students feel free to explore the nebulous limits of their powers and responsibilities while school administrators either compromise, give in, or become punitive, with few principles except momentary expedience to guide their actions. The result is a scenario calling for future outbursts, since the basis for grievances, real or imaginary, is seldom fully investigated, while future administrative reaction to further violence is neither established nor credible.

The teachers are pawns in a struggle in which they have little power to affect meaningful change. They bear the brunt of discontent they haven't caused and often don't understand. Not knowing for certain which of their actions or attitudes will irritate students and the community, and being equally uncertain of the backing they will receive from administrative echelons, they tend to exhibit the fear and uncertainty which itself becomes an invitation to student aggression.

Teachers and schools have certainly lost much of their sacrosanct status, due, in part, to conflicts with the community. There is reason to believe that some community members not only sanction aggressive pupil behavior against teachers and schools but actually encourage it. It is easily seen that the recent wave of teacher strikes further encourages erosion of the teacher's former "above-the-battle" status.

Prospects for the immediate future are not optimistic. College strife is likely to continue until a clear pattern for successfully handling grievances emerges. We can look forward to increasing dislocation at the high-school level. This is heralded by the following remark of the interorganizational secretary at the 1968 meeting of the Students for a Democratic Society: "Our high schools will be the new thrust. They are used as babysitting jails. They are used to trap people into stupid colleges to train them for jobs they don't want. They are oppressive." *(15)*

It does not take the gift of prophecy to expect accelerated problems in the junior high schools and elementary schools. The actions of an 11-year-old New York City pupil circulating a petition to oust the principal of his school may well presage a further breakdown of school authority with a concomitant rise in school violence *(11)*.

What can teachers and teachers' organizations do to counter school disruptions and their concomitant regressive educational and social consequences? Must the classroom teacher be the battered shuttlecock in power plays between the school administration and the community? Can teachers play a meaningful role in redirecting unguided social forces into educationally constructive channels?

These questions can have hopeful, encouraging answers only if teachers are willing to do five things.

First, they must build up their own personal "power base" in the community. This can be done by involving the parents in class activities via newsletters, personal get-together invitations, letters to parents that are sent on a personal rather than official basis, greater use of parents in class functions, and visitations to students' homes as an interested friend and not in the teacher role. All of this takes time and energy, both of which are in short supply after a full day's teaching, but it is a necessity in order to build up community rapport.

Second, administrators must be assured of complete teacher-organization support for any actions that must be taken to assure the safety of school personnel and property, while being told precisely what measures of self-defense will be undertaken by the teachers themselves if administrative support is not forthcoming.

Third, teachers must take the lead in demanding curricular adjustments relevant to the particular environment of the student body. This should be done before the demand arises and not in grudging response to a confrontation.

Fourth, students should not only be given a meaningful voice in school affairs, but should also be held responsible for the execution of decisions they help formulate. A step in this direction might be placing student officers on a salary basis as junior members of the school administration.

Fifth, and last, teachers should demand that community leaders be brought into the schools as paid aides and consultants and help to share the responsibility for school stability and other educational decisions.

A peaceful, learning environment will return to the schools when teachers stop being reactors to revolt and become initiators of action.

REFERENCES:

1. *New York Times,* March 5, 1964, p. 27.
2. *Ibid.,* March 6, 1964, p. 1.
3. *Ibid.,* Feb. 25, 1966, p. 15.
4. *Ibid.,* May 26, 1966, p. 41.
5. *Ibid.,* Jan. 25, 1968, p. 22.
6. *Ibid.,* April 8, 1968, p. 49.
7. *Ibid.,* Aug. 25, 1968, p. E 11.
8. *Ibid.,* Aug. 27, 1968, p. 33.
9. *Ibid.,* Dec. 7, 1968, p. 50.
10. *Ibid.,* Dec. 8, 1968, p. 52.
11. *Ibid.,* Dec. 10, 1968, p. 1.
12. *Ibid.,* Dec. 16, 1968, p. 43.
13. *Ibid.,* Dec. 17, 1968, p. 1.
14. *Ibid.,* Dec. 21, 1968, p. 30.
15. *Ibid.,* Dec. 30, 1968, p. 29.
16. *New York Times Index,* 1940 - 1968.
17. *U.S. News & World Report,* Dec. 2, 1968, p. 33.
18. *Ibid.,* p. 30.

Questions:

1. What do you feel are the main reasons for the violence in our schools (K-12)?

2. List the actions teachers should initiate in order to make the school a safe place.

SUBJECT INDEX

AUTHOR INDEX

A

ADAMS, William E. *(Black Studies in the Elementary Schools) (Black Leaders Speak Out on Black Education);* teacher, Elementary Division, Baltimore City Public Schools, and president, Public School Teachers Association.

ALLEN, James E., Jr. *(Crisis in City Schools);* former United States Commissioner of Education.

B

BACHTOLD, Louise M. *(Personality Differences Among High Ability Underachievers);* Assistant Professor, Child Development, Department of Applied Behavioral Sciences, University of the Pacific.

BAKAN, Rita *(Malnutrition and Learning);* Assistant Professor, Center for Urban Affairs, Justin Morrill College.

BECK, Armin *(Strategies for Change: Conditions for School Desegregation);* Director, Midwest Program for Equal Educational Opportunities and Associate Professor, Center for Inner City Studies, Northeastern Illinois State College, Chicago.

BLACKBURN, Dan *(The Impacted Ghetto);* staff writer.

BRAZZIEL, William F. *(Perspective on the Jensen Affair);* Professor of Higher Education, University of Connecticut.

BROZOVICH, Richard W. *(Characteristics Associated with Popularity Among Different Racial and Socioeconomic Groups of Children);* Educational Psychologist, Oakland Schools, Pontiac, Michigan.

BURROW, Will H. *(Performance of Head Start and Non-Head Start Participants at First Grade);* Director of Education and Training, Central Connecticut Regional Center, Meriden, Connecticut.

C

CAMPBELL, LAURA K. *(Black Leaders Speak Out on Black Education);* Assistant Principal in Charge of Stevenson Elementary School, Detroit, Michigan.

CAWLEY, John F. *(Performance of Head Start and Non-Head Start Participants at First Grade);* Professor of Education, University of Connecticut.

CHASE, William W. *(Design for Regenerating a City);* Deputy Director, Division of Facilities Development, Office of Education, Office of Construction Service.

CHING, Doris C. *(Urban Preschool Children);* Associate Professor, California State College, Los Angeles.

CLEAR, Delbert K. *(Decentralization Issues and Comments);* Assistant Professor, Department of Educational Administration and Supervision, University of Wisconsin—Milwaukee.

CLIFT, Virgil A. *(Further Considerations in the Education of the Disadvantaged);* Professor of Education, New York University School of Education.

COBBS, Price *(Black Leaders Speak Out on Black Education);* M.D., Assistant
Clinical Professor of Psychiatry, University of California; co-director, Pacific
Training Association.
COCHRAN, J. Otis *(Black Leaders Speak Out on Black Education);* Lecturer at
Yale University, Third Year Student at Yale Law School, and National
Chairman, Black American Law Students Association.
COHEN, Boaz *(Establishing A Science Curriculum for Aggressive Children);*
Teacher, Children's Day Treatment Program, St. Joseph's Hospital, Syracuse,
New York.
COHEN, Stewart *(The Ghetto Dropout – Analysis and Partial Solution);*
Assistant Professor of Educational Psychology, University of Illinois,
Urbana.
CUTLER, Marilyn H. *(Pacesetting Playgrounds: City Schools Grab the Lead);*

D

DeROCHE, Edward F. *(Methods, Materials, and the Culturally Disadvantaged);*
Associate Professor, Marquette University, Milwaukee, Wisconsin.
DIVOKY, Diane *(Project ASPIRE: Help for "Hopeless" Kids);* Information
Officer, Public Education Association, New York City; also free-lance writer.
DRAPER, Imogene H. *(The Slum Child);* English Teacher, John F. Kennedy
High School, Richmond, Virginia.
DUNCAN, Joseph C. *(Black Leaders Speak Out on Black Education);* Principal,
Jones Elementary School, Yanceyville, North Carolina.
DURHAM, Joseph T. *(Who Needs It? Compensatory Education);* Associate
Dean, College of Education, Illinois State University, Normal.

E

ERICKSON, Frederick D. *(Strategies for Change: Conditions for School
Desegregation);* Assistant Professor of Education, University of Illinois,
Chicago, and Director, Inter-Ethnic Communication Study Project, Univer-
sity of Illinois at Chicago Circle.
EZERSKY, Eugene *(Get Rid of Gymnasiums in Big City High Schools);* former
Assistant Director of Health and Physical Education, New York City Board
of Education and now on Faculty of New York University.

F

FANTINI, Mario *(The Ocean Hill-Brownsville Experiment);* Dean of Education
and Professor, State University of New York, New Paltz, New York.
FEATHERSTONE, Joseph *(Poor Education);* Editorial Writer for *The New
Republic.*
FEATHERSTONE, Richard L. *(Urban School Decentralization);* Chairman,
Department of Administration and Higher Education, College of Education,
Michigan State University.

G

GITTELL, Marilyn *(The Ocean Hill-Brownsville Experiment)*; Professor of Political Science and Director of the Institute for Community Studies, Queens College.

GOODSTEIN, Henry A. *(Performance of Head Start and Non-Head Start Participants at First Grade)*; Assistant Professor of Education, School of Education, University of Connecticut at Storrs.

GREELEY, Andrew M. *(The New Urban Studies – A Word of Caution)*; Program Director, National Opinion Research Center, University of Chicago.

GRIEDER, Calvin *(Busing: Wrong Prescription for Discrimination Ills)*; Professor of School Administration, University of Colorado at Boulder.

GROSS, Norman N. *(Reaching for the Dream: An Experiment in Two-Way Busing)*; Administrator, Title I, ESEA and Urban-Suburban Transfers, City School District, Rochester, New York.

H

HARDING, Alice Curry *(Early School Admissions)*; Education Journal Staff Writer.

HARE, Nathan *(Black Leaders Speak Out on Black Education)*; Publisher of *The Black Scholar;* Former Interim Chairman, Department of Black Studies, San Francisco State College.

HAVIGHURST, Robert J. *(Curriculum for the Disadvantaged)*; Professor of Education and Human Development; University of Chicago.

HERMAN, Barry E. *(Inner-City Teaching . . . Frustrating, Exciting and Rewarding)*; Principal of Winchester Community School in New Haven, Connecticut.

HEUSSENSTAMM, Frances K. *(How Can I Teach Black Children?)*; Associate Professor of Education and Art, California State College, Los Angeles.

HILL, Frederick W. *(Urban School Decentralization)*; Deputy Superintendent of Schools, New York City.

HORTON, Kathryn B. *(Language Development and Cultural Disadvantagement)*; Chief, Language Development Programs, Bill Wilkerson Hearing and Speech Center and Assistant Professor, Vanderbilt University, Department of Hearing and Speech Sciences.

HURT, N. Franklin *(Integrating American History)*; Assistant Dean of Continuing Education, Prairie State College, Chicago Heights, Illinois.

I

ITZKOFF, Seymour W. *(Decentralization: Dialectic and Dilemma)*; Associate Professor of Education and Director of the Smith College Day Schools, Smith College, Northampton, Massachusetts.

J

JERREMS, Raymond L. *(Racism: Vector of Ghetto Education)*; Principal, Fermi Elementary School, Chicago.

JONES, Howard L. *(Establishing a Science Curriculum for Aggressive Children);* Associate Professor of Science Education, University of Houston, Texas.

K

KRUMBEIN, Eliezer *(Strategies for Change: Conditions for School Desegregation);* Associate Professor of Education, University of Illinois at Chicago Circle.

KRUSZYNSKI, Eugene *(The Disadvantaged—The Nature of Urban Education);* Associate Professor of Secondary Education, San Francisco State College.

L

LARSON, Richard G. *(Compensatory Programs and Special Education: Is There a Difference?)*; Associate Professor, School of Education, University of Wisconsin, Milwaukee.

LEVIN, Henry M. *(Why Ghetto Schools Fail);* Associate Professor of Education and Economics, Stanford University.

LEVINE, Daniel U. *(Urban Education — Stratification, Segregation, and Children in the Inner-City School);* Professor of Education, University of Missouri, Kansas City.

M

McCONNELL, Freeman*(Language Development and Cultural Disadvantagement);* Director, Bill Wilkerson Hearing and Speech Center; Professor of Audiology, Vanderbilt University; Professor of Special Education, George Peabody College for Teachers.

METALITZ, Beatrice R. *(Kibbutzim for the Disadvantaged);* Kindergarten Teacher, Oakland Terrace Elementary School, Silver Spring, Maryland; Principal, Non-Affiliated Jewish Sunday School, Kensington, Maryland.

METZNER, Seymour *(The Urban Teacher: Saint, Sinner or Sucker?) (School Terrorism);* Director of the Learning Resource Center, Northridge, California; Associated with San Fernando State College.

MEYERS, Trienah *(The Extra Cost of Being Poor);* Staff Assistant to the Administrator of the Economic Research Service, U. S. Department of Agriculture, Washington, D. C.

MONTEZ, Philip *(Will the Real Mexican American Please Stand Up);* Western Regional Director, U. S. Commission on Civil Rights.

O

OLSON, James L. *(Compensatory Programs and Special Education: Is There A Difference?);* Professor, Department of Exceptional Education, University of Wisconsin, Milwaukee.

ORNSTEIN, Allan C. *(Decentralization: Problems and Prospects) (Discipline: A Major Function in Teaching the Disadvantaged);* Author of three books on the disadvantaged: *How to Teach Disadvantaged Youth* (McKay 1969),

Understanding and Teaching the Disadvantaged (McKay 1971), and *Educating the Disadvantaged* (Scarecrow 1972).

P

PAIGE, Joseph C. *(Problems in Teaching Science to the Urban Child);* Dean, Community Education, Federal City College, Washington, D. C.

PALMER-BROWN, Minta *(How Can I Teach Black Children?);* Associate Professor, Education, California State College, Los Angeles.

PEDRAM, Manouchehr *(A Unique Approach to Inner City Teacher Education);* Secondary Education Specialist, Mid-Continent Regional Education Laboratory, Kansas City, Missouri.

R

RASPBERRY, William *(Should Ghettoese Be Accepted?);* Columnist, *The Washington Post.*

READ, Merrill S. *(Malnutrition and Learning);* Program Director, Growth and Development, National Institute of Child Health and Human Development.

REDL, Fritz *(Aggression in the Classroom);* Distinguished Professor of Behavioral Science, Wayne State University.

REEVES, Gloria D. *(Preconditioned Panic Responses to Black Militancy);* School Social Worker, Detroit Public Schools, Detroit, Michigan.

S

SCHWARTZ, Albert V. *(On Teaching the Word "Black");* Assistant Professor of Education, Richmond College, Staten Island, New York.

SCUDDER, John R., Jr. *(Educational Uncle Tomism);* Professor of Philosophy and Education, Lynchburg College, Virginia.

SHEVIAKOV, George V. *(Anger in Children);* Author of many articles and books including *Anger in Children,* American Association of Elementary/ Kindergarten/Nursery Educators.

SMITH, Bertha R. *(Language Development and Cultural Disadvantagement);* Head Teacher, South Street Centenary Project, Nashville, Tennessee.

SMITH, William L. *(Black Leaders Speak Out on Black Education);* Director, Division of School Programs, Bureau of Educational Personnel Development, U. S. Office of Education, Washington, D. C.

STANFORD, Barbara Dodds *(Affective Aspects of Black Literature);* Department of English, Vashon High School, St. Louis, Missouri.

T

TAYLOR, Louise H. *(Stop Shortchanging Inner-City Schools);* Chicago State College, Chicago, Illinois.

THEIBERT, P. Richard *(Get Rid of Gymnasiums in Big City High Schools);* Athletic Director, Chapman College, California; Administrator of an Athletic Facilities Grant from Education Facilities Laboratory.

TRIESCHMAN, A. E. *(Temper Tantrums);* Director, Walker School, Needham, Massachusetts; Lecturer, Clark University, Worcester; Supervising Psychologist, Children's Hospital Medical Center, Boston.

W

WALTON, Sidney F., Jr. *(Black Leaders Speak Out on Black Education);* Instructor, Ethnic Studies Department, University of California, Berkeley Campus.

WILKINS, Roy, Jr. *(Black Leaders Speak Out on Black Education);* Executive Director, National Association for the Advancement of Colored People.

WOODARD, Samuel L. *(Black Power and Achievement Motivation);* Director, Program Implementation for the School District of Philadelphia, Pennsylvania.

PUBLICATION INDEX

American Education, Department of Health, Education, and Welfare, Office of Education, 400 Maryland Avenue, S.W., Washington, D.C. 20202.

American School and University, North American Publishing Company, 134 North Thirteenth Street, Philadelphia, Pa. 19107.

American School Board Journal, 1233 Central Street, Evanston, Illinois 60201.

Business Education Forum, National Business Education Association, 1201 Sixteenth Street, N.W., Washington, D.C. 20036.

Changing Education, American Federation of Teachers, AFL-CIO, 1012 – 14th Street, N.W., Washington, D. C. 20005.

Changing Times, The Kiplinger Washington Editors, Inc., 1729 H Street, N.W., Washington, D. C. 20006.

Childhood Education, Journal of the Association for Childhood Education International, 3615 Wisconsin Avenue, N.W., Washington, D.C. 20016.

Children, Department of Health, Education and Welfare, Office of the Secretary, Washington, D. C. 20201.

The Clearing House, Fairleigh Dickinson University, Teaneck, New Jersey.

Education, The University of Wisconsin–Milwaukee, Milwaukee, Wisconsin 53201.

Educational Forum, Kappa Delta Pi, Box A, West Lafayette, Indiana 47906.

Educational Leadership, Association for Supervision and Curriculum Development, 1201 Sixteenth Street, N.W., Washington, D.C. 20036.

Educational Record, American Council on Education, One DuPont Circle, Washington, D. C. 20036.

English Journal, The National Council of Teachers of English, 508 South Sixth Street, Champaign, Illinois 61820.

Exceptional Children, The Council for Exceptional Children, 1411 South Jefferson Davis Highway, Suite 900 – Jefferson Plaza, Arlington, Va. 22202.

Improving College and University Teaching, Oregon State University Press, P.O. Box 689, Oregon State University, Corvallis, Oregon 97331.

The Instructor, The Instructor Publications, Inc., Dansville, New York 14437.

Integrated Education: Race and Schools, 343 S. Dearborn Street, Chicago, Illinois 60604.

Journal of Educational Research, DEMBER Educational Research Services, Inc. Post Office Box 1605, Madison, Wisconsin 53701.

Journal of Health, Physical Education, Recreation (JOPHER), American Association for Health, Physical Education, and Recreation, 1201 Sixteenth Street, N.W., Washington, D.C. 20036.

Journal of Home Economics, American Home Economics Association, 1600 Twentieth Street, N.W., Washington, D.C. 20009.

Journal of Negro Education, Bureau of Educational Research, Howard University, Washington, D. C. 20001.

The Nation, Nation Associates, Inc., 333 Sixth Avenue, New York, New York 10014.

Nation's Schools, 1050 Merchandise Mart, Chicago, Illinois 60654.

The Negro Educational Review, P. O. Box 741, Nashville, Tennessee 37202.

The New Republic, 1244 — 19th Street, N.W., Washington, D. C. 20036.

Phi Delta Kappan, Phi Delta Kappa, International Headquarters Building, Eighth and Union, Bloomington, Indiana 47401.

Saturday Review, 380 Madison Avenue, New York, New York 10017.

Scholastic Teacher, Scholastic Magazines and Book Services, 50 West 44th Street, New York, New York 10036.

School and Society, The Society for the Advancement of Education, Inc., 1860 Broadway, New York, New York 10023.

The Science Teacher, National Science Teachers Association, 1201 Sixteenth Street, N.W., Washington, D. C. 20036.

Social Casework, 144 East 23rd Street, New York, New York 10010.

Today's Education, National Education Association of the United States, 1201 Sixteenth Street, N.W., Washington, D. C. 20036.

U.S. News & World Report, 2300 N Street, N.W., Washington, D.C. 20037.